Lecture Notes in Computer Science

Lecture Notes in Artificial Intelligence   14102

Founding Editor

Jörg Siekmann

Series Editors

Randy Goebel, *University of Alberta, Edmonton, Canada*
Wolfgang Wahlster, *DFKI, Berlin, Germany*
Zhi-Hua Zhou, *Nanjing University, Nanjing, China*

The series Lecture Notes in Artificial Intelligence (LNAI) was established in 1988 as a topical subseries of LNCS devoted to artificial intelligence.

The series publishes state-of-the-art research results at a high level. As with the LNCS mother series, the mission of the series is to serve the international R & D community by providing an invaluable service, mainly focused on the publication of conference and workshop proceedings and postproceedings.

Kamil Ekštein · František Pártl ·
Miloslav Konopík
Editors

Text, Speech, and Dialogue

26th International Conference, TSD 2023
Pilsen, Czech Republic, September 4–6, 2023
Proceedings

 Springer

Editors
Kamil Ekštein ⓘ
University of West Bohemia
Pilsen, Czech Republic

František Pártl ⓘ
University of West Bohemia
Pilsen, Czech Republic

Miloslav Konopík ⓘ
University of West Bohemia
Pilsen, Czech Republic

ISSN 0302-9743 ISSN 1611-3349 (electronic)
Lecture Notes in Artificial Intelligence
ISBN 978-3-031-40497-9 ISBN 978-3-031-40498-6 (eBook)
https://doi.org/10.1007/978-3-031-40498-6

LNCS Sublibrary: SL7 – Artificial Intelligence

This Springer imprint is published by the registered company Springer Nature Switzerland AG
The registered company address is: Gewerbestrasse 11, 6330 Cham, Switzerland

This book of proceedings is dedicated to the memory of Tino Haderlein (1974–2023). A long-time member of the TSD community, he was a devoted scientist, skilled researcher, selfless and dedicated colleague, reliable and conscientious TSD Program Committee member, but first of all, a good-hearted, kind, and lovely fellow. We will always miss you, Tino!

Preface

The annual **International Conference on Text, Speech and Dialogue** (TSD), which emerged in 1998, constitutes a recognized platform for presenting and discussing state-of-the-art technology and recent achievements in the computer processing of natural language. It has become a broad interdisciplinary forum, interweaving the topics of speech technology and language processing. The conference attracts researchers not only from Central and Eastern Europe but also from other parts of the world. Indeed, one of its goals has always been bringing together NLP researchers with various interests from different parts of the world and promoting their cooperation. One of the ambitions of the conference is, as its name suggests, not only to deal with dialogue systems but also to improve dialogue among researchers in areas of NLP, i.e., among the "text" and the "speech" and the "dialogue" people.

After several years of touring around Central Europe, TSD 2023 returned to Plzeň—one of its original home towns (that is because the two co-organizing institutions, Masaryk University and the University of West Bohemia, reside in Brno and Plzeň, respectively). Unfortunately, this year of the conference is again not entirely easy-going, not void of problems thanks to what is going on in the world. This time, no disease is raging; however, another—geopolitical—disaster affected the preparation and the pursuance of the conference. After a blatantly condemnable Russian act of international violence against Ukraine in February 2022, the TSD conference, which has always aimed to connect the East and the West, has received another bothersome blow of fate. The TSD Programme Committee consists of reputable and distinguished scientists from both Ukraine and Russia and Russian scientists submitted their papers to the conference. Needless to say, there were calls for immediate actions against the Russian members of the Programme Committee and implicit rejection of all submitted papers written by Russians. The TSD Programme Committee and the TSD Organizing Committee, of course, profoundly deplore Putin's unprecedented aggression against the sovereign state of Ukraine and its nation. However, we believe that science is far above politics, that international scientific cooperation is always the best way to understanding among nations, and that peace always comes from the brave hearts of good people on both sides of the border. That is why we kept the status quo and did not take any rash actions, and trusted our instincts about the people we know personally as the good ones.

In order to have a pleasant and calm place shielded from the heavinesses and burdens of contemporary life, we chose the cosy and suitably situated Primavera Hotel & Congress Centre in the Plzeň suburb Černice as the TSD 2023 venue. The conference took place on 4–6 September 2023, and its schedule and its topics were again co-ordinated with the Interspeech conference—TSD 2023 was listed as an Interspeech 2023 satellite event. Like its predecessors, TSD 2023 highlighted the importance of language and speech processing to both the academic and scientific world and their most recent breakthroughs in current applications. Both experienced researchers and professionals and newcomers in the field found the TSD conference a forum to meet and communicate with people sharing similar interests.

This volume contains a collection of submitted papers presented at the conference. Each of them was thoroughly reviewed in a double-blind process by at least three members of the reviewing team, consisting of 42 top specialists in the conference topic areas. A total of 31 papers out of 64 submitted, altogether contributed by 121 authors and co-authors, were selected by the Programme Committee for presentation at the conference and publication in this book. Theoretical and more general contributions were presented in common (plenary) sessions. Problem-oriented sessions, as well as panel discussions, then brought together specialists in narrower problem areas to exchange knowledge and skills resulting from research projects of all kinds.

Last but not least, we would like to express our gratitude to the authors for providing their papers on time, to the members of the conference reviewing team and the Programme Committee for their careful reviews and paper selection, and to the editors for their hard work preparing this volume. Special thanks go to the members of the Organizing Committee for their tireless effort and enthusiasm during the course of preparation of the conference.

We hope that everyone enjoyed this year's TSD and has benefitted from the event, and relished the social programme prepared by the members of the Organizing Committee. And you, dear reader, please, enjoy this book of proceedings...

The 26th International Conference on Text, Speech and Dialogue—TSD 2023—was organized by the Department of Computer Science and Engineering and the NTIS (New Technologies for the Information Society) P2 Research Centre of the Faculty of Applied Sciences, University of West Bohemia in Plzeň (Pilsen), Czechia, and co-organized by the Faculty of Informatics, Masaryk University in Brno, Czechia.

The conference website is located at https://www.kiv.zcu.cz/tsd2023/ or https://www.tsdconference.org/.

September 2023

Kamil Ekštein
Miloslav Konopík
František Pártl

Organization

Programme Committee

Elmar Nöth (General Chair)	Friedrich-Alexander-Universität Erlangen-Nuremberg, Germany
Rodrigo Agerri	University of the Basque Country, Spain
Eneko Agirre	University of the Basque Country, Spain
Vladimír Benko	Slovak Academy of Sciences, Slovakia
Archna Bhatia	Institute for Human and Machine Cognition, USA
Jan Černocký	Brno University of Technology, Czechia
Simon Dobrišek	University of Ljubljana, Slovenia
Kamil Ekštein	University of West Bohemia, Czechia
Karina Evgrafova	Saint Petersburg State University, Russia
Yevhen Fedorov	Cherkasy State Technological University, Ukraine
Volker Fischer	EML European Media Laboratory GmbH, Germany
Darja Fišer	University of Ljubljana, Slovenia
Lucie Flek	Philipps-Universität Marburg, Germany
Björn Gambäck	Norwegian University of Science and Technology, Norway
Radovan Garabík	Slovak Academy of Sciences, Slovakia
Alexander Gelbukh	National Polytechnic Institute, Mexico
Louise Guthrie	Institute for Human and Machine Cognition, USA
Tino Haderlein	Friedrich-Alexander-Universität Erlangen-Nürnberg, Germany
Jan Hajič	Charles University, Czechia
Eva Hajičová	Charles University, Czechia
Yannis Haralambous	IMT Atlantique, France
Hynek Hermansky	Johns Hopkins University, USA
Jaroslava Hlaváčová	Charles University, Czechia
Aleš Horák	Masaryk University, Czechia
Eduard Hovy	Carnegie Mellon University, USA
Maria Khokhlova	Saint Petersburg State University, Russia
Aidar Khusainov	Tatarstan Academy of Sciences, Russia
Daniil Kocharov	Saint Petersburg State University, Russia
Miloslav Konopík	University of West Bohemia, Czechia
Valia Kordoni	Humboldt University Berlin, Germany
Evgeny Kotelnikov	Vyatka State University, Russia

Pavel Král	University of West Bohemia, Czechia
Siegfried Kunzmann	Amazon Alexa Machine Learning, USA
Nikola Ljubešić	Jožef Stefan Institute, Slovenia
Natalija Loukachevitch	Lomonosov Moscow State University, Russia
Bernardo Magnini	Bruno Kessler Foundation − FBK, Italy
Václav Matoušek	University of West Bohemia, Czechia
Roman Mouček	University of West Bohemia, Czechia
Agnieszka Mykowiecka	Polish Academy of Sciences, Poland
Hermann Ney	RWTH Aachen University, Germany
Joakim Nivre	Uppsala University, Sweden
Juan Rafael Orozco-Arroyave	Universidad de Antioquia, Colombia
Maciej Piasecki	Wroclaw University of Science and Technology, Poland
Josef Psutka	University of West Bohemia, Czechia
James Pustejovsky	Brandeis University, USA
German Rigau	University of the Basque Country, Spain
Paolo Rosso	Polytechnic University of València, Spain
Leon Rothkrantz	Delft University of Technology, The Netherlands
Anna Rumshisky	UMass Lowell, USA
Milan Rusko	Slovak Academy of Sciences, Slovakia
Pavel Rychlý	Masaryk University, Czechia
Mykola Sazhok	International Research/Training Center for Information Technologies and Systems, Ukraine
Odette Scharenborg	Delft University of Technology, The Netherlands
Pavel Skrelin	Saint Petersburg State University, Russia
Pavel Smrž	Brno University of Technology, Czechia
Petr Sojka	Masaryk University, Czechia
Georg Stemmer	Intel Corp., USA
Marko Robnik-Šikonja	University of Ljubljana, Slovenia
Marko Tadić	University of Zagreb, Croatia
Jan Trmal	Johns Hopkins University, USA
Tamas Varadi	Hungarian Academy of Sciences, Hungary
Zygmunt Vetulani	Adam Mickiewicz University, Poland
Aleksander Wawer	Polish Academy of Science, Poland
Pascal Wiggers	Amsterdam University of Applied Sciences, The Netherlands
Marcin Wolinski	Polish Academy of Sciences, Poland
Alina Wróblewska	Polish Academy of Sciences, Poland
Victor Zakharov	Saint Petersburg State University, Russia
Jerneja Žganec Gros	Alpineon d.o.o., Slovenia

Organizing Committee (Plzeň Team)

Miloslav Konopík (Chair)	University of West Bohemia, Czechia
Václav Matoušek (Chair Emeritus)	University of West Bohemia, Czechia
Marluce Quaresma (Secretary)	University of West Bohemia, Czechia
Kamil Ekštein (PR/Comms. Manager, Webmaster, Proceedings Editor-in-Chief)	University of West Bohemia, Czechia
Roman Mouček (Chief Accountant/Financial Manager)	University of West Bohemia, Czechia
František Pártl (Technical Assistant, Proceedings Assistant Editor)	University of West Bohemia, Czechia
Ondřej Pražák (Technical Assistant)	University of West Bohemia, Czechia
Jan Rychlík (Social Events Manager)	University of West Bohemia, Czechia

Keynote Speakers

The organizers would like to thank the following respected scientists and researchers for delivering their keynote talks:

Philippe Blache, Director of Research at the Laboratoire Parole et Langage (LPL), Institute of Language, Communication and the Brain − CNRS & Aix-Marseille University, France

Ivan Habernal, Head of the Trustworthy Human Language Technologies (TrustHLT) Group − Department of Computer Science, Technische Universität Darmstadt, Germany

Juan Rafael Orozco-Arroyave, GITA Lab, School of Engineering, Universidad de Antioquia, Medellín, Colombia

Supporting Institution

The organizers would like to express their gratitude to the following institution for its continuous support and helpful attitude to the TSD conference:

International Speech Communication Association

https://www.isca-speech.org/iscaweb/

Plzeň, Czechia — Industrial Capital of West Bohemia
(About the Venue)

The city of Plzeň (or Pilsen in Germanic languages) is situated in the heart of West Bohemia at the confluence of four rivers: Úhlava, Úslava, Radbuza, and Mže. With its approx. 181,000 inhabitants, it is the fourth largest city in the Czech Republic and an important industrial, commercial, and administrative centre. It is also the capital of the Pilsen Region. In addition, it was elected the European Capital of Culture for 2015 by the Council of the European Union.

Plzeň is well-known for its brewing tradition. Pilsner beer is a planetwide legend. The trademark Pilsner Urquell has the best reputation all over the world thanks to the traditional recipe, high-quality hops from the famous Žatec hop fields, and crystal-clear groundwater from extraordinarily deep wells. Beer lovers will always appreciate a visit to the Brewery Museum or the Pilsner Urquell Brewery itself.

Plzeň is also the home of an industrial giant, Škoda. The Škoda Works used to be one of the largest European industrial conglomerates of the 20th century. They were founded in 1859 there, then in the Kingdom of Bohemia, Austrian Empire, by famous Czech engineer and industrialist knight Emil Škoda. Since then, the make Škoda with the distinctive winged arrow has been proudly put onto countless locomotives, tramways, trolleybuses, ships, aircraft, machine tools, steam turbines, and even nuclear reactors.

Apart from its delicious beer and advanced industrial production, Plzeň hides lots of cultural and historical treasures in its core. The city can boast the second-largest synagogue in Europe. The dominant feature of the old part of the city centre is certainly the 13th-century Gothic cathedral of St. Bartholomew, the loftiness of which is accentuated by its slim church spire. The spire was reconstructed into its modern shape after a fire in 1835 when it was hit by a lightning bolt during a night storm. It is the highest church spire in Czechia (102.34 m), and there is the possibility to go up and admire the view of the city. Not far from the cathedral, there is the splendid Renaissance Town Hall from 1558, later decorated with frescoes from 1908−12. The placement of the church within the grounds of the city square was also rather unique for its time. The church stands right across from the city hall. You will certainly also notice the Baroque spire of the Franciscan monastery. Moreover, plenty of pleasant cafes and pubs are situated on and around the main square.

There is also the beautiful Pilsen Historical Underground—under the city centre, a complex network of passageways and cellars can be found. The passages are about 14 km long, and visitors can see the most beautiful part of this labyrinth during the tour. A legend says that there is also a secret tunnel going to the Radyně Castle far behind the city limits.

It is also recommended to visit the City Zoological Garden, which has the second largest space for bears in Europe and keeps a few Komodo dragons, large lizards that exist in only a few zoos in the world.

In the surroundings of the city, there are some landmarks worth seeing, especially the Radyně Castle, the Kozel Chateau, and St. Peter's Rotunda in Starý Plzenec, which comes from the 10th century.

Plzeň is also an important centre of higher education: The University of West Bohemia in Plzeň provides a variety of courses for both Czech and international students. It is the only institution of higher education in this part of the country which prepares students for careers in engineering (electrical and mechanical), science (computer science, applied mathematics, physics, and mechanics), education (both primary and secondary), public health services, economics, philosophy, politics, archaeology, anthropology, foreign languages, law and public administration, art, and design. The Faculty of Medicine in Plzeň is one of five faculties of medicine of Charles University and educates physicians of numerous specializations, dentists, and highly qualified nurses.

Brief History of Plzeň

The new town of Plzeň (Pilsen) was founded at the confluence of four rivers—Mže, Radbuza, Úhlava, and Úslava—following a decree issued by the Czech king, Wenceslaus II Přemyslid. He did so in 1295. From the very beginning, the town was a busy trade centre located at the crossroads of two important trade routes. These linked the Czech lands with the German cities of Nürnberg and Regensburg.

In the 14th century, Plzeň was the third largest city after Prague and Kutná Hora. It comprised 290 houses in an area of 20 ha. Its population was 3,000 inhabitants. At the beginning of the 15th century, during the so-called Hussite Wars (1419–1434), Plzeň was unwaveringly on the Catholic side of the conflict. Therefore, it was besieged by Hussite troops led by radical Hussite priest Prokop Holý in July 1433. The Hussites besieged the town ineffectually for over nine months (among other reasons because of the existence of the large network of underground passages), and during one casual dauntless thrust of the Plzeň defenders, a camel was captured (and eaten later on) from the Hussite forces. That is how such an exotic (in Czech lands of those days) animal has appeared in the city coat of arms.

In the 16th century, after several fires that damaged the inner centre of the town, Italian architects and builders contributed significantly to the changing character of the city. The most renowned among them was Giovanni de Statia. The Holy Roman Emperor and the Czech king Rudolf II of Habsburg, resided in Pilsen twice between 1599 and 1600. It was at the time of the Estates' revolt. He fell in love with the city and even bought two houses neighbouring the town hall and had them reconstructed according to his taste. Later, in 1618, Pilsen was besieged and captured by Count Mansfeld's army.

Many Baroque-style buildings dating to the end of the 17th century were designed by Jakub Auguston. Sculptures were made by Kristian Widman. The historical heart of the city—almost identical to the original Gothic layout—was declared a protected historic city preserve in 1989.

Pilsen experienced tremendous growth in the first half of the 19th century. The City Brewery was founded in 1842, and the Škoda Works in 1859.

The historical core of the city of Plzeň is limited by the line of the former town fortification walls. These gave way, in the middle of the 19th century, to a green belt of town parks. Entering the grounds of the historical centre, one walks through streets that still respect the original Gothic urban layout.

All architecture lovers can also find more hidden jewels—objects appreciated for their artistic and historical value. These are burgher houses built by our ancestors in the styles of the Gothic, Renaissance, or Baroque periods. The architecture of these sights was successfully modeled by the reconstruction whirl of the end of the 19th century and the beginning of the 20th century.

Keynote Talks

Predictive Coding, Good-Enough Processing and Constructions: A Neuro-Cognitive Model for Dialogue

Philippe Blache ⓘ

Institute of Language, Communication and the Brain, France
LPL-CNRS, France
`blache@ilcb.fr`
`https://cv.hal.science/philippe-blache`

Abstract. Language understanding is a complex task, integrating different sources of information, from sounds and gestures to context. However, in spite of its complexity, this process is extremely fast and robust, performed in real time during conversations. Many studies have shown that this robustness and efficiency are made possible by different mechanisms: the ability to predict, the possibility of directly accessing entire pieces of meaning and the possibility to perform a "good-enough" processing, sufficient to access the meaning. These mechanisms, by substituting to the classical incremental and compositional architecture, facilitate the access to the meaning. However, existing models do not explain precisely when these facilitation mechanisms are triggered and whether they inhibit or on the contrary work in parallel with the standard ones.

I propose in this presentation a new model integrating both facilitation and standard mechanisms by revisiting the different stages of the processing: segmentation of the input, access to the corresponding meaning in long-term memory and integration to the interpretation under construction. This architecture is based on different features: unique representation of linguistic objects (independently from their granularities), control of the memory access (in particular thanks to search space reduction) and multiple-level prediction. This neuro-cognitive model provides a new framework explaining how deep and shallow mechanisms of language processing can cohabit. It is also a good candidate for explaining different effects of mismatch observed at the brain level.

Keywords: Language processing architecture · Understanding · Neuro-cognitive model.

Towards Privacy-Preserving Natural Language Processing

Ivan Habernal

Trusthworthy Human Language Technologies Department of Computer Science,
Technical University of Darmstadt
www.trusthlt.org
ivan.habernal@tu-darmstadt.de

Abstract. What does it mean for natural language processing (NLP) systems to protect privacy, and why should we even care? In this talk, we will explore privacy challenges and concerns in NLP and present possible solutions to address them. We will cover anonymization as well as formal techniques based on differential privacy both in training NLP models and in publishing data. Furthermore, we will also touch on legal and ethical implications when implementing privacy-preserving solutions in NLP.

Keywords: Privacy

1. Extended Abstract

In this talk, we are going to explore the topic of privacy in contemporary natural language processing. We will start with motivating examples showing why privacy matters in the first place. We will then adopt our working definition of privacy, differential privacy, which is a de-facto standard in private data analysis and has been recently gaining attention in the NLP community [3, 4]. We will then address some recent research questions tackled with colleagues from the Trustworthy Human Language Technologies group and beyond. First, how can we efficiently ensure differential privacy of training data fed into graph neural networks [6]? How about privacy of fine-tuning transformers across NLP tasks [11] or even pre-training transformer models with differential privacy [12] for domain adaptation? Second, we will tackle the problem of privacy in natural language texts, that is, can we 'privatize' sensitive texts and publish them without hesitation? We will show that the problem of text privatization is inherently hard [1]. We will highlight our open-source framework DP-Rewrite for conducting transparent and reproducible experiments [5] with the aim to avoid pitfalls of reported results which sometimes 'look too good to be true' [2], and show our approach to tighter privacy with pruning transformer models [7]. We will conclude with applications of privacy-preserving models or data publishing in domains such as mental health [10], crowdsourcing [9], and bias and fairness of large language models [8].

References

1. Habernal, I.: When differential privacy meets NLP: The devil is in the detail. In: Proceedings of the 2021 Conference on Empirical Methods in Natural Language Processing. pp. 1522–1528. Association for Computational Linguistics, Punta Cana, Dominican Republic (2021)
2. Habernal, I.: How reparametrization trick broke differentially-private text representation learning. In: Proceedings of the 60th Annual Meeting of the Association for Computational Linguistics (Volume 2: Short Papers). pp. 771–777. Association for Computational Linguistics, Dublin, Ireland (2022)
3. Habernal, I., Mireshghallah, F., Thaine, P., Ghanavati, S., Feyisetan, O.: Privacy-preserving natural language processing. In: Proceedings of the 17th Conference of the European Chapter of the Association for Computational Linguistics: Tutorial Abstracts. pp. 27–30. Association for Computational Linguistics, Dubrovnik, Croatia (2023)
4. Hu, L., Habernal, I., Shen, L., Wang, D.: Differentially private natural language models: Recent advances and future directions. arXiv preprint (2023)
5. Igamberdiev, T., Arnold, T., Habernal, I.: DP-Rewrite: Towards reproducibility and transparency in differentially private text rewriting. In: The 29th International Conference on Computational Linguistics. pp. 2927–2933. International Committee on Computational Linguistics, Gyeongju, Republic of Korea (2022)
6. Igamberdiev, T., Habernal, I.: Privacy-preserving graph convolutional networks for text classification. In: Proceedings of the Language Resources and Evaluation Conference. pp. 338–350. European Language Resources Association, Marseille, France (2022)
7. Igamberdiev, T., Habernal, I.: DP-BART for privatized text rewriting under local differential privacy. In: Findings of the Association for Computational Linguistics: ACL 2023. Association for Computational Linguistics, Toronto, Canada (2023)
8. Matzken, C., Eger, S., Habernal, I.: Trade-offs between fairness and privacy in language modeling. In: Findings of the Association for Computational Linguistics: ACL 2023. Association for Computational Linguistics, Toronto, Canada (2023)
9. Mouhammad, N., Daxenberger, J., Schiller, B., Habernal, I.: Crowdsourcing on sensitive data with privacy-preserving text rewriting. In: Proceedings of the 17th Linguistic Annotation Workshop. Association for Computational Linguistics, Toronto, Canada (2023)
10. Sawhney, R., Neerkaje, A.T., Habernal, I., Flek, L.: How much user context do we need? privacy by design in mental health NLP application. In: Proceedings of the International AAAI Conference on Web and Social Media. pp. 766–776. No. 17, AAAI Press, Limassol, Cyprus (2023)
11. Senge, M., Igamberdiev, T., Habernal, I.: One size does not fit all: investigating strategies for differentially-private learning across NLP tasks. In: Proceedings of the 2022 Conference on Empirical Methods in Natural Language Processing. pp. 7340–7353. Abu Dhabi, UAE (2022)
12. Yin, Y., Habernal, I.: Privacy-preserving models for legal natural language processing. In: Proceedings of the Natural Legal Language Processing Workshop 2022. pp. 172–183. Association for Computational Linguistics, Abu Dhabi, United Arab Emirates (2022)

Speech and Language Markers in Neurodegeneration

Juan Rafael Orozco-Arroyave

GITA Lab, Universidad de Antioquia UdeA, Medellín, Colombia
LME Lab, Friedrich-Alexander Universität, Erlangen-Nürnberg, Germany

Abstract. The progress in medicine achieved within the last decades has led humanity (especially in the northern hemisphere) to live longer. It is estimated that people in developed countries have increased their life expectancy until around 90 years. Given the fact that aging is the most documented risk factor for developing neurodegenerative diseases, this longevity phenomenon brings new challenges to science in terms of detection and monitoring of neurodegeneration. There exist methods for diagnosing and treating neurological disorders; however, they are either very expensive or invasive, requiring sophisticated machinery and well-trained expert clinicians to handle the devices and interpret the results. Recent advances in speech and language processing have shown how to enable unintrusive detection and monitoring of neurological disorders like Parkinson's and Alzheimer's. Classical approaches and modern methods like those based on language embeddings have been shown to be complementary in the task of detecting and monitoring neurological diseases. Even though their accuracy and sensitivity need to be improved to make these new approaches suitable for clinical practice on a regular basis, their simplicity in data collection and interpretation bring them as an inexpensive and promising biomarker to be used as a second opinion before deciding to make more sophisticated screenings. Among the challenges for future research, it is necessary to continue developing robust methods for speech recording under different acoustic conditions. Finally, since privacy is a significant concern, Federated Learning emerges as a promising approach in which privacy is preserved while physiological information of patients in different centers located at different latitudes is transferred and used to improve the performance of the whole system, enabling the possibility to create more robust and reliable approaches.

Keywords: Speech Processing · Language Processing · Parkinson's Disease · Alzheimer's Disease · Neurological Diseases

Acknowledgements

The organizers would like to give special thanks to the following scientists and researchers who substantially contributed to the successful completion of the TSD 2023 review process by voluntarily agreeing to deliver extra reviews:

Tomás Arias-Vergara, Friedrich-Alexander-Universität Erlangen-Nuremberg, Germany
Jan Lehečka, University of West Bohemia, Czechia
David Mareček, Charles University, Czechia
Jindřich Matoušek, University of West Bohemia, Czechia
František Pártl, University of West Bohemia, Czechia
Ondřej Pražák, University of West Bohemia, Czechia
Josef V. Psutka, University of West Bohemia, Czechia
Zbyněk Zajíc, University of West Bohemia, Czechia

Contents

Speech

Text

Japanese How-to Tip Machine Reading Comprehension by Multi-task Learning Based on Generative Model

Xiaotian Wang, Tingxuan Li, Takuya Tamura, Shunsuke Nishida, Fuzhu Zhu, and Takehito Utsuro[✉]

Degree Programs in Systems and Information Engineering, Graduate School of Science and Technology, University of Tsukuba, 1-1-1, Tennodai, Tsukuba, Ibaraki 305-8573, Japan
{s2320811,s2120816,s2120744,s2320778,s2220804,
utsuro.takehito.ge}@u.tsukuba.ac.jp
https://nlp.iit.tsukuba.ac.jp

Abstract. In the research of machine reading comprehension of Japanese how-to tip QA tasks, conventional extractive machine reading comprehension methods have difficulty in dealing with cases in which the answer string spans multiple locations in the context. In this paper, we trained a generative machine reading comprehension model of Japanese how-to tip by constructing a generative dataset based on the website "wikihow" as a source of information. We proposed two methods for multi-task learning to fine-tune the generative model, i.e., i) multi-task learning with generative and extractive hybrid training dataset, where both generative and extractive datasets are simultaneously trained on a single model, and ii) multi-task learning with inter-sentence semantic similarity and answer generation, where, drawing upon the answer generation task, the model additionally learns the distance between the sentences of question/context and the answer in the training examples. Evaluation experimental results showed that both of the multi-task learning models significantly outperformed that of the single-task learning model on the generative QA dataset. Especially, that with generative and extractive hybrid training dataset performed the best in terms of the manual evaluation result.

Keywords: QA Task · Machine Reading Comprehension · Generative Model · How-to Tip · mT5 · Multi-task Learning

1 Introduction

As shown in Fig. 1, a machine reading comprehension task in natural language processing is a task, given a question written in natural language and a context, to extract from the context the answer part of the question. In recent years, the advancement of deep learning technologies and the availability of large datasets has led to a number of achievements in the research field of machine reading comprehension. For example, it has been reported that, for machine reading comprehension of SQuAD [14][1], which is a

---

[1] https://rajpurkar.github.io/SQuAD-explorer/.

K. Ekštein et al. (Eds.): TSD 2023, LNAI 14102, pp. 3–14, 2023.
https://doi.org/10.1007/978-3-031-40498-6_1

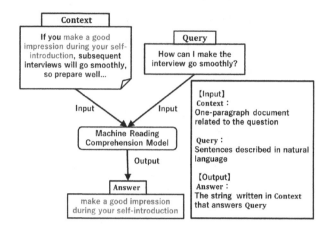

Fig. 1. The Framework of How-to Tip Machine Reading Comprehension

machine reading comprehension dataset created from articles in the English Wikipedia, machine reading comprehension outperforms humans. In addition, SQuAD 2.0 [13], a dataset containing "unanswerable" QA examples, has been created to take into account cases where the context does not contain the answer to the question.

In addition to SQuAD [13, 14], which targets factoid questions such as proper nouns and quantities, and machine reading comprehension datasets with answer possibilities[2], there has been a lot of research on non-factoid questions such as how things are done and why things are done. Compared to factoid type questions, which are relatively simple, non-factoid type questions are more challenging. Among various kinds of non-factoid knowledge which are the key to developing techniques for non-factoid QA tasks, Chen et al. [2] studied how to develop a dataset for training Japanese how-to tip (following Chen et al. [2], we use the simplified term "tip") QA models.

In general, the model and dataset for the usual machine reading comprehension task follow the method of extracting from the context the part of the question text that is the answer. However, as illustrated in Sect. 2, in tip machine reading comprehension, the answer string often spans multiple locations in the context. The method of fine-tuning of the BERT model [3] for machine reading comprehension tasks is not suitable for such cases. Therefore, in this paper, we apply a generative model, mT5 [18], to generate answers for tip questions, instead of an extractive model that extracts strings in context. We developed a question-and-answer dataset for generative machine reading comprehension by utilizing the Japanese version of "wikihow"[3], which is a comprehensive website that compiles tips. We then proposed two methods for multi-task learning to fine-tune the generative model. The first method is the multi-task learning with generative and extractive hybrid training dataset, where both generative and extractive datasets are simultaneously trained on a single model. The second method is the multi-task learning with inter-sentence semantic similarity and answer generation, where, draw-

---

[2] http://www.cl.ecei.tohoku.ac.jp/rcqa/.

[3] https://www.wikihow.jp/.

ing upon the answer generation task, the model additionally learns the distance between the sentences of question/context and the answer in the training examples. The evaluation results showed that both of the multi-task learning methods significantly outperformed single-task learning in generative question-and-answer examples. Between the two methods for multi-task learning, that with generative and extractive hybrid training dataset performed the best in terms of the manual evaluation result.

Our contributions are as follows:

1. We employed the mT5 [18] which is an encoder-decoder model based on the Transformer [17] as a generative model for machine reading comprehension and applied it to how-to tip machine reading comprehension.
2. We developed a question-and-answer dataset for generative machine reading comprehension by utilizing the Japanese version of "wikihow", which is a comprehensive website that compiles tips.
3. We proposed two methods for multi-task learning to fine-tune the generative model, i.e., i) multi-task learning with generative and extractive hybrid training dataset, where both generative and extractive datasets are simultaneously trained on a single model, and ii) multi-task learning with inter-sentence semantic similarity and answer generation, where, drawing upon the answer generation task, the model additionally learns the distance between the sentences of question/context and the answer in the training examples.
4. The evaluation results demonstrated that both of the multi-task learning methods significantly outperformed single-task learning in generative question-and-answer examples. Especially, multi-task learning with generative and extractive hybrid training dataset performed the best in terms of the manual evaluation result.

2 Difference Between Extractive and Generative Types in Machine Reading Comprehension

The machine reading comprehension task in SQuAD [14], a representative dataset for machine reading comprehension of the factoid type, is to extract from the context the parts that are the answers to the questions. In the Japanese tip QA dataset [2], question-and-answer examples are also created by means of designing questions in accordance with short articles used as contexts and by extracting corresponding answers from the contexts. In this paper, we refer to this method as "Extractive Machine Reading Comprehension".

Devlin et al. proposed BERT model [3], which is a typical extractive machine reading comprehension model used in extractive machine reading comprehension tasks. In BERT, a bi-directional encoder mechanism with Transformer [17] predicts the start and end positions of the answer in the machine reading comprehension task, and outputs the span between the two positions as the answer to the question.

On the other hand, in this paper, we refer to the method of machine reading comprehension that generates answers as "Generative Machine Reading Comprehension". There exist research examples of generative machine reading comprehension [1] that do not require context, but only input questions to a pre-trained and fine-tuned model to

Table 1. Specific Examples of Predictions by the Models (mBERT and mT5, English Translation of Japanese Examples)

	Example 1	Example 2
Question	How do I make my own temporary tattoo sheet?	How do I find the best quote to use at the beginning of an essay?
Context	The fluidity of the gel pen ink makes it easy to adhere from the seal to the skin once the design is complete. Draw your own design on tracing paper or parchment paper with a pencil, then color it in with a gel pen. Try to get as much ink on the line as possible, but...	If you use famous quotes that many people use verbatim, that alone will bore the reader. It will also even seem as if the author is not taking the project seriously or does not think much of the reader
Reference Answer	Draw the design using a dark-colored gel pen	Avoid clichés and quotes you see often
mBERT Answer	Draw your own design on tracing paper or parchment paper with a pencil	use famous quotes that many people use verbatim
mT5 Answer	Use a gel pen to draw your design of choice on tracing paper or parchment paper	Consider whether to use the quotation verbatim.

generate sentences that serve as answers. In this paper, however, we perform generative machine reading comprehension in a setting that assumes the input of context.

For the generative machine reading comprehension task, we apply a generative machine reading comprehension model with the ability to generate answers, where the model is with an encoder of Transformer [17] that converts input text into an internal representation, and a decoder mechanism of Transformer that summarizes the output of the encoder and further produces a variable-length output. A representative example of such a generative model is T5 [12]. This paper uses a model, in which fine-tuning is performed for downstream tasks on a model that has been pre-trained using a vast amount of training data for various tasks. So far, it is known that T5 achieved high performance on extractive machine reading comprehension tasks when applied to SQuAD [14].

To illustrate the differences in the properties of both models, this paper compares the performance of BERT [3] (mBERT) and T5 [12] (mT5 [18]) pre-trained with multilingual texts. Specifically, for the extractive model, fine-tuning of mBERT was performed using 1,614 extractive tip QA data (807 answerable examples and 807 non-answerable examples) developed by Chen et al. [2]. For the generative model, mT5 [18] was fine-tuned by using the 10,000 generative tip QA data created in Sect. 3, using the method described in Sect. 4.2 as well as following the evaluation procedure of Sect. 5.1. Then, we evaluated the performance of the tip machine reading comprehension models by inputting the questions and contexts of the evaluation examples of the generative question-and-answer data into both models. Table 1 shows specific examples of the evaluation of both models. Example 1 in Table 1 shows that mBERT can only extract the parts of the context that are just fragments of answers, whereas mT5 can summarize answer fragments scattered in multiple locations in the context, or can complete word endings. Example 2 in Table 1 shows that mBERT ignores the second half of the context that contains a negative message, but extracts a part of the first half of the context as the answer, which only contains a positive message. mT5, on the other hand, does not ignore the second half of the context that contains a negative message, but generates answers referring to the overall context information including the negative message in the second half of the context. Thus, overall, with the ability to generate answers considering the whole context information, it can be concluded that mT5 outperforms mBERT in the task of tip machine reading comprehension with the generative question-and-answer data.

3 Generative Question-and-Answer Dataset

In this section, we describe how to use Japanese wikihow[4] as a source information to create a QA dataset on generative machine reading comprehension methods.

Wikihow is a comprehensive website that compiles tips and guides across 19 diverse topics such as cars, family, and health. While previous research conducted by Koupaee et al. [8] utilized a dataset derived from the English version of wikihow for summarization purposes, this study adopts a distinct approach by using the article's title and subtitle as questions, and the summary of the article text as answers. An example of the structure of the website's tip column is presented below as an illustration (English translation of Japanese examples).

Title: The way to wash jeans that do not fade easily
Subtitle: Care after washing
Summary: Spray water with a mist instead of washing
Context: If you start to notice sweat, stains, or odor on your jeans, do not immediately put them in the washing machine. First, spray water with a mist to remove the odor. Washing jeans once every 4~5 weeks is sufficient. Prepare a misting sprayer and add water and vodka in a 1:1 ratio. Placing jeans that have been sprayed with water in the freezer overnight will further reduce odor.

The above web column is formatted into QA example data on the generative machine reading comprehension method used in this study as follows.

Question: About the way to wash jeans that do not fade easily, what should I do with care after washing?
Context: If you start to notice sweat, stains, or odor on your jeans, do not immediately put them in the washing machine. First, spray water with a mist to remove the odor. Washing jeans once every 4~5 weeks is sufficient. Prepare a misting sprayer and add water and vodka in a 1:1 ratio. Placing jeans that have been sprayed with water in the freezer overnight will further reduce odor.
Answer: Spray water with a mist instead of washing.

In order to remove examples that were difficult to answer, filtering was performed based on the length of the example. The length here is uniformly measured as the number of morphemes in the sentence that is segmented by MeCab[5]. As filtering criteria,

---

[4] https://www.wikihow.jp/.

[5] https://github.com/neologd/mecab-ipadic-neologd.

Table 2. Statistics of the Training Examples of Generative How-to Tip Dataset Before and After Filtering

	Number of examples	Average length of contexts (# of morphemes)	Average length of answers (# of morphemes)	BLEU (by the baseline mT5 of a single-task learning)
Before filtering	23, 937	108.75	9.92	8.0
After filtering	10, 000	66.97	11.52	9.0

Table 3. The Number of Examples of QA Datasets

(a) Generative QA Dataset

	Total number of examples
Training Set	10, 000
Validation Set	1, 509
Evaluation Set	235

(b) Generative and Extractive QA Dataset

	Total number of examples (# of Generative Type / # of Extractive Type)
Training Set	20, 000(10, 000/10, 000)
Validation Set	1, 509(1, 509/1, 509)
Evaluation Set	235(235/0)

we excluded examples where the context was less than twice the length of the question or more than 10 times the length of the question, and examples where the concatenated question and context exceeded the maximum length of 512 morphemes of the input sentence, in accordance with the specification of the mT5 model of huggingface[6] used in the experiments. Before filtering, the total number of examples is 25,681, from which we first remove 1,509 validation examples as well as 235 evaluation examples that satisfy the length criteria of filtering described above, where 23,937 training examples remain. Filtering was performed to those 23,937 training examples. Statistics of the training examples of the dataset before and after filtering is shown in Table 2. Among all the datasets used in the evaluation of this paper, Table 3(a) summarizes the statistics of the QA dataset on generative machine reading comprehension methods created by performing the filtering in this section, where the overall dataset is divided into training, validation, and evaluation sets. When the baseline mT5 of a single-task learning described in Sect. 5.1 is evaluated against the 235 evaluation examples, as shown in Table 2, the filtering resulted in 1.0 point increase in the BLEU score for the performance of the mT5 model that was trained on the generative tip QA dataset.

4   Multi-task Learning in Generative How-To Tip Machine Reading Comprehension

Multi-task learning is a technique that enhances accuracy by enabling a single model to be simultaneously trained on multiple tasks that are related to the target task. This section introduces two multi-task learning approaches to generative tip machine reading comprehension.

---

[6] https://huggingface.co/google/mt5-base.

4.1 Multi-task Learning with Generative and Extractive Hybrid Training Dataset

T5 [12], which employs a text-to-text input/output format, enables the simultaneous execution of multi-task learning on multiple tasks by establishing distinct prefixes for each task and subsequently appending them to the onset of examples. This capability has been inherited by mT5 [18], the multilingual iteration of T5. The first method for multi-task learning to fine-tune the generative model is the multi-task learning with generative and extractive hybrid training dataset, where both generative and extractive datasets are simultaneously trained on a single model.

The reason for selecting generative and extractive machine reading comprehension as the subjects for multi-task learning is because they possess common factors or useful characteristics. Additionally, generative machine reading comprehension is more challenging than extractive, and for difficult tasks, learning can be easier by obtaining information from simpler tasks. Furthermore, for the dataset in use, since the data has content shared between the two tasks, it is desired to perform multiple tasks of generative and extractive machine reading comprehension on this data. Therefore, the generative question-answer examples created in Sect. 3 were used as data for the generative task, and the reference answers to these examples were added to the beginning of the context and used as data for the extractive task. Both sets of data were mixed in equal proportions and inputted into the generative model for multi-task learning.

4.2 Multi-task Learning with Inter-sentence Semantic Similarity and Answer Generation

The second method for multi-task learning to fine-tune the generative model is the multi-task learning with inter-sentence semantic similarity and answer generation. Inter-sentence semantic similarity measure has been incorporated in numerous machine learning studies, and previous work by Tymoshenko et al. [16] has linked them to machine reading comprehension tasks. Therefore, drawing upon the answer generation task performed by mT5, we introduce a method that additionally learns the distance between the sentences of question/context and the answer in the training examples. The objective is to produce answers that are more akin to the input of the question/context.

The details of the model are delineated in Fig. 2. Utilizing the Siamese Network framework, Sentence-BERT [15] has demonstrated outstanding performance in the task of inter-sentence semantic similarity. We use the mT5 encoder's embedding layer for the inter-sentence semantic similarity task. In order to avoid having more than one types of sentence embeddings in answer generation tasks and to avoid the protracted training duration, we have devised a structure akin to the Siamese Network, employing the embedding layer of the mT5 encoder to perform the task of inter-sentence semantic similarity.

Furthermore, with regards to the loss function, for the inter-sentence semantic similarity task proposed in this section, we applied the Multiple Negative Ranking Loss function [5], which is used in situations where only positive examples are present, as all instances in the training data were treated as positive examples. In the implementation, we referred to the algorithm within the script of the Multiple Negative Ranking

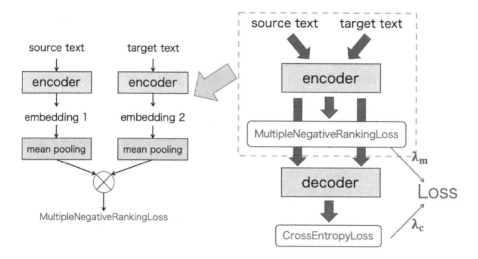

Fig. 2. Architecture of the Model for Multi-task Learning of Semantic Similarity and Answer Generation

Loss function of the sentence-transformers library[7] and implemented the function. For the answer generation task, on the other hand, the default Cross Entropy Loss of the mT5 model is used. The loss function for the inter-sentence semantic similarity task is denoted as L_m, while that for the answer generation task is denoted as L_c. By computing the weighted sum of the two tasks' loss functions as the model's overall loss function, multi-task learning of the generative model is performed using the following equation.

$$Loss = \lambda_m L_m + \lambda_c L_c$$

5   Evaluation

5.1   Evaluation Procedure

In this section, we describe our experiments and evaluation using the generative QA dataset created in Sect. 3. The detailed number of examples for each dataset is shown in Table 3, where Table 3(a) shows those of the generative QA dataset, while Table 3(b) shows those of the generative-extractive hybrid QA dataset. The generative model used was mT5[8], a multilingual version of T5 [12]. In this paper, we conducted experiments using the generative tip machine reading comprehension dataset created in Sect. 3[9], employing two proposed methods as described in Sect. 4.

---

[7] https://github.com/UKPLab/sentence-transformers/blob/master/sentence_transformers/losses/MultipleNegativesRankingLoss.py.

[8] https://huggingface.co/google/mt5-base.

[9] In fine-tuning, the model for the minimum validation loss is selected where the maximum number of epochs is 40. The learning rate was set to 0.00005, and the batch size was set to 16.

As shown in Table 3, each dataset is divided into training, validation, and evaluation sets. For the multi-task learning using the generative-extractive hybrid training dataset described in Sect. 4.1, QA examples related to extraction are created by adding the reference answer for QA examples related to generation to the beginning of the context. As shown in Table 3(b), 10,000 training and 1,509 validation examples related to extraction are created with this procedure. We used the evaluation results of mT5 of a single-task learning trained using only the generative QA dataset as a baseline[10], and compared it with the proposed methods.

In the experiments using the proposed method of multi-task learning, which is based on inter-sentence semantic similarity and answer generation described in Sect. 4.2, utilizing the formula of the proposed loss function, we conducted experiments with the combinations of λ_m and λ_c ranging from $\lambda_m = 0.95$ and $\lambda_c = 0.05$ to $\lambda_m = 0.05$ and $\lambda_c = 0.95$ with 0.05 increments in between.

We employed BLEU [11][11] and ROUGE-L [9][12] for automatic evaluation. However, since the evaluation results by BLEU and ROUGE-L only take into account the level of agreement between the predicted and reference answers in terms of token-level literal matching, we also performed manual evaluation[13]. Manual evaluation focused on determining the validity of the generated sentences as the answer when the context is given. Statistical significance is tested with mteval Toolkit[14] for BLEU and with Welch's t-test for ROUGE-L and manual evaluation.

5.2 Evaluation Results

The evaluation results are shown in Table 4, where the proposed two methods of multi-task learning yielded better performance than the model of the single-task learning.

The evaluation result based on BLEU is calculated by taking the geometric mean of the 1~4-gram matches between the predicted answers of the model and the reference answers (called bleu-n in Table 4), with a penalty applied for short generated sentences (BP; brevity penalty). While the bleu-n scores show that the multi-task learning approach based on inter-sentence semantic similarity and answer generation outperform the other approaches, the BLEU scores of the two multi-task learning approaches are the same due to the influence of BP. Additionally, the manually-evaluated results also indicate that the multi-task learning approach based on generative and extractive hybrid training dataset is superior. In terms of the ROUGE-L, the evaluation results also demonstrated that both of the multi-task learning methods significantly outperformed the single-task learning in generative question-and-answer examples. In the comparison of the ROUGE-L scores of the two approaches to the multi-task learning, that based on inter-sentence semantic similarity and answer generation outperformed that based on generative and extractive hybrid training dataset. Overall, it can be concluded that the

---

[10] The learning rate was set to 0.00003, and the batch size was set to 24. Other hyper parameters are the same as those of the multi-task learning.

[11] https://github.com/mjpost/sacrebleu.

[12] https://github.com/google-research/google-research/tree/master/rouge.

[13] Manual evaluation was done by the first author of the paper.

[14] https://github.com/odashi/mteval.

Table 4. Results of the Generative Model (mT5) Evaluated with the QA Datasets of Table 3 (Evaluation Sets). G-Examples stands for Generative Examples of Table 3(a), while G&E-Examples stands for Generative and Extractive Examples of Table 3(b). In addition, the abbreviation (A/B) in manual evaluation refers to (The number of correct answers by manual judgment/The number of evaluation examples). † stands for significant ($p < 0.05$) difference with the BLEU or ROUGE-L or Manual Evaluation of Single-Task learning approach.

(a) Result of Generative Model fine-tuned by Single-Task Approach

Dataset	Task	bleu-1	bleu-2	bleu-3	bleu-4	BP	BLEU	ROUGE-L	Manual Evaluation
G-Examples	Single-Task	43.7	19.6	10.0	5.5	0.611	9.0	33.78	92/235

(b) Result of Generative Model fine-tuned by Multi-task Approach of Answer Generation and Answer Extraction

Dataset	Task	bleu-1	bleu-2	bleu-3	bleu-4	BP	BLEU	ROUGE-L	Manual Evaluation
G&E-Examples	Multi-Task	43.1	21.1	11.3	6.7	0.868	**14.2**†	37.79†	**154/235**†

(c) Results of Generative Model fine-tuned by Multi-task Approach of Semantic Similarity and Answer Generation

Dataset	Loss Weight λ_m, λ_c	bleu-1	bleu-2	bleu-3	bleu-4	BP	BLEU	ROUGE-L	Manual Evaluation
	0.35 , 0.65	43.2	**21.8**	**12.4**	**7.0**	0.823	13.9†	37.64†	141/235†
G-Examples	0.25 , 0.75	**43.7**	21.6	12.1	6.7	0.855	**14.2**†	**38.28**†	150/235†
	0.10 , 0.90	42.5	20.7	11.8	6.5	**0.878**	14.1†	37.98†	149/235†

multi-task learning with generative and extractive hybrid training dataset performed the best in terms of the manual evaluation result.

The evaluation results of models trained using the multi-task learning approach based on inter-sentence semantic similarity and answer generation are presented by listing the top 3 results[15] of the BLEU scores and the ROUGE-L scores obtained from the combinations of λ_m and λ_c. The results with high BLEU scores and ROUGE-L scores are concentrated within the range of $\lambda_m < \lambda_c$. This is because the relationship between L_m and L_c becomes $L_m \gg L_c$ during the training convergence because of the difference of the characteristics of the loss functions of the two tasks of the inter-sentence semantic similarity and answer generation[16]. To reduce the influence of L_m, setting $\lambda_m < \lambda_c$ can help suppress the effect of L_m in the inter-sentence semantic similarity task. However, setting λ_m too small would eliminate the effect of L_m, leading to a decrease in model performance.

6   Related Work

Bajaj et al. have done a relevant research, named MS MARCO [1], which is a vast machine reading comprehension dataset that sources its information from Bing and

---

[15] The top 3 results of the BLEU scores and the ROUGE-L scores are the same between the two metrics.

[16] Roughly speaking, even at the end of the training convergence, the similarity between the sentences of question/context and the answer in the validation examples tend to be relatively low, making L_m relatively larger, while the answers predicted by the model to the validation examples tend to be very close to the reference answers, making L_c much smaller than L_m.

Cortana search histories. By using MS MARCO, a generative machine reading comprehension task that generates abstractive answers based on context[17] starts to emerge, and ROUGE-L and BLEU-1 are used as evaluation criteria for generative machine reading comprehension. While Nishida et al. [10] proposed an encoder-decoder model with Transformer [17] for this task and achieved the top rank on the leader board at the time of publication of the paper [10] (currently ranked 5th in June 2023, excluding the human baseline, and the four models and papers above it have not yet been published). Other datasets that feature abstractive answers in the task of generative machine reading comprehension include DuReader [4] and NarrativeQA [7].

As a study on machine reading comprehension at scale that is closely related to generative machine reading comprehension, Izacard and Grave [6] proposed a method in which the top search result contexts and questions are independently fed into the encoder, while the resulting representations of the top search result contexts and questions obtained from the encoder are concatenated and input into the decoder. This demonstrates the significance of generative machine reading comprehension methods in the task of machine reading comprehension at scale.

7   Conclusion

In this study, we employed the mT5 [18] as a generative model for machine reading comprehension and applied it to how-to tip machine reading comprehension. We developed a question-and-answer dataset for generative machine reading comprehension by utilizing the Japanese version of wikihow. Then, we proposed two methods for multi-task learning to fine-tune the generative model. The evaluation results demonstrated that both of the multi-task learning methods significantly outperformed the single-task learning in generative question-and-answer examples. Future work includes applying the proposed multi-task learning approaches to other datasets of generative machine reading comprehension such as MS MARCO [1], NarrativeQA [7], and DuReader [4].

Acknowledgements. This work was supported by JSPS KAKENHI Grant Number 21H00901.

References

1. Bajaj, P., et al.: MS MARCO: a human generated machine reading comprehension dataset. arXiv preprint arXiv:1611.09268 (2016)
2. Chen, T., Li, H., Kasamatsu, M., Utsuro, T., Kawada, Y.: Developing a how-to tip machine comprehension dataset and its evaluation in machine comprehension by BERT. In: Proceedings of the 3rd FEVER, pp. 26–35 (2020)
3. Devlin, J., Chang, M.W., Lee, K., Toutanova, K.: BERT: pre-training of deep bidirectional transformers for language understanding. In: Proceedings of the NAACL-HLT, pp. 4171–4186 (2019)
4. He, W., et al.: DuReader: a Chinese machine reading comprehension dataset from real-world applications. In: Proceedings of the Workshop on Machine Reading for Question Answering, pp. 37–46 (2018)

---

[17] Question Answering Task of MS MARCO at https://microsoft.github.io/msmarco/.

5. Henderson, M.L., et al.: Efficient natural language response suggestion for smart reply. arXiv preprint arXiv:1705.00652 (2017)
6. Izacard, G., Grave, E.: Leveraging passage retrieval with generative models for open domain question answering. In: Proceedings of the 16th EACL, pp. 874–880 (2021)
7. Kočiský, T., et al.: The NarrativeQA reading comprehension challenge. Trans. Assoc. Comput. Linguist. **6**, 317–328 (2018)
8. Koupaee, M., Wang, W.Y.: WikiHow: a large scale text summarization dataset. arXiv preprint arXiv:1810.09305 (2018)
9. Lin, C.Y.: ROUGE: a package for automatic evaluation of summaries. In: Proceedings of the Workshop on Text Summarization Branches Out, pp. 74–81 (2004)
10. Nishida, K., et al.: Multi-style generative reading comprehension. In: Proceedings of the 57th ACL, pp. 2273–2284 (2019)
11. Papineni, K., Roukos, S., Ward, T., Zhu, W.J.: Bleu: a method for automatic evaluation of machine translation. In: Proceedings 40th ACL, pp. 311–318 (2002)
12. Raffel, C., et al.: Exploring the limits of transfer learning with a unified text-to-text transformer. J. Mach. Learn. Res. 1–67 (2020)
13. Rajpurkar, P., Jia, R., Liang, P.: Know what you don't know: unanswerable questions for SQuAD. In: Proceedings of the 56th ACL (Volume 2: Short Papers), pp. 784–789 (2018)
14. Rajpurkar, P., Zhang, J., Lopyrev, K., Liang, P.: SQuAD: 100,000+ questions for machine comprehension of text. In: Proceedings of the EMNLP, pp. 2383–2392 (2016)
15. Reimers, N., Gurevych, I.: Sentence-BERT: sentence embeddings using Siamese BERT-networks. In: Proceedings of the EMNLP and 9th IJCNLP, pp. 3982–3992 (2019)
16. Tymoshenko, K., Moschitti, A.: Cross-pair text representations for answer sentence selection. In: Proceedings of the EMNLP, pp. 2162–2173 (2018)
17. Vaswani, A., et al.: Attention is all you need. arXiv preprint arXiv:1706.03762 (2017)
18. Xue, L., et al.: mT5: a massively multilingual pre-trained text-to-text transformer. In: Proceedings of the NAACL-HLT, pp. 483–498 (2021)

One Model to Rule Them All: Ranking Slovene Summarizers

Aleš Žagar[(✉)] and Marko Robnik-Šikonja

Faculty of Computer and Information Science, University of Ljubljana,
Večna pot 113, 1000 Ljubljana, Slovenia
{ales.zagar,marko.robnik}@fri.uni-lj.si

Abstract. Text summarization is an essential task in natural language processing, and researchers have developed various approaches over the years, ranging from rule-based systems to neural networks. However, there is no single model or approach that performs well on every type of text. We propose a system that recommends the most suitable summarization model for a given text. The proposed system employs a fully connected neural network that analyzes the input content and predicts which summarizer should score the best in terms of ROUGE score for a given input. The meta-model selects among four different summarization models, developed for the Slovene language, using different properties of the input, in particular its Doc2Vec document representation. The four Slovene summarization models deal with different challenges associated with text summarization in a less-resourced language. We evaluate the proposed SloMetaSum model performance automatically and parts of it manually. The results show that the system successfully automates the step of manually selecting the best model.

Keywords: Text summarization · low-resource languages · meta-model · Slovene language

1 Introduction

Text summarization identifies the essential information in a document or a collection of documents and presents it in a concise and coherent manner. In spite of the long efforts of natural language processing (NLP), text summarization is still a challenging task. With the explosive growth of digital information, summarizing large volumes of text into a shorter, more manageable form is becoming increasingly important.

There are two main approaches to text summarization: extractive and abstractive. Extractive summarization selects a subset of sentences or phrases from the original text that best represents the content. The selected sentences are combined to form a summary. Abstractive summarization, on the other hand, generates new sentences that capture the meaning of the original text. Extractive summarization is simpler and faster than abstractive summarization, but it can

© The Author(s), under exclusive license to Springer Nature Switzerland AG 2023
K. Ekštein et al. (Eds.): TSD 2023, LNAI 14102, pp. 15–24, 2023.
https://doi.org/10.1007/978-3-031-40498-6_2

result in summaries that contain redundant and repetitive content. Abstractive summarization is more challenging and requires more advanced natural language processing techniques, but it can produce human-like summaries.

State-of-the-art technology for text summarization has seen a significant shift in recent years with the rise of transformer neural network architectures, such as T5 [13] and GPT-3 [1]. This resulted in the summarization models whose summaries closely resemble those written by humans, with few repetitions and inaccuracies. These models are also capable of processing increasingly long content, enabling the creation of summaries for larger volumes of text. Consequently, state-of-the-art automatic summaries can be clear and easy to comprehend for end-users.

In the context of the less-resourced morphologically-rich Slovene language, text summarization is even more challenging than in English, due to limited availability of resources and data, as well as research. We produced four Slovene summarization models with different properties and trained them on different training data[1]. Our four models encompass two extraction summarizers (one based on a simple word frequency sentence selection, the other being graph-based), an abstractive T5-based model, and a hybrid extractive-abstractive model. In general, the T5-based transformer model works best but may not generalize well for all types of input text. Therefore, we address the problem of which summarization model is the most appropriate for a given text, based on text length and genre.

We propose a novel Slovene summarization system (named SloMetaSum), consisting of extractive, abstractive, and hybrid summarizers and a meta-model that selects among them. The proposed meta-system consists of a fully connected neural network that analyzes the input content and recommends the most suitable summarization model for a given text. To achieve this, SloMetaSum uses the Doc2Vec [7] numerical representation of documents and predicts the ROUGE scores for each of the summarizers. By using a combination of approaches, the system can effectively generate high-quality summaries that are informative and easy to understand for many types of text, regardless of their length and genre[2].

Our contributions are:

- We have developed four summarization models that can effectively summarize text of varying lengths and genres, making them versatile for a range of applications.
- We overcame the challenges of the low-resourced Slovene language, and created high-performing models for summarizing Slovene text.
- We have also created a meta-model that can recommend the best-suited summarization model for a given text based on factors such as length, complexity, level of abstraction, and intended use case.

---

[1] Within the scope of the RSDO project: https://www.cjvt.si/rsdo/.
[2] The demo is available at https://slovenscina.eu/en/povzemanje. The code repositories are available at https://github.com/azagsam/metamodel and https://github.com/clarinsi/SloSummarizer.

The rest of the paper is organized as follows. We present related research in Sect. 2. Section 3 describes the datasets. In Sect. 4, we describe summarization systems and the meta-model. We present our experiments and discuss the findings in Sect. 5. Section 6 concludes and recommends future research.

2 Related Work

Early approaches to text summarization relied on statistical frequencies of words, sentence position, and sentences containing keywords [12]. These approaches aimed to extract important sentences or phrases from a text and generate a summary by concatenating them. Abstractive methods involved deleting less important words from the text to create a summary [6].

Graph-based methods have been another popular approach to text summarization. In this approach, the document is represented as a graph, where sentences are nodes, and edges represent the relationships between them. The graph is then used to generate a summary by selecting the most important sentences. This method has been explored in several works [3,10].

With the advent of neural networks, there has been an increasing interest in developing abstractive summarization techniques. Early neural abstractive systems used methods such as LSTM and other recurrent neural networks [11, 14]. However, transformer-based architectures have emerged as state-of-the-art models for abstractive text summarization [9,18]. These models use self-attention mechanisms to selectively focus on important parts of the text and can generate more fluent and coherent summaries compared to earlier methods.

While several approaches have been proposed for text summarization, many of them are designed to handle specific genres or types of text. In this work, our goal is to build a summarization system that can handle every type of text and genre with every possible property that can appear in the real world. This includes texts of varying lengths, topics, styles, and summaries that capture the most important information in the text. Achieving this goal requires developing a robust and adaptable model that can learn to summarize texts of diverse types and produce high-quality summaries.

3 Datasets

In this section, we describe the datasets we used in our research. Below, we provide a short description of the datasets, with their statistics contained in Table 1.

The STA dataset (general news articles from the Slovenian Press Agency) consists of 366,126 documents and the first paragraph of each article was used as a proxy for summary since the dataset does not contain hand-written human summaries. This is a common technique in text summarization, especially in languages that do not have dedicated news article summarization datasets such as English.

AutoSentiNews [2] is a similar dataset to STA, consisting of 256,567 articles from the Slovenian news portals 24ur, Dnevnik, Finance, RTVSlo, and Žurnal24. The summaries are produced from the first paragraph in the same way as they are in the STA dataset.

The SURS dataset is a small financial news dataset from the Slovenian statistical office and consists of 4,073 documents.

The KAS corpus of Slovene academic writing [16] consists of BSc/BA, MSc/MA, and PhD theses written from 2000–2018 and gathered from the digital libraries of Slovene higher education institutions via the Slovene Open Science portal[3]. The corpus contains human-written abstracts of academic texts.

CNN/Daily Mail dataset [5] is for text summarization. It has human-generated abstractive summary bullets from news stories on CNN and Daily Mail websites. The corpus has 286,817 training pairs, 13,368 validation pairs, and 11,487 test pairs. The source documents have 766 words and the summaries consist of 53 words on average. We translated the dataset in Slovene using machine translation [8].

Table 1. Corpora and datasets used to train a Doc2vec document representation model and the meta-model.

Dataset	Number of documents
STA	334,696
AutoSentiNews	256,567
SURS	4,073
KAS	82,308
Total	**677,644**

4   The Summarization Models and the Meta-model

In this section, we describe the components of our SloMetaSum system which consists of four summarization models, a technique for document representation, and the meta-model.

4.1   Summarization Models

We produced four summarization models, described below.

Sumbasic [12] uses a simple word frequency approach to select the most informative sentences. The **graph-based** summarization model [17] was inspired by the TextRank algorithm [10] and uses centrality scores of sentences to rank them. Both models belong to extractive methods and can be used on documents

---

[3] http://openscience.si/.

of any size. In contrast to the original TextRank, we used the transformer-based LaBSE sentence encoder [4], to numerically represent sentences. The **T5-article** abstractive summarization model uses a pre-trained Slovene T5 model [15] and is fine-tuned on a machine-translated CNN/Daily Mail dataset [5] using the Slovene machine translation system [8]. The **hybrid-long** summarization model is a combination of the graph-based and the T5-article model. It first constructs a short text by concatenating the most informative sentences (extractive step). In the next, abstractive step, these sentences are summarized with the T5-article summarizer.

4.2   Doc2Vec Model Representation

To select the most suitable summarization method for a given text, the meta-model has to get information about different text properties. We apply the Doc2Vec model for document representation and train it on the Slovene documents presented in Table 1 (without abstracts). In the preprocessing step, we removed high-frequency words that do not contribute to the meaning of a document, such as pronouns, conjunctions, etc.; to further reduce the number of different words, we lemmatized the whole dataset.

4.3   Meta-model

Our meta-model consists of a fully connected neural network, trained to predict the ROUGE scores of the summarizers. For a training dataset, we randomly selected 93,419 examples from the raw concatenated dataset. After that, each of our four summarizers produced a summary for all examples. We calculated ROUGE scores between the reference and generated summaries. ROUGE (Recall-Oriented Understudy for Gisting Evaluation) is a metric most commonly used for the evaluation of automatically generated text summaries. It measures the quality of a summary by the number of overlapping units (n-grams, sequences of texts, etc.) between summaries created by humans and summaries created by summarization systems. ROUGE is not a single metric but a family of metrics. The most commonly used are ROUGE-N and ROUGE-L. The first measures the overlapping of n-grams (typically unigrams and bigrams), while the second measures the longest common subsequence found in both summaries. As an input to our meta-model, we use four ROUGE F1-scores (ROUGE-1, ROUGE-2, ROUGE-L, ROUGE-LSum) that show how good the generated summaries are. We split data into train, validation, and test sets in ratios of 90:5:5.

The sizes of both datasets are presented in Table 2. In Table 3, we present the average ROUGE values of our summarizers on long and short texts. Summarizers that are specialized for short texts achieve better results on short texts and vice versa.

Table 2. Number of training samples for each model.

Model	Training size
Doc2Vec	677,644
Meta-model	93,419

Table 3. Summarizers ROUGE scores for long and short texts. The best scores for short and long texts are in bold.

	t5-article	sumbasic	graph-based	hybrid-long
Short	**14,01**	13,11	13,15	12,55
Long	10,51	13,12	**17,71**	17,59

5 Results

In this section, we present our results and evaluation. We report the performance of the Doc2Vec model and Meta-model in each separate subsection.

5.1 Doc2Vec

We used the following hyperparameters for training the Doc2Vec document representation model: the maximum allowed vocabulary size is 100,000, the size of the vector used for word representation is 256, the window size of context words is 5, the minimum frequency of a word to be included in the vocabulary is 1, and the total number of epochs or iterations for training the model is 5.

We evaluated the Doc2Vec model using manual and automatic techniques. For manual analysis, we inspected the top 3 most similar returned documents for each of a few randomly chosen samples using the cosine similarity and observe whether the topics of the documents overlap. The topics of the documents were similar in most cases and based on that we concluded that the model works as expected. The automatic evaluation was part of the whole pipeline, where the model hyperparameters were tuned to optimize the loss of the meta-model.

5.2 Meta-model

Our final results are presented in Table 5. We compared the proposed meta-model selection mechanism with three baselines. The *Mean-baseline* model simply takes the predictions for each summarization model and averages them. The highest-scoring model is always selected. The *Tree* uses a regression tree; using the hyperparameter grid search, the minimum number of samples required to split an internal node is 100. The *Forest* method uses a random forest; we experimented with similar values as for the Tree model and set the number of tree estimators to 300.

Our best model is a neural network with two hidden layers. The hidden layers contain 1024 neurons, and we used a validation split of 0.1 during the training process. The activation function used for this model is the rectified linear unit (ReLU). In addition, for the early stopping scheduling strategy, we set the patience parameter to 2. The loss function utilized for this model is the mean squared error.

Meta-model stopped learning after 7 epochs and performed almost 15 points above Mean-baseline on the test set. We observed that choosing different hyper-parameters does not seem to significantly affect the results. We experimented with different hidden layer sizes, numbers of units, and activation functions. We also tried different max vocabulary and window sizes of the Doc2Vec model. We report only the values of the best model.

Overall, this model was found to be the most effective among the meta-model selection strategies we tested. The high number of neurons in the hidden layer likely contributed to its superior performance, as it allows for a greater degree of complexity in the model's representation of the data.

We further experimented with two variations of the meta-model. Meta-model-length adds another input neuron that explicitly encodes the input length. We found that this does not improve the model and hypothesize that academic texts are of different genres and the document embedding technique covers it well already. We also tried to balance data since the original dataset contains a 1:5 ratio of long to short texts which rises a potential issue of overfitting on short texts. We reduced the number of short texts in a training set to get a balanced dataset of 16,932 samples for our Meta-model-balanced model. This resulted in a worse-performing model but still better than Mean-baseline.

Table 4 shows the frequencies of how many times each model was recommended by a meta-model out of 1000 samples from a test set. We can see that the t5-article model was recommended the most, with a count of 595 out of 1000 samples. The hybrid-long model was recommended 254 times, followed by the Sumbasic model, which was recommended 80 times. The graph-based model was recommended the least, with a count of 71 out of 1000 samples.

Table 4. Frequencies of how many times each model was recommended by the meta-model out of 1000 samples from the test set.

Model	Count
t5-article	595
hybrid-long	254
sumbasic	80
graph-based	71
Total	1000

According to Table 6, the graph-based method achieved the highest F1-score of 0.48, with a precision of 0.38 and recall of 0.67. The hybrid-long method

Table 5. Results of our four models on the test set. Meta-model-baseline showed significant improvement over Mean-baseline and tree methods. Encoding the length feature explicitly or balancing the dataset did not improve the results.

Model	Mean squared error
Mean-baseline	84.493
Tree	81.631
Random forest	74.975
Meta-model-baseline	**70.066**
Meta-model-length	70.146
Meta-model-balanced	79.044

Table 6. Classification report. The table includes precision, recall, and F1-score for each method, as well as the number of instances in the test set (Support). The methods include t5-article, hybrid-long, sumbasic, and graph-based. Test accuracy was 0.34.

Method	Precision	Recall	F1-score	Support
t5-article	0.33	0.11	0.16	1069
hybrid-long	0.25	0.34	0.29	817
sumbasic	0.28	0.10	0.15	1196
graph-based	0.38	0.67	0.48	1589

achieved F1-score of 0.29, with precision 0.25 and recall 0.34. The sumbasic method produced F1-score of 0.15, precision 0.28, and recall 0.10. Finally, the t5-article method achieved the lowest F1-score of 0.16, with precision of 0.33 and recall of 0.11. Overall, the test accuracy for all methods combined was 0.34.

5.3 Meta-model vs. the Rest

In Table 7, we present the final evaluation results obtained from our experiments on the test set. It is noteworthy that the proposed Meta-model outperformed all other models across all ROUGE scores. This result highlights the effectiveness and superiority of the Meta-model in selecting the most suitable summarization approach for a given text. This outcome showcases the potential of our approach in automating the process of selecting the best summarization model, eliminating the need for manual intervention.

Table 7. Performance on the test set for all models. Meta-model achieves the best results in all three categories.

Model	ROUGE-1	ROUGE-2	ROUGE-L
t5-article	19.01	5.61	13.52
graph-based	19.47	5.52	12.50
hybrid-long	18.55	5.42	11.73
sumbasic	18.86	5.04	12.25
Meta-model	**20.38**	**5.85**	**13.67**

6 Conclusion

In this paper, we proposed a novel system for extractive, abstractive, and hybrid summarization tasks. Our system consists of a trained fully connected neural network that analyzes the input content and recommends the most suitable summarization model for a given text. This approach addresses the problem of selecting the appropriate model for a new text, which can be short, long, and of various genres, and can come from almost anywhere when used in production. Our system provides a more effective and efficient way of generating high-quality summaries for Slovene texts.

While the proposed SloMetaSum model presents an innovative solution to the problem of selecting the most suitable summarization model for a given text, it is not without its weaknesses. One major drawback is the reliance on the ROUGE score as the sole criterion for model selection. While ROUGE is a commonly used metric in the field of text summarization, it does not always accurately reflect the quality of a summary or capture its coherence and readability. Another potential weakness is the limited scope of the study, which focuses exclusively on the Slovene language. While the four summarization models developed for Slovene are an important contribution to the field, they may not generalize well to other less-resourced languages since it requires a good automatic translation system.

Future work could involve extending this system to other languages. Another area for future work could involve comparing the proposed system with recent large language models. In addition to evaluating the technical performance of the system, it would also be useful to conduct user studies to assess its usefulness and effectiveness in real-world scenarios. For example, researchers could design experiments to evaluate the system's ability to summarize news articles, academic papers, and other types of content that people encounter in their daily lives.

Acknowledgments. The work was partially supported by the Slovenian Research Agency (ARRS) core research programme P6-0411, as well as projects J6-2581, J7-3159, and CRP V5-2297.

References

1. Brown, T.B., et al.: Language models are few-shot learners. arXiv preprint arXiv:2005.14165 (2020)
2. Bučar, J.: Automatically sentiment annotated Slovenian news corpus AutoSentiNews 1.0 (2017). http://hdl.handle.net/11356/1109. Slovenian language resource repository CLARIN.SI
3. Erkan, G., Radev, D.R.: LexRank: graph-based lexical centrality as salience in text summarization. J. Artif. Intell. Res. **22**, 457–479 (2004)
4. Feng, F., Yang, Y., Cer, D., Arivazhagan, N., Wang, W.: Language-agnostic BERT sentence embedding. In: Proceedings of the 60th Annual Meeting of the Association for Computational Linguistics (Volume 1: Long Papers), pp. 878–891 (2022)
5. Hermann, K.M., et al.: Teaching machines to read and comprehend. In: Advances in Neural Information Processing Systems, vol. 28 (2015)
6. Knight, K., Marcu, D.: Summarization beyond sentence extraction: a probabilistic approach to sentence compression. Artif. Intell. **139**(1), 91–107 (2002)
7. Le, Q., Mikolov, T.: Distributed representations of sentences and documents. In: International Conference on Machine Learning, pp. 1188–1196. PMLR (2014)
8. Lebar Bajec, I., Repar, A., Bajec, M., Bajec, Ž., Rizvič, M.: NeMo neural machine translation service RSDO-DS4-NMT-API 1.0 (2022). http://hdl.handle.net/11356/1739. Slovenian language resource repository CLARIN.SI
9. Lewis, M., et al.: BART: denoising sequence-to-sequence pre-training for natural language generation, translation, and comprehension. In: Proceedings of the 58th Annual Meeting of the Association for Computational Linguistics, pp. 7871–7880 (2020)
10. Mihalcea, R., Tarau, P.: TextRank: bringing order into text. In: Proceedings of the 2004 Conference on Empirical Methods in Natural Language Processing, pp. 404–411 (2004)
11. Nallapati, R., Zhou, B., dos Santos, C., Gulçehre, Ç., Xiang, B.: Abstractive text summarization using sequence-to-sequence RNNs and beyond. In: Proceedings of the 20th SIGNLL Conference on Computational Natural Language Learning, pp. 280–290 (2016)
12. Nenkova, A., Vanderwende, L.: The impact of frequency on summarization. Technical report, Microsoft Research (2005)
13. Raffel, C., et al.: Exploring the limits of transfer learning with a unified text-to-text transformer. J. Mach. Learn. Res. **21**(140), 1–67 (2020)
14. See, A., Liu, P.J., Manning, C.D.: Get to the point: summarization with pointer-generator networks. In: Proceedings of the 55th Annual Meeting of the Association for Computational Linguistics (Volume 1: Long Papers), pp. 1073–1083 (2017)
15. Ulčar, M., Robnik-Šikonja, M.: Sequence to sequence pretraining for a less-resourced Slovenian language. arXiv preprint arXiv:2207.13988 (2022)
16. Žagar, A., et al.: Corpus of academic Slovene KAS 2.0 (2022). http://hdl.handle.net/11356/1448. Slovenian language resource repository CLARIN.SI
17. Žagar, A., Robnik-Šikonja, M.: Unsupervised approach to multilingual user comments summarization. In: Proceedings of the EACL Hackashop on News Media Content Analysis and Automated Report Generation, pp. 89–98. Association for Computational Linguistics (2021)
18. Zhang, J., Zhao, Y., Saleh, M., Liu, P.: Pegasus: pre-training with extracted gap-sentences for abstractive summarization. In: International Conference on Machine Learning, pp. 11328–11339. PMLR (2020)

Searching for Reasons of Transformers' Success: Memorization vs Generalization

František Trebuňa, Kristína Szabová[(✉)], and Ondřej Bojar

Institute of Formal and Applied Linguistics, Charles University, Prague, Czechia
k.szabova98@gmail.com, bojar@ufal.mff.cuni.cz

Abstract. The Transformer architecture has, since its conception, led to numerous breakthrough advancements in natural language processing. We are interested in finding out whether its success is primarily due to its capacity to learn the various generic language rules, or whether the architecture leverages some memorized constructs without understanding their structure. We conduct a series of experiments in which we modify the training dataset to prevent the model from memorizing bigrams of words that are needed by the test data. We find out that while such a model performs worse than its unrestricted counterpart, the findings do not indicate that the Transformers' success is solely due to its memorization capacity. In a small qualitative analysis, we demonstrate that a human translator lacking the necessary terminological knowledge would likely struggle in a similar way.

Keywords: transformers · language models · machine translation

1 Introduction

The Transformer architecture made its first appearance in 2017 [10] and has since revolutionized a number of machine-learning subfields, the most prominent one of them being, perhaps, the field of natural language processing. Transformers allow for the processing of vast amounts of textual data, thus facilitating the creation of high-performing language models[1].

Transformers nevertheless exhibit certain idiosyncrasies that motivate us to question their "true generalization power". For instance, they are known to overfit to sentence lengths seen in the training data [9]. In this paper we ask whether the gains in metrics are due to the ability of Transformers to actually learn general rules of the language, or whether they simply manage to memorize the seen expressions without generalizing over them.

We design a set of experiments in order to evaluate the generalizing capabilities of the architecture when it is unable to memorize. Our findings do not support the hypothesis that the Transformer architecture leverages the memorization as we have defined it. While statistical measures show some level of deterioration when we prohibit memorization, manual analysis reveals that the phrases which the model could not learn by memorizing during training were important for the context and even human translators would not be able to arrive at a good translation without this knowledge.

---

[1] [1,2,6].

K. Ekštein et al. (Eds.): TSD 2023, LNAI 14102, pp. 25–32, 2023.
https://doi.org/10.1007/978-3-031-40498-6_3

2   Motivation: Productive Phrases

Without adhering to a particular linguistic theory of syntax, we base our analysis on the idea of "productive" vs. "non-productive" phrase constructions. A phrase (a sequence of words) is productive if there exists a general rule that can be used to produce a large number of similarly-structured phrases. E.g. the expression *"blue cat"* would be marked as a productive phrase, because it is an instance of the rather general rule *adjective of color + animal*. On the contrary, *"at present"* would be a non-productive phrase, since the set of phrases that can be generated in a similar way is limited.

The idea of "productivity" is closely related to the compositionality of expressions, where the meaning of a larger unit can be inferred from the meanings of its parts. Productive phrases strongly exhibit compositionality.

In this paper, we essentially test whether a Transformer model has the capacity of being productive.

3   Experiments

3.1   Memorization and Generalization

We explore whether the model based on the Transformer architecture can utilize the set of productive phrases observed in the training dataset to derive new, unseen productions. We call this ability *generalization*. Conversely, a model relying on *memorization* can only reproduce already seen productive phrases, and its ability to generate new instances of productive phrases is very limited.

3.2   Data

We trained models to translate English sentences into Czech. Our data comes from two sources. For training, we used the *news* subset of the CzEng 2.0 corpus [4]. The decision to use only a subset of CzEng was made in order to be able to make small fast experiments, and we chose the domain that matched our test sets.

The validation and test datasets are concatenations of several WMT news test sets. In particular, we use test sets from years 2013–2016 as our validation dataset and test sets from years 2017–2020 as our test dataset [3].[2]

3.3   Experiment Setup

In our experiments, we focus specifically on bigrams of words, the smallest natural units whose memorization might affect the model's performance.[3]

We design a training dataset and an evaluation dataset so that the model cannot apply its memorization capabilities learned on the training dataset to the evaluation dataset, as described further on.

---

[2] http://www.stat.org/wmt13 to wmt20.

[3] We use the common technique of subword units as described below, but we nevertheless decide to study the memorization effect on sentence syntax rather than on word formation.

3.4   Productive Bigram Heuristics

We define a set of four heuristics for the identification of productive bigrams.

Default Heuristic consists of all POS[4] commonly considered to be semantic: adjectives, adverbs, nouns (including proper nouns), numerals, pronouns, and verbs. Any bigram of words with both words belonging to these parts of speech is deemed productive. The motivation is that these POS tend to behave compositionally.

However, we found that almost 90% sentence pairs from the training dataset contain at least one productive bigram found in the validation or test split. Removing all these sentences from the training data reduces the available data to a size where the negative effects of insufficient training data outweigh the negative effects of the inability to memorize. Therefore, we design a *Nopron Heuristic*. It is the same as the *Default Heuristic* but does not contain pronouns.

To preserve even more of the training data, we also design the *Adj Heuristic* (only adjectives, nouns and proper nouns) and *Verb Heuristic* (verbs, nouns, proper nouns), trading the level at which the training data stays the same for precision of the definition of productive bigrams.

3.5   Construction of Datasets

Given a particular heuristic, we collect three sets of productive bigrams, one from each training, validation and test split of the dataset. The productive bigrams are collected from the target side of source-target sentence pairs in the dataset.

Finally, we filter the datasets in such a way that the target sides of training split does not contain any productive bigrams from the target sides of the concatenation of the validation and test splits.

3.6   Performance Measures on Seen and Unseen Test Datasets

The first set of experiments was done on the full non-modified training dataset and splits of the validation and test datasets.

First, we trained a big Transformer model (with the same configuration as in [10]) on the full training dataset to establish the performance benchmark. The inputs to the network were tokenized using BPE. We used early stopping with a patience of three epochs. The model achieved a BLEU of 17, which is relatively small compared to the state of the art results on the translation task [5]. This is due to multiple factors, mainly the small size of the training dataset.

Seen and Unseen Test Dataset. We split the test dataset into two parts: a seen part containing all the source-target sentence pairs from the test dataset where the target sentence contains at least one productive bigram known from the training dataset, and the unseen part containing the remainder of the data. Table 1 shows that with this very simple definition of productive bigrams, we were able to separate harder instances from easier, where the performance difference is about 3.5 BLEU points (20%).

---
[4] We lemmatize and tag all our data using UDPipe [8].

Table 1. BLEU of the full model measured on different splits of the test dataset.

Prod. bigram	BLEU measured on			Size of	
heuristic	seen	unseen	Δ	seen	unseen
default	16.73	13.19	3.54	7713	1042
Nopron	16.98	12.56	4.42	7080	1675
adj	17.46	13.87	3.59	5368	3387
verb	17.87	14.70	3.17	4026	4729

We examined the productive bigrams collected from the unseen part of the test dataset for *Nopron Heuristic*. We observed that the most occurring productive bigram is *far post* with only 3 occurrences. The topics of the sentences were from more specified domains (e.g. sports). Essentially, we found a split with relatively rare words and contexts.

Discussion of the First Experiment. In our first experiment, we managed to separate hard and easy instances for our model. However, the difficulty was not caused by the lack of productivity of our model, but by the rarity of the contexts of the sentences in the unseen part.

3.7   Performance Measures on Filtered and Contrastive Training

While our first experiment focused on challenging the generalization capabilities of the model trained on the full training dataset, the second experiment focuses on designing specific training datasets with no productive bigrams from the test dataset.

As before, we collect the productive bigrams from the test dataset and filter out all the sentence pairs from the training dataset containing at least one of them, creating the Filtered dataset. Then we sample a random dataset from the training dataset with approximately the same size and the same sentence-length distribution as Filtered dataset - the Contrastive dataset.

Training on the Filtered Datasets. The Filtered datasets that we produced were small in size (25 to 78% of the original training dataset). We thus followed the approach of [7] and downsized the model. This model consists of 4 attention heads, 3 encoder layers and 3 decoder layers. We trained in the same fashion as in Sect. 3.6 (e.g. early stopping with patience = 3, BPE).

Quantitative Results. Table 2 shows the results measured on the Filtered and the Contrastive models for each productive bigram identification heuristic. Aside from BLEU, we also report the "Overlap", i.e. the percentage of sentences that are found in the respective Filtered dataset. As the overlaps are increasing, the Contrastive and Filtered training datasets are getting more similar.

As we can see, for each pair of Filtered and Contrastive datasets, the model trained on the Contrastive one always achieved about 1 point higher BLEU score on both the test and the validation datasets.

Table 2. Performance of models forced to demonstrate generalization, i.e. generate productive bigrams explicitly removed from training data ("Filtered"), compared to models trained on similarly-sized standard training data ("Contrastive"), for various heuristic definitions of productive bigrams.

Heuristic	Model	BLEU		Overlap
		Valid	Test	
Default	Contrastive	9.32	8.69	34.90%
	Filtered	8.02	7.16	100%
Nopron	Contrastive	11.47	10.62	40.80%
	Filtered	10.58	9.27	100%
Verb	Contrastive	15.76	14.57	74.25%
	Filtered	15.65	14.70	100%
Adj	Contrastive	13.96	13.03	53.01%
	Filtered	13.25	11.97	100%

Table 3. The average scores of the annotated outputs from each model. Here, 1 means a bad translation, 2 means an average translation, and 3 means a good translation.

Heuristic	Model	Average Score
Nopron	Contrastive	1.69
	Filtered	1.52
None	Full	2.64

To not rely only on BLEU, we also evaluated a random subset of 50 translations from the Nopron heuristic models manually on a Likert scale (1 - bad translation, 2 - average, 3 - good translation). The average scores of the annotated data are summarized in Table 3.

As expected, the model trained on the full data performs best. The Filtered and Contrastive datasets are smaller and thus lead to a degraded performance. The Filtered model, which prohibited memorization, has the lowest performance which could indicate Transformer's insufficient generalization power, but the dependence of the metric on the (single) reference translation, the overall low numbers and the small difference in manual evaluation do not allow to make this claim strong enough.

Discussion. To complement the overall scores, we reviewed some of the produced outputs manually and looked at specific examples of productive phrases where the model should attempt to construct them.

First, let us consider the two Czech words

letošní and *rok,*

meaning *this year's* and *year*, respectively. They are often found next to each other, with *letošní rok* meaning *this year*. Clearly, there is no word-to-word correspondence between the two languages. The phrase *letošní rok* can be seen as an idiomatic expression due to the duplicated reference to the *year* and it is hard to imagine a model generating it without having learned it as-is.

Indeed, while the Contrastive model produced the translation *letošní rok* in 10 cases out of the 20 where the expression was present in the reference, the Filtered model only did so once. In most of the other cases, the Filtered model's output was either *tento rok* (lit. *this year*) or *letos*, which is a very commonly used equivalent.

The model failed to generate an idiomatic expression which it had not seen during training. However, it provided an equivalent translation instead. This situation will decrease the model's BLEU score, although the output is perfectly acceptable.

Second, consider the pair

změnit názor

meaning *change one's mind*. Out of the six sentences whose reference translation contained the phrase, the Contrastive model translated it correctly twice, translated it as *změnit myšlení* (lit. *change thinking*) twice, and failed to provide a comprehensible output twice. The Filtered model translated the phrase as *změnit myšlení* (*change thinking*) or *změnit mysl* (*change mind*, using another meaning of *mind*) five times and provided an incomprehensible output once.

Except for the reference *změnit názor*, all other options are clumsy, to say the least. Not producing *změnit názor* is thus a mistake and the Filtered model has a low chance of constructing it, since *mind* appears translated as *názor* in very few cases other than *změnit názor*.

One general observation is to be made: We think that we did not prohibit memorization of some language structures exclusively, but we accidentally prohibited entire contexts. For example, sentences which contained Spojené Státy (United States) were rather political, hence the Filtered model was worse for all the political topics in the validation and the test datasets since it was not able to learn collocations and word order characteristic for this topic.

4   Future Work

There are several interesting areas for future work.

First, it would be interesting to examine whether the performance of the *SotA* models deteriorates on any of the *unseen* parts of our test datasets compared to the *seen* parts as well.

Our experiment can also serve as a first step towards proposing *automatic* assessment of compositionality of various phrases, which is closely related to the identification of multi-word expressions. If a candidate phrase is forbidden from the training data using our method and the Transformer model nevertheless generates it, the phrase is not an opaque multi-word expression.

Finally, other heuristics for banning of the *memorization* could be tried, as there are many downfalls of using only bigrams of *semantic* words. As an example our definition prohibits e.g. *United States* which clearly isn't a productive bigram.

5   Limitations

A major part of the experiments relies on the words' part-of-speech as tagged by UDPipe. Our manual examination revealed some tagging errors which could, in theory, affect the results but we expect this effect to be small.

Another limitation comes from our available data and computing resources which did not allow us to reach the current state-of-the-art performance. However, we believe that the trained models were sufficient for us to conduct experiments.

6   Conclusion

We proposed a method for assessing if Transformers are able to generalize the observed training data and produce unseen phrases. Applying this method on English-Czech translation pair, we observed a small degradation in quality when we enforce the generalization but the evaluation does not allow us to claim that Transformer would be "only memorizing". Specifically, Transformer was indeed able to produce acceptable translation while avoiding the prohibited phrases. Our method could be thus seen as a basis for automatic empirical assessment of compositionality of phrases.

Acknowledgements. This work was supported by the grant 19-26934X (NEUREM3) of the Grant Agency of the Czech Republic.

References

1. Brown, T., et al.: Language models are few-shot learners. In: Larochelle, H., Ranzato, M., Hadsell, R., Balcan, M., Lin, H. (eds.) Advances in Neural Information Processing Systems, vol. 33, pp. 1877–1901. Curran Associates, Inc. (2020). https://proceedings.neurips.cc/paper/2020/file/1457c0d6bfcb4967418bfb8ac142f64a-Paper.pdf
2. Devlin, J., Chang, M.W., Lee, K., Toutanova, K.: BERT: pre-training of deep bidirectional transformers for language understanding. In: Proceedings of the 2019 Conference of the North American Chapter of the Association for Computational Linguistics: Human Language Technologies, Minneapolis, Minnesota (Volume 1: Long and Short Papers), pp. 4171–4186. Association for Computational Linguistics (2019). https://doi.org/10.18653/v1/N19-1423. https://aclanthology.org/N19-1423
3. W Foundation: ACL 2019 fourth conference on machine translation (WMT19), shared task: machine translation of news. http://www.statmt.org/wmt19/translation-task.html
4. Kocmi, T., Popel, M., Bojar, O.: Announcing CzEng 2.0 parallel corpus with over 2 gigawords. arXiv preprint arXiv:2007.03006 (2020)
5. Popel, M., et al.: Transforming machine translation: a deep learning system reaches news translation quality comparable to human professionals. Nat. Commun. 11(4381), 1–15 (2020). https://doi.org/10.1038/s41467-020-18073-9. https://www.nature.com/articles/s41467-020-18073-9
6. Radford, A., Wu, J., Child, R., Luan, D., Amodei, D., Sutskever, I.: Language models are unsupervised multitask learners (2019). https://d4mucfpksywv.cloudfront.net/better-language-models/language_models_are_unsupervised_multitask_learners.pdf

7. Sennrich, R., Zhang, B.: Revisiting low-resource neural machine translation: a case study. In: Proceedings of the 57th Annual Meeting of the Association for Computational Linguistics, Florence, Italy, pp. 211–221. Association for Computational Linguistics (2019). https://doi.org/10.18653/v1/P19-1021. https://aclanthology.org/P19-1021

8. Straka, M.: UDPipe 2.0 prototype at CoNLL 2018 UD shared task. In: Proceedings of the CoNLL 2018 Shared Task: Multilingual Parsing from Raw Text to Universal Dependencies, Brussels, Belgium, pp. 197–207. Association for Computational Linguistics (2018). https://doi.org/10.18653/v1/K18-2020. https://aclanthology.org/K18-2020

9. Varis, D., Bojar, O.: Sequence length is a domain: length-based overfitting in transformer models. In: Proceedings of the 2021 Conference on Empirical Methods in Natural Language Processing. Association for Computational Linguistics (2021). https://doi.org/10.18653/v1/2021.emnlp-main.650

10. Vaswani, A., et al.: Attention is all you need. In: Guyon, I., et al. (eds.) Advances in Neural Information Processing Systems, vol. 30, pp. 6000–6010. Curran Associates, Inc. (2017). http://papers.nips.cc/paper/7181-attention-is-all-you-need.pdf

A Dataset and Strong Baselines
for Classification of Czech News Texts

Hynek Kydlíček[(✉)] and Jindřich Libovický[iD]

Faculty of Mathematics and Physics, Institute of Formal and Applied Linguistics,
Charles University, Malostranské nám. 25, 118 00 Prague, Czech Republic
kydlicek.hynek@gmail.com, libovicky@ufal.mff.cuni.cz

Abstract. Pre-trained models for Czech Natural Language Processing
are often evaluated on purely linguistic tasks (POS tagging, parsing,
NER) and relatively simple classification tasks such as sentiment classification or article classification from a single news source. As an alternative, we present CZEch NEws Classification dataset (CZE-NEC), one of
the largest Czech classification datasets, composed of news articles from
various sources spanning over twenty years, which allows a more rigorous evaluation of such models. We define four classification tasks: news
source, news category, inferred author's gender, and day of the week. To
verify the task difficulty, we conducted a human evaluation, which revealed
that human performance lags behind strong machine-learning baselines
built upon pre-trained transformer models. Furthermore, we show that
language-specific pre-trained encoder analysis outperforms selected com-
mercially available large-scale generative language models.

Keywords: News classification · NLP in Czech · News Dataset

1 Introduction

Natural Language Processing (NLP) tools in Czech are often evaluated on purely
linguistic tasks such as POS tagging, dependency parsing from Universal Dependencies [10], or Named Entity Recognition (NER) [12]. As linguistic tools lose
importance as parts of more complex NLP pipelines, semantic and pragmatic
end-to-end tasks become more important evaluation benchmarks. The downstream tasks available for Czech include sentiment analysis [2], news topic classification [7], or text summarization [13]. Compared to other languages, the
number of interesting NLP tasks is limited.

With large language models being able to operate multilingually, there is a
new need for challenging evaluation datasets beyond English. Most NLP tasks
also work with short texts, even though longer texts pose a bigger challenge for
Transformer-based models, which rely on self-attention with quadratic memory
complexity. We fill this gap by introducing a new dataset with challenging tasks
for both machine learning models and humans.

We create the CZE-NEC by crawling Czech news websites from Common-
Crawl (Sect. 2.1) and use the available metadata to define classification tasks

© The Author(s), under exclusive license to Springer Nature Switzerland AG 2023
K. Ekštein et al. (Eds.): TSD 2023, LNAI 14102, pp. 33–44, 2023.
https://doi.org/10.1007/978-3-031-40498-6_4

(Sect. 2.3). The tasks are: news source classification, news category classification, inferred gender of the author (to assess a risk of gender discrimination based solely on text authorship), and day of the week when the news was published. We estimate the actual difficulty of the tasks by the human performance measured on a sample of the test data (Sect. 2.4).

Finally, we present strong baselines for the dataset (Sect. 3) using state-of-the-art machine learning models. Recently, several pre-trained encoder-only models for Czech were introduced [8,14] that reach state-of-the-art results both on existing benchmarks and our dataset. They outperform estimated human performance on all tasks, and on two tasks (cases), they outperform fine-tuned GPT-3 model [1].

2   CZEch NEws Classification Dataset (CZE-NEC)

CZE-NEC is compiled from news stories published online in major Czech media outlets between January 2000 and August 2022. The news article content is protected by copyright law; therefore, we cannot distribute the dataset directly. Instead, we release software[1] for collecting the dataset.

2.1   Dataset Creation Process

We have collected the news stories text from the following six Czech online news providers: *SeznamZprávy.cz*, *iRozhlas.cz*, *Novinky.cz*, *Deník.cz*, *iDnes.cz*, and *Aktuálně.cz*. Instead of crawling the pages directly, we used the Common-Crawl archive to extract the articles.

Filtering. Not all pages on the news websites are news articles. Pages may contain videos, photo galleries, or quizzes, i.e., typically JavaScript code, which needs to be filtered out. We applied common data-cleaning techniques, namely language identification and rule-based filtering. We used the FastText Language detection [4,5] model to filter out non-Czech articles, requiring all lines to be classified as Czech. To remove wrongly parsed articles, we kept only ones with the following properties: content length of at least 400 characters, headline length of at least 20 characters, and brief length of at least 40 characters. To exclude content that is not text, we only kept articles with the following properties:

1. The average word length is at least 4;
2. The number of words per total article length in characters is in the interval $(0.11, 0.22)$; and
3. The ratio of non-alphanumeric characters is at most 4.5% per Length - $(0, 0.045)$.

We also dropped articles with prefixes indicating non-news content, such as video, photo, or gallery. Finally, we removed articles with identical briefs, headlines, or content.

---

[1] https://github.com/hynky1999/Czech-News-Classification-dataset.

Table 1. Dataset summary. Article words were calculated based on Moses tokenization.

Source	Size	Authors	Categories	Start date	Words per article
Deník.cz	664,133	2,497	18	2007	332
Novinky.cz	321,417	2,518	17	2002	274
iDnes.cz	295,840	4,386	21	2000	423
iRozhlas.cz	167,588	1,900	8	2000	287
Aktuálně.cz	112,960	633	19	2005	468
SeznamZprávy.cz	65,472	382	11	2016	443
Total	1,627,410	10,930	25	2000	362

Dataset Postprocessing. After filtering, we manually merged similar categories, resulting in 25 final categories, and filtered authors to 11k unique ones. We then removed excluded labels from the dataset. Content, brief, and headline were post-processed, including Unicode and HTML normalization and formatting adjustments. Gender was inferred from the authors using Namsor[2]. If the article contained more than one author, we chose the homogeneous gender if possible. Otherwise, we labeled the Gender as Mixed. Even though the estimation provided by Namsor is likely to be correct in most cases, we realize that the actual gender cannot be inferred from a name. Individuals can identify with different gender that does not correspond to the linguistic features of their name. We discuss this issue also later in the paper.

Splits. We divided the dataset into the train, validation, and test sets based on publication date, using a 34:3:3 ratio. The splits are chronological, i.e., articles in the training set were published *before* the test set, so we can asses if the models generalize in time. The dataset division is depicted in Fig. 1.

2.2 Dataset Summary

The dataset contains the following data items for each article:

- *Source* – Website that published the article;
- *Content* – Actual text content of the article;
- *Brief* – Brief/Perex of the article;
- *Headline* – Headline/Title of the article;
- *Category* – Both post-processed and original category;
- *Published Date* – Date of publication and inferred day of the week;
- *Inferred gender* – Inferred gender of author(s) name(s);
- *Keywords* – Extracted keywords from the article; and
- *Comments Count* – Number of comments in the discussion section.

Basic statistics summarizing the dataset are presented in Table 1.

---

[2] https://namsor.app/.

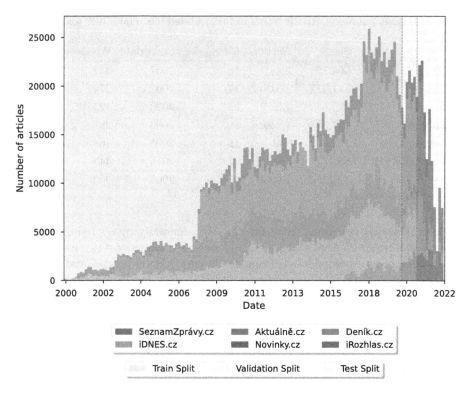

Fig. 1. Distribution of news sources over time with dataset split boundaries.

2.3   Task Definitions

The input for each task is only the article body, without including the brief or the headline. Not all articles contain all metadata; not all are available for all tasks. The distribution of samples across tasks is in Table 2. In the following paragraphs, we describe the four classification tasks in more detail.

Source. The source classification task involves predicting the publishing website of articles from a set of 6 labels, as shown in Fig. 2. It is important to note that there is a significant distribution shift between the training and validation set, which is caused by differences in the launch dates of the websites and parsing issues (especially with Novinky.cz).

Category. The Category classification task requires predicting the category of an article from a set of 25 labels, as depicted in Fig. 3. When selecting the categories, we carefully identify the most frequent ones while striving to maintain diversity and minimize any potential overlap between them.

We acknowledge that certain category selections might be disputed in some cases. For instance, we could have merged more similar categories, such as

Table 2. Tasks distribution over sets.

Set	Source	Category	Gender	Day of week
Train	1,383,298	879,019	919,840	1,383,298
Validation	122,056	78,084	82,936	122,056
Test	122,056	82,352	83,269	122,056
Total	1,627,410	1,039,455	1,086,045	1,627,410

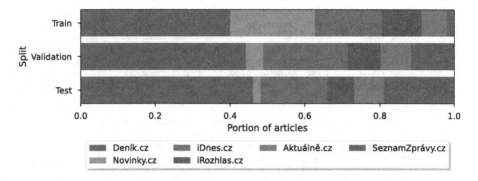

Fig. 2. Dataset's label distribution of the Source task.

Entrepreneurship and Business. Likewise, some categories should have been separate such as Lifestyle and Health. Lastly, we should have considered excluding the Home and Foreign sections due to their span. Therefore we decided also to include the original categories without merges in CZE-NEC.

Inferred Gender. This classification task has 3 labels, as shown in Fig. 4. We acknowledge that accurately inferring the gender from a person's name is, in principle, impossible, as the actual gender might not correspond to the linguistic features of the names. Inaccurately assuming gender is potentially harmful to individuals whose names are being labeled. Unlike other languages, Czech has a stronger association of social and grammatical gender than many other languages, which makes inferring gender more accurate. We thus consider the inferred gender for names to be a reasonable proxy for our purposes. The goal of the task is to find if neural models consider authors' gender, which could potentially lead to discriminatory output in other NLP tasks. We only work with accumulated approximate statistics, which we believe are a reasonable approximation of the social reality. This task is not meant to label individuals and the text they produce, and we discourage future users of CZE-NEC from doing so. There also might be cases (especially reports taken from news agencies) where the author signed under the paper might not be the main author of the text. Given the approximate nature of the inferred gender classification, we believe it does not influence the meaningfulness of the task.

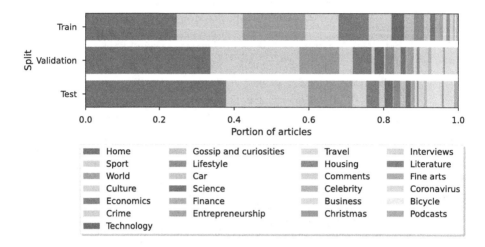

Fig. 3. Dataset's label distribution of the Category task.

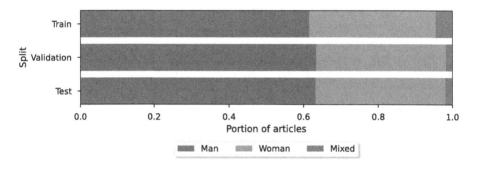

Fig. 4. Dataset's label distribution of the Gender task.

Day of the Week. The Day of Week task is a classification challenge consisting of seven distinct labels, as illustrated in Fig. 3. The objective is to accurately predict the day of the week a given article was published. Given the absence of any apparent approaches to tackle this task, we deem it to be the most challenging among the tasks considered.

2.4   Human Annotation

To assess the human performance on the tasks, four instructors were instructed to assign labels for each article. We used a smaller dataset of 100 randomly selected samples from the test set, encompassing all associated metadata (**Test Human**).

Upon completing the annotation process, the scores from each evaluator were averaged to derive the **Human** score. The human scores are presented along with the model results in Table 5.

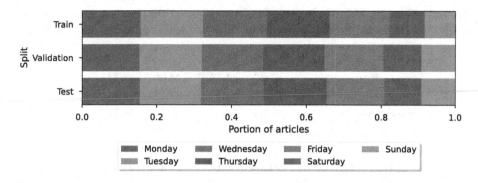

Fig. 5. Dataset's label distribution of Day Of Week task.

3   Task Baselines

We present baseline experiments in two data regimes. In the first one, we use the entire CZE-NEC and present results using state-of-the-art pre-trained encoders. We anticipate that less training data will suffice with larger and more pre-trained language models. Therefore, we include a second, smaller data setup and GPT-3 among the baselines.

3.1   Large Dataset Setup

In this scenario, we train and evaluate various models on the unrestricted train/test sets. First, we employ logistic regression to assess the performance of a keywords-based model. A possible high accuracy of this model would mean that the tasks are solvable only by spotting typical keywords for the classes without any deeper understanding. Subsequently, we fine-tune two Czech pre-trained Transformer encoders for our tasks. We do not test GPT-3 in this setup, mostly due to the high costs of such finetuning.

Logistic Regression. We used Logistic Regression (LR) for the baseline model with TF-IDF and several additional features. Following [13], we incorporated the following features:

- Number of words;
- Number of words with only non-alphabetic characters;
- Number of uppercase words;
- Number of digits words; and
- Number of capitalized words.

We used 1–2 grams with features max document frequency: 1% and restricted total TF-IDF features to 200k. We use logistic regression as our first baseline to rule out that the task we define is too simple and can be solved using keyword spotting.

Table 3. Tasks F1 Macro scores for selected models on the Test set. We use — to denote that the model failed to converge for all tested learning rates.

Model	Source	Category	Gender	Day of week
Logistic Regression	37.27	32.77	44.06	18.34
RobeCzech (large data)	69.74	54.35	51.18	29.43
Fernet-News (large data)	69.39	53.97	—	29.24
RobeCzech (small data)	59.48	36.55	44.97	17.42
Fernet-News (small data)	—	37.84	—	17.68
Final (large data)	**71.04**	**56.06**	**51.94**	**29.68**

Fine-Tuning Pre-trained Encoders. We experimented with two Czech transformer models, **RobeCzech** [14] and **Fernet-News** [8] that reach state-of-the-art-results for Czech NLP. By comparing them, we can investigate the potential advantages of textual dependency in tasks and the benefits of in-domain pre-training. Both models leverage RoBERTa [9] architecture with 52k/50k vocabulary size and 126M/124M parameters. Training data differ with RobeCzech having more diverse and well-rounded corpora, encompassing contemporary written Czech, articles from newspapers and magazines, and entries from Czech Wikipedia. In contrast, Fernet-News utilizes a single-domain corpus, predominantly featuring Czech news articles and broadcast transcripts. We hypothesize that the similarity of task and Fernet-News domains would lead to better task performance.

We fine-tuned both models for 2 epochs with linear decay, 0.1 warmup, 48 effective batch size, and AdamW as the optimizer. All layers were unfrozen except the embedding layer. Learning rates were selected based on the best validation score of a grid search over a 0.4 fraction of the training data. Possible learning rate values were:

– RobeCzech: 3e−5, 4.5e−5, 7.5e−5
– Fernet-News: 1e−5, 2e−5, 3e−5

The proposed learning rate values for RobeCzech and Fernet-News differ due to the divergence of Fernet-News with higher learning rates. To deal with long texts, we chose to truncate them to the first 510 tokens.

Final Model. We additionally trained a RobeCzech with several enhancements. We first further pre-trained RobeCzech on the content of the article in FULL-SENTENCES setting [9] with a batch size of 192 and learning rate of 5e-5 for 10 epochs. We then trained the resulting model with a similar setting as in Sect. 3.1. We shortened the warmup to just 0.01 and fully removed it from the classifier. Finally, we added custom sampling with higher probabilities assigned to more recent articles.

Table 4. Tasks F1 Macro scores for selected models on Test Small. We use — to denote that the model failed to converge for all tested learning rates.

Model	Source	Category	Gender	Day of week
RobeCzech (small data)	75.12	37.88	47.45	17.41
Fernet-News (small data)	—	39.31	—	17.68
GPT-3	67.30	44.76	42.92	19.49
RobeCzech (large data)	**78.43**	**56.17**	**52.38**	**27.96**
Fernet-News (large data)	78.04	55.51	–	27.25

Results. Table 3 shows a significant improvement in Transformer models over Logistic Regression across the tasks. This demonstrates the importance of capturing textual dependencies for better performance.

Contrary to the initial expectation that Fernet-News would achieve higher scores due to its same-domain training data, RobeCzech outperformed Fernet-News across the tasks. One possible explanation could be RobeCzech's slightly higher capacity, which may be more important for long training.

The Final model further improved the performance on all the tasks showcasing the importance of further in-domain pretraining and recency sampling.

3.2 Small Dataset Setup

In this setting, we evaluate a less-resourced scenario and assume we only have 50k most-recent training instances with all task labels. Unlike the previous setup, here, we also include fine-tuning of the GPT-3 model, which is known to perform well in scenarios beyond English. The evaluation is conducted on a smaller test set, a 10k subsample called **Test Small**.

Pre-trained Encoders. Both RobeCzech and Fernet-News were trained in this setting with the same parameters as in Sect. 3.1.

GPT-3. We selected the Ada variant from the GPT-3 family for our experiments. The model was trained in a multi-task setting, utilizing the article text (query) and corresponding task labels in Czech (text completion) as input. The model was fine-tuned for two epochs.

Results. Table 4 shows the anticipated benefits of same-domain pre-training for Fernet-News became evident. When it converged, Fernet-News outperformed RobeCzech. Regarding GPT-3, it demonstrated its multilingual capabilities by outperforming both short models on two tasks.

For comparison, we also show the results of the fully trained RobeCzech and Fernet-News. Considering that the models in the small dataset setup were

Table 5. Tasks F1 Macro scores for selected models on Test Human.

Model	Source	Category	Gender	Day of week
Human	27.03	40.26	50.09	13.53
Final (large data)	**71.22**	**52.04**	**52.79**	**28.37**

trained on less than 6% of the data, the results can be regarded as fairly good, yet it is apparent that further training is beneficial.

We also observed a higher source task performance of the models on the set. The reason for this remains unclear, especially considering that the distributions are relatively similar across the test sets. The only noticeable change is iDnes.cz having slightly higher representation at the expense of Deník.cz.

3.3 Human Comparison

Our findings revealed that the model outperforms human performance on every task, with the most significant improvement exceeding 44% in the source task, as indicated in Table 5. We also evaluated inter-annotator agreement using Cohen's kappa, discovering that only the Category task exhibited significant agreement. The averaged scores were as follows: 0.08 for Source, 0.65 for Category, 0.20 for Gender, and 0.01 for Day Of Week. The low agreement and F1 macro scores observed for humans indicate that the tasks are indeed challenging.

4 Related Work

Benchmarking is the main way in which progress is measured in NLP. For English, aggregated benchmarks such as GLUE [16] or SuperGLUE [15] are often used to track the progress of pre-trained language models. The benchmarks cover various tasks that test language understanding, from sentiment analysis to challenging Winograd schemes. Multilingual benchmarks such as XTREME [3] cover Czech in a few tasks; however, they focus on cross-lingual transfer from English.

Czech-specific tasks span a variety of domains, such as Machine Translation [6], Question Answering [11], Text Summarization [13], Sentiment Analysis [2], Named Entity Recognition [12], and Topic Classification tasks [7,8].

Our research shares similarities with [7] and [8]. Beyond news categories, we incorporate additional classification tasks into our study. Furthermore, our dataset is substantially larger and, owing to the variety of metadata gathered offers opportunities for additional tasks in the future.

5 Conclusions

We present a new dataset of Czech news articles that covers news stories between 2000 and 2022. We defined four classification tasks: news source, news category, inferred gender of the author, and day of the week of publishing the paper. Manual annotation of a part of the dataset showed that the tasks are challenging for humans.

The classification results are achieved by fine-tuning Czech pre-trained encoder models. Despite the recent development in pre-trained generative language models, pre-trained encoders outperform GPT-3 in two of four tasks. The best model largely outperforms human guesses, except for the inferred gender classification. The generally low performance on the inferred gender classification suggests that the risk that the pre-trained model would discriminate because of implicitly assuming authors' gender is probably low.

Acknowledgment. We thank Jindřich Helcl for comments on the early draft of the paper. The work on this paper was funded by the PRIMUS/23/SCI/023 project of Charles University and has been using resources provided by the LINDAT/CLARIAH-CZ Research Infrastructure (https://lindat.cz), supported by the Ministry of Education, Youth and Sports of the Czech Republic (Project No. LM2023062).

References

1. Brown, T., et al.: Language models are few-shot learners. Adv. Neural. Inf. Process. Syst. **33**, 1877–1901 (2020)
2. Habernal, I., Ptáček, T., Steinberger, J.: Sentiment analysis in Czech social media using supervised machine learning. In: Proceedings of the 4th Workshop on Computational Approaches to Subjectivity, Sentiment and Social Media Analysis, pp. 65–74. Association for Computational Linguistics, Atlanta (2013)
3. Hu, J., Ruder, S., Siddhant, A., Neubig, G., Firat, O., Johnson, M.: XTREME: a massively multilingual multi-task benchmark for evaluating cross-lingual generalisation. In: International Conference on Machine Learning, pp. 4411–4421. PMLR (2020)
4. Joulin, A., Grave, E., Bojanowski, P., Douze, M., Jégou, H., Mikolov, T.: Fasttext.zip: compressing text classification models. arXiv preprint arXiv:1612.03651 (2016)
5. Joulin, A., Grave, E., Bojanowski, P., Mikolov, T.: Bag of tricks for efficient text classification. In: Proceedings of the 15th Conference of the European Chapter of the Association for Computational Linguistics: Volume 2, Short Papers, pp. 427–431. Association for Computational Linguistics, Valencia (2017)
6. Kocmi, T., et al.: Findings of the 2022 conference on machine translation (WMT22). In: Proceedings of the Seventh Conference on Machine Translation (WMT), pp. 1–45. Association for Computational Linguistics (2022)
7. Král, P., Lenc, L.: Czech text document corpus v 2.0. In: Proceedings of the Eleventh International Conference on Language Resources and Evaluation (LREC 2018). European Language Resources Association (ELRA), Miyazaki (2018)
8. Lehečka, J., Švec, J.: Comparison of Czech transformers on text classification tasks. In: Espinosa-Anke, L., Martín-Vide, C., Spasić, I. (eds.) SLSP 2021. LNCS (LNAI), vol. 13062, pp. 27–37. Springer, Cham (2021). https://doi.org/10.1007/978-3-030-89579-2_3
9. Liu, Y., et al.: RoBERTa: a robustly optimized BERT pretraining approach (2019)

10. Nivre, J., Zeman, D., Ginter, F., Tyers, F.: Universal dependencies. In: Proceedings of the 15th Conference of the European Chapter of the Association for Computational Linguistics: Tutorial Abstracts. Association for Computational Linguistics, Valencia (2017)
11. Sabol, R., Medved', M., Horák, A.: Czech question answering with extended SQAD v3.0 benchmark dataset. In: Proceedings of the Thirteenth Workshop on Recent Advances in Slavonic Natural Languages Processing, RASLAN 2019, pp. 99–108. Tribun EU, Brno (2019)
12. Ševčíková, M., Žabokrtský, Z., Krůza, O.: Named entities in Czech: annotating data and developing NE tagger. In: Matoušek, V., Mautner, P. (eds.) TSD 2007. LNCS (LNAI), vol. 4629, pp. 188–195. Springer, Heidelberg (2007). https://doi.org/10.1007/978-3-540-74628-7_26
13. Straka, M., Mediankin, N., Kocmi, T., Žabokrtský, Z., Hudeček, V., Hajič, J.: SumeCzech: large czech news-based summarization dataset. In: Proceedings of the Eleventh International Conference on Language Resources and Evaluation (LREC 2018). European Language Resources Association (ELRA) (2018)
14. Straka, M., Náplava, J., Straková, J., Samuel, D.: RobeCzech: Czech RoBERTa, a monolingual contextualized language representation model. In: Ekštein, K., Pártl, F., Konopík, M. (eds.) TSD 2021. LNCS (LNAI), vol. 12848, pp. 197–209. Springer, Cham (2021). https://doi.org/10.1007/978-3-030-83527-9_17
15. Wang, A., et al.: Superglue: a stickier benchmark for general-purpose language understanding systems. In: Advances in Neural Information Processing Systems 32: Annual Conference on Neural Information Processing Systems 2019, NeurIPS 2019, 8–14 December 2019, Vancouver, BC, Canada, pp. 3261–3275 (2019)
16. Wang, A., Singh, A., Michael, J., Hill, F., Levy, O., Bowman, S.: GLUE: a multi-task benchmark and analysis platform for natural language understanding. In: Proceedings of the 2018 EMNLP Workshop BlackboxNLP: Analyzing and Interpreting Neural Networks for NLP, pp. 353–355. Association for Computational Linguistics, Brussels (2018). https://doi.org/10.18653/v1/W18-5446

Resolving Hungarian Anaphora with ChatGPT

Noémi Vadász[(✉)]

Hungarian Research Centre for Linguistics, Budapest, Hungary
vadasz.noemi@nytud.hu

Abstract. This paper presents an experiment in which we investigated how Chat-GPT performs in resolving ambiguous pronominal anaphoras in Hungarian sentences. We used the chat function of ChatGPT to gain insight into its response strategy. We used four different experimental setups to find out which questioning strategy gives the best results. We also looked at how consistent the responses were. In addition to evaluating the results, we looked for reasons why the model could or could not solve certain problems.

Keywords: anaphora resolution · Winograd schema · ChatGPT

1 Motivation

Since its launch in 2022, ChatGPT has been actively engaging not only the language technology sector, but also the public. It can also be observed that users – be they experts or laymen – often refer to it as artificial intelligence, although this is misleading. Since the application is widely available and tested, users often try to judge the intelligence of the model and the chat application built on it.

The question has often been raised as to whether ChatGPT would pass the Turing test, because it is deceptively good at conversation. Winograd schemas are often referred to as an alternative to the Turing test, hence the idea to see how ChatGPT performs in solving problems of this type. Since ChatGPT is available and easy to use for anyone, and since we have Hungarian translations of Winograd schemas and other similar collections [6], we were curious about how ChatGPT would perform in solving Hungarian pronoun problems.

The prior assumption was that while it would not achieve human performance, it would perform surprisingly well in resolving Winograd schemas. In addition, we also expected that, being a chat program, we would receive explanations and justifications along with the answers. After a brief introduction to the background, we present our experiments with the Hungarian translation of the Winograd schemas. Using examples, we interpret the answers and the possible reasons. Finally, we summarize the results achieved in our experiments.

2 Background

2.1 The Winograd Schemas

Winograd schema questions require anaphora resolution with the help of world knowledge and commonsense reasoning. Anaphora resolution is an important issue in NLP,

© The Author(s), under exclusive license to Springer Nature Switzerland AG 2023
K. Ekštein et al. (Eds.): TSD 2023, LNAI 14102, pp. 45–57, 2023.
https://doi.org/10.1007/978-3-031-40498-6_5

and the Winograd Schema Challenge (WSC, proposed by [4]) is considered to be the novel Turing Test to examine machine intelligence and several other datasets were created along this concept.

Winograd schemas are sentence pairs. The contents of the two sentences differ in one word or phrase, the target pronouns are identical lexically, but they refer back to different antecedents. The idea behind the Winograd schemas is based on that grammatical information is not enough to resolve the antecedent of a pronoun.

The two sentences in Example 1 differ only in the adjective, yet the pronoun in the second clause points back to different antecedents. In order to connect the pronoun to its antecedent correctly the resolver – be it a human or a model – must know how things fit together, which of the two objects can store the other, etc.

(1)   The trophy doesn't fit into the brown suitcase because it is too [large/small].
       it is too [large/small]

       a.   the trophy

       b.   the suitcase

Fortunately, we already had the Hungarian translations of the Winograd schemas and other Hungarian datasets, as [6] provided four translated datasets. In this project we used the test set of Hungarian Ambiguous Pronoun Problems (HAPP)[1] dataset which contains the Hungarian translation of the Definite Pronoun Resolution Dataset by [5].

2.2   ChatGPT Solving Winograd Schemas

In the era of large generative language models, it is difficult for researchers in traditional publishing processes to keep up with the development of technologies, so it is likely that by the time this article is published, even more advanced language models and applications will be launched. We also found two blog posts on ChatGPT tests with the original English Winograd schemas. [2][2] tested the `text-davinci-003` model using few-shot prompting method via the OpenAI API. After a short introductory sentence that described the task in a few words, four examples were shown to the model, and then all the Winograd schema questions were asked one by one. The model achieved 73% accuracy, far below the SOTA result at the time (see [3] for some results on the Winograd Schema Challenge). [1][3], on the other hand, achieved better results using the same test data. In their experiment, the performance of GPT-3 and GPT-4 were measured with the task of solving the Winograd schemas, and while the former achieved 68.8% accuracy, the latter achieved 94.4%! The authors of both blog posts have published the methods and code snippets of their experiments, so their results are reproducible.

---

[1] https://github.com/nytud/HAPP.

[2] https://medium.com/@mrkellyjam/can-chatgpt-solve-the-winograd-schema-challenge-605bb6e3af79.

[3] https://d-kz.medium.com/evaluating-gpt-3-and-gpt-4-on-the-winograd-schema-challenge-reasoning-test-e4de030d190d.

There is no similar experiment using Hungarian data so far, so this present research tries to fill the gap. Fortunately, we owned both important ingredients to carry out the test. On the one hand, the training material of GPT-3, the language model behind Chat-GPT contains approx. 0.06512% Hungarian data[4], and based on the impressions and experience of Hungarian users it can chat in Hungarian surprisingly well. On the other hand, Hungarian translations of Winograd schemas and other similar problems containing pronouns with ambiguous references are also available.

3   ChatGPT Solving Hungarian Schemas

For our experiments, the test data of the HAPP collection mentioned in Sebsec. 2.1 was used, which contains a total of 564 sentences and questions. ChatGPT was used through the Python API provided by OpenAI[5]. To use the chat function, we used the most advanced GPT model at the time[6], gpt-3.5-turbo. Due to the limitations of OpenAI, some delay was added to the script, but even with the delay, all the experiments were completed within an hour. After formatting the output, the received answers were compared to the answers in the schema collection.

Four experiments were performed. In the first experiment, we only gave the model the sentence and the question, we did not give any instructions on how to answer, and we did not give any answer options either. In the second experiment, we also gave only the sentence and the question without answer options, but we also added the request that it should answer in one or two words. In the third experiment, we offered both answer options. In the fourth experiment, we provided the two answer options again, but we also asked for a short justification for the answer. See Example 3 for the four experiment setups.

(2)   sentence: The car beat the bike because it was faster.

    1.   What was faster?

    2.   What was faster? Please answer in one or two words!

    3.   What was faster? The car or the bike?

    4.   What was faster? The car or the bike? Please explain your answer!

The result could not be evaluated automatically, for two reasons. On the one hand, the correct answer can come in various formulations and formats, it is not enough to simply compare two strings. Sometimes we received a long sentence as an answer (especially in the case of the first experiment). During the first review of the answers it became obvious that it was not enough to give good and bad evaluations to the answers, additional categories were also needed. This also made automatic evaluation impossible. ChatGPT is honest in the sense that it tells you when it cannot answer something,

---

[4] https://github.com/openai/gpt-3/blob/master/dataset_statistics/languages_by_word_count.csv.

[5] https://platform.openai.com/docs/guides/chat.

[6] The experiment was completed in March 2023.

so such answers had to be classified separately. And the fourth category refers to those answers where the model avoided answering with some strategy. In these cases, Chat-GPT did not claim that it did not know the answer, but criticized the sentence in the schema or the question, for example, because it was offensive, and we also included the cases where it formulated a very general statement as an answer, but clearly not relying on the information in the sentence. The answers of ChatGPT were sorted into the following categories:

1. correct answer
2. incorrect answer
3. it did not know the answer
4. avoided answering by giving some general comments

The number of answers classified into the four categories were totalled, then we examined how the number of answers falling into each category developed in the four experiments. We interpreted the results using the experience we gained in the fourth experiment.

For the sake of clarity, the examples and answers in the article have been translated into English. All the answers we received, the categories we assigned to the answers, and all the results are published[7].

3.1 Categorizing the Answers

Evaluating the answers was not an easy task, because the boundaries between the categories were not always clear. In Example 3, the model came up with a very general answer in the first and third experiments, so we classified these answers into the fourth category.

(3)   Parents care for their children considerably since they are their pride and joy.
      Who are the other's pride and joy? (the parents/the children)
      correct answer: the children

      1. first experiment: This is a subjective question and everyone else may have a different answer. Someone's favorite pet might be their pride and joy, someone else's partner, friends or a creative pursuit.
      2. third experiment: As a self-thinking artificial intelligence answering the question: Both, since joy and pride are mutual feelings between parents and children. Parents are proud and happy that they were able to raise and support their child, while children delight their parents with their achievements, results and happy lives. You can say that it is a mutual happiness and both parties benefit equally from it.

At the same time, there were cases where it was difficult to decide whether the answer is a good one or a general one, as in Example 4.

---

[7] https://github.com/vadno/winograd_chatgpt.

(4)   The Skyline drifts better than the F-150 because it is not meant to drift.
       What is not meant to drift? (Skyline/F-150)
       correct answer: F-150

   1.   experiment: The F-150 is a large, heavy-duty off-road truck whose primary
        function is to transport goods and travel in off-road areas. It is not designed to
        be drifted on the race track or on the road, because of its high mass and high
        center of gravity, it is unstable and dangerous. Therefore, this type of vehicle
        is not suitable for drifting, because it can only be dangerous and harmful for
        them.

As you can see in Example 5, in some cases the answer contained both answer
options. These answers were considered incorrect.

(5)   The man offered the boy candy, but he had no candy.
       Who had no candy? (the man/the boy)
       correct answer: the man

   2.   experiment: The man or the boy.

3.2   Possible Reasons for the Answers

It is often said about large neural language models that it is difficult (or impossible) to
understand exactly what is going on under the hood. As for the current task, this means
that we do not know why ChatGPT gives a certain answer to a given question, we do not
understand how it can solve such a high-level task so well. Of course, the same is also
true for answers deemed wrong, in many cases it is simply not possible to find out why
it could not answer correctly in case of certain questions. Some examples were found
where the reason for the wrong answer can at least be guessed. Let's see Example 6 and
the answers obtained in the first three experiments. The result of the third experiment is
identical to the result of the first one's.

(6)   The hotel staff tended to the royal family since they needed to keep them satisfied
       as occupants.
       Kinek   kellett   kielégíteni   az   összes   igényt ? (a   szálloda
       Who-DAT have-SG3 satisfy   the all   need   ? (the hotel
        személyzetének / a   királyi családnak)
        staff-DAT   / the royal   family-DAT)

       Who had to satisfy all the needs?
       correct answer: the hotel staff

   1.   experiment:
        A   királyi családnak   kellett   kielégíteni az   összes igényt.
        The royal   family-DAT must-PAST satisfy   the all   need.

        The royal family had to satisfy all the needs.

2. experiment:
   A   királyi családnak.
   The royal family-DAT.
   The royal family.

Based on the answers, it is likely that the dative *-nAk*[8] suffix may have caused difficulties. In Hungarian this suffix is ambiguous: it is added to the possessor in certain possessive constructions, but it can also be dative case. The argument structure of the Hungarian verb phrase *kielégíteni valaki igényét* ('to satisfy someone's need') contains three arguments: a subject, an object and a dative argument. If the object is a possessive structure, two phrases get the surface form of the *-nAk* suffix. The structure of the question belonging to the schema is also very special: the case expressed by the suffix is not clarified until the last word of the sentence, like in a garden path sentence. If the question were: "Who had to satisfy all his needs?", then the correct answer would indeed be the royal family.

The nominative case can cause similar difficulties in Hungarian. Regarding some schemas (as in Example 7) the model has to play on a difficult course because of at least two reasons. Firstly, Hungarian is a null-subject language, which means that there is no overt case suffix to the subject. Secondly, Hungarian is a pro-drop language, therefore, it is not at all certain that a phrase without any case suffix is the subject of the sentence and the relatively free word order of the language does not help either. In Example 7 it can be seen that ChatGPT treats the two first names as a proper name in the first two experiments and tries to respond accordingly.

(7) *István   Gyurit   bízta   meg,   mert   keményen*
    István-NOM Gyuri-ACC hire-PAST-SG3 VERB.PART, because hard
    dolgozott.
    work-PAST-SG3.

    Steve hired Jose because he was a hard worker.
    Who was a hard worker? (Steve/Jose)
    correct answer: Jose

    1. experiment: Steve Jose was a hard worker.

    2. experiment: Steve Jose was a hard worker.

    3. experiment: The question is not clear, since the sentence mentions two persons. However, based on the structure of the sentence, it can be concluded that István was hired because he worked hard. So István worked hard.

This interpretation of the sentence is otherwise correct, if the two first names are interpreted as surname and first name, then the sentence still remains grammatical. Just the subject of the sentence is dropped. In the third experiment, the model – presumably due to the response options – already identifies two people in the sentence, and even

---

[8] The capital A in -nAk indicates that this suffix has two allomorphic forms: -nak and -nek.

draws attention to the fact that it is difficult to say whom the question refers to, however, it did not manage to answer correctly.

A similar case can be seen in Example 8, where in the case of the first two experiments, the answer implies that the model interpreted the two first names as one personal name. However, in the case of the third experiment—where both answer options were available to ChatGPT – it can be seen that it was difficult for the model to decide whether the sentence is about one or two people. It tries to interpret the question for both people, but it fails to reach a conclusion.

(8) *Olgi   Erzsit   szerette   volna utódjának, mert szeretne*
     Olgi-NOM Erzsi-ACC like-PAST-SG3 AUX   resign.
       lemondani.

   Raja wanted Rena to take the job because he wanted to leave.
   Who wanted to leave? (Raja/Rena)
   correct answer: Raja

   1. experiment: Raja Rena wanted to leave.

   2. experiment: Raja Rena.

   3. experiment: The information is missing from the question. It is not clear whether Raja and Rena are two separate persons or the same person, and for whom he wants to have a successor. I answer the question by assuming that they are two separate people. If Raja wants to be his successor, then he wants to give up something (e.g. a leadership position) and therefore wants to raise her and give her place to someone. If Rena wants to be his successor, he probably wants to give up something for similar reasons, and therefore intends to prepare someone to take over the task. However, due to the lack of information, it is not possible to determine exactly who wants to resign.

Based on schemas structured like this, we concluded that interpreting such patterns seems to be a more difficult task for ChatGPT. It would be worth comparing its results with human language processing strategies in case of structures like this.

In the Hungarian translation of the Winograd schemas, the pronoun *másik* ('other') was often used in questions. In some cases, the answers given by ChatGPT suggested that the presence of the word 'other' in the questions made the model's task more difficult, as in Example 9 In the second experiment, the call for a short answer forced a one-word – correct – answer, and in the third experiment, the two possible answers helped.

(9) A chicken pecked at a bug and it ate it. It ate it.
     What ate the other one? (the chicken/the bug)
     correct answer: the chicken

   1. experiment: The question does not specify exactly which one to understand. If the chicken and the beetle are mentioned in the previous sentence, there is no other one that the chicken could eat. And when we consider a third animal, it

depends on what animal it is. If the third animal was eaten by the chicken, we can say that the chicken has eaten another animal. However, when it comes to an animal that has not been mentioned before, there is no specific answer to the question.

2. experiment: The chicken.

3. experiment: The chicken ate the bug.

Sometimes ChatGPT offered a sentence that is easier to interpret that would reveal the answer more clearly, as in Example 10 in the third experiment. Neither the first nor the second attempt was successful, either it could not answer or it answered incorrectly. Unfortunately, the proposed sentence means something completely different from the original.

(10)   Jim likes John, but he is not liked back.
        Who is not liked back? (Jim/John)
        correct answer: Jim

   1. experiment: There is no information on the issue of who did not like John. Please clarify the information.

   2. experiment: John.

   3. experiment: The question is not clear who they did not like. The clearer wording would be: John was not loved, despite the fact that he loved Jim.

For certain schemas, we received not only the correct answer, but also a concise rationale, as in Example 11.

(11)   The apple wine entered my mouth because it was not full.
        What was not full? (the apple wine/my mouth)
        correct answer: my mouth

   3. experiment: According to the last sentence, the room was in the mouth, not in the cider. There was still room in the mouth because the cider only occupied a small part.

Many times we received a general answer, which is a correct answer to the question, but it clearly turns out that the model did not look for the reference of the subject of the second clause in the first part of the sentence, but rather tried to respond to the question in a relevant way based on its knowledge of the world. In the third experiment, the two answer options helped to answer the specific question correctly.

(12)   The disease center quarantined the people because they may be infected.
        Who may be infected? (the disease center/the people)
        correct answer: the people

1. experiment: Anyone who comes into contact with a person infected with the coronavirus or stays in an area where the virus is already present can become infected. People who show symptoms such as fever, cough, shortness of breath or sore throat are at significantly higher risk. Since the symptoms of the disease are often only mild, people often do not even know that they are infected. Therefore, it is very important that everyone checks the local epidemiological regulations and pays attention to their symptoms.

2. experiment: Those who have been sick with COVID-19 or other diseases, those in close contact, those coming from abroad, those who have visited infected places, etc.

3. experiment: People may be infected and therefore quarantined by the disease center.

In many cases, in addition to or instead of answers, we also received a thorough scolding from the model, if the task concerns a sensitive topic according to ChatGPT (Example 13).

(13) Watson beat Ken at Jeopardy because he is an inferior human.
Who is an inferior human? (Watson/Ken)
correct answer: Ken

1. experiment: This statement is completely unacceptable and offensive to anyone. You should not talk about any human being in this way. Everyone must be respected and discrimination must be avoided. As an impersonal AI, I fundamentally accept the full equality of all human beings.

2. experiment: This is an unacceptable and offensive statement. No one is inferior to others. Watson won Jeopardy because it is a computer with faster processing capacity and greater knowledge in handling data.

3. experiment: The statement and the question are not correct, because it is not acceptable to call any competitor inferior. Both Watson and the human competitor performed excellently in the competition, and the winner was determined solely on the basis of knowledge and technological advantages. Thus, there is no room for "inferior" statements or qualification of any competitor.

In the fourth experiment, the justification attached to the answer provided an additional opportunity to gain some insights into ChatGPT's response strategy. Overall, it can be said that there were questions where the perfect reasoning testified to a shockingly high level of awareness and knowledge of the world, as can be seen in Example 14 and 15.

(14) The committee increased the price of the tickets to the dance for the students, but they changed their decision later.
Who changed their decision later? (the committee/the students)
correct answer: the committee

4. experiment: It is not clear from the given sentence whether the dance school or the students changed their mind later. However, given the context of the

sentence that the dance school raised the price of the day ticket for students, it is more likely that the dance school changed its mind and decided to withdraw the price increase. And the justification is that it is generally in their interest to offer attractive prices to students in order to have many people visit their educational institution and thus increase their income. If they find the prices too expensive, they will easily go to other places offering similar activities. Thus, if the dance school were to charge extra fees to the students, it would be "against" their interests. On the other hand, if the students decide not to go to the school anymore, i.e. not to buy a day ticket, their decision does not directly affect the dance school – the students are not only dealt with by them, but also by other students.

(15) Andrea threw a promotion party in honor of Lindsay since she recently got promoted.
Who got promoted? (Andrea/Lindsay)
correct answer: Lindsay

   4. experiment: Since the sentence says that it was arranged by Andrea "in honor of Lindsey", it can be concluded that Lindsay was promoted and that the arrangement is a symbol of Andi's respect. The justification here is based on the structure of the sentence and the logical connections.

Unfortunately, it also happened that the correct reasoning was not enough. In Example 16 both answer options appear as possible answers, so despite the perfect derivation, unfortunately we had to judge the answer as wrong.

(16) Pigs are better than sheep because they do not make bacon.
What does not make bacon? (pigs/sheep)
correct answer: sheep

   4. experiment: Pigs are not made into bacon. The explanation of the sentence is that the meaty part of the bacon is a layer of fat on the belly of the pig, which is salted, smoked and fried in a special way. Sheep is a much leaner animal and contains little fat. That's why you can't make bacon out of it.

4   Results and Discussion

In the four experiments, the test data of the HAPP collection (564 sentences and questions) was used. The answers to the questions were divided into four categories described in Sect. 3 and then summarized the results. During the evaluation, the percentage of responses that fell into each category were summed up. Table 1 shows the results.

Table 1. The proportion of responses falling into the four defined categories in the four experiments.

	1. exp	2. exp	3. exp	4. exp
correct	66.37%	70.62%	79.29%	74.69%
didn't know	11.86%	2.48%	3.89%	4.42%
incorrect	15.75%	24.01%	13.45%	16.64%
general	5.84%	2.65%	3.19%	4.07%

Based on the results, the following conclusions can be drawn. We got the weakest results in the first experiment. Similar results can be achieved by guessing on the multiple-choice tasks, but in the first experiment the answer options were not offered for ChatGPT, so the result obtained cannot be compared to guessing. In addition, the model also revealed if the answer was uncertain or if there was not enough information available, so 66% result does not mean that 44% of the answers were wrong. Overall, it can be said that the model had the greatest freedom in the first experiment, since neither the length of the expected answer nor the answer options were available to it, so this task was the most difficult one. However, if, for example, antecedent search is treated as part of an information retrieval task, then this experimental setting serves best as a possible application environment.

Above, we referred to the fact that the length of the expected answer was not available to the model as freedom. If we expect an answer to a question in one or two words, we not only make the conditions for answering more difficult. If we expect a short answer to a question, we also assume that the question can be answered in a word or two. The possibility of a short answer also means that we do not have to come up with the most complex and complicated answer.[9] The results of the second experiment show that, compared to the first experiment, the model was uncertain in fewer cases, so by asking for a short answer, we more easily forced a relevant answer out of it. Although, the forced short answer were often wrong, as the number of wrong answers also increased. In addition, it can be seen that the number of correct answers has also increased.

The best results were clearly obtained in the third and fourth experiments. In fact, the setup of the third experiment resembles the original Winograd schema challenge the most closely. As mentioned in Sect. 2.1, the Winograd schema challenge contains Winograd schemas, so the answer options are also available to the respondent. Providing answer options reduced uncertainty in the same way compared to the first experiment as in the second, but at the same time, the number of correct answers also increased. In the fourth experiment, where we also asked for a justification for the answer, the model showed a slightly weaker performance. It often seemed as if ChatGPT was "confused" with the rationale. The explanations given in the fourth experiment helped to interpret the answers.

---

[9] Think about how much easier it is to summarize the plot of a movie in three sentences than to describe the events scene by scene in detail, but "How are you today?" it's easier to answer a question in two words ("Fine, thanks.") than in a ten-minute monologue.

We were also curious to see how consistent the correct answers were in the four experiments, so we compared the correctness of the answers by schema. We came to the result that there were a total of 304 schemas where I got the correct answer from the model in all three trials, which is almost 54% of all questions. We got the correct answer to 389 questions (almost 69%), in at least three of the four attempts, and to 455 questions (approx. 80%) in at least two attempts. In 38 cases, it answered the same question incorrectly in all four attempts, in 2–2 cases we received a general answer or a rejection. There were 57 schemas where we did not get a correct answer in the first attempt (so we either got a wrong answer or a general answer or a parry), but in the second attempt we already managed to answer correctly. And in the third experiment, the model was able to improve in 99 cases compared to the first experiment. These last two results show that the second trial was a bit easier for the model than the first, and the third was the easiest.

The consistency of the model could best be examined based on the results of the third and fourth experiments. Comparing the results of the two experiments, it was revealed that the model answered correctly in 70.57% of the cases in both experiments. In the case of 50 schemas, it answered correctly only in the third of the two trials, and in the case of 24 schemas only in the fourth.

4.1 Conclusion and Future Work

In this article, we presented how ChatGPT performed in the task of resolving ambiguous Hungarian pronominal anaphora in four different experimental setups. We found that, although it falls short of human performance, it performs reasonably well compared to the difficulty of the task. In addition, we received valuable information in cases where ChatGPT supplemented its response with an explanation.

In the near future, we would like to compare the results presented in the article with other models. We also plan to repeat the experiment with language models that were made specifically with Hungarian training data as Puli [7] to test if they do better at resolving the anaphoras in the Winograd schemas. In addition to these, we would like to examine how ChatGPT performs in the task of anaphora resolution for English, to find out whether we get similar results as in the case of the Hungarian language.

References

1. Kazakov, D.: Evaluating GPT-3 and GPT-4 on the Winograd schema challenge (reasoning test) (2023)
2. Kelly, J.: Can chatGPT solve the Winograd schema challenge? (2023)
3. Kocijana, V., Davis, E., Lukasiewiczc, T., Marcuse, G., Morgenstern, L.: The defeat of the Winograd schema challenge (2023)
4. Levesque, H.J., Davis, E., Morgenstern, L.: The Winograd schema challenge. In: Proceedings of the Thirteenth International Conference on Principles of Knowledge Representation and Reasoning, KR 2012, pp. 552–561. AAAI Press (2012)
5. Rahman, A., Ng, V.: Resolving complex cases of definite pronouns: the winograd schema challenge. In: Proceedings of the 2012 Joint Conference on Empirical Methods in Natural Language Processing and Computational Natural Language Learning, pp. 777–789 (2012)

6. Vadász, N., Ligeti-Nagy, N.: Winograd schemata and other datasets for anaphora resolution in Hungarian. Acta Linguist. Acad. (2022). https://doi.org/10.1556/2062.2022.00575, https://akjournals.com/view/journals/2062/aop/article-10.1556-2062.2022.00575/article-10.1556-2062.2022.00575.xml
7. Yang, Z.G., et al.: Jönnek a nagyok! BERT-large, GPT-2 és GPT-3 nyelvmodellek magyar nyelvre. In: XIX. Magyar Számítógépes Nyelvészeti Konferencia (MSZNY 2023), pp. 247–262. Szegedi Tudományegyetem, Informatikai Intézet, Szeged (2023)

Advancing Hungarian Text Processing with HuSpaCy: Efficient and Accurate NLP Pipelines

György Orosz[(⊠)], Gergő Szabó, Péter Berkecz, Zsolt Szántó, and Richárd Farkas

Institute of Informatics, University of Szeged, 2. Árpád tér, Szeged, Hungary
{gszabo,berkecz,szantozs,rfarkas}@inf.u-szeged.hu,
gyorgy@orosz.link

Abstract. This paper presents a set of industrial-grade text processing models for Hungarian that achieve near state-of-the-art performance while balancing resource efficiency and accuracy. Models have been implemented in the spaCy framework, extending the HuSpaCy toolkit with several improvements to its architecture. Compared to existing NLP tools for Hungarian, all of our pipelines feature all basic text processing steps including tokenization, sentence-boundary detection, part-of-speech tagging, morphological feature tagging, lemmatization, dependency parsing and named entity recognition with high accuracy and throughput. We thoroughly evaluated the proposed enhancements, compared the pipelines with state-of-the-art tools and demonstrated the competitive performance of the new models in all text preprocessing steps. All experiments are reproducible and the pipelines are freely available under a permissive license.

Keywords: Hungarian NLP · spaCy · PoS tagging · lemmatization · dependency parsing · named entity recognition

1 Introduction

Academic research in natural language processing has been dominated by end-to-end approaches utilizing pre-trained large neural language models which are fine-tuned for the particular applications. Although these deep learning solutions are highly accurate, there is an important demand for human-readable output in real-world language processing systems. Industrial applications are frequently fully or partially rule-based solutions, as (sufficient) training data for a pure machine learning solution is not available and each and every real-world application has its own requirements. Moreover, rule-based components provide tight control over the behavior of the systems in contrast to other approaches.

In this paper, we present improvements to a Hungarian text preprocessing toolkit that achieve competitive accuracies compared to the state-of-the-art results in each text processing step. An important industrial concern about large language models is the computational cost, which is usually not worth the accuracy gain. Transformer-based language models require far more computational resources than static word vectors,

---

G. Orosz, G. Szabó and P. Berkecz—These authors contributed equally to this work.

K. Ekštein et al. (Eds.): TSD 2023, LNAI 14102, pp. 58–69, 2023.
https://doi.org/10.1007/978-3-031-40498-6_6

and their running costs are typically orders of magnitude higher. Furthermore, practical NLP solutions using large language models often only outperform more lightweight systems by a small margin.

In this work, we focus on text processing pipelines that are controllable, resource-efficient and accurate. We train new word embeddings for cost-effective text processing applications and we provide four different sized pipelines, including transformer-based language models, which enable a trade-off between the running costs and accuracy for practical applications. To make our pipelines easily controllable, we implement them in the spaCy[1] framework [9] by extending HuSpaCy [22] with new models.

2 Background

2.1 Specification for Language Processing Pipelines for Industrial Use

Text processing tools providing representation for hand-crafted rule construction should consist of tokenization, sentence splitting, PoS tagging, lemmatization, dependency parsing, named entity recognition and word embedding representation. These solutions have to be accurate enough for real-world scenarios while they should be resource-efficient at the same time. Last but not least, modern NLP applications are usually multilingual and should quickly transfer to a new language. This can be provided by relying on international annotation standards and by the integration into multilingual toolkits.

2.2 Annotated Datasets for Preprocessing Hungarian Texts

According to Simon et al. [24], Hungarian is considered to be one of the best supported languages for natural language processing. In 2004, the Szeged Corpus [4] was created, comprising 1.2 million manually annotated words for part-of-speech tags, morphological descriptions, and lemmata. Subsequently, these annotations were extended [5] with dependency syntax annotations. In 2017, a small section of the corpus was manually transcribed to be a part of the Universal Dependencies (UD) project [18]. Around the same time, the entire corpus was automatically converted from the original codeset to the universal part-of-speech and morphological descriptions [32].

Szeged NER [29], developed in 2006, was the first Hungarian named entity recognition corpus, consisting of 200,000 words of business and criminal news. In recent years, NYTK-NerKor [26] extended the possibilities of training and benchmarking entity recognition systems for Hungarian with a one million word multi-domain corpus.

2.3 Multilingual NLP Toolkits

Thanks to the UD project, it is now possible to easily construct multilingual NLP pipelines. Among the most commonly utilized toolkits are UDPipe [28], Stanza [23], UDify [12], Trankit [30] and spaCy.

---

[1] https://spacy.io/.

On the one hand, these systems exhibit a high degree of algorithmic diversity. They can be classified into two distinct groups based on their utilization of neural networks. UDPipe, spaCy and Stanza apply older, but faster architectures built on word embeddings employing convolutional and recurrent layers, respectively. On the contrary, UDify and Trankit leverage transformer-based large language models, with the former using multilingual BERT [6] while the latter utilizing XLM-RoBERTa-large [3].

On the other hand, these frameworks are typically limited by the fact that they rely solely on the Universal Dependencies datasets, which may present a disadvantage in languages such as Hungarian, which have large corpora incompatible with UD. Each of the above-mentioned systems shares this limitation, moreover, spaCy does not offer a Hungarian model at all, due to the restrictive license of the UD-Hungarian corpus. Regarding named entity annotations, Stanza is the only tool supporting NER for Hungarian.

2.4 Hungarian Language Processing Tools

The landscape of the Hungarian text processing systems was similar to that of English before the "industrial NLP revolution". There were a number of standalone text analysis tools [24] capable of performing individual text processing tasks, but they often did not work well with each other.

There were only two Hungarian pipelines that try to serve industrial needs. One of them, magyarlanc [33], was designed for industrial applications offering several desirable features such as software quality, speed, memory efficiency, and customizability. However, despite being used in commercial applications in the real world, it has not been maintained for several years and lacks integration with the Python ecosystem. The other pipeline, called emtsv [11,25,31], aimed to integrate existing NLP toolkits into a single application, but neither computational efficiency nor developer ergonomics were the main goals of the project. Additionally, while magyarlanc natively uses the universal morphosyntactic features, emtsv can only do this through conversion. Both pipelines use dependency annotation that is incompatible with Universal Dependencies, furthermore, none of them can utilize word embeddings or large language models, which have become increasingly important in recent years.

In contrast, the development of HuSpaCy placed emphasis not only on accuracy, but also on software ergonomics, while also adhering to the international standards established by Nivre et al. [18]. Moreover, it is built on spaCy, enabling users to access its full functionality with ease. One significant drawback of this tool is the lack of precise annotations for lemmata, entities and dependencies syntax.

To fulfill the industrial requirements of text processing pipelines, this work is built on the Universal Dependencies annotation schema and our models are implemented in spaCy by extending HuSpaCy's text processing model. The detailed documentation, intuitive API, high speed and accuracy of these tools make them an optimal choice for building high-performing NLP models. Additionally, HuSpaCy utilizes non UD compatible corpora as well, which allows for a comprehensive analysis of Hungarian texts.

3 Methods

3.1 HuSpaCy's Internals

HuSpaCy's main strength lies in the clever usage of available Hungarian linguistic resources and its multi-task learning capabilities inherited from spaCy. Its machine learning approach can be summarized as "embed, encode, attend, predict" shown in Fig. 1 and detailed by [10,22]. Tokens are first embedded through the combination of lexical attributes and word vectors, then context encoding is performed by stacked CNN [13] layers[2]. Finally, task specific layers are used parallelly in a multi-task learning setup.

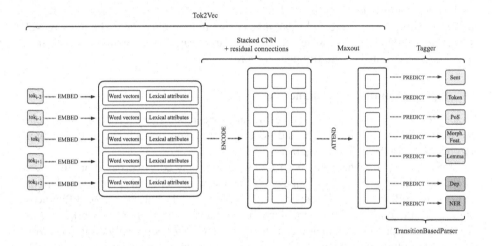

Fig. 1. The "embed, encode, attend, predict" architecture of spaCy

Orosz et al. [22] used a three step approach for fully utilizing annotated Hungarian datasets. First, they pre-train the tagger, the lemmatizer and the sentence boundary detection components on a silver standard UD annotated corpus (cf. [32]). Then, the Tok2Vec layers of this model are reused by both the NER and the parsing components: the dependency parser and the morphosyntactic taggers are fine-tuned on the UD-Hungarian dataset, the lemmatizer is trained on the entire Szeged Corpus, while the entity recognizer is further trained on the combination of the NYTK-NerKor and the Szeged NER datasets.

3.2 Improving on the Underlying Language Models

HuSpaCy's model is built on word2vec [14] word embeddings, which are known to have limitations in providing meaningful representations for out-of-vocabulary words.

---

[2] These steps are usually referred to as the Tok2Vec layers.

This is particularly problematic for morphology-related tasks in agglutinative languages. To enhance this simple approach, a more fine-grained method that uses subword embeddings can be employed. fastText [2] is a widely-used extension of word2vec that learns sub-token embeddings. In this study, we utilized floret[3] which is a spaCy-compatible fork of fastText. To train new word vectors, we used the Hungarian Webcorpus 2.0 [17]. Two sets of word embeddings were constructed: a 100-dimensional and a 300-dimensional one.

In recent years, there has been a growing interest in transformer-based large language models (LLM), as evidenced by their high performance in text processing models (e.g. [8,17]). With the advent of spaCy' s native support for such architectures and the availability of pre-trained language models for Hungarian, it is now possible to train transformer-based NLP pipelines for Hungarian. Our research is based on two widely used LLMs that provide support for Hungarian. One of these is huBERT [17], which has a BERT-like architecture and was trained using monolingual data. The other model is XLM-RoBERTa-large, which has a much larger capacity compared to the former model and was trained on multilingual corpora.

3.3 Pipeline Component Enhancements

In addition to the use of more powerful language models, we propose fundamental changes to the lemmatization and dependency parsing models, as well as minor improvements to the entity recognizer.

HuSpaCy' s lemmatizer has been replaced by a new edit-tree-based architecture, recently available in the spaCy framework[4]. This new model builds on the foundations laid out by Müller et al. [15] (called the Lemming model), but has minor differences from it. On the one hand, this reimplementation fully utilizes the framework's multi-task learning capabilities, which means that the lemmatizer is not only co-trained with PoS and morphological tagging, but also with sentence boundary detection. On the other hand, spaCy' s version lacks standard support for morphological lexicons which Lemming benefited from.

We have improved this model in two steps. 1. A simple dictionary learning method is put in place to memorize frequent *(token, tag, lemma)* triplets of the training data which are then used at prediction time to retrieve the roots of words. 2. A common weakness of Hungarian lemmatization methods is addressed. Computing the lemmata of sentence-starting tokens can be challenging for non-proper nouns, as their roots are always lowercase. Thus, we force the model to use the true casing of such words. For example, when computing the root of the sentence starting *Ezzel* 'with this' token, our method checks its PoS tag (that is ideally PRON) first, so that it can use the lowercase wordform for generating and looking up edit-trees.

Moving on, the dependency syntax annotation component is replaced with a model that has higher accuracy for many languages. Although spaCy' s built-in transition-based parser [10] has high throughput, it falls short on providing accurate predictions. Graph-based architectures are known to have good performance for dependency parsing (e.g. [1]), making such methods good enhancement candidates. Furthermore, a

---

[3] https://explosion.ai/blog/floret-vectors.

[4] https://explosion.ai/blog/edit-tree-lemmatizer.

spaCy-compatible implementation of Dozat and Manning's model [7] (referred to as the Biaffine parser) has recently been made available, thus we could easily utilize it in our experiments.

Finally, the named entity recognizer has been fine-tuned to provide more accurate entity annotations. This was primarily achieved by using beam-search in addition to the transition-based NER module.

4 Experiments and Results

This section presents the results of several experiments that demonstrate the improvements of our changes and show competitive results compared to well-established baselines. We evaluated pipelines developed on datasets used by the creators of HuSpaCy: the Hungarian part of the Universal Dependencies corpus[5] was utilized to benchmark the sentence boundary detector, the lemmatizer, the PoS and morphological taggers, and the dependency parser, while the entity recognizer is benchmarked on the combination of the NYTK-NerKor and the Szeged NER corpora (similar to [22] and [27]). To account for the instability of spaCy's training process we report the maximum result of three independent runs.

4.1 Evaluation of Architecture Improvements

The lemmatization accuracy of the original model has been greatly improved through a number of steps discussed in Sect. 3.3. As evidenced in Table 1, incorporation of the new neural architecture along with sub-word embeddings produced significant improvements. Furthermore, changing the default behavior of the edit-tree lemmatizer by allowing it to evaluate more than one candidate (see the row `topk=3`) also resulted in a slightly better performance. In addition, the integration of true-casing led to a considerable improvement, and the use of lemma dictionaries also significantly improved lemmatization scores.

Table 1. Lemmatization accuracy on the UD-Hungarian test set of different ablation settings. Rows marked with a "+" indicate a new feature added on top of the previous ones. `topk` is a hyperparameter of the lemmatization model controlling the number of edit-trees considered to be evaluated.

	Lemma Accuracy
HuSpaCy	95.53%
+ Edit-tree lemmatizer	95.90%
+ `floret` 300d vectors	96.76%
+ `topk=3`	97.01%
+ True-casing	97.30%
+ Learned dictionary	97.58%

---

[5] Experiments are performed at the v2.10 revision.

Entity recognition tasks often encounter a challenge in the form of a considerable number of out-of-vocabulary tokens, leading to decreased performance. However, the utilization of floret vectors has proven to be effective in addressing this issue, as indicated by the results in Table 2. Additionally, the use of beam search allowed the model to take prediction history into account, which slightly improved its efficiency.

Table 2. Evaluation of the entity recognition model improvements on the combination of the Szeged NER and NYTK-NerKor corpora. The rows starting with "+" signify the inclusion of a new feature in addition to the existing ones.

	NER F_1-score
HuSpaCy	83.68
+ floret 300d vectors	85.53
+ Beam search	85.99

The results in Table 3 indicate that the improved text representations and the new parsing architecture offer substantial improvements over HuSpaCy's outcomes. However, it is worth noting that spaCy's CNN-based base model is not fully compatible with the Biaffine parser's architecture. Therefore, parsing improvements were benchmarked on top of a transformer-based encoder architecture using huBERT. The results show that the use of floret vectors is beneficial to predict morphosyntactic characteristics and dependency relations, while the use of huBERT-based text representations substantially improves performance across all subtasks. Furthermore, the Biaffine parser significantly outperforms its transition-based counterpart, as evidenced by its better attachment scores.

Table 3. Evaluation of text parsing improvements on the UD-Hungarian test set. "+" indicate a new feature added on top of the existing ones.

	PoS Acc.	Morph. Acc.	UAS	LAS
HuSpaCy	96.58%	93.23%	79.39	74.22
HuSpaCy + floret 300d vectors	96.55%	93.93%	80.36	74.89
HuSpaCy + huBERT	98.10%	96.97%	89.95	83.94
+ Biaffine parser	98.10%	96.97%	90.31	87.23

4.2   Comparison with the State-of-the-Art

In addition to parsing and tagging correctness, resource consumption is an important consideration for industrial NLP applications. Therefore, following the approach of Orosz et al. [22] we conducted a benchmark study to compare both the accuracy and memory usage as well as the throughput of our models with text processing tools available for Hungarian.

Table 4. Text parsing accuracy of the novel pipelines compared to HuSpaCy, Stanza, UDify, Trankit and `emtsv`. Results for non-comparable models are shown in italics.

	Sent. F_1-score	PoS Acc.	Morph. Acc.	Lemma Acc.	UAS	LAS	NER F_1-score
emtsv	*98.11*	*89.19%*	*87.95%*	*96.16%*	*–*	*–*	**92.99**
Trankit	*98.00*	*97.49%*	*95.23%*	*94.45%*	*91.31*	*87.78*	*–*
UDify	–	96.15%	90.54%	88.70%	88.03	83.92	–
Stanza	97.77	96.12%	93.58%	94.68%	84.05	78.75	83.75
HuSpaCy	97.54	96.58%	93.23%	95.53%	79.39	74.22	83.68
md	97.88	96.26%	93.29%	97.38%	79.25	73.99	85.35
lg	98.33	96.91%	93.93%	97.58%	79.75	74.78	85.99
trf	99.33	**98.10%**	**96.97%**	98.79%	90.31	87.23	91.35
trf_xl	**99.67**	97.79%	96.53%	**98.90%**	90.22	86.67	91.84

Table 5. Resource usage (All benchmarks are run on the same environment having AMD EPYC 7F72 CPUs and NVIDIA A100 GPUs) of the new models and state-of-the-art of text processing tools available for Hungarian. Throughput is measured as the average number of processed tokens per second, while memory usage columns records the peak value of each tool.

	Throughput		Memory Usage (GB)
	CPU	GPU	
emtsv	113	–	3.9
Trankit	434	2119	3.7
UDify	129	475	3.2
Stanza	30	395	5.3
HuSpaCy	1525	6697	3.5
md	2652	3195	1.4
lg	847	3128	3.2
trf	273	2605	4.8
trf_xl	82	2353	18.9

First of all, an important result of this study is a base model (referred to as `lg`), which achieves a good balance between accuracy and resource usage as seen in Tables 4 and 5. This pipeline is built on top of the 300d `floret` vectors and incorporates all the enhancements described above, except for the new parser. Evaluation data demonstrates that the `lg` pipeline consistently outperforms Stanza in all tasks except syntactic dependency relation prediction, which can be explained by the superior parsing model of the latter tool.

We present the results of a medium-sized model (`md`) as well that is a reduced version of the `lg` pipeline utilizing the smaller (100d) word embeddings. Surprisingly, the `md` pipeline delivers performance similar to that of the larger model. Furthermore, the medium-sized model achieves scores comparable to or higher than those of HuSpaCy, despite requiring half the memory and exhibiting much higher throughput on CPU.

Transformer-based pipelines using the graph based dependency parser have the highest scores across all language analysis tasks. Remarkably, despite its smaller capacity, the model based on huBERT (trf) achieves the highest attachment scores for dependency parsing, while the one using XLM-RoBERTa-large (trf_xl) provides slightly more accurate PoS tags and named entities.

It is important to consider that not all third-party pipelines in Table 4 are directly comparable to our results, due to differences in the versions of the UD-Hungarian dataset used to train and evaluate their models. To ensure a fair comparison, Stanza and UDify have been retrained. On the other hand, we obtained the results of Trankit from [30] since it would be a demanding task to fine-tune this model. Furthermore, the results of emtsv's text parsing components [19–21] cannot be deemed reliable either (cf. [22]), since its components use a different train-test split of the Szeged Corpus. However, this tool's entity recognition module (emBERT [16]) was evaluated by Simon et al. [27] using the same settings as in our paper, thus we rely on their assessment. Additionally, state-of-the-art results are also shown in Table 4. With regard to highest dependency parsing scores, the results of the multilingual Trankit system are produced by a parsing model similar to that of ours. As for named entity recognition, emBERT attains the best F_1 scores by utilizing a Viterbi encoder that eliminates invalid label sequences from the outputs of the underlying model.

Regarding computational requirements, Table 5 presents findings that demonstrate how floret embeddings can effectively decrease the memory usage of models without compromising their accuracy and throughput. However, it is apparent that enhancing pipeline accuracy frequently results in slower processing speed, as can be observed from the lg, trf and trf_xl models. Additionally, our tests also showed that most of the readily available NLP pipelines are not adequately optimized to handle large workloads, which is evident from their low throughput values.

5   Conclusion

This paper has introduced new industrial-grade text processing pipelines for Hungarian and presented a thorough evaluation showing their (close to) state-of-the-art performance. We have shown that new architectures for lemmatization and dependency parsing and the use of improved text representation models significantly improve the accuracy of HuSpaCy. The presented models have not only demonstrated high performance in all text preprocessing steps, but the resource consumption of three of our models' (md, lg, trf) makes them suitable for solving practical problems. All of our experiments are reproducible and the models are freely available under a permissive license.

For future work, we consider the following areas of improvement. 1. Transformer-based pipelines are optimized for accuracy but this could limit their usability due to reduced computational efficiency. We would like to investigate optimizing their size to enhance their resource usage. 2. We would like to include more silver standard data to further improve the parsing and tagging scores, as the corpus used to train and evaluate text parsing components is limited in size. 3. Our models are mostly trained on news-related corpora, which makes user-generated text processing a difficult task. In order to address this challenge, we intend to integrate automatic data augmentation into the training process as a solution.

Acknowledgments. The authors would like to thank Gábor Berend for his valuable suggestions. HuSpaCy research and development is supported by the European Union project RRF-2.3.1-21-2022-00004 within the framework of the Artificial Intelligence National Laboratory.

References

1. Altıntaş, M., Tantuğ, A.C.: Improving the performance of graph based dependency parsing by guiding bi-affine layer with augmented global and local features. Intell. Syst. Appl. **18**, 200190 (2023)
2. Bojanowski, P., Grave, E., Joulin, A., Mikolov, T.: Enriching word vectors with subword information. Trans. Assoc. Comput. Linguist. **5**, 135–146 (2017)
3. Conneau, A., et al.: Unsupervised cross-lingual representation learning at scale. In: Proceedings of the 58th Annual Meeting of the Association for Computational Linguistics, pp. 8440–8451 (2020)
4. Csendes, D., Csirik, J., Gyimóthy, T.: The szeged corpus: a POS tagged and syntactically annotated Hungarian natural language corpus. In: Sojka, P., Kopeček, I., Pala, K. (eds.) TSD 2004. LNCS (LNAI), vol. 3206, pp. 41–47. Springer, Heidelberg (2004). https://doi.org/10.1007/978-3-540-30120-2_6
5. Csendes, D., Csirik, J., Gyimóthy, T., Kocsor, A.: The szeged treebank. In: Matoušek, V., Mautner, P., Pavelka, T. (eds.) TSD 2005. LNCS (LNAI), vol. 3658, pp. 123–131. Springer, Heidelberg (2005). https://doi.org/10.1007/11551874_16
6. Devlin, J., Chang, M.W., Lee, K., Toutanova, K.: BERT: pre-training of deep bidirectional transformers for language understanding. In: Proceedings of NAACL-HLT, pp. 4171–4186 (2019)
7. Dozat, T., Manning, C.D.: Deep biaffine attention for neural dependency parsing. In: International Conference on Learning Representations (2017)
8. Enevoldsen, K., Hansen, L., Nielbo, K.: DaCy: a unified framework for Danish NLP. arXiv preprint arXiv:2107.05295 (2021)
9. Honnibal, M.: Introducing spaCy (2015). https://explosion.ai/blog/introducing-spacy
10. Honnibal, M., Goldberg, Y., Johnson, M.: A non-monotonic arc-eager transition system for dependency parsing. In: Proceedings of the Seventeenth Conference on Computational Natural Language Learning, pp. 163–172. Association for Computational Linguistics, Sofia (2013)
11. Indig, B., Sass, B., Simon, E., Mittelholcz, I., Vadász, N., Makrai, M.: One format to rule them all - the emtsv pipeline for Hungarian. In: Proceedings of the 13th Linguistic Annotation Workshop, pp. 155–165. Association for Computational Linguistics, Florence (2019)
12. Kondratyuk, D., Straka, M.: 75 languages, 1 model: parsing universal dependencies universally. In: Proceedings of the 2019 Conference on Empirical Methods in Natural Language Processing and the 9th International Joint Conference on Natural Language Processing (EMNLP-IJCNLP), pp. 2779–2795 (2019)
13. Lecun, Y., Bottou, L., Bengio, Y., Haffner, P.: Gradient-based learning applied to document recognition. Proc. IEEE **86**(11), 2278–2324 (1998)
14. Mikolov, T., Chen, K., Corrado, G., Dean, J.: Efficient estimation of word representations in vector space (2013)

15. Müller, T., Cotterell, R., Fraser, A., Schütze, H.: Joint lemmatization and morphological tagging with lemming. In: Proceedings of the 2015 Conference on Empirical Methods in Natural Language Processing, pp. 2268–2274. Association for Computational Linguistics, Lisbon (2015)
16. Nemeskey, D.M.: Egy emBERT próbáló feladat. In: XVI. Magyar Számítógépes Nyelvészeti Konferencia (MSZNY2020), pp. 409–418. Szeged (2020)
17. Nemeskey, D.M.: Natural language processing methods for language modeling. Ph.D. thesis, Eötvös Loránd University (2020)
18. Nivre, J., et al.: Universal dependencies v2: an evergrowing multilingual treebank collection. In: Proceedings of the Twelfth Language Resources and Evaluation Conference, pp. 4034–4043. European Language Resources Association, Marseille (2020)
19. Novák, A.: A new form of humor – mapping constraint-based computational morphologies to a finite-state representation. In: Proceedings of the Ninth International Conference on Language Resources and Evaluation (LREC 2014), pp. 1068–1073. European Language Resources Association (ELRA), Reykjavik (2014)
20. Novák, A., Siklósi, B., Oravecz, C.: A new integrated open-source morphological analyzer for Hungarian. In: Proceedings of the Tenth International Conference on Language Resources and Evaluation (LREC 2016), pp. 1315–1322. European Language Resources Association (ELRA), Portorož (2016)
21. Orosz, G., Novák, A.: PurePos 2.0: a hybrid tool for morphological disambiguation. In: Proceedings of the International Conference Recent Advances in Natural Language Processing RANLP 2013, pp. 539–545. INCOMA Ltd., Shoumen, BULGARIA, Hissar (2013)
22. Orosz, G., Szántó, Z., Berkecz, P., Szabó, G., Farkas, R.: HuSpaCy: an industrial-strength Hungarian natural language processing toolkit. In: XVIII. Magyar Számítógépes Nyelvészeti Konferencia (2022)
23. Qi, P., Zhang, Y., Zhang, Y., Bolton, J., Manning, C.D.: Stanza: a Python natural language processing toolkit for many human languages. In: Proceedings of the 58th Annual Meeting of the Association for Computational Linguistics: System Demonstrations (2020)
24. Simon, E., Lendvai, P., Németh, G., Olaszy, G., Vicsi, K.: A Magyar Nyelv a Digitális Korban - the Hungarian Language in the Digital Age. Georg Rehm and Hans Uszkoreit (Series Editors): META-NET White Paper Series. Springer, Heidelberg (2012)
25. Simon, E., Indig, B., Kalivoda, Á., Mittelholcz Iván, S.B., Vadász, N.: Újabb fejlemények az e-magyar háza táján. In: Berend, G., Gosztolya, G., Vincze, V. (eds.) XVI. Magyar Számítógépes Nyelvészeti Konferencia, pp. 29–42. Szegedi Tudományegyetem Informatikai Tanszékcsoport, Szeged (2020)
26. Simon, E., Vadász, N.: Introducing NYTK-NerKor, a gold standard Hungarian named entity annotated corpus. In: Ekštein, K., Pártl, F., Konopík, M. (eds.) TSD 2021. LNCS (LNAI), vol. 12848, pp. 222–234. Springer, Cham (2021). https://doi.org/10.1007/978-3-030-83527-9_19
27. Simon, E., Vadász, N., Lévai, D., Dávid, N., Orosz, G., Szántó, Z.: Az NYTK-NerKor több szempontú kiértékelése. XVIII. Magyar Számítógépes Nyelvészeti Konferencia (2022)
28. Straka, M.: UDPipe 2.0 prototype at CoNLL 2018 UD shared task. In: Proceedings of the CoNLL 2018 Shared Task: Multilingual Parsing from Raw Text to Universal Dependencies, pp. 197–207. Association for Computational Linguistics, Brussels (2018)
29. Szarvas, György., Farkas, Richárd, Kocsor, András: A multilingual named entity recognition system using boosting and C4.5 decision tree learning algorithms. In: Todorovski, Ljupčo, Lavrač, Nada, Jantke, Klaus P.. (eds.) DS 2006. LNCS (LNAI), vol. 4265, pp. 267–278. Springer, Heidelberg (2006). https://doi.org/10.1007/11893318_27
30. Van Nguyen, M., Lai, V., Veyseh, A.P.B., Nguyen, T.H.: Trankit: a light-weight transformer-based toolkit for multilingual natural language processing. EACL **2021**, 80 (2021)

31. Váradi, T., et al.: E-magyar - a digital language processing system. In: Proceedings of the Eleventh International Conference on Language Resources and Evaluation (LREC 2018). European Language Resources Association (ELRA), Miyazaki (2018)

32. Vincze, V., Simkó, K., Szántó, Z., Farkas, R.: Universal dependencies and morphology for Hungarian - and on the price of universality. In: Proceedings of the 15th Conference of the European Chapter of the Association for Computational Linguistics: Volume 1, Long Papers, pp. 356–365. Association for Computational Linguistics, Valencia (2017)

33. Zsibrita, J., Vincze, V., Farkas, R.: magyarlanc: a toolkit for morphological and dependency parsing of Hungarian. In: Proceedings of Recent Advances in Natural Language Processing 2013, pp. 763–771. Association for Computational Linguistics, Hissar (2013)

ParaDiom – A Parallel Corpus of Idiomatic Texts

Gregor Donaj[(⊠)] and Špela Antloga

University of Maribor, Faculty of Electrical Engineering and Computer Science,
Koroška c. 46, 2000 Maribor, Slovenia
{gregor.donaj,s.antloga}@um.si
http://www.feri.um.si/

Abstract. This paper present ParaDiom – a parallel corpus with 2000 Slovene and English text segments. The text segments are rich with manually annotated idiomatic expressions, which poses a challenge for machine translation systems. We describe the definition of idiomatic expressions, the sampling of the corpus sentences, the annotation scheme, and the general characteristics of the finished corpus. The motivation for this corpus is to have a test set for machine translation systems to evaluate their performance on figurative language. In the last part of the paper, we demonstrate an example use of the corpus in a machine translation experiment.

Keywords: idiomatic expression · corpus · machine translation

1 Introduction

Recent advances in neural network architecture, training design, the availability of large parallel corpora, and hardware capabilities have increased the quality of neural machine translation systems. However, there are still some areas or specific types of text where machine translation struggles–one example is translating idiomatic expressions. Recently, Vieira et al. [27] conducted a survey in the UK asking how users would describe the machine translation system of the future. Some expected it to be able to recognize idiomatic expressions and also produce idiomatic translations. Participants also emphasized some cultural aspects and nuances. Those can also be connected to the use of figurative language.

To assess the performance of machine translation systems, we need evaluation sets which contain aligned parallel sentences in two or more languages. Although many such sets exist, they often contain sentences randomly sampled from general domain corpora or text in specific domains. To our knowledge, there is no prior parallel annotated corpus for Slovene that is specifically designed to assess the performance of machine translation systems on figurative speech.

In this paper, we present ParaDiom – a parallel corpus with annotated idiomatic expressions designed as a test set for machine translation for the English-Slovene language pair with the possibility to extend the corpus to other languages. The source sentences are sampled from existing corpora, each containing at least one idiomatic expression, while translations to the target language are not guaranteed to contain idiomatic

K. Ekštein et al. (Eds.): TSD 2023, LNAI 14102, pp. 70–81, 2023.
https://doi.org/10.1007/978-3-031-40498-6_7

expressions. All idiomatic expressions in the source sentences and the translations are manually annotated by a single annotator.

To illustrate a potential use of the corpus, we show a preliminary experiment with two machine translation systems and highlight some findings from a manual evaluation of the translations.

1.1 Definition of Idiomatic Expressions

Finding a comprehensive definition that includes various forms of what can constitute idiomatic expressions can be challenging. These expressions are often defined as sequences of words involving some degree of semantic idiosyncrasy or noncompositionality. In phraseology, 'idioms' are defined as a dominant subtype within the category of the phraseological unit as a lexicalized, reproducible word group in common use, which has syntactic and semantic stability and may carry connotations, but whose meaning cannot be derived from the meanings of its constituents [14], e.g., "to be hand in glove" means "to have a very close relationship", but its meaning cannot be deduced from the literal meanings of the words "hand" and "glove."

Another term used in phraseological research to denote a multiword expression (MWE) with a fully or partially figurative meaning is 'phraseological unit'. In some Slavonic and German linguistic traditions, it is used as a superordinate term for multiword lexical items [13]. 'Phraseme' is also used as a superordinate term (e.g., in [20], as well as in Slovene phraseological research, e.g., [18]), though not in the Anglo-American tradition. Other terms also encountered in the phraseological literature are 'multiword lexical unit' [4], 'fixed expression' [25], 'fixed phrase' [26] and 'phrasal lexeme' [21].

In Slovene studies [11], MWEs are divided into 1) phraseological units (PUs), in which at least one component carries the meaning that differs from one of its denotative dictionary senses and expresses figurativeness, and 2) all other multiword expressions, which are characterized by a certain degree of fixedness and denote a meaning that can be predicted from the meanings of their elements. PUs are further divided by syntactic structure: the clausal type (including proverbs) and the phrasal type (all non-verbal PUs). Verbal MWEs (VMWEs) are determined by their morphosyntactic features (ibid.); an MWE is classified as a VMWE if it includes a verbal element and functions as a predicate. However, that would make it unclear how to classify examples in which the verbal MWE does not function as a predicate, e.g., "hočeš nočeš" "like it or not", which includes two verbal elements but functions as an adverbial phrase. The problem of categorizing MWEs according to their morphological structure and syntactic function was resolved in PARSEME shared task [24] through the definition that the main criterion for VMWEs is that their syntactic head in the prototypical form is a verb, regardless of the fact whether it can or cannot fulfill other syntactic roles.

In ParaDiom, the terms 'idiom' and 'idiomatic expressions' are used to refer to a two- or multiword lexical item whose meaning is conventionalized and not predictable from the meaning of its constituent words. We have adopted PARSEME's approach to define MWEs based on the part of speech that constitutes their syntactic head in the prototypical form (verb, adjective, noun, adverb). We implemented it in our annotation scheme, excluding light verb constructions and verb-particle constructions.

A special type of idiomatic expression, 'similes', are figures of speech that describe one thing by comparing it with another and suggesting similarities between them, although they are clearly different. Similes follow the same structure as comparative, e.g., "my hands were cold like ice". In Paradiom, we included conventional similes that tend to be fixed and have idiom status, e.g., "priden kot mravljica" "hardworking as an ant", "hiter kot strela" "as quick as lightning", but in the process of annotation we also found novel, context-depending similes, e.g., "nositi se kot pav, ki osvaja" "to carry yourself like a peacock that's hitting on someone" instead of conventionalized "nositi se kot pav" "to carry yourself like a peacock".

1.2 Idiomatic Expressions in Machine Translation

Idiomatic expressions and other multiword expressions pose a challenge for machine translation. The reason for this is that they often can not be translated literally. A frequently used example is the English idiom "It's raining cats and dogs." This idiom is easily understood by native English speakers, but it is not literary translated into other languages. Using the literal translation of idioms can create confusion, as the meaning can not be determined from the meaning of the words of the idiom. For example, the Slovene idiom "iti po gobe" literally translates to "going to get mushrooms," while it means that someone dies or something fails. Idiomatic expressions are very often culture-specific because they refer to a unique denotatum belonging to the national culture, e.g., "zaščiten kot kočevski medved" translates to "protected as a bear from Kočevje[1]." Contrary to this, some idioms originate from word history or literature and are understood in many languages, e.g., "The die is cast" or "Tilting at windmills."

Modern machine translation systems are based on large amounts of training data. If enough examples of an idiom and a proper translation are present in the training data, the system might be able to produce a correct translation. Ducar and Schocket found, for example, that Google Translate performs well with frequent idioms but not with rate ones [8].

Identifying and translating idiomatic expressions are connected research areas. Saini and Modh [23] found that existing machine translation systems perform poorly on Gujarati idioms and proposed a dictionary-based approach for translation idioms. Dhariy et al. [5] also found that example-based translation improves the performance in translating sentences with idioms and other ambiguities.

Ghoneim and Diab [12] demonstrated a way of integrating idioms and other multiword expressions into statistical machine translation and gained improvement in experiments between English and Arabic. Similarly, Ebrahim et al. [9] presented a method to detect and integrate phrasal verbs as multiword expressions into statistical machine translation.

Such research has shown that idiom detection and text preprocessing can benefit machine translation. However, detecting figurative speech elements is challenging, especially for expressions that can be used literally and idiomatically. Recent research from Abarna et al. [1] showed a model based on a knowledge graph to distinguish between the literal and idiomatic use of phrases. Similar work was done by Briskilal and Subalalitha [3].

---

[1] Kočevje is a region in Slovenia.

2   The ParaDiom Corpus

2.1   Source Corpora

The sentences in ParaDiom were sampled from three source corpora. Slovene sentences were sampled from ccGigafida 1.0 corpus, and English sentences were sampled from the annotated ParlaMint 2.1 corpus and The Corpus of Late Modern English Texts 3.1. We selected those source corpora for their size and availability under Creative Commons licenses, which was a requirement in the funding agreement for the corpus. Also, ccGigafida and ParlaMint are available in XML-TEI format with part-of-speech and lemma annotations.

Gigafida is a reference corpus of written Slovene with approximately 1.1 billion tokens in its latest version [17]. It is the largest corpus of Slovene, but it is only freely available through web concordancers. ccGigafifda contains sampled sentences from Gigafida and amounts to approximately 103 million words. It is available for download under a Creative Commons license on the CLARIN.SI repository.[2]

ParlaMint [10] is a set of corpora containing debates from 17 European parliaments. The corpus from the British parliament contains approximately 109 million words from debates from both the House of Commons and the House of Lords. It is also available for download under a Creative Commons license on the CLARIN.SI repository.[3]

The Corpus of Late Modern English Texts (CLMET) [6] is a collection of public domain texts from 1710 to 1920 with approximately 34 million words. It is available on the CLARIND-UdS repository.[4] Unlike the previous two corpora, it is not available in XML-TEI format, but file IDs are provided, and paragraph boundaries are annotated. To enable sentence sampling, the corpus was annotated and lemmatized using the Stanza NLP Library [22] and converted to XML-TEI format.

2.2   Sentence Sampling

To sample sentences, a list of idiomatic expressions was first compiled. For Slovene, the list includes 71 idioms and 29 similes, and for English, 83 idioms and 9 similes. Both lists were prepared with the words in their lemmatized form and, in some cases, with several possible idiom forms, e.g., "call the shots" and "call the tune" or "the last straw" and "the final straw." Entries in the lists contain only the mandatory elements of the idiomatic expressions. Lemmas were used to account for different morphological forms of idiomatic expressions. The Slovene list was compiled by selecting expressions from the Dictionary of Slovenian Phrasemes [16], and the English list using the online Cambridge Learners and other online sources.

Parts of the idiomatic expression that are not invariant were replaced with wild-card stand-ins to allow different forms. E.g., in the idiom "pulling one's leg," the word "one's" was replaced with a wildcard since it can be replaced with other personal pronouns or a person's name.

---

[2] http://hdl.handle.net/11356/1035.
[3] http://hdl.handle.net/11356/1431.
[4] https://fedora.clarin-d.uni-saarland.de/clmet/clmet.html.

Next, sentences from the source corpora were sampled if they contained all lemmas of the idiomatic expression in the same order while allowing a limited number of other words between the words in the idiomatic expression. This enables us to sample sentences where optional parts of the idiom are present or other words are inserted, e.g., "bear in mind" vs. "bear this in mind."

Sentences, where elements from the idiomatic expressions were used in a literal sense, were manually excluded. To keep the corpus more representative of a general domain, we also excluded sentences from ParlaMint that contained several parliamentary-specific words. For each idiomatic expression, 8 to 12 sentences were added to the corpus. Finally, 1000 sentences from each language were selected. In the English part, 841 sentences were from ParlaMint and 151 from CLMET. During sampling, sentence boundaries were determined based on the existing XML-TEI tags. Sentence and token ID tags were preserved to create a mapping table from ParaDiom to the source corpora.

2.3 Translation

The sampled sentences in both languages were divided into two equal parts so that sentences sampled for each idiomatic expression appeared in both parts.

For both languages, the first part was manually translated by a professional translation agency. Because most of the English text is from parliamentary debates, it can contain specific terms, e.g., Lord or Bill. Since some of these terms might be ambiguous without context, the translators were informed of the source of the text. Other than that, the translators were given no specific instructions on how to translate the sentences.

The second part was translated using machine translation and manual post-editing. In the post-editing processes, the sentences were corrected to be accurate translations of the source text and grammatically correct. Changes regarding writing style or sentence structure were not made.

Given the source language and the translation method, the ParaDiom corpus was divided into four parts (each part contained two files – one for each language):

1. sentences from the Slovene corpus and post-edited machine translations to English,
2. sentences from the Slovene corpus and manual translations to English,
3. sentences from the English corpora and post-edited machine translations to Slovene,
4. sentences from the English corpora and manual translations to Slovene.

The texts from all files were again annotated with part-of-speech tags and lemmas, and converted into XML-TEI format. Tagging for English was done using the Stanza NLP library [22], and for Slovene using the CLASSLA fork of Stanza [19]. Tagging was also done for the source language sentences already tagged in the source corpora since this has been done with older and less accurate taggers.

It should be noted that some, mostly longer, sentences from the source languages were translated into two sentences in the other language. In such cases, they were kept together within one sentence element in the XML-TEI structure to preserve alignment between both languages. Therefore, sentences in the final corpus should be considered text segments rather than grammatical sentences.

During tagging, new ID tags in the XML-TEI format were created with a sentence-level mapping table from the source corpora IDs to the ParaDiom IDs.

2.4   Annotation

We used the Q-CAT annotation tool [2] to manually annotate idiomatic expressions in Slovene and English. The annotated nounal, adjectival, and adverbial idioms were given the label MWE ID (idiomatic multiword expression), verb idioms MWE VID (verbal idiomatic multiword expression), similes MWE SIM (simile), and proverbs MWE P (proverb). Figure 1 shows an annotated example sentence in the tool.

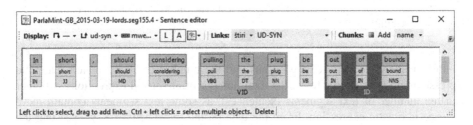

Fig. 1. A sentence from ParlaMint opened Q-CAT with two manually annotated idiomatic expressions (one MWE VID and one MWE ID).

While annotating idiomatic expressions, we paid attention to their invariant form (type and sequence of components and the relation between them, e.g., "keep one's eye on the ball" vs. "eye on the ball"), but also taking into account the limited variability of the components of the idiom, e.g., "keep one's *eyeball on the ball"; the mandatory and optional components in its textual realization, e.g., "a labour of love" vs. "a real labour of love"; modifications in syntactic structure, e.g., "skočiti si v lase" "to jump in each other's hair" vs. "ne biti si v laseh" "to not be in each other's hair"; permissible alternations, e.g., "trgovanje z belim blagom" "white-goods trading (meaning human trafficking)" vs. "trgovec z belim blagom" (human trafficker); and renovations, e.g., "polniti si tako baterije kot bančni račun" "charge one's batteries as well as their bank account".

We annotated only mandatory components of the idiomatic expression, which we identified based on the Dictionary of Slovenian Phrasemes [16] and for English as specified in the Cambridge Learners Dictionary. All dictionary entries list invariant form, mandatory and optional components of the idiomatic expression. If we identified idioms that are not listed in the mentioned dictionaries, we defined the invariant form of the idiom and its mandatory and optional components according to the analysis of the use of the specific idiom in corpora.

2.5   Publication and Corpus Statistics

The ParaDiom Corpus is freely available under the Creative Commons BY-NC-SA 4.0 license on the CLARIN.SI repository website [7]. It is published in XML-TEI format with an additional mapping file linking the sentence IDs in ParaDiom to sentence IDs in the source corpora. Figure 2 shows an example sentence from the final corpus.

```
<s xml:id="ParaDiom-en-3.s1005">
  <w lemma="that" pos="DT" xml:id="ParaDiom-en-3.s1005.t1">That</w>
  <w lemma="fall" pos="VBD" xml:id="ParaDiom-en-3.s1005.t2">fell</w>
  <w lemma="by" pos="IN" xml:id="ParaDiom-en-3.s1005.t3">by</w>
  <w lemma="the" pos="DT" xml:id="ParaDiom-en-3.s1005.t4">the</w>
  <w join="right" lemma="wayside" pos="NN" xml:id="ParaDiom-en-3.s1005.t5">wayside</w>
  <pc pos="." xml:id="ParaDiom-en-3.s1005.t6">.</pc>
  <linkGrp type="MWE" corresp="#ParaDiom-en-3.s1005">
    <link ana="mwe:VID" target="ParaDiom-en-3.s1005.t2 ParaDiom-en-3.s1005.t3
                                 ParaDiom-en-3.s1005.t4 ParaDiom-en-3.s1005.t5" />
  </linkGrp>
</s>
```

Fig. 2. A sentence from ParaDiom part 3 English text. The full MSD tag has been omitted in the figure for readability.

Table 1 shows the size of the corpus and the number of all annotated idiomatic expressions. In both source texts, the total number of annotated expressions is higher than the number of text segments (sentences), as some text segments contain more than one idiomatic expression. From the data on the translated texts, we see that the number of annotated expressions is much lower since idiomatic expressions were often translated into literal descriptions of them.

Table 1. Corpus size and the number of annotations for the source text and the translation.

	English source	Slovene source	English translations	Slovene translations
Text segments	1,000	1,000	1,000	1,000
Words	16,461	17,022	19,615	13,317
MWE ID	477	220	155	106
MWE VID	510	512	210	128
MWE SIM	76	295	166	73
MWE P	2	3	0	0
MWE total	1,065	1,030	531	307

2.6 Expansion Possibilities

The file structure in the final corpus is designed to enable easy expansions. The main files are named "Paradiom-XX-Y.xml," where XX is the language code, and Y is the corpus part. Sentences are aligned based on the sentence IDs in the main files, which have the format "Paradiom-XX-Y-sZZZZ," where ZZZZ is the consecutive sentence number (see Fig. 2). The sentence numbers in the corpus range from 1 to 2000 and are unique across the corpus parts, i.e., each new part of the corpus continues incrementing the number from the previous part.

If the corpus would be expanded by adding more sentences in the same language pair, they should be added to both files in the existing corpus parts based on the source language and translation type. For example, more Slovene sentences with post-edited machine translations to English can be added to part 1 (files "ParaDiom-sl-1.xml" and

"ParaDiom-en-1.xml") with sentence numbers from 2001 onwards. A similar expansion can be done for the other three corpus parts.

If the corpus would be expanded by adding more languages, additional files would be necessary. The additional files would depend on the source of the sentences. For example, if the Slovene sentences were manually translated into a third language, the file "ParaDiom-de-2.xml" would be added with the existing sentence numbers.

The second possibility of adding a third language is to add sentences from this language and translate them into Slovene, English, or both. In this case, two additional parts of the corpus should be created – one part where sentences would be manually translated and one part with post-edited machine translations. In this case, sentence numbers from 2001 onwards should be used.

3   Example Use: Machine Translation Experiments

3.1   Translation System

A preliminary machine translation experiment was performed to demonstrate using ParaDiom as a test set for machine translation. We trained two machine translation systems for each translation direction (Slovene to English and English to Slovene). The two systems differ in the training corpus used.

We trained the first system on the ParaCrawl corpus, version 8.[5] It contains 7.5 million aligned parallel text segments in the Slovene-English language pair. The segments were sampled from different web pages. We consider this corpus to be a general domain corpus of written languages. The corpus contains 136 million words on the English side and 121 on the Slovene.

We trained the second system on the OpenSubutitles corpus, version 2018.[6] It contains approximately 18 million aligned parallel text segments. The corpus contains 129 million words on the English side and 98 on the Slovene. The average text segment in this corpus is considerably shorter than in ParaCrawl, making the sizes of these two corpora more comparable regarding word count.

We performed standard preprocessing: normalization, tokenization, and truecasing. We split the words in the corpus into subword units based on the byte pair encoding algorithm with a joined vocabulary and 32,000 merge operations.

On both corpora, a small portion of the training set with 4000 randomly sampled segments was used as a validation set.

We trained neural machine translation (NMT) models with Marian NMT [15] for 20 epochs. We selected the transformer architecture and model hyperparameters based on the wmt2017-transformer example.[7] We selected the best-performing model based on the BLEU scores during validation.

---

[5] https://opus.nlpl.eu/ParaCrawl-v8.php.

[6] https://opus.nlpl.eu/OpenSubtitles-v2018.php.

[7] https://github.com/marian-nmt/marian-examples/tree/master/wmt2017-transformer.

Table 2. BLEU results for all systems. All differences between ParaCrawl and OpenSubtitles systems are statistically significant (bootstrap resampling test, all p-values less than 0.001).

Corpus part	Training set	BLEU (en-sl)	BLEU (sl-en)
1	ParaCrawl	27.64	37.30
1	OpenSubtitles	21.22	28.25
2	ParaCrawl	23.07	30.07
2	OpenSubtitles	18.56	27.00
3	ParaCrawl	32.93	28.82
3	OpenSubtitles	26.56	23.61
4	ParaCrawl	29.69	25.76
4	OpenSubtitles	23.07	20.98

3.2 Evaluation

We used SacreBLEU for automatic evaluation and present the results in Table 2. On average, models trained with the ParaCrawl corpus performed 5.75 BLEU points better. This is a surprising result as we expected figurative speech to be more present in subtitles than on web pages. However, the better performance might be due to this model performing better in general, not only on text with figurative speech.

The results obtained on the machine-translated and post-edited parts of the corpus are, on average, 3.52 BLEU points better than on the manually translated parts. This aligns with our expectation that machine translation output is more similar to post-edited machine translation output than manually translated text. However, these results must be examined more carefully. Although sentences were randomly divided between different translation methods, we can not exclude that one of the parts of the test set poses a more demanding test set for machine translation in general.

From previous research experience, we expected that translation from Slovene to English would give better scores than from English to Slovene. This is the case for parts 1 and 2 of the corpus, where the original sentences were in Slovene and translated into English. These results are 8.03 BLEU points better on average. However, for parts 3 and 4 of the corpus, the translation scores from English to Slovene are, on average, 3.27 BLEU points better.

A qualitative analysis can be performed on examples from the machine translations. Figure 3 show four translation examples from Slovene to English. In example (a), the expression was correctly translated. However, in this example, the same comparison is used for this simile in English and Slovene. Here, the literal translation is, in fact, correct.

In example (b), the Slovene idiom "delati cirkus" was literary translated by the system built on the OpenSubtitles corpus. The system built on the ParaCrawl corpus made a correct translation, although not identical to the reference translation. Example (c) shows a similar situation with another idiom. Example (d) shows an example where the idiom "Zaščiten kot kočevski medved" was incorrectly translated by both models.

The presented results only illustrate the possible use of the ParaDiom corpus. In order to properly explore the performance of machine translation on figurative speech, carefully designed experiments and a systematic analysis of the results are needed.

---

a) src: Fant je **hiter kot blisk**.
   ref: The boy is **as fast as lightning**.
   tOS: The boy is   **quick as lightning**.
   tPC: Boy's **as fast as lightning**.

---

b) src: Ne boš zaradi tega **delal cirkusa**?
   ref: Aren't you going to **make a fuss**   out of it?
   tOS: Will   you not   <u>make a circus</u>   for this?
   tPC: You're not gonna   **make a big deal** about it?

---

c) src: Izjava je torej **čista kot solza**.
   ref: So the statement is   as **clean as a whistle**.
   tOS: The statement is therefore <u>pure as tear</u>.
   tPC: So   it's   **clean as a whistle**.

---

d) src: Do takrat pa so **zaščiteni kot kočevski medvedje**.
   ref: Until then, they'll **be untouchable**.
   tOS: Until then   they are   <u>protected as Kočevje bears</u>.
   tPC: Until then, they're   <u>protected like cosmic bears</u>.

Fig. 3. Translation examples from Slovene to English. Displayed are the source text (src), reference translations (ref.), translation with the OpenSubtitles models (tOS), and translations with ParaCrawl models (tPC). Idiomatic expressions are bold and literal translations of idiomatic expressions are in red and underlined. (Color figure online)

4 Conclusion

In this work, we described the build processes for the ParaDiom corpus, which contains manual annotations of idiomatic expressions. The corpus can be used for experiments in idiom detection in English and Slovene or qualitative analysis of translation tendencies of figurative language. Its primary intended use is a test set for machine translation on the English-Slovene language pair with an emphasis on figurative language. The expandable structure of the corpus makes it possible to extend machine translation experiments to other languages in the future.

Future work includes a planned upgrade of the corpus by adding manually created word alignments. Such alignments would enable automatic evaluations for machine translation, specifically on the idiomatic expressions instead of the whole corpus. Still, some manual examination of the results would be needed.

Acknowledgements. This work was supported by CLARIN.SI and the Slovenian Research Agency (research core funding No.P2-0069-Advanced Methods of Interaction in Telecommunications).

The authors thank the creators of the ParaCrawl project (paracrawl.eu) and OpenSubtitles (www.opensubtitles.org) for their corpora and OPUS (opus.nlpl.eu) for their service. The authors also thank the HPC RIVR (www.hpc-rivr.si) consortium for the use of the HPC system VEGA on the Institute of Information Science (IZUM).

References

1. Abarna, S., Sheeba, J., Devaneyan, S.P.: An ensemble model for idioms and literal text classification using knowledge-enabled BERT in deep learning. Measur. Sens. **24**, 100434 (2022)
2. Brank, J.: Q-CAT corpus annotation tool (2019). http://hdl.handle.net/11356/1262, slovenian language resource repository CLARIN.SI
3. Briskilal, J., Subalalitha, C.: An ensemble model for classifying idioms and literal texts using BERT and RoBERTa. Inf. Process. Manage. **59**(1), 102756 (2022)
4. Cowie, A.P.: Multiword lexical units and communicative language teaching. In: Arnaud, P.J.L., Béjoint, H. (eds.) Vocabulary and Applied Linguistics, pp. 1–12. Palgrave Macmillan UK, London (1992)
5. Dhariya, O., Malviya, S., Tiwary, U.S.: A hybrid approach for Hindi-English machine translation. In: 2017 International Conference on Information Networking (ICOIN), pp. 389–394. IEEE (2017)
6. Diller, H.J., De Smet, H., Tyrkkö, J.: A European database of descriptors of English electronic texts. Eur. Engl. Messenger **19**, 21–35 (2011)
7. Donaj, G., Antloga, Š.: Parallel corpus of idiomatic text ParaDiom 1.0 (2022). http://hdl.handle.net/11356/1714. slovenian language resource repository CLARIN.SI
8. Ducar, C., Schocket, D.H.: Machine translation and the L2 classroom: pedagogical solutions for making peace with google translate. Foreign Lang. Ann. **51**(4), 779–795 (2018)
9. Ebrahim, S., Hegazy, D., Mostafa, M.G.H.M., El-Beltagy, S.R.: Detecting and integrating multiword expression into English-Arabic statistical machine translation. Procedia Comput. Sci. **117**, 111–118 (2017)
10. Erjavec, T., et al.: The ParlaMint corpora of parliamentary proceedings. Lang. Resour. Eval. **57**(1), 415–448 (2022)
11. Gantar, P., Krek, S., Kuzman, T.: Verbal multiword expressions in Slovene. In: Mitkov, R. (ed.) EUROPHRAS 2017. LNCS (LNAI), vol. 10596, pp. 247–259. Springer, Cham (2017). https://doi.org/10.1007/978-3-319-69805-2_18
12. Ghoneim, M., Diab, M.: Multiword expressions in the context of statistical machine translation. In: Mitkov, R., Park, J.C. (eds.) Proceedings of the Sixth International Joint Conference on Natural Language Processing, pp. 1181–1187. Asian Federation of Natural Language Processing, Nagoya, Japan (2013)
13. Gläser, R.: Terminological problems in linguistics, with special reference to neologisms. In: Hartmann, R.R.K. (ed.) LEXeter '83 Proceedings, pp. 345–351. Max Niemeyer Verlag, Tübingen, Germany (Sep 1983)
14. Gläser, R.: The stylistic potential of phraseological units in the light of genre analysis. In: Cowie, A.P. (ed.) Phraseology: Theory, Analysis, and Applications, chap. 9, pp. 128–143. Oxford University Press, Oxford (1998)
15. Junczys-Dowmunt, M., et al.: Marian: fast neural machine translation in C++. In: Proceedings of ACL 2018, System Demonstrations, pp. 116–121. Association for Computational Linguistics, Melbourne, Australia (2018)
16. Keber, J.: Slovar Slovenskih Frazemov. Založba ZRC, ZRC SAZU, Ljubljana (2011)
17. Krek, S., et al.: Gigafida 2.0: the reference corpus of written standard Slovene. In: Proceedings of the Twelfth Language Resources and Evaluation Conference, pp. 3340–3345. European Language Resources Association, Marseille, France (2020)
18. Kržišnik, E.: Idiomatska beseda ali frazeološka enota. Slavistična revija **58**(1), 83–94 (2010)
19. Ljubešić, N., Dobrovoljc, K.: What does neural bring? Analysing improvements in morphosyntactic annotation and lemmatisation of Slovenian, Croatian and Serbian. In: Proceedings of the 7th Workshop on Balto-Slavic Natural Language Processing, pp. 29–34. Association for Computational Linguistics, Florence, Italy (2019)

20. Mel'cuk, I.: Phrasemes in language and phraseology in linguistics. In: Everaert, M., Erik-Jan van der Linden, A.S., Schreuder, R., Schreuder, R. (eds.) Idioms: Structural and Psycological Perspectives, pp. 167–232. Hillsdale: Lawrence Erlbaum Associates (1995)

21. Naciscione, A.: Stylistic use of phraseological units in discourse. John Benjamins Publishing Company, Amsterdam, Philadelphia (2010)

22. Qi, P., Zhang, Y., Zhang, Y., Bolton, J., Manning, C.D.: Stanza: a Python natural language processing toolkit for many human languages. In: Proceedings of the 58th Annual Meeting of the Association for Computational Linguistics: System Demonstrations, pp. 101–108. Association for Computational Linguistics (2020)

23. Saini, J.R., Modh, J.C.: GIdTra: a dictionary-based MTS for translating Gujarati bigram idioms to English. In: 2016 Fourth International Conference on Parallel, Distributed and Grid Computing (PDGC), pp. 192–196. IEEE, Waknaghat, India (2016)

24. Savary, A., et al.: The PARSEME shared task on automatic identification of verbal multiword expressions. In: Markantonatou, S., Ramisch, C., Savary, A., Vincze, V. (eds.) Proceedings of the 13th Workshop on Multiword Expressions (MWE 2017), pp. 31–47. Association for Computational Linguistics, Valencia, Spain (2017)

25. Svensson, M.H.: A very complex criterion of fixedness: Noncompositionality. In: Granger, S., Meunier, F. (eds.) Phraseology: An Interdisciplinary Perspective, pp. 81–93. John Benjamins Publishing Company, Philadelphia (2008)

26. Verstraten, L.: Fixed phrases in monolingual learners' dictionaries. In: Arnaud, P.J.L., Béjoint, H. (eds.) Vocabulary and Applied Linguistics, pp. 28–40. Palgrave Macmillan UK, London (1992)

27. Vieira, L.N., O'Sullivan, C., Zhang, X., O'Hagan, M.: Machine translation in society: insights from UK users. Language Resources and Evaluation (2022)

Measuring Sentiment Bias in Machine Translation

Kai Hartung[1(✉)], Aaricia Herygers[1], Shubham Vijay Kurlekar[1], Khabbab Zakaria[1],
Taylan Volkan[1], Sören Gröttrup[1], and Munir Georges[1,2]

[1] AImotion Bavaria, Technische Hochschule Ingolstadt, Ingolstadt, Germany
{kai.hartung,aaricia.herygers,shubhamvijay.kurlekar,tav9580,
khabbab.zakaria, soeren.groettrup,munir.georges}@thi.de
[2] Intel Labs, Munich, Germany

Abstract. Biases induced to text by generative models have become an increasingly large topic in recent years. In this paper we explore how machine translation might introduce a bias in sentiments as classified by sentiment analysis models. For this, we compare three open access machine translation models for five different languages on two parallel corpora to test if the translation process causes a shift in sentiment classes recognized in the texts. Though our statistic test indicate shifts in the label probability distributions, we find none that appears consistent enough to assume a bias induced by the translation process.

Keywords: Machine translation · sentiment classification · bias

1 Introduction

With the increasing use of artificial intelligence also came a rise in research into its trustworthiness and fairness [24]. These studies have shown that models in various fields contain biases. For instance, in computer vision a range of biases has been investigated, followed by novel mitigation techniques [42]. Similarly, biases have been found and mitigated [45] in speech recognition and recommender systems [5].

In order to avoid perpetuating social biases and further contribute to discrimination, researchers have also studied biases in machine translation (MT). For example, Prates et al. [31] conducted a case study into Google Translate by translating sentences such as "He/She is an engineer", with varying occupations, from gender-neutral languages into English. They found that, especially for job titles in the fields of science, technology, engineering, and mathematics, the English gendered pronoun tended to be male. Following these results, Escudé et al. [9] experimented with a debiasing method and a gender-neutral MT system [49]. The study showed that a system that learned gender information disregarded contextual gender information, providing wrong translations. The gender-neutral system, however, did take the sentential gender information, providing correct translations, enabling it to achieve a higher BLEU [28] performance.

Another type of bias is *sentiment bias*, in which case a sentiment classification or sentiment analysis (SA) model provides a sentence with a sentiment (e.g., positive or negative) which may change when the phrasing or a certain word changes. In [16], a language generation model was used to generate sentences with varying occupations, countries, and gendered names. Through counterfactual evaluation [13], the study revealed

K. Ekštein et al. (Eds.): TSD 2023, LNAI 14102, pp. 82–93, 2023.
https://doi.org/10.1007/978-3-031-40498-6_8

that there were systematic differences in the sentiments across the varying inputs. For example, sentences containing the word 'baker' had a more positive sentiment than those containing the word 'accountant'.

This paper thus seeks to measure sentiment bias in machine translation. The following sections describe related work (Sect. 2), followed by a description of our analysis (Sect. 3), the used models (Sect. 4) and corpora (Sect. 5). The results are presented and discussed in Sect. 6, followed by a conclusion in Sect. 7.

2   Related Work

As MT is essentially a task on natural language processing in one language and generation in another, this section briefly describes related work on biases in natural language processing. Extended literature overviews on such biases are provided in [3,38].

In [47] the authors studied language as support for visual recognition tasks. Specifically, they investigated the data as well as the models for two tasks: multi-label object classification and visual semantic role labeling. They found that the dataset contained a gender bias, which was amplified when used to train a model (e.g., 'cooking' was 30% more likely to be accompanied by 'woman' than 'man' in the training set, followed by a 70% more likely association after training). In order to counter this effect, the authors proposed to provide a balanced gender ratio for each of the activities, i.e., put constraints on the corpus level, within a framework called 'Reducing Bias Amplification'. This approach was able to decrease the bias by over 40% for both studied tasks.

Furthermore, Zhao et al. [48] studied gender coreference (e.g., "The physician called the secretary and told *him/her* to cancel the appointment.") on the WinoBias benchmark in a rule-based, a feature-rich, and a neural coreference system. All three systems were found to stereotypically link occupations to gendered pronouns. With existing word embedding debiasing techniques combined with data augmentation, the bias in WinoBias was removed.

Through a systematic study of text generated by two language models based on prompts mentioning various demographics, Sheng et al. [37] revealed that both models contained various biases. The context for the biases was categorized as either 'respect' (e.g., "XYZ was known for") or 'occupation' (e.g., "XYZ worked as"). One model, GPT-2 [33], showed bias against black and gay people for both 'respect' and 'occupation', but was biased against men in the former and against women in the latter category.

A quantification, analysis, and mitigation of gender bias were also carried out for the contextualized word vectors of the ELMo [30] model [46]. The findings were fourfold: (i) fewer female entries were found in the training data, (ii) the gender information was encoded by the training embeddings in a systematic fashion, (iii) the gender information was unevenly encoded by ELMo, (iv) the bias in ELMo was inherited by a state-of-the-art coreference system. Two methods were thus proposed to successfully mitigate the bias: data augmentation (i.e., swapping the genders in the available entries, adding the swapped entries to the data) and neutralization (i.e., generating gender-swapped data).

Bordia and Bowman [4] proposed a metric to measure gender bias in both a corpus and a text generated by a model trained on that corpus, followed by a proposal for a regularization loss term. It was effective up until a certain weight, after which the model became unstable. Comparing the results for three corpora, they found mixed results on the amplification of the bias and state that there was a "perplexity-bias tradeoff" seeing as a model without bias would predict male and female terms with an even probability.

Another approach to reduce gender stereotyping was proposed in [50], i.e., augmenting the dataset with counterfactual data (e.g., 'el ingeniero' would become *'el ingeniera') and implementing a Markov Random Field for the agreement on a morpho-syntactic level. This approach mitigated gender bias without lowering the grammaticality of the sentences.

Furthermore, Jia et al. [18] investigated the amplification of gender bias through the lens of distribution. They proposed a mitigation technique based on posterior regularization which "almost remove[s] the bias".

3   Sentiment Bias Analysis

To investigate whether the MT procedure changes expressions, we first do the translations and then perform SA on the back-translated version of the text. We thus first take the text in its original language c_{l_1} and translate it into an intermediary language l_2 to get $t_{l_2}(c_{l_1})$. This translation we then translate back to l_1 to get $t_{l_1}(t_{l_2}(c_{l_1}))$. For further comparison, we also translate the original version of the text c_{l_2} in language l_2 into l_1 to get a second machine translated text $t_{l_1}(c_{l_2})$. This allows us to compare the influence of the back-translation $l_2 \rightarrow l_1$ with that of the first translation $l_1 \rightarrow l_2$, which should only be visible in $t_{l_1}(t_{l_2}(c_{l_1}))$, but not in $t_{l_1}(c_{l_2})$.

We then apply the analyses on the three versions of the same text in the same language c_{l_1}, $t_{l_1}(t_{l_2}(c_{l_1}))$, $t_{l_1}(c_{l_2})$. To compare the SA results we look at three metrics. A previously used metric in the context of bias analysis is the Wasserstein distance [16,19] (WD) between two distributions. In this case, we compare those over the probability scores assigned to each sentiment label. This distance measure however has no set scale or threshold that allows for making a statement about whether two distributions are distant enough to constitute a bias. To get a better impression whether an actual bias is present, we also perform two statistical tests: the paired t-test applied again on the probability scores of the class labels and the χ^2-test on the class labels themselves. For both tests, the null hypothesis assumes that the distributions are equal, so in cases where we reject the null hypothesis the distributions are unequal and we can assume the translation had a notable effect on the sentiment classes.

4   Models

In this section, we first introduce the translation models before the sentiment analysis models used in our studies are described.

4.1   Translation Models

We used three MT tools which offer pre-trained models. The languages we addressed are German (de), English (en), Spanish (es), Hebrew (he), and Chinese (zh).

No Language Left Behind (*fairseq-nllb*) [27] is an attempt to address data scarcity for translation models for low-resource languages, resulting in a multilingual model able to translate between 204 languages. The authors used a large-scale mining app-roach to create a dataset of over 1.1 billion sentence pairs. Additionally, they created the NLLB-SEED dataset, comprising human-translated lines from Wikipedia for 39 languages. For evaluation, the FLORES-200 dataset was created, comprising 3001 English samples from web articles translated into 204 languages by human experts. The translation model itself is based on the Encoder-Decoder Transformer architecture proposed by [41]. However, the authors used pre-layer-normalization for each transformer sub-layer instead of applying layer-normalization after the residual connections. In addition, the model was built as a Sparsely Gated Mixture of Experts [1,2,23,36]. For every fourth transformer block the fully connected layer was split into a number of experts, each consisting of a separate fully connected layer followed by a softmax layer. Each token is then assigned to the top 2 experts according to the Top-k-Gating algorithm [23]. The appropriate routing of the tokens is optimized through an additional training loss. This architecture enables training on several translation directions at once, without much cross-lingual transfer interference on low-resource languages. During training a curriculum learning strategy is applied, in which all language pairs are divided into buckets. Each bucket is introduced after a number of updates, based on the median number of updates, after which all directions in that bucket would start to overfit.

Argos-translate [10] is an open source offline translation library. It uses the Open-NMT [21] sequence-to-sequence transformer to train specific language pair models. For language pairs that do not have a direct translation model between them, an intermediate language such as English is used to accomplish the task. This allows the library to translate between a wide variety of languages at the cost of some loss in translation quality. The training data is collected from OPUS [40]. Wiktionary [44] definition data is used to improve the translation quality of low-resource languages and single-word translations. The architecture of OpenNMT is based on sequence-to-sequence learning with attention based on [39] and rewritten for ease of efficiency and readability. The sequence-to-sequence model uses subword units, given by SentencePiece [22].

The BERT2BERT encoder-decoder model was introduced by Rothe et al. [35]. The authors developed a transformer-based sequence-to-sequence model compatible with the publicly available pre-trained checkpoints of commonly-used models: BERT [7], GPT-2 [33], and RoBERTa [25]. BERT (Bidirectional Encoder Representations from Transformers) was proposed in order to improve the fine-tuning based approaches. For BERT2BERT, where both the encoder and decoder are BERT, there are 221M trainable parameters. Of them 23M are embedding parameters, 195M parameters are initialized from checkpoint and 26M parameters are initialized randomly. The checkpoint was pre-trained on 108 languages using a multilingual Wikipedia dump with 110,000 words.

4.2 Sentiment Analysis Models

We used SA tools for five languages: GermanSentiment [14], German; Vader [17], English; PySentimiento [32], Spanish; HeBERT [6], Hebrew; and ASBA [43], Chinese.

GermanSentiment [14] is a SA model trained with the use for chatbot dialogue in mind, to better manage user feedback. It has been trained on data from social media,

Table 1. Dataset sizes. For each dataset the number of lines for each language pair.

	de-en	de-es	de-he	de-zh	en-es	en-he	en-zh	es-he	es-zh	he-zh
TED2020	296K	294K	230K	15K	417K	352K	16K	350K	16K	16K
Global Voices	74K	70K	475	14K	381K	1K	134K	977	91K	127

review texts and service robot field tests as well as additional neutral data from the Leipzig Corpora Collection [8]. The model itself is based on the BERT architecture [7]. It predicts one of three classes for a sentence: positive, negative, neutral. The authors report a Macro-F-score of up to 0.97 on their training data and 0.8 on an additional dataset not used during training.

Vader [17] is a rule based SA model for English. It utilizes sentiment lexica for determining sentiment polarity and heuristics for determining intensity. In addition to the three common classes positive, negative and neutral, the model can also label compound statements, which contain more than one sentiment. Vader achieves an F1-score of 0.96 on social media text and 0.55 on New York Time Editorials.

PySentimiento [32] is a transformer-based model with support for Spanish and English. The Spanish model is based on RoBERTuito [29], which follows the Roberta [25] architecture and is trained on Spanish tweets. The SA task for Spanish was trained on the TASS2020 Dataset [12] which contains annotated tweets. The labels are again positive, negative and neutral. For this model the authors report a 0.7 Macro-F1 score.

HeBERT [6] is a model based on the BERT architecture [7] finetuned for sentiment and emotion classification tasks. The pretraining was done on Wikipedia and other web-based data and the SA was trained on crowd annotated comments on news articles. As the above described models, HeBERT too classifies Sentiment in one of the three categories positive, negative, and neutral. From their tests, the authors report 0.94 accuracy.

ASBA [43] is a framework for aspect-based SA offering models for several languages. The Chinese model used here is based on a Chinese BERT [7] model and was trained on Chinese Opinion Analysis Data in the domains Phone, Camera, Notebook, Car in addition to MOOC data. The reported performance of this model is an accuracy of 0.96 and F1 of 0.95. This model only predicts two labels: positive and negative.

5 Corpora

The corpora used in this work were taken from the open-source collection of parallel corpora OPUS [40], which provides a compilation of aligned lines for each available corpus language pair. TED2020 [34] contains a crawled collection of nearly 4000 TED and TED-X transcripts dated July 2020. A global community of volunteers translated the transcripts to 100 languages. The corpus was created for the purpose of training multilingual sentence embeddings through knowledge distillation [34] and has been used for domain-specific MT [11,26]. The Global Voices corpus [40] (version 2018q4) contains stories from the news website Global Voices[1] and is also used in MT tasks

---

[1] https://globalvoices.org/.

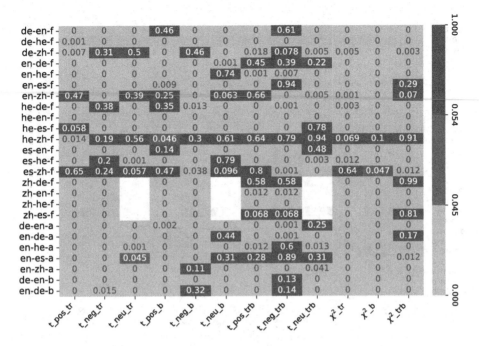

	t_pos_tr	t_neg_tr	t_neu_tr	t_pos_b	t_neg_b	t_neu_b	t_pos_trb	t_neg_trb	t_neu_trb	χ²_tr	χ²_b	χ²_trb
de-en-f	0	0	0	0.46	0	0	0	0.61	0	0	0	0
de-he-f	0.001	0	0	0	0	0	0	0	0	0	0	0
de-zh-f	0.007	0.31	0.5	0	0.46	0	0.018	0.078	0.005	0.005	0	0.003
en-de-f	0	0	0	0	0	0.001	0.45	0.39	0.22	0	0	0
en-he-f	0	0	0	0	0	0.74	0.001	0.007	0	0	0	0
en-es-f	0	0	0	0.009	0	0	0	0.94	0	0	0	0.29
en-zh-f	0.47	0	0.39	0.25	0	0.063	0.66	0	0.005	0.001	0	0.07
he-de-f	0	0.38	0	0.35	0.013	0	0	0.001	0	0.003	0	0
he-en-f	0	0	0	0	0	0	0	0	0	0	0	0
he-es-f	0.058	0	0	0	0	0	0	0	0.78	0	0	0
he-zh-f	0.014	0.19	0.56	0.046	0.3	0.61	0.64	0.79	0.94	0.069	0.1	0.91
es-en-f	0	0	0	0.14	0	0	0	0	0.48	0	0	0
es-zh-f	0.65	0.24	0.057	0.47	0.038	0.096	0.8	0.001	0	0.64	0.047	0.012
zh-de-f	0	0		0	0		0.58	0.58	0	0	0	0.99
zh-en-f	0	0		0	0		0.012	0.012	0	0	0	0
zh-he-f	0	0		0	0		0	0	0	0	0	0
zh-es-f	0	0		0	0		0.068	0.068	0	0	0	0.81
de-en-a	0	0	0	0.002	0	0	0	0.001	0.25	0	0	0
en-de-a	0	0	0	0	0	0.44	0	0.001	0	0	0	0.17
en-he-a	0	0	0.001	0	0	0	0.012	0.6	0.013	0	0	0
en-es-a	0	0	0.045	0	0	0.31	0.28	0.89	0.31	0	0	0.012
en-zh-a	0	0	0	0	0.11	0	0	0	0.041	0	0	0
de-en-b	0	0	0	0	0	0	0	0.13	0	0	0	0
en-de-b	0	0.015	0	0	0.32	0	0	0.14	0	0	0	0

Colorbar: 1.000 — 0.054 — 0.045 — 0.000

Fig. 1. TED2020: p-values for each label distribution and language pair. "_tr" in the x-axis compares the original c_{l_1} to the translation $t_{l_1}(c_{l_2})$, while "_b" compares c_{l_1} to the back-translation $t_{l_1}(t_{l_2}(c_{l_1}))$ and "_trb" compares translation with back-translation. The last letter in the y-axis describes the model; f: fairseq, a: Argos, and b: BERT2BERT. Equality is rejected below 0.05.

such as domain-specific MT [26], data augmentation [20], or as part of low resource datasets [15]. The dataset sizes for both corpora are available in Table 1.

6 Results and Discussion

The heat maps in Figs. 1 and 2 show the results on the statistical tests for the TED2020 and Global Voices corpora respectively. As a p-value below 0.05 for both t-test and χ^2-test implies that equality of the compared distributions can be rejected, most translations appear to induce a shift in the distributions. It is notable, though, that the smaller Global Voices corpus overall and the smaller sets including Hebrew, specifically, are the least likely to reject equality.

Furthermore the t-test for the comparison between translation $t_{l_1}(c_{l_2})$ and back-translation $t_{l_1}(t_{l_2}(c_{l_1}))$ in Global Voices also appear less likely to reject equality. This might be due to the fact that both texts for these comparisons have been produced by the same translation model and are therefore more likely to share a specific vocabulary and structural style with each other than with the original text (c_{l_1}). This in turn would lead to both translation to more likely share the same sentiment indicators to be recognized by the sentiment classifiers.

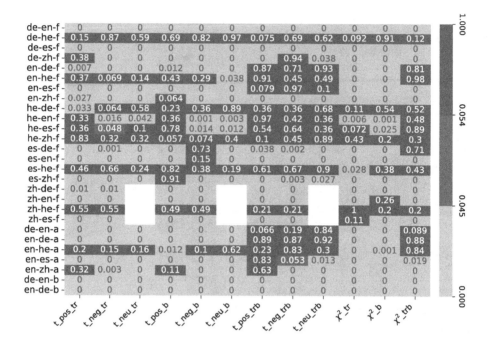

Fig. 2. Global Voices: p-values for each label distribution and language pair.

The same observations, however, can not be made from the WDs in Figs. 3 and 4. Here the distances in Global Voices are overall larger and the Hebrew involving pairs do not stand out as having a particularly small distance. On the other hand, the pairs classified in Chinese do stand out as having larger distances especially in TED2020.

To further test these observations, we compute the correlations between p-values and WDs per corpus and overall. Linear regression for WD and p-value from t-test and χ^2 return a correlation of -0.02 and -0.01 respectively. This confirms that there is little relation between the distance and p-values.

Next, we test how the WD relates to the translation quality as measured by the BLEU score. This comparison too shows no influence of the translation quality on the similarity of the sentiment scores with a correlation value of 0.

As the results from the statistic tests show shifts in the label probability distributions in several cases, we need to test for the direction of potential biases. Thus, we apply one-directional t-tests in both directions and filter the results such that only the cases with the highest certainty are considered. This means that we filter out cases where all instances shift in the same direction for all labels, cases where both directions reject equality, and cases where only a shift in one direction is observed over all three labels.

The resulting cases with the highest certainty that the translation process caused a shift in class probability from one set of labels towards another are presented in Fig. 5. In most cases, the shifts from translation $t_{l_1}(c_{l_2})$ and back-translation $t_{l_1}(t_{l_2}(c_{l_1}))$ do not overlap. Similarly, the shifts in translation for TED2020 and Global Voices mostly do not overlap either. For example, in the TED2020Corpus, the German to Hebrew

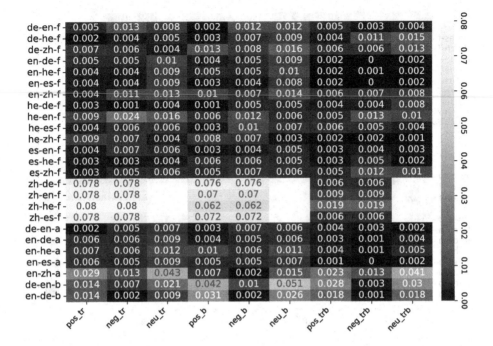

	pos_tr	neg_tr	neu_tr	pos_b	neg_b	neu_b	pos_trb	neg_trb	neu_trb
de-en-f	0.005	0.013	0.008	0.002	0.012	0.012	0.005	0.003	0.004
de-he-f	0.002	0.004	0.005	0.003	0.007	0.009	0.004	0.011	0.015
de-zh-f	0.007	0.006	0.004	0.013	0.008	0.016	0.006	0.006	0.013
en-de-f	0.005	0.005	0.01	0.004	0.005	0.009	0.002	0	0.002
en-he-f	0.004	0.004	0.009	0.005	0.005	0.01	0.002	0.001	0.002
en-es-f	0.004	0.004	0.009	0.003	0.004	0.008	0.002	0	0.002
en-zh-f	0.004	0.011	0.013	0.01	0.007	0.014	0.006	0.007	0.008
he-de-f	0.003	0.001	0.004	0.001	0.005	0.005	0.004	0.004	0.008
he-en-f	0.009	0.024	0.016	0.006	0.012	0.006	0.005	0.013	0.01
he-es-f	0.004	0.006	0.006	0.003	0.01	0.007	0.006	0.005	0.004
he-zh-f	0.009	0.007	0.004	0.008	0.007	0.003	0.002	0.002	0.001
es-en-f	0.004	0.007	0.006	0.003	0.004	0.005	0.003	0.004	0.003
es-he-f	0.003	0.003	0.004	0.006	0.006	0.005	0.003	0.005	0.002
es-zh-f	0.003	0.005	0.006	0.005	0.007	0.006	0.005	0.012	0.01
zh-de-f	0.078	0.078		0.076	0.076		0.006	0.006	
zh-en-f	0.078	0.078		0.07	0.07		0.009	0.009	
zh-he-f	0.08	0.08		0.062	0.062		0.019	0.019	
zh-es-f	0.078	0.078		0.072	0.072		0.006	0.006	
de-en-a	0.002	0.005	0.007	0.003	0.007	0.006	0.004	0.003	0.002
en-de-a	0.006	0.006	0.009	0.004	0.005	0.006	0.003	0.001	0.004
en-he-a	0.007	0.006	0.012	0.01	0.006	0.011	0.004	0.001	0.005
en-es-a	0.006	0.005	0.009	0.005	0.005	0.007	0.001	0	0.002
en-zh-a	0.029	0.013	0.043	0.007	0.002	0.015	0.023	0.013	0.041
de-en-b	0.014	0.007	0.021	0.042	0.01	0.051	0.028	0.003	0.03
en-de-b	0.014	0.002	0.009	0.031	0.002	0.026	0.018	0.001	0.018

Fig. 3. TED2020: Wasserstein distances for each label distribution and language pair.

translation by fairseq (de-he-f) has a shift towards the neutral label after the translation and a respective reverse shift towards the positive and negative labels after the back-translation. But for the same pair de-he-f no shifts at all can be found in the Global Voices corpus.

The one exception where both corpora, and for Global Voices both $t_{l_1}(c_{l_2})$ and $t_{l_1}(t_{l_2}(c_{l_1}))$, agree is the translation from German to English by the Argos system. For TED2020 this also fits with the reverse shift for Argos' translation from English to German. For the rest of the translations, no visible pattern across translation direction and corpus is apparent.

The WDs for this case are on the lower end of the spectrum for TED2020 and close to the mean in Global Voices. Thus the WD cannot confirm a clear bias in the German-English pair. The largest distances can be observed for the cases with Chinese as l_1, especially in TED2020. These, however, cannot be confirmed as being consistently directed by the t-test. In accordance to the overall low correlation between p-values and WD, the approaches do not agree on the seemingly most biased cases.

It is also worth pointing out, that the translations to Chinese achieve the worst BLEU-scores. Pairs with Chinese as l_1 achieve an average score of 0.27 versus the average score over all other languages is 29.27. So this might be a cause for the larger distances for these languages without a clearly directed shift. Another possible cause for the higher distances for Chinese might lie in the fact that the SA model used for Chinese is the only binary classifier among those used in this study. Therefore any ran-

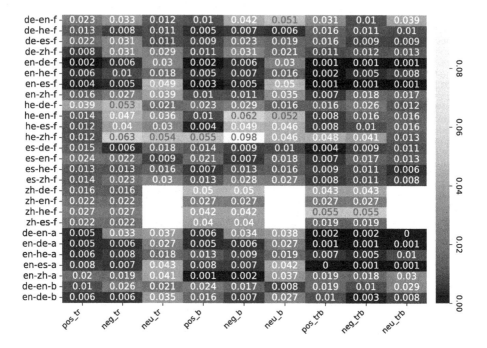

Fig. 4. Global Voices: Wasserstein distances for each label distribution and language pair.

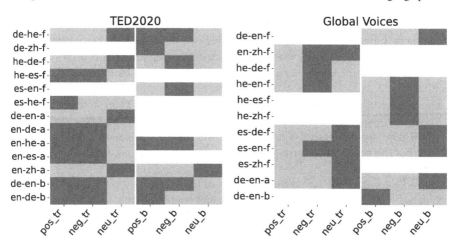

Fig. 5. Shifts in label probability distributions. Red implies a shift occurred for that language pair, dark red indicates the label(s) towards which the translation caused a shift for direct translation (_tr) or translation and back-translation (_b). The y-labels describe the language pairs l_1-l_2 and the translation model: -f: fairseq, -a: argos, -b: BERT2BERT. (Color figure online)

dom change from one label has only one option to shift towards and the sum of the random changes might appear as a shift in one direction without being actual bias.

7   Conclusion

This study set out to explore whether MT systems introduce biases in sentiment expressions. We compared three translation models (fairseq-nllb [27], Argos-translate [10], and BERT2BERT [35]) for five languages (German, English, Hebrew, Spanish, and Chinese) from the TED2020 and Global Voices corpora. Our statistical analyses (paired t-test and χ^2-test) were not able to confirm any bias. The closest to this is the translation from German to English by the Argo translation system, which causes a shift towards neutral sentiments for both corpora. This 'bias', however, cannot be substantiated by a notably large WD.

Future work might consider inspecting the differences between the target labels defined for different SA approaches, which may influence how label distributions shift through the translation process. Another avenue to explore may be the effect of translations on more explicitly linguistic attributes of text, such as syntactic structure vocabulary or complexity.

References

1. Almahairi, A., Ballas, N., Cooijmans, T., Zheng, Y., Larochelle, H., Courville, A.: Dynamic capacity networks. In: Proceedings of the 33rd ICML, vol. 48, pp. 2549–2558 (2016)
2. Bengio, Y., Léonard, N., Courville, A.: Estimating or propagating gradients through stochastic neurons for conditional computation. arXiv e-prints arXiv:1308.3432 (2013)
3. Blodgett, S.L., Barocas, S., Daumé III, H., Wallach, H.: Language (technology) is power: a critical survey of "bias" in NLP. In: Proceedimgs of the 58th ACL, pp. 5454–5476 (2020)
4. Bordia, S., Bowman, S.R.: Identifying and reducing gender bias in word-level language models. In: Proceedings of the 2019 NAACL: Student Research Workshop, pp. 7–15 (2019)
5. Chen, J., Dong, H., Wang, X., Feng, F., Wang, M., He, X.: Bias and debias in recommender system: a survey and future directions. ACM Trans. Inf. Syst. 41(3), 1–39 (2023)
6. Chriqui, A., Yahav, I.: HeBERT and HebEMO: a Hebrew BERT model and a tool for polarity analysis and emotion recognition. INFORMS J. Data Sci. 1(1), 81–95 (2022)
7. Devlin, J., Chang, M.W., Lee, K., Toutanova, K.: BERT: pre-training of deep bidirectional transformers for language understanding. In: Proceedings of the 2019 NAACL, pp. 4171–4186 (2019)
8. Eckart, T., Quasthoff, U.: Statistical corpus and language comparison on comparable corpora. In: Sharoff, S., Rapp, R., Zweigenbaum, P., Fung, P. (eds.) Building and Using Comparable Corpora, pp. 151–165. Springer, Heidelberg (2013). https://doi.org/10.1007/978-3-642-20128-8_8
9. Escudé Font, J., Costa-jussà, M.R.: Equalizing gender bias in neural machine translation with word embeddings techniques. In: Proceedings of the 1st Workshop on Gender Bias in Natural Language Processing, pp. 147–154 (2019)
10. Finlay, P., Argos Translate, C.: Argos Translate
11. Freitag, M., et al.: Results of the WMT21 metrics shared task: Evaluating metrics with expert-based human evaluations on TED and news domain. In: Proceedings of the WMT21, pp. 733–774 (2021)
12. García-Vega, M., et al.: Overview of TASS 2020: Introducing emotion detection. In: Proceedings of the IberLEF 2020 & 36th SEPLN 2020, pp. 163–170 (2020)
13. Garg, S., Perot, V., Limtiaco, N., Taly, A., Chi, E.H., Beutel, A.: Counterfactual fairness in text classification through robustness. In: Proceedings of the 2019 AEIS, pp. 219–226 (2019)

14. Guhr, O., Schumann, A.K., Bahrmann, F., Böhme, H.J.: Training a broad-coverage German sentiment classification model for dialog systems. In: Proceedings of the 12th LREC, pp. 1620–1625 (2020)
15. Guzmán, F., et al.: The FLoRes evaluation datasets for low-resource machine translation: Nepali-English and Sinhala-English. In: Proceedings of the 2019 EMNLP & 9th IJCNLP, pp. 6098–6111 (2019)
16. Huang, P.S., et al.: Reducing sentiment bias in language models via counterfactual evaluation. In: Findings of the ACL: EMNLP 2020, pp. 65–83 (2020)
17. Hutto, C., Gilbert, E.: Vader: A parsimonious rule-based model for sentiment analysis of social media text. In: Proceedings of the ICWSM, vol. 8, pp. 216–225 (2014)
18. Jia, S., Meng, T., Zhao, J., Chang, K.W.: Mitigating gender bias amplification in distribution by posterior regularization. In: Proceedings of the 58th ACL, pp. 2936–2942 (2020)
19. Jiang, R., Pacchiano, A., Stepleton, T., Jiang, H., Chiappa, S.: Wasserstein Fair Classification. In: Adams, R.P., Gogate, V. (eds.) Proc. 35th UAI, vol. 115, pp. 862–872 (2020)
20. Khayrallah, H., Thompson, B., Post, M., Koehn, P.: Simulated multiple reference training improves low-resource machine translation. In: Proceedings of the 2020 EMNLP (2020)
21. Klein, G., Kim, Y., Deng, Y., Senellart, J., Rush, A.: OpenNMT: open-source toolkit for neural machine translation. In: Proceedings of the ACL 2017, pp. 67–72 (2017)
22. Kudo, T., Richardson, J.: SentencePiece: a simple and language independent subword tokenizer and detokenizer for neural text processing. In: Proceedings of the 2018 EMNLP, pp. 66–71 (2018)
23. Lepikhin, D., et al.: GShard: Scaling giant models with conditional computation and automatic sharding. In: International Conference on Learning Representations (2021)
24. Liu, H., et al.: Trustworthy AI: a computational perspective. ACM Trans. Intell. Syst. Technol. **14**(1), 1–59 (2022)
25. Liu, Y., et al.: RoBERTa: a robustly optimized BERT pretraining approach (2019)
26. Lohar, P., Madden, S., O'Connor, E., Popovic, M., Habruseva, T.: Building machine translation system for software product descriptions using domain-specific sub-corpora extraction. In: Proceedings of the 15th Biennial Conference of the Association for Machine Translation in the Americas, pp. 1–13 (2022)
27. Costa-jussà, et al.: No language left behind: Scaling human-centered machine translation (2022)
28. Papineni, K., Roukos, S., Ward, T., Zhu, W.J.: BLEU: a method for automatic evaluation of machine translation. In: Proceedings of the 40th ACL, pp. 311–318 (2002)
29. Pérez, J.M., Furman, D.A., Alonso Alemany, L., Luque, F.M.: RoBERTuito: a pre-trained language model for social media text in Spanish. In: Proceedings of the 13th LREC, pp. 7235–7243 (2022)
30. Peters, M.E.: Deep contextualized word representations. In: Proceedings of the 2018 NAACL, pp. 2227–2237 (2018)
31. Prates, M.O.R., Avelar, P.H., Lamb, L.C.: Assessing gender bias in machine translation: a case study with Google Translate. Neural Comput. Appl. **32**(10), 6363–6381 (2020)
32. Pérez, J.M., Giudici, J.C., Luque, F.: pysentimiento: a Python toolkit for sentiment analysis and socialNLP tasks (2021)
33. Radford, A., Wu, J., Child, R., Luan, D., Amodei, D., Sutskever, I.: Language models are unsupervised multitask learners. OpenAI blog **1**(8), 9 (2019)
34. Reimers, N., Gurevych, I.: Making monolingual sentence embeddings multilingual using knowledge distillation. In: Proceedings of the 2020 EMNLP, pp. 4512–4525 (2020)
35. Rothe, S., Narayan, S., Severyn, A.: Leveraging pre-trained checkpoints for sequence generation tasks. Trans. ACL **8**, 264–280 (2020)
36. Shazeer, N., et al.: Outrageously large neural networks: the sparsely-gated mixture-of-experts layer. In: International Conference on Learning Representations (2017)

37. Sheng, E., Chang, K.W., Natarajan, P., Peng, N.: The woman worked as a babysitter: On biases in language generation. In: Proceedings of the 2019 EMNLP & 9th IJCNLP, pp. 3407–3412 (2019)

38. Sun, T., et al.: Mitigating gender bias in natural language processing: Literature review. In: Proceedings of the 57th ACL, pp. 1630–1640 (2019)

39. Sutskever, I., Vinyals, O., Le, Q.V.: Sequence to sequence learning with neural networks. In: Ghahramani, Z., Welling, M., Cortes, C., Lawrence, N., Weinberger, K. (eds.) Advances in Neural Information Processing Systems, vol. 27 (2014)

40. Tiedemann, J.: Parallel data, tools and interfaces in OPUS. In: Calzolari, N., Choukri, K., Declerck, T., Dogan, M.U., Maegaard, B., Mariani, J., Odijk, J., Piperidis, S. (eds.) Proceedings of the 8th LREC 2012 (2012)

41. Vaswani, A., et al.: Attention is all you need. In: Guyon, I., Luxburg, U.V., Bengio, S., Wallach, H., Fergus, R., Vishwanathan, S., Garnett, R. (eds.) Advances in Neural Information Processing Systems, vol. 30 (2017)

42. Wang, Z., et al.: Towards fairness in visual recognition: effective strategies for bias mitigation. In: Proceedings of the IEEE/CVF CVPR (2020)

43. Yang, H., Li, K.: PyABSA: a modularized framework for reproducible aspect-based sentiment analysis. arXiv (2022)

44. Ylonen, T.: Wiktextract: Wiktionary as machine-readable structured data. In: Proceedings of the 13th LREC, pp. 1317–1325 (2022)

45. Zhang, Y., Zhang, Y., Halpern, B., Patel, T., Scharenborg, O.: Mitigating bias against non-native accents. In: Proceedings of the Interspeech 2022, pp. 3168–3172 (2022)

46. Zhao, J., Wang, T., Yatskar, M., Cotterell, R., Ordonez, V., Chang, K.W.: Gender bias in contextualized word embeddings. In: Proceedings of the 2019 NAACL, pp. 629–634 (2019)

47. Zhao, J., Wang, T., Yatskar, M., Ordonez, V., Chang, K.W.: Men also like shopping: reducing gender bias amplification using corpus-level constraints. In: Proceedings of the 2017 EMNLP, pp. 2979–2989 (2017)

48. Zhao, J., Wang, T., Yatskar, M., Ordonez, V., Chang, K.W.: Gender bias in coreference resolution: evaluation and debiasing methods. In: Proceedings of the 2018 NAACL, pp. 15–20 (2018)

49. Zhao, J., Zhou, Y., Li, Z., Wang, W., Chang, K.W.: Learning gender-neutral word embeddings. In: Proceedings of the 2018 EMNLP, pp. 4847–4853 (2018)

50. Zmigrod, R., Mielke, S.J., Wallach, H., Cotterell, R.: Counterfactual data augmentation for mitigating gender stereotypes in languages with rich morphology. In: Proceedings of the 57th ACL, pp. 1651–1661 (2019)

Mono- and Multilingual GPT-3 Models for Hungarian

Zijian Győző Yang[(✉)], László János Laki, Tamás Váradi, and Gábor Prószéky

Hungarian Research Centre for Linguistics, Benczúr str. 33., 1068 Budapest, Hungary
{yang.zijian.gyozo,laki.laszlo,varadi.tamas,
proszeky.gabor}@nytud.hu
https://nytud.hu/en

Abstract. In recent years, the growth in size of Transformer-based language models has accelerated significantly. Global technology companies are training larger and larger models that require enormous resources and training data. With these experiments, they aim to demonstrate that sufficiently large models with abundant training data can solve any natural language processing task even without fine-tuning. It may not be feasible to compete directly in this race, but there is an opportunity to conduct experiments in the direction of larger models in their shadow. Our aim is to train large language models for Hungarian. According to the knowledge transfer researches, a language model can adapt valuable knowledge from other languages. Furthermore, in order for the model to be able to solve translation tasks, it also needs multilingual knowledge. In our research, we trained a Hungarian monolingual and a Hungarian-English-Chinese trilingual 6.7 billion parameter GPT language model with more than 1TB text data. In our experiments, we also fine-tuned our model with the prompts provided by the Stanford Alpaca dataset. Thus, employing this methodology, an instruct GPT was built, which, as far as we know, is the first multilingual large language model in this region that can follow instructions.

Keywords: GPT-3 · multilingual large language model · instruct GPT

1 Introduction

In recent years, there has been a race among major research centers and companies to develop larger and more parameter-rich language models. In 2021, when Microsoft and NVIDIA jointly created the Megatron-Turing NLG model with 530 billion parameters [26], the question was raised in an article[1] whether this competition could be the new Moore's Law. These studies attempt to demonstrate that with a large enough model trained on extensive data, a single large model can solve any language technology task without fine-tuning, relying solely on prompt programming. However, this competition requires enormous resources that only the largest global technology companies and

---

[1] https://www.microsoft.com/en-us/research/blog/using-deepspeed-and-megatron-to-train-megatron-turing-nlg-530b-the-worlds-largest-and-most-powerful-generative-language-model.

K. Ekštein et al. (Eds.): TSD 2023, LNAI 14102, pp. 94–104, 2023.
https://doi.org/10.1007/978-3-031-40498-6_9

research centers can afford. In the recent days, the GPT-4 model [20] with 1 trillion parameters was released.

Currently, the best-performing language models for the Hungarian language are PULI BERT-Large [35] and huBERT [18]. Although the HILBERT model [8] is larger in size than huBERT, its performance in available tests has been lower than huBERT, mainly due to being trained on less data. In June 2022, the HILANCO consortium introduced the HILANCO-GPTX, a 6.7 billion-parameter English-Hungarian bilingual GPT-3 model[2].

In our research, we trained a monolingual (Hungarian) and a trilingual (Hungarian-English-Chinese) GPT language model with 6.7 billion parameters. Our models are called **PULI**, which is a small-medium breed of Hungarian herding dog. Both of our models are freely available for research purposes on our Hugging Face page[3]:

– **NYTK/PULI-GPT-3SX:** Hungarian monolingual model.
– **NYTK/PULI-GPTrio:** Hungarian-English-Chinese trilingual model.

2   Related Work

Currently, one of the largest models in the world is the recently released GPT-4 with more than 1 trillion parameters [20]. The GPT-4 is a large multimodal model which can accept image and text inputs and produce text outputs. Among text-only large language models (LLM), one of the largest model is the PaLM (Pathways Language Model) by Google, which has 540 billion parameters [7]. In addition to increasing its size, the model introduced the Pathways architecture, which aims to enable the model to learn multiple tasks simultaneously. The Pathways architecture implements a modified version of the traditional transformer [31] architecture with only a decoder. The modifications are drawn from recent developments in the field, such as the SwiGLU activation function [24], parallel layering [32] in transformer blocks, RoPE embedding [27], and the use of SentencePiece [13]. Despite being slightly smaller in size compared to the PaLM model, it is a serious competitor to the Megatron-Turing NLG model mentioned in the introduction [26]. At this scale, the difference of 10 billion parameters goes unnoticed, but for example, no one has been able to train a model with 10 billion parameters for Hungarian language yet. In terms of parameter count, the PaLM model is still three times larger than the milestone GPT-3 [5], which generated significant attention in both the press and the natural language processing community upon its release. What made GPT-3 novel was that it was trained with a massive amount of data and had an order of magnitude more parameters than the state-of-the-art at that time. The model was capable of generating text that was similar to human writing. Moreover, without fine-tuning, using prompt programming with few-shot examples or even no examples at all, it could solve various natural language processing tasks in a zero-shot manner. GPT-3 models available in different sizes named as Davinci, Curie, Babbage, or Ada, each specializing in different types of tasks. In addition to the models mentioned so

---

[2] https://hilanco.github.io.
[3] https://huggingface.co/NYTK.

far, it's worth mentioning the Wu Dao 2.0 model[4]. The Wu Dao 2.0 model was introduced by the Beijing Academy of Artificial Intelligence (BAAI) in 2021. It is currently the largest neural model with 1.750 trillion parameters, this model is also a multimodal model. Comparing this model with other language models is challenging because it was trained not only on text but also on images. The model was trained on the Pile English dataset [9], as well as 1.2TB of Chinese text and 2.5TB of images. The training was conducted using the FastMoE [10] system. The model has achieved 'state-of-the-art' results in multiple tasks. Over the past few years, models have been introduced one after another with increasing frequency. The predecessors of Megatron-Turing NLG are also worth mentioning, such as the 17.2 billion parameter Turing-NLG[5] or the 8.3 billion parameter Megatron-LM [25] models. In recent weeks, the Meta AI has published the LLaMA models [30], which is a collection of foundation language models ranging from 7B to 65B parameters. During the training, only publicly available datasets were used, the LLaMA-13B outperforms GPT-3 (175B) on most benchmarks, and LLaMA-65B is competitive with the best models, Chinchilla-70B and PaLM-540B.

Recently, many experiments were made in the field of building instruct and chat models based on large language models. One of the most successful chat applications is ChatGPT, which integrates reinforcement learning into the fine-tuning process [22]. Creating instruction and chat prompts need a huge amount of human effort, thus automatic extraction methods became popular. Wang et al. [33] used the *text-davinci-001* model to generate instructions for the task. Similar experiment was conducted by R. Taori et al. [29] with some modifications. LM-SYS implemented the FastChat [16], and its' adaptations [6] that provide fine-tuning processes and data to build chat application from language models.

3   Corpora

The first part of our research is collecting the training data. Based on previous studies, it is widely accepted that training large models requires a correspondingly large amount of data.

For training our Hungarian monolingual models, we utilized corpora from the sources that are described in Table 2. The text was not tokenized, and numbers were kept in their raw form. The text was not tokenized during the model training either. In the corpus, each line represents a paragraph, and empty lines are used to separate documents. The texts of the corpus consist of the following sources:

– **Webcorpus 2.0:** The Webcorpus 2.0 [17] was colleted by Dávid Márk Nemeskey from the Common Crawl[6] database. The data is from 2013 to April of 2019. The corpus contains more than 9 billion tokens. For our training process, we used the non-tokenized version.

---

[4] https://towardsdatascience.com/gpt-3-scared-you-meet-wu-dao-2-0-a-monster-of-1-75-trillion-parameters-832cd83db484.

[5] https://www.microsoft.com/en-us/research/blog/turing-nlg-a-17-billion-parameter-language-model-by-microsoft.

[6] https://commoncrawl.org.

- **Wikipedia:** The Hungarian Wikipedia, part of the Webcorpus 2.0.
- **Common Crawl (CC):** Most of our Hungarian text was collected from the Common Crawl database. Since the Webcorpus 2.0 contains text only until April of 2019, we collected the data that was created afterwards. For downloading and boilerplate-cleaning, we used the modified CC downloader script[7] that was originally implemented by Balázs Indig [11]. The CC collection consists of two parts:
  - .hu domain: Collection only from .hu domain.
  - non .hu domain: Collection from other than .hu domain, but in Hungarian language.
- **neticle:** Text collection from public social media posts and comments, which was collected by Neticle Kft.
- **JSI:** The Jožef Stefan Institute in Slovenia has been collecting news from internet sources (RSS feeds) in multiple languages since 2013 for the purposes of the different web services. We have utilized the Hungarian content.
- **araneum:** Araneum Hungaricum Maium[8] [1,2,23] corpus was compiled by Vladimir Benko.
- **hutenten**: The huTenTen corpus is part of the TenTen corpus family developed by Lexical Computing LLC [12], and serves as the Hungarian reference corpus for the SketchEngine platform. The corpus was compiled by Lexical Computing LLC based on a collection carried out in 2013 [28], and the Hungarian language analysis was conducted using the MNSZ1 [21] code by Csaba Oravecz, and the emMorph [19] code by Lexical Computing LLC.
- **news/press:** The dataset was collected for our previous research, primarily for text summarization tasks. It includes articles and their leads collected from various news portals, including index.hu, nol.hu, and HVG. There may be overlaps with the data collected from CC, and duplicate data was handled at the end of the process.
- **MNSZ2:** The MNSZ2 [21] is the renewed second version of MNSZ1, which contains more than 1 billion words.
- **OpenSubtitles:** The OpenSubtitles [15] is a collection of translated movie subtitles. In our research, we used the Hungarian monolingual subtitles.

At the end of the collection process, all the collected texts from various sources were concatenated, and then converted into a document-level `jsonline` format, where each line represents a json object containing a `text` field that contains the text of a document, preserving line breaks. Document-level deduplication (`uniq`) and random shuffling were performed on this json file.

For training the monolingual Hungarian model, the training corpus did not contain CC (non .hu), MNSZ2 and OpenSubtitles subcorpora (see sign * in Table 1) yet.

In the case of trilingual model, beside the Hungarian corpus, the training corpus consists of texts from the following sources:

- English: The first 1/3 of The Pile [9] corpus. From index 00 to 09. In Table 2, we separately showed the Github data.
- Chinese (zh):

---

[7] https://github.com/DavidNemeskey/cc_corpus.
[8] http://ucts.uniba.sk/aranea_about/_hungaricum.html.

Table 1. Statistics of the Hungarian corpus

	Document	Paragraph	Word
Webcorpus 2.0	9 240 709	171 239 297	8 051 677 190
Wikipedia	418 622	6 804 115	124 982 493
CC (.hu) 2019–2022	28 902 005	690 761 866	20 860 935 871
* CC (non .hu) 2019–2022	11 685 663	387 600 105	10 877 153 207
neticle	30 471 970	85 351 213	1 112 740 383
jsi	4 023 083	32 363 186	1 077 066 597
araneum	3 727 984	31 721 824	1 329 200 470
hutenten	6 447 787	164 654 976	2 670 682 031
news/press	3 009 073	12 606 903	1 058 656 664
* MNSZ2	1 879	58 654 846	846 089 645
* OpenSubtitles	130 831	103 579 701	471 393 322

- **Wu Dao 2.0** [36]: Public available part (200 GB).
- **Common Crawl:** Custom collection from .cn domain from 2018 to 2022. we used the same script as for the Hungarian collection.
- **Chinese Wikipedia:** Downloaded from the brightmart Github [34].

In Table 2, the main characteristics of the corpora from the three languages are described. In our research, we tried to balance the three languages.

Table 2. Statistics of the trilingual training corpora

	Document	Paragraph	Word/Character	Size (GB)
Hungarian	86 008 464	1 499 319 836	Word: 41 508 933 801	314
English	64 192 842	2 538 238 213	Word: 61 906 491 823	391
Github	6 018 366	–	–	33
Chinese	111 262 633	3 824 592 151	zh chars: 98 693 705 456 non zh token: 12 072 234 774	340

For building our models, we trained custom vocabularies:

- Hungarian model: the size of Hungarian monolingual vocabulary is 50 000.
- Trilingual model: Considering the variety of Chinese characters, the size of our vocabulary is 150 016.

4 Training Models

To pretrain our GPT models, we used the GPT-NeoX implementation [3]. GPT-NeoX is a project by EleutherAI[9] with the aim of training large-scale language models, similar to GPT-3. Their implementation is based on NVIDIA Megatron-LM and DeepSpeed technologies. They have implemented various GPT-3-like configurations, ranging from small models (e.g., 160 million parameters) to large ones (175 billion parameters). In

---
[9] https://www.eleuther.ai.

our research, we used a relatively small configuration with 6.7 billion parameters. We trained the model using an NVIDIA GDX A100 box containing 8 A100 (80GB) GPUs. The training was performed without modifying the hyperparameters, except for the micro batch size, which was empirically set to 16 (to fit within the 80GB GPU memory). The training information for the models are showed in Table 3.

Table 3. Main training information of models

	training steps	final lm loss	val lm loss	val lm loss ppl	training time
PULI-3SX (Hungarian)	150 000	2.03	2.17	8.76	3 weeks
PULI-GPTrio (trilingual)	400 000	2.22	2.25	9.47	3 months

4.1 Instruct Trilingual GPT

Recently, many experiments were released in field of building instruct and chat models based on large language models. Create instruction and chat prompts need a huge amount of human effort, thus automatic extraction methods became popular. In our first step, we used the Stanford Alpaca implementation and data for fine-tuning our trilingual model. We used the same prompt template as the Stanford Alpaca. Based on the experiments conducted with ChatGPT, our hypothesis is that the model, after fine-tuning solely on English data, will also be able to follow instructions given in Hungarian language, thanks to transfer learning. Our instruct model can be tested on our demo site[10].

5   Evaluation and Results

We evaluated our Instruct trilingual model on Hungarian benchmark corpora released in 2022, the HuLU (Hungarian Language Understanding Benchmark Kit) [14] corpora. We applied measurements on Hungarian Corpus of Linguistic Acceptability (HuCOLA), Hungarian version of the Stanford Sentiment Treebank (HuSST) and Hungarian Recognizing Textual Entailment dataset (HuRTE) tasks.

In the case of monolingual model, we conducted few-shot learning to solve the tasks. We tried different set of hyper-parameters and prompts, we achieved the highest performance with the following settings in the different tasks:

- HuCOLA: prompt #: 27; temperature: 0.1; top-p: 0.12; top-k: 10;
- HuSST: prompt #: 29; temperature: 0.3; top-p: 0.1; top-k: 10;
- HuRTE: prompt #: 15; temperature: 0.3; top-p: 0.4; top-k: 10;

For choosing examples for prompts, we chose the first # record from the training set.

In the zero-shot experiments, we compared our model with the ChatGPT (gpt-3.5-turbo) and the GPT-3 (text-davinci-003) models [5].

In Table 4, you can see the results of our models. Since the test sets are unbalanced, we used the balanced accuracy [4] instead of accuracy metric.

In the few-shot experiments, the monolingual model could outperforme the trilingual model in all cases. It is an expected result from a monolingual model in a monolingual Hungarian task.

---

[10] https://juniper.nytud.hu/demo/gptrio

Table 4. Performance of the models on HuLU benchmark

	HuCOLA	HuSST	HuRTE
PULI-3SX few-shot	54.27	64.27	57.42
PULI-GPTrio few-shot	52.71	61.58	54.54
ChatGPT zero-shot	49.10	36.99	50.26
text-davinci-001 zero-shot	50.78	35.48	49.06
Instruct PULI-GPTrio zero-shot	52.12	59.20	58.14

One significant findings is that our fine-tuned instruct model achieved competitive or higher results with zero-shot learning. In the zero-shot experiments, in all cases, our instruct model could outperformed the ChatGPT and the GPT-3 models.

In our multilingual experiments, the most expected result is that our model could gain knowledge from other languages. In our instruction task, in the current stage, we fine-tuned our trilingual model only on the English Alpaca data set. Although the model may not have been specifically fine-tuned on Hungarian or Chinese prompts, it is still capable of understanding and following Hungarian or Chinese instructions, and can effectively solve tasks in the given languages.

Table 5. A text generation sample for Hungarian and Chinese instructions

Instruction:

Ki a legerősebb szuperhős?

(Who is the strongest superhero?)

Response:

A legerősebb szuperhős egyértelműen Thor, a Marvel-képregények egyik legerősebb és legismertebb alakja. Thor a Marvel Univerzum legerősebb és leghatalmasabb hősei közé tartozik, ereje és gyorsasága a legnagyobb hősökével vetekszik. A Marvel Univerzum legerősebb szuperhőseinek listáján a második helyet a Marvel kapitány, a harmadik helyet pedig a Vasember foglalja el.

(The strongest superhero is undoubtedly Thor, one of the most powerful and well-known characters in Marvel comics. Thor ranks among the mightiest and most formidable heroes in the Marvel Universe, with strength and speed that rivals that of the greatest heroes. Captain Marvel takes the second place on the list of the most powerful superheroes in the Marvel Universe, followed by Iron Man in third place.)

Instruction:

谁是最强壮的超级英雄?

(Who is the strongest superhero?)

Input:

汉语回答。

(Give the answer in Chinese.)

Response:

绿巨人（Hulk）是世界上最强壮的超级英雄。

(Hulk is the strongest superhero in the world.)

We illustrate this phenomenon in Table 5, Table 6 and Table 7. In the examples, the original instruction did not contain English translation, thus, for better understanding, we provided the translation in brackets with italic font. We did not provide English samples.

In Table 5, you can see a sample for text generation. In the case of Chinese, we had to add an additional instruction in the input part: 汉语回答。, which means 'Give the answer in Chinese.'. Without this instruction, the answer were given in English. Based on this sample, we can observe that after fine-tuning the model in English-only prompt data set, it has become capable of providing relevant answers, but in many cases, it responded in the English language.

Table 6. A NER sample for Hungarian and Chinese instructions

Instruction:
Listázd ki a személyneveket az alábbi szövegből!
(List the personal names from the text below.)
Input:
Dr. Kovács Péternek van egy autója és szereti Győzikét!
(Dr. Péter Kovács has a car and likes Győzike!)
Response:
Dr. Kovács Péter, Győzike.

Instruction:
列出以下句子中的汉语人名！
(List the Chinese names in the following sentences!)
Input:
这部由瑞恩·高斯林 (Ryan Gosling) 和艾玛·斯通 (Emma Stone) 主演的电影获得了各大奖项的提名。
(This film, starring Ryan Gosling and Emma Stone, has been nominated for various awards.)
Response:
瑞恩·高斯林 (Ryan Gosling) 、艾玛·斯通 (Emma Stone)

In Table 6, you can see an sample for solving named entity recognition (NER) task. In this example we ask our model to list the person names from the text. In the Hungarian sample, in the sentence you can see the name 'Győzikét', which is in the accusative form. The lemma of this name is 'Győzike', which was correctly extracted by our model. We also tried this task with ChatGPT, but it returned 'Győziké', an incorrect lemma, as it ignores the quite regular variation in the stem vowel. This example demonstrates the added value of using the larger amount of data for training model in a given language.

One of the biggest advantages of the transfer learning is that our model can generate programming code (see in Table 7) with Hungarian instruct, which our monolingual model cannot do, since the Hungarian corpus does not contain programming codes.

Table 7. Sample for code generating

Instruction:

Generálj egy python kódot, ami összead két számot!

(Generate a python code that add two numbers.)

Response:

```
def add_two_numbers(a, b):
    return a + b
```

Table 8. Samples for translation

Instruction:

```
Fordítsd le magyar nyelvre!
```

(Translate it into Hungarian language.)

Input:

```
The find also grants insight into the evolution of feathers in birds.
```

Response:

```
A talált lelet emellett betekintést nyújt a madarak tollazatának alakulásába is.
```

Instruction:

把它翻译成中文

(Translate it into Chinese.)

Input:

```
The find also grants insight into the evolution of feathers in birds.
```

Response:

它还揭示鸟类的羽毛是如何演变的。

Last but not least, a multilingual task like translation also requires multilingual knowledge, which our model has become capable of acquiring (see Table 8).

6   Conclusion and Future Work

The present paper described two GPT-3 models, one monolingual (PULI-GPT-3SX – Hungarian), the other trilingual (PULI-GPTrio – Hungarian, English and Chinese) each having 6.7 billion parameters. The trilingual model was further fine-tuned with the Alpaca instruction dataset to produce an instruct GPT model. The results proved that our hypothesis about cross-lingual transfer learning operating with the trilingual model was correct. Despite their size, the performance of our models were quite promising. Our instruct GPT model in zero-shot experiments outperformed ChatGPT on some Hungarian tests in the HuLU benchmark datasets.

So far, we have only applied experiments with fine-tuning our trilingual model on Stanford Alpaca prompts. We plan to proceed by translating and cleaning the Standord Alpaca prompts into Hungarian. Using the translated prompts, we plan to fine-tune our monolingual model to be able to follow Hungarian instructions with high quality. In addition, we will fine-tune our model for chatting. Last but not least, we will improve the performance of our models by applying reinforcement learning methods.

References

1. Benko, V.: Aranea: yet another family of (comparable) web corpora. In: Sojka, P., Horák, A., Kopeček, I., Pala, K. (eds.) TSD 2014. LNCS, pp. 247–256. Springer International Publishing, Cham (2014). https://doi.org/10.1007/978-3-319-10816-2_31
2. Benko, V.: Compatible sketch grammars for comparable corpora. In: Abel, A., Vettori, C., Ralli, N. (eds.) Proceedings of the 16th EURALEX International Congress, pp. 417–430. EURAC research, Bolzano, Italy (2014)
3. Black, S., et al.: GPT-NeoX-20B: an open-source autoregressive language model. In: Proceedings of the ACL Workshop on Challenges & Perspectives in Creating Large Language Models (2022). https://arxiv.org/abs/2204.06745
4. Brodersen, K.H., Ong, C.S., Stephan, K.E., Buhmann, J.M.: The balanced accuracy and its posterior distribution. In: 2010 20th International Conference on Pattern Recognition, pp. 3121–3124 (2010). https://doi.org/10.1109/ICPR.2010.764
5. Brown, T., et al.: Language models are few-shot learners. In: Larochelle, H., Ranzato, M., Hadsell, R., Balcan, M.F., Lin, H. (eds.) Advances in Neural Information Processing Systems, vol. 33, pp. 1877–1901. Curran Associates, Inc. (2020)
6. Chenghao Fan, Z.L., Tian, J.: Chinese-vicuna: a Chinese instruction-following llama-based model (2023). https://github.com/Facico/Chinese-Vicuna
7. Chowdhery, A., et al.: PaLM: scaling language modeling with pathways (2022)
8. Feldmann, Á., et al.: HILBERT, magyar nyelvű BERT-large modell tanítása felhő környezetben. In: XVII. Magyar Számítógépes Nyelvészeti Konferencia, pp. 29–36. Szegedi Tudományegyetem, Informatikai Intézet, Szeged, Magyarország (2021)
9. Gao, L., et al.: The Pile: an 800GB dataset of diverse text for language modeling (2020)
10. He, J., Qiu, J., Zeng, A., Yang, Z., Zhai, J., Tang, J.: FastMoE: a fast mixture-of-expert training system (2021)
11. Indig, B.: Közös crawlnak is egy korpusz a vége - Korpuszépítés a CommonCrawl.hu domainjából. In: Vincze, V. (ed.) XIV. Magyar Számítógépes Nyelvészeti Konferencia (MSZNY 2018), p. 125–134. Szegedi Tudományegyetem Informatikai Intézet, Szegedi Tudományegyetem Informatikai Tanszékcsoport, Szeged (2018)
12. Jakubíček, M., Kilgarriff, A., Kovář, V., Rychlý, P., Suchomel, V.: The TenTen corpus family. In: 7th International Corpus Linguistics Conference CL 2013, pp. 125–127. Lancaster (2013)
13. Kudo, T., Richardson, J.: SentencePiece: a simple and language independent subword tokenizer and detokenizer for neural text processing. In: Proceedings of the 2018 Conference on Empirical Methods in Natural Language Processing: System Demonstrations, pp. 66–71. Association for Computational Linguistics, Brussels, Belgium (2018). https://doi.org/10.18653/v1/D18-2012, https://aclanthology.org/D18-2012
14. Ligeti-Nagy, N., et al.: HuLU: magyar nyelvű benchmark adatbázis kiépítése a neurális nyelvmodellek kiértékelése céljából. In: XVIII. Magyar Számítógépes Nyelvészeti Konferencia, pp. 431–446. JATEPress, Szeged (2022)
15. Lison, P., Tiedemann, J.: OpenSubtitles2016: extracting large parallel corpora from movie and TV subtitles. In: Proceedings of the Tenth International Conference on Language Resources and Evaluation (LREC 2016), pp. 923–929. European Language Resources Association (ELRA), Portorož, Slovenia (2016)
16. LM-SYS: Fastchat (vicuna: An open-source chatbot) (2023). https://github.com/lm-sys/FastChat
17. Nemeskey, D.M.: Natural Language Processing Methods for Language Modeling. Ph.D. thesis, Eötvös Loránd University (2020)
18. Nemeskey, D.M.: Introducing huBERT. In: XVII. Magyar Számítógépes Nyelvészeti Konferencia, pp. 3–14. Szegedi Tudományegyetem, Informatikai Intézet, Szeged, Magyarország (2021)

19. Novák, A., Siklósi, B., Oravecz, C.: A new integrated open-source morphological analyzer for Hungarian. In: Calzolari, N., et al. (eds.) Proceedings of the Tenth International Conference on Language Resources and Evaluation (LREC 2016). European Language Resources Association (ELRA), Paris, France (2016)
20. OpenAI: GPT-4 Technical Report (2023)
21. Oravecz, C., Váradi, T., Sass, B.: The Hungarian Gigaword corpus. In: Proceedings of the Ninth International Conference on Language Resources and Evaluation (LREC 2014), pp. 1719–1723. European Language Resources Association (ELRA), Reykjavik, Iceland (2014)
22. Ouyang, L., et al.: Training language models to follow instructions with human feedback (2022)
23. Rychlý, P.: Manatee/Bonito - a modular corpus manager. In: 1st Workshop on Recent Advances in Slavonic Natural Language Processing, pp. 65–70. Masarykova univerzita, Brno (2007)
24. Shazeer, N.: GLU Variants Improve Transformer (2020)
25. Shoeybi, M., Patwary, M., Puri, R., LeGresley, P., Casper, J., Catanzaro, B.: Megatron-LM: training multi-billion parameter language models using model parallelism (2019)
26. Smith, S., et al.: Using DeepSpeed and Megatron to Train Megatron-Turing NLG 530B, A Large-Scale Generative Language Model (2022)
27. Su, J., Lu, Y., Pan, S., Murtadha, A., Wen, B., Liu, Y.: RoFormer: enhanced transformer with rotary position embedding (2021)
28. Suchomel, V., Pomikálek, J.: Efficient web crawling for large text corpora. In: Kilgarriff, A., Sharoff, S. (eds.) Proceedings of the seventh Web as Corpus Workshop (WAC7), pp. 39–43. Lyon (2012)
29. Taori, R., et al.: Stanford alpaca: an instruction-following llama model (2023). https://github.com/tatsu-lab/stanford_alpaca
30. Touvron, H., et al.: LLaMA: Open and efficient foundation language models. arXiv preprint arXiv:2302.13971 (2023)
31. Vaswani, A., et al.: Attention is all you need. In: Guyon, I., et al. (eds.) Advances in Neural Information Processing Systems, vol. 30, pp. 5998–6008. Curran Associates, Inc. (2017)
32. Wang, B., Komatsuzaki, A.: GPT-J-6B: a 6 billion parameter autoregressive language model (2021). https://github.com/kingoflolz/mesh-transformer-jax
33. Wang, Y., et al.: Self-instruct: aligning language model with self generated instructions (2022)
34. Xu, B.: NLP Chinese corpus: large scale Chinese corpus for NLP (2019). https://doi.org/10.5281/zenodo.3402023
35. Yang, Z.G., et al.: Jönnek a nagyok! BERT-large, GPT-2 és GPT-3 nyelvmodellek magyar nyelvre. In: XIX. Magyar Számítógépes Nyelvészeti Konferencia (MSZNY 2023), pp. 247–262. Szegedi Tudományegyetem, Informatikai Intézet, Szeged, Hungary (2023)
36. Yuan, S., et al.: Wudaocorpora: a super large-scale Chinese corpora for pre-training language models. AI Open **2**, 65–68 (2021). https://doi.org/10.1016/j.aiopen.2021.06.001

The Unbearable Lightness of Morph Classification

Vojtěch John and Zdeněk Žabokrtský[(⊠)]

Faculty of Mathematics and Physics, Institute of Formal and Applied Linguistics,
Charles University, Malostranské náměstí 25, 118 00 Prague, Czech Republic
zabokrtsky@ufal.mff.cuni.cz

Abstract. In light of the recent push for the creation and unification of large morphologically annotated resources, there is a call for (preferably language-independent, low-resource) methods of morph classification. This paper reports on a pilot experiment on morph classification of the Czech language. We have performed two experiments - root morph recognition and complete morph classification. By exploiting simple quantitative methods and - in some cases - available Czech morphological resources, we have achieved morph-level precision of respectively 96.7% and 88.3%.

Keywords: morphology · morphological analysis · morph classification · DeriNet

1 Introduction

The standard NLP task of morphological segmentation, i.e. dividing words into sequences of the smallest possible meaning-bearing units called morphemes[1], has recently seen a fair share of renewed interest. Recent development in morphological analysis of underresourced languages and/or multilingual morphological analysis (e.g. [1] or [9]). The state-of-the-art methods of morphological segmentation are however usually based on neural networks [1], and hence are neither easily generalizable to languages with fewer resources nor straightforwardly usable for further morphological analysis. As there is a push for the creation and unification of morphologically annotated resources [3,26], and as adding morphological and syntactic information seems to improve the quality of machine translation for morphologically rich and underresourced languages [8], a need arises for new methods for language-independent low-resource methods of morph classification.

Up to now, there has been relatively little attention paid to the task. Classification of morphs aims to classify the individual morphs given already segmented words, the possible granularity of the classification ranging from the simple binary distinction *free morpheme - bounded morpheme* to e.g. the very complex and fine-grained Leipzig glossing rules [7]. To our best knowledge, there has been no recent attempt to tackle automated classification of morphs of the Czech language apart from [5], where the

---

[1] Or morphs, if we speak about particular forms that appear in words.

© The Author(s), under exclusive license to Springer Nature Switzerland AG 2023
K. Ekštein et al. (Eds.): TSD 2023, LNAI 14102, pp. 105–115, 2023.
https://doi.org/10.1007/978-3-031-40498-6_10

DeriNet derivational lexicon is used for root morph identification; however, this is just quickly mentioned in the article and the results are neither evaluated nor discussed. Furthermore, to this date, there is a very limited amount of reasonably-high-quality morphologically annotated Czech data available (apart from the UniMorph project [3], whose unsuitability for our purposes we will discuss in the next section).

In this paper, we report on a pilot experiment concerned with the classification of morphs of the Czech language. Firstly, we try to show how the root and non-root morphs of pre-segmented words are surprisingly well distinguishable using simple quantitative approaches and a small corpus of other pre-segmented words; we also propose classification methods that exploit existing Czech derivational resources. Secondly, we report on a work in progress in which we propose to use the root morph identification methods as a basis for complete morpheme classification of pre-segmented words, exploiting the available Czech derivational and morphological resources.

It will be noticed that the proposed methods differ both in their generality and the demands on resources. Namely, we also use two additional resources: the Czech derivational network DeriNet [24,25] and MorfFlex [12] (for lemmatization and part-of-speech tagging). Nevertheless as according to [5] similarly constructed derivational networks are available for at least 11 languages and lemmatization and part-of-speech tagging are among the best-explored topics in NLP, we feel confident that these additional requirements are not so stringent as to make possible adaptations or generalizations of our approach to other languages too costly.

2 Related Work

2.1 Terminology

In the following text, we use the terminology as described in [26]. A morpheme is the smallest (in the sense of non-subdivisible) sequence of graphemes associated with a definite meaning. In individual words, morphemes are present in particular forms – morphs [13]. The morphs can be further characterized. We can distinguish free morphemes that can be used as separate words), and bound morphemes that cannot[2]. Alternatively, the morphemes are either lexical (with more or less general lexical meaning) or grammatical (with inflectional meaning).

Based on these two distinctions, we distinguish root morphemes (free lexical morphemes; e.g. *kůň, plav*), derivational affixes (bound lexical morphemes, e.g. *pro-, -tel*), inflectional affixes (bound grammatical morphemes, e.g. *nej-, -ý*) and function words (free grammatical morphemes, e.g. *s, a*). According to their position relative to the root morpheme (resp. morph), we may divide affixes into prefixes preceding the root morph, interfixes between the root morphs or suffixes following the root. We could also take into account postfixes - morphemes that appear after inflectional suffixes.

---

[2] It should be noted that these terms, while universally used, are not completely suitable for the Czech language, where many of the morphs cannot be used as separate words because words that contain them demand an inflectional affix in every form (e.g. "pín", the root morph for "odepínat"–"to bind", which alone is not a valid word in Czech); even though they would otherwise be classified as root morphs.

2.2 Data Resources

There are several kinds of relevant data resources. First, there are morphological lexicons. For Czech, there are two main lexicons, unfortunately not available in machine tractable form: *Retrográdní morfematický slovník češtiny* [21] and *Bázový morfematický slovník češtiny* [20]. Furthermore, the Czech language is included in the UniMorph project [3]. Nevertheless, the Czech data in UniMorph, automatically extracted from MorfFlex [12], are segmented in a way that is incompatible with our proposed morph classification. Namely, the root in the UniMorph segmentation actually seems to be the lemma or the root of the derivational tree (often including non-inflectional prefixes). For the morphological segmentation, there are 38 000 manually segmented Czech words in the data used for the SIGMORPHON 2022 shared task [1].

In addition, several of the available derivational resources already contain at least some kind of morphological segmentation and classification. A survey of this type of resource can be found in [26]. A good example of the kind of morphological resource we have in mind is the manually created CroDeriV lexicon [22]. It contains over 14 000 Croatian words (except two nouns all verbs) segmented to morphs. The morphs are classified as prefixes, stems, suffixes or endings.

The granularity of the classification included in the data differs: the Dictionary of Morphemes of the Russian Language [16] contains over 74 000 segmented Russian lemmas with labeled root morphs (and not affixes). Furthermore, for many languages, either no such resources exist or - as they are created automatically or semi-automatically-they are not straightforwardly usable as a source of gold data, such as in the case of the German morphological derivational lexicon Derivbase [27] or the recent multilingual derivational and inflectional database MorphyNet [2]. This database also includes Czech data; they are however incompletely and quite often inaccurately segmented. Therefore, however useful this resource might prove to be for practical purposes, we are reluctant to employ it for our pilot experiment (especially as the gold data).

The Czech derivational network DeriNet [25] contains a rough morphological segmentation (resp. for 250 000 of the lemmas the root morphs are labeled). The methods by which the root morphs are labeled are nevertheless much similar to some of the methods we try (and therefore cannot be used as the gold data); furthermore, the relevant articles [5, 25] do not mention the final accuracy of the method.

2.3 Morphological Segmentation and Classification

Some of the classical approaches to morphological analysis either already include, or could be straightforwardly extended to include, the classification of morphs. Thus Goldsmith's unsupervised morphological segmentation [10] uses minimum description length and several simple heuristics to generate candidate stems and suffixes. Unsupervised morphology induction like Schone and Jurafsky [19] or more recently the word-embedding-based induction proposed by Soricut and Och [23] use automatically extracted affixes for morphological rules induction.

For languages for which well-annotated and sufficiently large resources of the abovementioned type are available, supervised machine learning can be used for both the tasks - morphological segmentation and classification of morphs. Recently, Bolshakova and Sapin [6] employed a neural model for morphological segmentation and classification of Russian, achieving over 90% word-level classification accuracy.

In comparison, the state-of-the-art results for the Czech language are not so promising. The Czech derivational network DeriNet has been used for morphological segmentation (and partial classification) [5] with the achieved word-level segmentation accuracy of 58.9 % (the number is only illustrative - the accuracy of root morph recognition was not measured). This might be caused by the lack of available relevant Czech data (almost no available data for morpheme classification, till recently ([1,26]) also for segmentation).

3 Data

We use four data resources in total. First, we use a small set of fully manually segmented and annotated words (316 words in total), which we further subdivide into the dev set and test set (each containing 158 words).[3] The morphs are annotated by their type, similarly to the CroDeriV [22]. The classes are as follows:

- **R** - root morphs,
- **P** - derivational prefixes,
- **S** - derivational suffixes,
- **I** - inflectional affixes,
- **N** - interfixes,
- **O** - postfixes.

Secondly, mainly as "training data" (for feature extraction of morphs), we use 10 438 manually segmented Czech non-compound words with manually selected root morphs. Thirdly, in some of our experiments, we use the DeriNet Czech derivational lexicon. It contains over 1M Czech lexemes connected by over 800 000 derivational relations. We also use the MorfFlex lexicon [12], which contains 125 348 899 simple lemma - tag - form triples. The tags, as described in [11], are very fine-grained and contain morphological as well as syntactic information.

4 Evaluation

There are two possible levels of evaluation—word-level evaluation and morph-level evaluation. The word-level evaluation measures are less fine-grained, but they offer some desirable properties (e.g. the instances might be weighted by the number of occurrences of a given word in the corpus, or unweighted - giving each word equal weight. Imagine two extreme scenarios - A) half of the annotations is completely right, the other half is completely wrong; and B) half of the morphs in every word is annotated right and the other half is wrong. While e.g. unweighted word-level precision of the first example would be 50% and the precision of the second one would be 0%, while the morph-level precision of both examples would be 50%.

For both of our experiments, we have selected five simple evaluation measures: Word-level accuracy and morph-level precision, recall, F-measure and accuracy. It

---

[3] https://github.com/johnvojtech/morph_analysis/blob/main/data/completed_hand_annotation. tsv.

should be noted however that since we use a very small test set, the word-level accuracy, while included for illustration and completeness, should be nevertheless regarded with some caution.

5   Experiment 1: Root Morph Selection

5.1   Methods

In our first experiment, our goal is to identify the root morph of the word. We started with three baseline heuristics. We also - as a 0-th baseline - tried to label every morph as an affix (since affixes are more common than roots) - $r0$. For all following heuristics, we compute the morph features on test set + training data, i.e. the 10k segmented words, without the annotation of the root morph.

First, we selected all the longest morphs of the segmented words. Secondly, we selected the morph with the least occurrences in our dictionary on the intuition that, since compounds is infrequent in Czech, root morphs are usually combined with (a limited number of) affixes, while affixes can combine with (a big number of) root morphs. This method was used in the annotation of DeriNet [25] with the first one as the tiebreaker. Thirdly, we estimate the left and right conditional entropy of the morphs and select the morph with the smallest difference between the two. This was motivated by the observation that while the roots usually appear in between two affixes at the beginning/end of the word, the affixes usually appear only on one side of the root morph, while on the other side, there is either the beginning/end of the word or another affix; thus, one would expect the difference between the left and right entropy to be quite high in the case of affixes and quite low in the case of root morphs. Finally, we combine all these three heuristics - we normalize them (so all three sum to 1) and minimize their unweighted sum; instead of the length we use 1/length (so that we may minimize it).

Further, we experimented with methods based on the derivational network DeriNet [25]. First, for each word, we found the unmotivated lemma (or "root lemma") of the derivational tree[4] (in DeriNet) and all its children, computed the edit distance between each morph and these words and selected the morph with the shortest edit distance. This we use either by itself ($r5$) or in combination with the previous three heuristics ($r6$) in the same way as in ($r4$). Lastly, instead of taking into account only the unmotivated lemma of the current word's derivation tree and its children, we computed the longest common substring of all descendants of the unmotivated lemma, (including replacing any character with a wildcard to - very roughly - deal with possible allomorphy; thus e.g. the common substring of "sit" and "sat" would be "s?t") and then apply $r6$.

In all of the ($r5$–$r7$), if the processed word is not found in the DeriNet, we use the $r4$ method. For comparison with a supervised approach, we also trained the CRF tagger implemented in NLTK [4] on the training data (with annotated root morphs); that is, we treat the segmented words as sentences and the morphs as tagged words.

---

[4] A tree structure, were derivationally related words are organised according to derivational history; the root of the tree represents the unmotivated lemma.

5.2 Results

As we announced in the introduction, the simple quantitative methods gave surprisingly good results (see Table 1). Every method apart from just taking the longest morphs (r1) achieved higher precision than the CRF tagger. As all of the methods (also apart from r1) were restricted to selecting exactly one root morph, the achieved F-measure is also surprisingly good (94.4%). We can also note that even the best of the fully-unsupervised methods (i.e. not using DeriNet) achieves comparable F-measure with the supervised CRF tagger.

Table 1. Evaluation of root morph identification.

	Word-level accuracy	Morph-level precision	Morph-level recall	Morph-level f-measure	Morph-level accuracy
CRF tagger	89.9	90.4	**94.7**	92.5	96.3
r0	–	–	–	–	68.9
r1	68.4	81.1	84.5	82.7	89.5
r2	86.1	92.4	86.9	89.6	93.9
r3	86.1	93.9	86.9	89.6	93.9
r4	88.6	94.9	89.3	92.0	95.4
r5	88.0	94.3	88.7	91.4	95.0
r6	90.5	96.8	91.1	93.9	96.4
r7	**91.1**	**97.4**	91.7	**94.4**	**96.8**

6 Experiment 2: Morph Classification

6.1 Methods

In our second experiment, we try to expand our root morph recognition methods to a fully-fledged morphological classifier. The most important part of this is the distinction between root morphs, the derivational affixes and the inflectional affixes.

6.2 Baselines

We have implemented two baseline morph classifiers, supervised and unsupervised one. As our first, supervised baseline (Baseline 1), we assign to each morph the tag that is most commonly associated with the morph in our development set; if it is not present there, we label it as a root morph (it is the most frequent label in the dev set). As our second, unsupervised baseline (Baseline 2), we designed two versions of a simple unsupervised heuristics-based classifier. First, we decide for each morph in a given word whether it could be a derivational affix, inflectional affix or a root morph (by heuristics described in the following subsections). In the second iteration, we assign to each of the positions the tag that is most common for the morph in the processed data. In the B version we consider as possible inflectional morphs only the first and last morphs of the word.[5]

---

[5] In all our baseline solutions we ignore the interfixes and postfixes.

Derivational Affixes. Using DeriNet, we take the morphs in which the segmented word fully differs from the root lemma; i.e., we compute the minimum edit distance between the word and the root lemma, and label the characters that would be added or rewritten during the minimal edit. We regard all the morphs, that consist only of such characters, as derivational morphs. This heuristics is very rough in that most of the Czech lemmas contain an inflectional affix, which in this way could also get classified as a derivational affix.

Inflectional Affixes. For each tag in MorfFlex [12], we take a thousand word-forms corresponding to the same tag; also for every word form present in the data, we take all the other word forms. The inflectional affixes are those that are (more or less) common for common tags, but different for the different forms. Namely, we try to extract an ending common for all the words tagged by the same tag; if that fails, we consider every ending common for at least one-fifth of the examples. If even that fails, we try to find the longest uncommon substring (including wildcard characters) for all the forms of the segmented word.

Roots. For root morph recognition we use the DeriNet-based r7 method from the previous section.

6.3   Finetuning CRF Taggers

To exploit the transition probabilities between words, we have (as in the first experiment) used the bidirectional LSTM-CRF tagger as described in [14]. The CRF tagger used in NLTK does not permit finetuning, so we have used the implementation from the bi-lstm-crf Python package [15]. First, we have trained it on the 10k training set with the manually annotated root morphs. Then, we finetuned it on the small development set (which contains 158 annotated words). This approach (Semi-supervised CRF), however, presupposes the rather large data with annotated root morphs. However, since we have developed methods of root morph recognition, we could use them for creating the training data.

In our second CRF tagger-based experiment (Supervised CRF), we have used the large training data stripped of the manual annotation and annotated automatically, using our most successful DeriNet-based method (*r7*). Thirdly, we have trained the CRF tagger only on the dev set (Small CRF). Finally, we have pre-trained the CRF tagger on the training data annotated by both of our baseline solutions (and again finetuned on the dev set).

6.4   Evaluation and Results

In the second experiment, we evaluate only the word-level and morph-level accuracy (Table 2). The results were somewhat surprising. First of all, no version of the CRF tagger was better than one of our unsupervised baselines, which has achieved 88 % morph-level accuracy. Secondly, while both pretraining the CRF tagger on root identification and on data annotated by the baseline methods seems to have significant impact

Table 2. Evaluation of full classification of morphs.

	Morph-level accuracy	Word-level accuracy
Baseline 1	83.7%	55%
Baseline 2A	76.6%	18%
Baseline 2B	**88.3%**	**70%**
Small CRF	72.9%	42 %
Supervised CRF	75.7%	44%
Semi-supervised CRF	79.7%	54%
Baseline 1 + CRF	84.6%	63%
Baseline 2A + CRF	61.2%	37%
Baseline 2B + CRF	80.8%	57%

Table 3. Example output (Baseline 2B)

Segmented word	Assigned signature	Correct signature
styd nou t	RSI	RSI
při prav i t	PRSI	PRSI
pol ovič n í	RRSI	RSSI
ne roz trh a l i	IPRSSI	IPRSSI
po prsk a t	PRSI	PRSI
maž	R	R
z kypř e t	PRSI	PRSI
o hod n ot i t	PRSSSI	PRSSSI
obe še l	PRS	PRI
sáh l a	SSI	RSI

on their accuracy, there is no clear correspondence between overall quality of the pre-training data and the overall quality of the CRF tagger results. Thirdly, there is a big difference in accuracy between the two versions of our unsupervised baseline.

Sometimes, the taggers make mistakes that could be fairly easily filtered out (but always not so easily corrected), as having a suffix before a root, a word without a root (see the last example in Table 3) or a sequence like "Root - Prefix - Suffix". Introduction of simple rules might therefore significantly increase the final accuracy. One such example causes the large difference between the accuracy of the two versions of Baseline 2. Closer look at the data reveals that most of the errors of the version A of the unsupervised baseline solution consisted in misidentification of derivational suffixes as inflectional, which might be easily filtered out by the restriction on the position of the inflectional affix, as used in the B version; the real accuracy of the A version might however be higher, as in some cases the identification of derivational suffixes in the manually annotated test set is spurious (e.g. *u klid n i l i* is assigned the signature *PRSSSI* in the test set and *PRSIII* by the baseline solution; but the suffix -*l*, expressing past tense, might be said to be inflectional).

Table 4. Errors in morph classification (except rare categories, i.e. infixes and postfixes)

System/Error (Correct:Assigned)	R:S	R:P	R:I	S:R	S:P	S:I	I:R	I:P	I:S	P:R	P:I	P:S
Baseline 1	0	0	1	17	2	11	6	0	28	9	0	2
Baseline 2A	0	3	1	5	3	74	8	11	14	4	1	1
Baseline 2B	0	4	0	5	5	4	8	11	18	4	0	1
Small-data CRF	11	43	5	19	0	22	11	5	19	8	0	1
Supervised CRF	36	16	0	24	3	18	1	6	10	9	0	4
Semi-supervised CRF	7	25	0	25	2	17	6	6	6	4	0	0
Baseline 1 + CRF	6	9	6	17	4	11	6	5	4	7	0	6
Baseline 2A + CRF	7	42	7	42	12	39	8	11	19	9	0	2
Baseline 2B + CRF	3	14	8	16	0	19	6	5	0	7	1	1

7   Conclusion

We have shown that applying simple quantitative methods on comparatively small and/or unannotated segmented data is sufficient for a high-quality root morph identification in Czech and that these results can be further improved by exploiting the DeriNet derivational lexicon. In our second experiment, we used our root morph identification methods to create training data and to train an LSTM-CRF tagger. It appears that the quality of the output can be increased by pre-training the tagger on root morph identification or morph data classified by a good-enough baseline solution. Furthermore, the simple supervised baseline was as good as the CRF taggers, while one of the unsupervised baselines has been significantly more accurate.

In the future, we would like to better utilize Czech resources like MorfFlex and DeriNet either for further morphological analysis (e.g. the derivational affixes would appear in many derivational trees in DeriNet but on the lower levels, while root morphs would appear in only a few trees and on all levels; most the inflectional affixes would not appear at all or at no specific level). Also, the morphological tags present in MorfFlex might be useful - the given tag would probably strongly predict the presence of corresponding endings (as opposed to derivational affixes and root morphs). These could then be used either for designing specific tagging methods or for enlarging the training data for machine-learning-based taggers.

Secondly, we would like to extend our approaches to a multi-lingual setting. We would especially like to use Universal features included in the Universal Dependencies [18]; these could be also used for more fine-grained morphological analysis in the future. However, there are also many derivational [17] multilingual resources that could be used for the classification of morphs in a similar way to DeriNet.

Acknowledgements. This work has been using data, tools and services provided by the LINDAT/CLARIAH-CZ Research Infrastructure (https://lindat.cz), supported by the Ministry of Education, Youth and Sports of the Czech Republic (Project No. LM2018101).

We are grateful to Magda Ševčíková and three anonymous reviewers for their helpful comments and suggestions. We thank Šárka Dohnalová for annotating a data sample with classification of morphs.

References

1. Batsuren, K., et al.: The SIGMORPHON 2022 shared task on morpheme segmentation. In: Proceedings of the 19th SIGMORPHON Workshop on Computational Research in Phonetics, Phonology, and Morphology, pp. 103–116. Association for Computational Linguistics, Seattle, Washington (2022). https://doi.org/10.18653/v1/2022.sigmorphon-1.11, https://aclanthology.org/2022.sigmorphon-1.11
2. Batsuren, K., Bella, G., Giunchiglia, F.: MorphyNet: a large multilingual database of derivational and inflectional morphology. In: Proceedings of the 18th SIGMORPHON Workshop on Computational Research in Phonetics, Phonology, and Morphology, pp. 39–48. Association for Computational Linguistics (2021). https://doi.org/10.18653/v1/2021.sigmorphon-1.5, https://aclanthology.org/2021.sigmorphon-1.5
3. Batsuren, K., et al.: UniMorph 4.0: Universal Morphology (2022)
4. Bird, S.: NLTK: the natural language toolkit. In: Proceedings of the COLING/ACL 2006 Interactive Presentation Sessions, pp. 69–72. Association for Computational Linguistics, Sydney, Australia (2006). https://doi.org/10.3115/1225403.1225421, https://aclanthology.org/P06-4018
5. Bodnár, J., Žabokrtský, Z., Ševčíková, M.: Semi-supervised induction of morpheme boundaries in Czech using a word-formation network. In: Sojka, P., Kopeček, I., Pala, K., Horák, A. (eds.) TSD 2020. LNCS (LNAI), vol. 12284, pp. 189–196. Springer, Cham (2020). https://doi.org/10.1007/978-3-030-58323-1_20
6. Bolshakova, E.I., Sapin, A.S.: Building a combined morphological model for Russian word forms. In: Burnaev, E., et al. (eds.) AIST 2021. Communications in Computer and Information Science, vol. 1086, pp. 45–55. Springer-Verlag, Berlin (2021). https://doi.org/10.1007/978-3-030-39575-9_16
7. Comrie, B., Haspelmath, M., Bickel, B.: The Leipzig glossing rules: conventions for interlinear morpheme-by-morpheme glosses. Max Planck Institute for Evolutionary Anthropology (2008). https://books.google.cz/books?id=e8B7AQAACAAJ
8. Donaj, G., Sepesy Maučec, M.: On the use of morpho-syntactic description tags in neural machine translation with small and large training corpora. Math. **10**(9) (2022). https://doi.org/10.3390/math10091608, https://www.mdpi.com/2227-7390/10/9/1608
9. Goldman, O., et al.: The MRL 2022 shared task on multilingual clause-level morphology. In: Proceedings of the The 2nd Workshop on Multi-lingual Representation Learning (MRL), pp. 134–146. Association for Computational Linguistics, Abu Dhabi, United Arab Emirates (Hybrid) (2022). https://aclanthology.org/2022.mrl-1.14
10. Goldsmith, J.: Unsupervised learning of the morphology of a natural language. Comput. Linguist. **27**(2), 153–198 (2001). https://doi.org/10.1162/089120101750300490, https://aclanthology.org/J01-2001
11. Hajič, J., et al.: Prague dependency treebank - consolidated 1.0. In: Proceedings of the Twelfth Language Resources and Evaluation Conference, pp. 5208–5218. European Language Resources Association, Marseille, France (2020). https://aclanthology.org/2020.lrec-1.641
12. Hajič, J., Hlaváčová, J., Mikulová, M., Straka, M., Štěpánková, B.: MorfFlex CZ 2.0. LINDAT/CLARIN digital library at the Institute of Formal and Applied Linguistics (ÚFAL), Faculty of Mathematics and Physics, Charles University (2020). http://hdl.handle.net/11234/1-3186

13. Haspelmath, M.: The morph as a minimal linguistic form. Morphology **30**(2), 117–134 (2020). https://doi.org/10.1007/s11525-020-09355-5
14. Huang, Z., Xu, W., Yu, K.: Bidirectional LSTM-CRF Models for Sequence Tagging (2015)
15. Ji, D.: Bi-LSTM-CRF (2019). https://github.com/jidasheng/bi-lstm-crf
16. Kuznetsova, A., Efremova, T.: Dictionary of Morphemes of the Russian Language. Firebird Publications, Incorporated (1986). https://books.google.cz/books?id=RPw7AAAACAAJ
17. Kyjánek, L., Žabokrtský, Z., Ševčíková, M., Vidra, J.: Universal derivations 1.0, a growing collection of harmonised word-formation resources. Prague Bull. Math. Linguist. **115**, 5–30 (2020). https://doi.org/10.14712/00326585.003
18. Nivre, J., et al.: Universal dependencies v2: an evergrowing multilingual treebank collection. In: Proceedings of the Twelfth Language Resources and Evaluation Conference, pp. 4034–4043. European Language Resources Association, Marseille, France (2020). https://aclanthology.org/2020.lrec-1.497
19. Schone, P., Jurafsky, D.: Knowledge-free induction of inflectional morphologies. In: Second Meeting of the North American Chapter of the Association for Computational Linguistics (2001). https://aclanthology.org/N01-1024
20. Šiška, Z.: Bázový morfematický slovník češtiny. Univerzita Palackého, Pedagogická fakulta (1998). https://books.google.cz/books?id=MZMWAAAACAAJ
21. Slavíčková, E.: Retrográdní morfematický slovník češtiny: s připojenými inventárními slovníky ceských morfémů kořenových, prefixálních a sufixálních. Academia (1975)
22. Šojat, K., Srebačić, M., Tadić, M., Pavelić, T.: CroDeriV: a new resource for processing Croatian morphology. In: Proceedings of the Ninth International Conference on Language Resources and Evaluation (LREC 2014), pp. 3366–3370. European Language Resources Association (ELRA), Reykjavik, Iceland (2014). http://www.lrec-conf.org/proceedings/lrec2014/pdf/1074_Paper.pdf
23. Soricut, R., Och, F.: Unsupervised morphology induction using word embeddings. In: Proceedings of the 2015 Conference of the North American Chapter of the Association for Computational Linguistics: Human Language Technologies, pp. 1627–1637. Association for Computational Linguistics, Denver, Colorado (2015). https://doi.org/10.3115/v1/N15-1186, https://aclanthology.org/N15-1186
24. Vidra, J., Žabokrtský, Z., Kyjánek, L., Ševčíková, M., Dohnalová, Š.: DeriNet 2.0. LINDAT/CLARIAH-CZ digital library at the Institute of Formal and Applied Linguistics (ÚFAL), Faculty of Mathematics and Physics, Charles University (2019). http://hdl.handle.net/11234/1-2995
25. Vidra, J., Žabokrtský, Z., Ševčíková, M., Kyjánek, L.: DeriNet 2.0: towards an all-in-one word-formation resource. In: Proceedings of the Second International Workshop on Resources and Tools for Derivational Morphology, pp. 81–89. Charles University, Faculty of Mathematics and Physics, Institute of Formal and Applied Linguistics, Prague, Czechia (2019). https://aclanthology.org/W19-8510
26. Žabokrtský, Z., et al.: Towards universal segmentations: UniSegments 1.0. In: Proceedings of the Thirteenth Language Resources and Evaluation Conference, pp. 1137–1149. European Language Resources Association, Marseille, France (2022). https://aclanthology.org/2022.lrec-1.122
27. Zeller, B., Šnajder, J., Padó, S.: DErivBase: inducing and evaluating a derivational morphology resource for German. In: Proceedings of the 51st Annual Meeting of the Association for Computational Linguistics (Volume 1: Long Papers), pp. 1201–1211. Association for Computational Linguistics, Sofia, Bulgaria (2013). https://aclanthology.org/P13-1118

A German Parallel Clausal Coordinate Ellipsis Corpus that Aligns Sentences from the TüBa-D/Z Treebank with Reconstructed Canonical Forms

Denis Memmesheimer[(✉)] and Karin Harbusch

Computer Science Faculty, University of Koblenz, 56070 Koblenz, Germany
{denismemmesheimer,harbusch}@uni-koblenz.de

Abstract. This paper presents a new German resource for coordinated sentences, including asyndetons. The aim is to align cases of *Clausal Coordinate Ellipsis (CCE)* with the ellipsis-reconstructed sentences. The latter are called *canonical forms*. CCE is a challenging linguistic phenomenon in which constituents can be omitted under certain conditions. Often, several elision phenomena occur simultaneously. Even state-of-the-art constituency parsers have difficulties with CCE sentences. Although CCE examples occur in sufficient numbers in both written and spoken corpora, they are often among those with the lowest F1 scores. We surmise that elided verbforms, in particular, lead to incorrect hypotheses about phrase boundaries. Our new parallel corpus is designed to support the development of effective models for machine learning or natural language processing components that can automatically reconstruct CCE phenomena.

Keywords: Coordination · ellipsis reconstruction · canonical form

1 Introduction

Ellipsis in coordinated sentences plays an integral role in written and spoken German (e.g., eight percent of sentences in the TIGER corpus [1] exhibit CCE constructions [9]; in spoken German, however, all CCE types occur less frequently [6]).

This paper describes a new German resource for coordinated sentences with Clausal Coordinate Ellipsis (CCE), a challenging linguistic phenomenon where at least one constituent in the second conjunct can be omitted (cf. example (1); here, the finite and the nonfinite verbform are elided due to *Long Distance Gapping*). In addition, CCE covers the elision of at least one word in the first conjunct (cf. example (2); here, *Backward Conjunction Reduction (BCR)* ignores the boundaries of the noun-phrase constituent $[151_{Card} Mark_N]_{NP}$ (i.e., it elides the last two words in the first conjunct; in the example, BCR occurs together with *Gapping*). In Sect. 3.2, we illustrate all phenomena in detail using English examples; however, we focus on the specific German constraints of each phenomenon—e.g., BCR variants in French [25] are not licensed in German). In the following, we underline the so-called *remnants*, i.e., the counterparts of each elision, which are not necessarily identical[1] in morphological form to the reconstructed

---

[1] Here, we follow the terminology in [7] where all identity types for CCE are outlined in detail.

K. Ekštein et al. (Eds.): TSD 2023, LNAI 14102, pp. 116–128, 2023.
https://doi.org/10.1007/978-3-031-40498-6_11

ones. The two examples show that both conjuncts can only be analyzed semantically if the elided constituents are reconstructed. When using existing treebanks, constituency parsers often generate incorrect structures because they lack cues encoded in the training data to prioritize the correct CCE variant. Our new parallel corpus is designed to support the development of effective models for machine learning or natural language processing components that are able to automatically reconstruct the CCE phenomena.

(1) *Die Männer waren verletzt,   die Frauen waren$_g$ nicht verletzt$_g$.*
The men   were wounded, the women were   not   wounded.

(2) *MS- und Krebskranke   erhielten dafür   151 Mark$_b$ zusätzlich$_b$,*
MS- and cancer_patients received for_this 151 Deutschmarks additionally,

Aids-Kranke erhielten$_g$ dafür$_g$ 179 Mark   zusätzlich.
Aids-patients received   for_this 179 Deutschmarks additionally.
'MS- and cancer patients additionally received for this 151 Deutschmarks,
Aids patients 179 Deutschmarks, respectively.'

The two example sentences above are taken from TüBa-D/Z [27]. In Sect. 2, we give an overview of how CCE is encoded in the different German treebanks. Based on these observations and our goal to support CCE analysis, we motivate why we based our parallel CCE corpus on a collection of sentences with at least one coordination in TüBa-D/Z. We also discuss what is an appropriate format for "learning CCE" from a corpus. In Sect. 3, we outline the encoding format in detail. In our corpus, we explicitly indicate that in certain cases, the reconstructions of CCE phenomena can be seen as competing interpretations alongside NP-/PP- or VP-coordinations. The two examples shown above do not permit any local interpretation. However, cases like in the examples (3) and (4) are encoded with both variants as the gold standard. In the two examples, the local variant is first delineated by the non-clausal constituent in square brackets. In turn, the subscript "f"/"fg" for the CCE variant indicates that the phenomenon can be classified as *Forward Conjunction Reductions (FCR)* (which can only occur in a fixed word order) or *Gapping*, assuming that the word order of the first conjunct is preserved in this n-ary ($n = 4$) case of CCE.

(3) *Steckt hinter dem Wechsel der   Fakultät [ein Mentor oder eine Gruppe]$_{SB}$?*
Is   behind the change of_the faculty a   mentor or   a   group?
Steckt hinter dem Wechsel der Fakultät ein Mentor oder steckt hinter dem Wechsel der Fakultät$_{fg}$ eine Gruppe?

(4) *Sie [hatte keine Papiere, erhielt keinen Lohn und schuftete tagelang, pausenlos]$_{VP}$;*
She had no   papers, got   no   wage and toiled for_days, nonstop
Sie hatte keine Papiere, sie$_f$ erhielt keinen Lohn und sie$_f$ schuftete tagelang, sie$_{fg}$ schuftete$_{fg}$ pausenlos;

The paper is structured as follows. In Sect. 2, we review previous research on ellipsis annotation in German treebanks in order to select the most appropriate one for (semi-)automatic production of canonical forms. Section 3 defines the clausal coordinate ellipsis phenomena and the annotation process employed to construct our new corpus. Section 4 presents a case study to illustrate how we checked the accuracy of all manually added information. In Sect. 5, we draw conclusions and address future work.

2   Related Work

For German, a variety of treebanks is available. A recent survey conducted by Dipper and Kübler [3] identifies TIGER and TüBa-D/Z as the most influential. In what follows, we will also discuss The German Reference Corpus (DeReKo; [19]), The Hamburg Dependency Treebank [4], Europarl [17], JRC-Acquis [28], and the Parallel Meaning Bank (PMB) [15]. The following review aims at finding a suitable encoding format that enables users to systematically evaluate CCE phenomena. In other words, it should be easy to retrieve/quantify specific elliptical constructions in each treebank.

Obviously, a format that provides input and output data for training all types of models, including statistical and machine learning models for CCE constructions, would be most advantageous. Without sufficient relevant input data, models will not have the necessary information to learn and make accurate predictions/decisions. Similarly, without output data, models cannot be evaluated for their performance and effectiveness. By *input*, we refer to the reduced sentences. Here, we use the term *non-canonical* to refer to the transliterated spoken/written text. By *output*, we refer to the fully reconstructed sentences—called the *canonical form*. The contrastive pair of terms is independent of individual treebank encoding formats (cf. Harbusch et al. [11]; similarly, but using a variant of Categorial Grammar for English, see [18], and for a psycholinguistic perspective in German, see Matzke et al. [21]). The primary goal of our treebank study is to determine whether corresponding canonical and non-canonical sentences can be obtained—ideally, automatically spelled out as input/output data.

Elliptical structures involve the omission of repeating constituents—not necessarily in their fully inflected form (cf. Gapping requires the reconstructed finite verbform to coincide with the subject in the second conjunct in the canonical form). The examples in the introductory section present the canonical form where the non-canonical version is represented by strikethrough wordforms with subscripts specifying the individual CCE phenomena; underlining allows easy identification of the remnants – inevitably necessary for any elision as an explicitly mentioned counterpart. In all treebanks, the non-canonical sentences are presented as string of leaves. In the structural descriptions, more or less explicit clues allow for the identification of elisions.

First, we examine the two most influential German treebanks: TIGER and TüBa-D/Z[2]. TIGER provides approximately 50,000 syntactic trees, while TüBa-D/Z is considerably larger. It contains over 120,000 trees. Both corpora are taken from German newspapers. TIGER is characterized by a very flat structure within noun phrases, which leaves certain generalizations implicit or even underspecified. In contrast, TüBa-D/Z employs a more hierarchical structure, which allows for more general queries (see [3]).

With respect to ellipses, TIGER uses *secondary edges* to explicitly indicate that a substructure is virtually the child of a node in the other conjunct as well. Figure 1 shows a case with three secondary edges in TIGER (cf. the sentence-initial MOdifier; the finite verbform with edge label HD; and the whole object clause with edge label OC below the S-node of the left conjunct below CS, which spans both ConJuncts). All secondary edges (in green) end at the S-node of the second conjunct to represent

---

[2] TüBa-D/S uses a very similar encoding scheme for spoken dialogues (see [26]). However, it does not provide either morphological or lemma specifications. So we focus on TüBa-D/Z.

Gapping. It is important to note that neither the linearization of the virtual constituents in the other conjunct nor inflectional accommodations are provided by secondary edges. Thus, the very elaborate concept of secondary edges in TIGER does not fully specify the canonical form. The underspecification of word order is desirable for Gapping, which is not limited to an identical word order in both conjuncts in German.

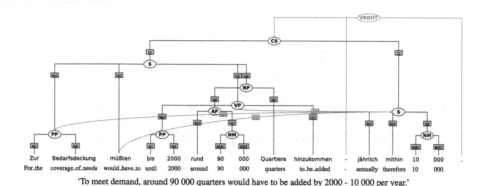

Fig. 1. Syntax tree with secondary edges (in green) from the TIGER treebank. (Color figure online)

TüBa-D/Z encodes the fixed placement of the verbal elements in a clause by topo-logical field categories (e.g., VF=frontfield, LK=left clause bracket, MF=midfield, VC-=verb complement, and NF=endfield below a SIMPX-node). There is no explicit encod-ing of ellipsis in TüBa-D/Z. Often, the syntactic category FKOORD is indicative of all kinds of ellipsis. However, it is important to stress that this category does not give rise to all elided constituents. The example in Fig. 2 illustrates a case of Gapping. FKO-ORD (in red) represents that all constituents above the categorial node should occur in both FKONJuncts. However, there is no indication for the fact that the subject (labeled ON) *sie* 'she' is also gapped. The fully reconstructed sentence: *[Besonders ... müsse] sie erreichbar sein und [besonders$_{fg}$ ... müsse$_{fg}$] sie$_{fg}$ telephonieren können.* can be classified either as a Gapping (with word order as in the left conjunct) or as an FCR phenomenon, where the word order has to be preserved (cf. subscript "fg").

Although TüBa-D/Z provides fewer clues for identifying elisions, we have chosen it as an interim solution over TIGER because of its richer encoding format and its consis-tent, albeit incomplete, encoding of CCE phenomena via the categorial node FKOORD.

DeReKo[3] is automatically annotated with various tools. Since we consider the encoding quality by human lexicographers in TüBa-D/Z to be higher than the auto-matically generated labels in DeReKo, we maintain our decision for TüBa-D/Z.

Represented as dependency structures, the Hamburg Dependency Treebank pro-vides 261,821 German sentences, Europarl 2,233,022 sentences. For both treebanks[4],

---

[3] https://www.ids-mannheim.de/digspra/kl/projekte/korpora/archiv-1/ with 50,6 billion words (2.2.2021).

[4] Inspect with https://weblicht.sfs.uni-tuebingen.de/Tundra.

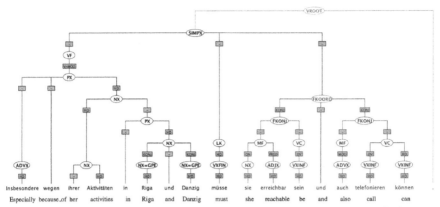

Fig. 2. Example from TüBa-D/Z that does not allow for the search within the complete range of CCE phenomena.

we examined the encoding/retrieval of CCE in coordinations. In all cases where a phrase is missing, the remaining parts of the phrase are represented as fragments. However, the format does not provide homogeneous cues that clearly identify the constituents to be reconstructed. Thus, we judged the reconstruction of canonical sentences to be more difficult/manual than in TüBa-D/Z.

JRC-Acquis is a freely available parallel corpus. It covers all twenty official languages of the European Union (EU). According to the authors, pairwise paragraph alignment information has been produced by two different aligners. More than 190 language-pair combinations are available. After a thorough inspection, we decided that the format is not suitable for the automatic reconstruction of canonical sentences.

Finally, we examined the Parallel Meaning Bank. It consists of sentences with corresponding syntactic and semantic representations for the languages: English, Dutch, German, Italian, Japanese, and Chinese. PMB provides fine-grained meaning representations for words, sentences, and texts. It aims to provide the most likely interpretation for a sentence, with a minimal use of underspecification. Version 4.0 (22.10.2021) comprises 2,844 German sentences. The corpus was found to be too small to capture all CCE phenomena. In the long run, the resource's sophisticated semantic encoding format of the resource may prove advantageous.

Thus, the final decision coincides with our preliminary choice of TüBa-D/Z. In the next section, we provide detailed information about our corpus.

3   Corpus Design and Annotations

Here, we outline the annotation format of our new corpus. First, we define more formally the cases of Clausal Coordinate Ellipsis that occur in German—but illustrated with English examples for better understanding. Then we present the new CCE corpus, in particular what information we have added to the sentences from TüBa-D/Z.

3.1 Annotated CCE Phenomena and Their Annotation Label

In the literature, four main types[5] of clause-level coordinative ellipsis are distinguished (see, e.g., [8, 12, 24]). Indicative of CCE is at least one missing constituent in one clausal conjunct that is present in the other one (dubbed *remnant* in the introduction; underlined in all examples). According to [8], CCE covers the following phenomena:

1. *Gapping* (cf. example (5)) and its special variants called *Stripping*, *Long Distance Gapping (LDG)* and *Subgapping* elide at least the verb in the second conjunct. However, the remnant and the reconstructed elided finite verbform do not have to match in their morphological features because of the subject-verb agreement with the subject in the second conjunct[6] (cf. examples (6) and (8)). Gapping often covers several constituents in the first conjunct. The case where only one of them remains is called Stripping. In German, a so-called *Stripping* particle—like *auch* 'as well'—must be added (see example (6))—which is not the case in Polish [11]. In LDG, the second conjunct consists of constituents stemming from different clauses (i.e., verb levels; see example (7); here, the main clause and the complement are elided). In Subgapping, not all verbs are elided (see example (8)).
2. *Forward Conjunction Reduction (FCR)* elides complete constituents with identical grammatical function in the two conjuncts in the left-periphery of the second conjunct (cf. example (9) and the relative clause in example (10); here, we illustrate the locality restriction of the periphery to the same clause by explicit S-brackets).
3. *Backward Conjunction reduction (BCR)*, also called *Right Node Raising (RNR)*, is almost a mirror image of FCR in German. It omits the right periphery of the second conjunct in the first conjunct; however, it can cut into constituents, i.e., it works word-by-word (lemma-identically) in the right periphery (see example (11); note that the example (13) in the following section is not a case of BCR together with FCR/Gapping because the latter cannot cut into the PP-constituent).
4. *Subject Gap in clauses with Finite/Fronted verb (SGF)* (see example (12)) elides the subject in the second conjunct if there is subject-verb inversion in the first conjunct. In German, the first constituent cannot be an object – which is not the case in Estonian, Hungarian, Polish, and Russian.

In the following examples, the italicized text with a subscript should be omitted. Here, we avoid strikethrough to improve readability. The subscripts indicate the elliptical mechanism at work: "g"=all types of Gapping, "f"=FCR, "b"=BCR, "s"=SGF. The reason for lumping all types of Gapping together stems from the assumption that gapping can be implemented as a recursive procedure, working top-down from the sentence root, as long as the verbform can be elided in the currently examined clause (cf. the procedure described in [7]). Only for Stripping, the Stripping particle must either be added in the case of ellipsis generation, or it must be identified during parsing. All other variants only correlate remnants and their elided counterparts per clause level. The examples in this section sketch only a single phenomenon. However, several CCE phenomena can occur at the same time (see example (2) in the Introduction section).

---

[5] SGF is not necessarily judged as an ellipsis phenomenon (see, e.g., [13] for a psycholinguistic argument).

[6] Originally, in [14], this licensing condition was referred to as *lemma-identity*.

(5) Henry <u>lives</u> in Boston and Peter *[lives]*$_g$ in Chicago.

(6) Henry <u>lives in Boston</u> and all his children *[live in Boston]*$_g$, too.

(7) My wife <u>wants to buy</u> a car, my son *[wants to buy]*$_g$ a motorcycle.

(8) The driver <u>was</u> killed and the passengers *[were]*$_g$ severely wounded.

(9) [^{S}<u>My sister</u> lives in Berlin and *[my sister]*$_f$ works in Frankfurt.]

(10) Amsterdam is the city [^{S}<u>where</u> Jan lives and *[where]*$_f$ Piet works].

(11) Anne arrived before one *[o'clock]*$_b$, and Susi left after three <u>o'clock</u>.

(12) Why did <u>you</u> leave but *[you]*$_s$ didn't warn me?

3.2   The CCE-Corpus Design

Our corpus should serve the purpose of evaluating a CCE-reconstruction process during parsing. So, we started by annotating the test part of TüBa-D/Z, i.e., the last 5,000 sentences. In the long run, we want to extend the set to all CCE constructions in TüBa-D/Z and other German corpora mentioned in the previous section. In the following, we present the two steps to obtain the parallel CCE corpus.

Step 1 (Search for all coordinated clauses – including asyndetons – in TüBa-D/Z). To obtain all CCE phenomena in TüBa-D/Z, we retrieve all sentences in TüBa-D/Z with a coordinating conjunction, or two (R-)SIMX encoded as siblings (asyndetons). The search returns 1,803 trees to examine. For all matches, we book-keep the unique sentence number from TüBa-D/Z in order to be able to supplement our corpus with either the XML structure provided by TüBa-D/Z or any syntactic tree structure generated by specific lowering procedures to get rid of crossing branches, respectively, to meet the conditions of different evaluation contexts.

Our treebank-search pattern intentionally overgeneralizes. Purely non-clausal cases (coordinations within ADJ, ADV, NP, PP, etc. phrases) will be identified in a subsequent task of this step. Example (13) illustrates such a case. Here, the NP-coordination is nested in a PP, i.e., FCR/Gapping is blocked. For these cases without CCE interpretation, the non-canonical sentence and an identical canonical version are paired in our corpus. We decided to leave the cases in the corpus, but to mark the whole sentence with "NoCCE". When evaluating the generation results, it is interesting to investigate if and which false locality assumptions are produced for a coordination. In addition, all cases are examined for possible CCE interpretations (see example (14) in the next step). All corresponding canonical forms are also listed as gold-standard variants.

(13) *Die   kommen [mit [Zeit und Ruhe]*$_{NP}$]*$_{PP}$ *nicht klar.*
    They come   with time and peace   not   clear.
    'They cannot handle time and peace.'

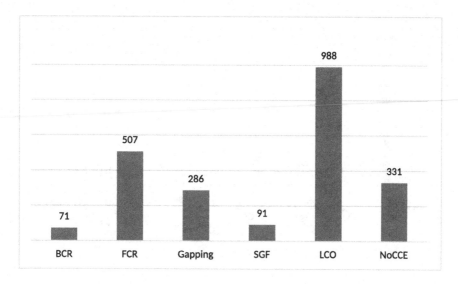

Fig. 3. Frequencies of individual CCE phenomena in our parallel CCE corpus.

Step 2 (Reconstruction of the CCE cases by assigning subscripts to the canonical form). All cases with at least one clausal coordination were manually inspected to encode subscripts for all variants of possible CCE phenomena (to improve reliability, both authors independently annotated the list; discrepancies and intricate cases beyond the CCE definition (cf. the corpus studies into CCE phenomena cited in the introduction) were corrected by mutual agreement).

(14) *Sie verloren Arbeit, [sie verloren]$_{fg}$ Wohnung und [sie verloren]$_{fg}$ Familie.*
      They lost   work,   [they lost]   housing and [they lost]   family.

As shown in the examples (3) and (4) in the introduction, cases with different analysis options are stored separately (cf. the columns "Gold 1", ..., "Gold n" in our corpus, where $n \leq 3$)[7]. In example (14), FCR or Gapping for the direct object is indicated by the subscript "fg" as one of the gold-standard option. In addition, another variant encodes the NP-coordination of *Arbeit, Wohnung und Familie* 'work, housing, and family' as the direct object. As mentioned above for "NoCCE"-variants, the sentence remains unaltered as canonical form. However, we classify these cases as "LCO" (= LocalCoOrdination) to distinguish such cases from "NoCCE".

To quickly focus on specific CCE phenomena in our corpus, we additionally provide the columns "FCR", "Gapping", 'BCR", "SGF", "LCO", and "NoCCE" filled with "0" or "1", respectively. Thus, one can easily extract a sub-corpus limited to the phenomena of current interest. For instance, example (13) has only a "1" in the "NoCCE" column, while (14) has a "1" in the "FCR", "Gapping", and "LCO" columns.

---

[7] In the CCE corpus, we do not spell out all word-order variants for Gapping, but rather adhere as closely as possible to the order in the first conjunct.

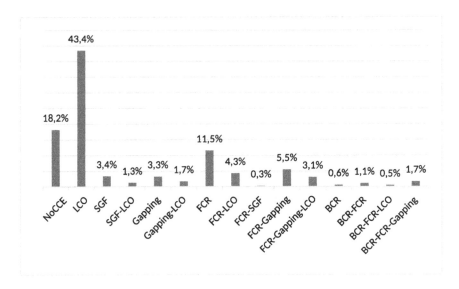

Fig. 4. Co-occurrence of CCE phenomena in parallel corpus.

3.3   A Brief Summary of the Features of Our Parallel CCE Corpus

As mentioned above, we currently cover the last 5,000 sentences of TüBa-D/Z with
at least one coordination (a total of 1,803 cases — including asyndetons). We have
assigned the canonical sentences with respect to a CCE phenomenon and/or with an
interpretation as local constituent coordination in NPs, PPs, or VPs, respectively.

Figure 3 shows the number of individual CCE phenomena in our collection. It is
important to note that the totals do not add up to the total number of sentences because
multiple phenomena can be active in the same sentence. Also, we provide all gold-
standard options at the same time. In the next section, we discuss the accuracy, i.e., the
correctness and completeness of the individual CCE encoding variants (cf. Figure 4 for
the frequencies of combinations of CCE phenomena in our parallel corpus).

4   An Evaluation with Our Parallel Corpus Approving Its Accuracy

To improve the accuracy of our corpus, we employ an indirect approach here: using a
constituency parser with parse-forest CCE-expansions. The hypothesis is that poor parsing results coincide with incomplete or incorrect canonical form encodings. Therefore,
these sentences are rechecked.

Constituency parsing of CCE sentences is challenging even for state-of-the-art parsers [16,23]. Additional procedures extend the derivation forest of the probabilistic
parser (using context-free rules resulting from a procedural extinction of XML-encoded
branch crossings, e.g., for punctuation; due to space limitations, we do not describe the

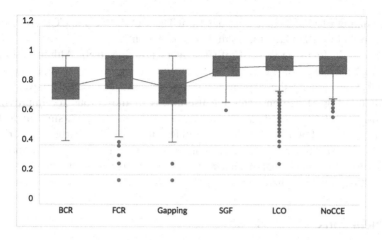

Fig. 5. Achieved BLEU-scores of canonical forms automatically reconstructed by OPIELLE per CCE phenomenon.

procedures here). OPIELLE[8] [22] reverses the procedure in Natural Language Genera-tion (NLG; see, e.g., [5]), where coordinative ellipsis is supposed not to result from the application of declarative grammar rules for clause formation, but from a procedural component that may block the overt expression of certain constituents (cf. ELLEIPO, a high-accurate CCE-generator [10]).

OPIELLE uses the tree forest produced by a constituency parser trained on 82,243 sentences of the TüBa-D/Z corpus—not overlapping with the CCE corpus. Triggered by a coordination, OPPIELLE examines the type of coordination to propose the best reconstructed canonical form. Empty spans, labeled with the adapted inflected form of the hypothesized remnant, represent elisions in the chart. These newly created neigh-borhoods can invoke further context-free rules that produce the canonical form of the input sentence. How to hypothesize empty spans in the parser's chart and how to verify these hypotheses—especially, when different phenomena occur simultaneously—must be omitted here for reasons of space.

The evaluation of OPIELLE uses *BLEU scores* (cf. [2]; for recent results in machine translation, see, e.g., [20]). Currently, we get 0.924 on the aligned corpus. Figure 5 visualizes the accuracy of the canonical forms generated by OPIELLE per CCE phe-nomenon category, measured in BLEU scores. Several rounds of detailed checking of all mismatches lead mainly to more local interpretation variants that we had overlooked

---

[8] OPIELLE stands for ELLEIPO read in reverse, indicating that it reverses the generation pro-cess. However, it is important to note that OPIELLE has to hypothesize the scope of a coor-dination along with all possible canonical forms, whereas ELLEIPO only tests conditions for omitting given constituents in the predefined scope of conjuncts. Due to space limitations, we have to skip all the details here. The advantages of OPIELLE are: (1) reusing a parser's initial chart data structure, and (2) using an efficient dynamic programming algorithm to produce reconstructed syntax trees for an entire input sentence. These factors contribute to the efficient production of canonical forms.

when translating FKOORD constructions from TüBa-D/Z. Specific CCE constructions are easier to find by analyzing the conjuncts in isolation.

Let us briefly focus on the task of CCE reconstruction itself. Although sentences with CCE phenomena are present in sufficient quantities in both written and spoken corpora, they are among the sentences with the lowest F1 scores. The evaluation of OPIELLE (cf. Fig. 5) demonstrates the usefulness of the corpus for improving the performance of a CCE-identification and -reconstruction during parsing. Importantly, OPIELLE produces few false positives. Similarly, the SGF reconstruction works very well. FCR suggestions are correct to a greater extent. On the other hand, Gapping and BCR pose more challenges. Upon closer inspection, it was verified that the system correctly hypothesizes CCE phenomena.

5 Conclusions

In summary, we have discussed which German treebank is best suited to represent the canonical forms of CCE phenomena to be provided in our parallel CCE corpus. We decided to extend TüBa-D/Z, a large treebank with a manually assigned/checked rich inventory and an ellipsis-encoding format that can be semi-automatically extended to canonical forms. In addition, we manually checked for the completeness of yielding all gold-standard options.

Exemplarily, we illustrated the usefulness of the new resource by sketching a component that extends the derivations of a constituency parser by the reconstructed elided words "borrowed" from the other conjunct (either the first or the second, or even both conjuncts at the same time). Our preliminary results suggest that further research on CCE may lead to additional improvements in a wide range of natural language processing tasks based on constituency parsing. As for future work, we are trying to increase the BLEU score of OPIELLE along with continuous improvements of the parallel corpus. As mentioned before, we are working on a broader collection of coordinations in TüBa-D/Z.

References

1. Brants, S., et al.: TIGER: linguistic interpretation of a German corpus. Res. Lang. Comput. **2**(4), 597–620 (2004)
2. Callison-Burch, C., Osborne, M., Koehn, P.: Re-evaluating the role of BLEU in machine translation research. In: Proceedings of the 11th Conference of the European Chapter of the Association for Computational Linguistics (EACL), Trento, Italy, pp. 249–256 (2006)
3. Dipper, S., Kübler, S.: German treebanks: TIGER and TüBa-D/Z. In: Ide, N., Pustejovsky, J. (eds.) Handbook of Linguistic Annotation, pp. 595–639. Springer, Dordrecht (2017). https://doi.org/10.1007/978-94-024-0881-2_22
4. Foth, K., Köhn, A., Beuck, N., Menzel, W.: Because size does matter: the Hamburg dependency treebank. Fachbereich Informatik, Universität Hamburg, Germany, Technical report (2014)
5. Gatt, A., Krahmer, E.: Survey of the state of the art in natural language generation: core tasks, applications and evaluation. J. AI Res. **61**(1), 65–170 (2018)

6. Harbusch, K.: Incremental sentence production inhibits clausal coordinate ellipsis: a treebank study into Dutch and German. Dialogue Discourse **2**(1), 313–332 (2011)

7. Harbusch, K., van Breugel, C., Koch, U., Kempen, G.: Interactive sentence combining and paraphrasing in support of integrated writing and grammar instruction: a new application area for natural language sentence generators. In: Proceedings of the 11th European Workshop on Natural Language Generation (ENLG), pp. 65–68. Saarbrücken, Germany (2007)

8. Harbusch, K., Kempen, G.: ELLEIPO: a module that computes coordinative ellipsis for language generators that don't. In: Proceedings of the 11th EACL: Posters & Demonstrations, Trento, Italy, pp. 115–118. (2006)

9. Harbusch, K., Kempen, G.: Clausal coordinate ellipsis in German: the TIGER treebank as a source of evidence. In: Proceedings of the 16th Nordic Conference of Computational Linguistics (NODALIDA 2007), Tartu, Estonia, pp. 81–88 (2007)

10. Harbusch, K., Kempen, G.: Generating clausal coordinate ellipsis multilingually: a uniform approach based on postediting. In: Proceedings of the 12th ENLG, Athens, Greece, pp. 138–145 (2009)

11. Harbusch, K., Memmesheimer, D., Franek, J., Kwasnik, W.: Polish clausal coordination with and without ellipsis. In: Guz, W., Szymanek, B. (eds.) Canonical and non-canonical structures in Polish, vol. 12, pp. 97–121. Wydawnictwo KUL, Lublin, Poland (2018)

12. Haspelmath, M.: Coordination. In: Shopen, T., (ed.) Language Typology and Linguistic Description, vol. 2, pp. 1–51, 2 edn. Cambridge University Press, Cambridge (2007)

13. Kempen, G.: Clausal coordination and coordinative ellipsis in a model of the speaker. Linguistics **47**(3), 653–696 (2009)

14. Kempen, G., Huijbers, P.: The lexicalization process in sentence production and naming: indirect election of words. Cognition **14**, 185–209 (1983)

15. Khullar, P., Majmundar, K., Shrivastava, M.: NoEl: an annotated corpus for noun ellipsis in English. In: Proceedings of the Twelfth Language Resources and Evaluation Conference, pp. 34–43. European Language Resources Association, Marseille, France (2020)

16. Kitaev, N., Cao, S., Klein, D.: Multilingual constituency parsing with self-attention and pre-training. In: Proceedings of the 57th Annual Meeting of the Association for Computational Linguistics, Florence, Italy, pp. 3499–3505 (2019)

17. Koehn, P.: Europarl: a parallel corpus for statistical machine translation. In: Proceedings of Machine Translation Summit X: Papers, Phuket, Thailand, pp. 79–86 (2005)

18. Kubota, Y., Levine, R.: Against ellipsis: arguments for the direct licensing of 'noncanonical' coordinations. Linguist. Philos. **38**, 521–576 (2015)

19. Kupietz, M., Lüngen, H., Diewald, N.: Das Gesamtkonzept des Deutschen Referenzkorpus DeReKo. In: Deppermann, A., Fandrych, C., Kupietz, M., Schmidt, T. (eds.) Korpora in der germanistischen Sprachwissenschaft: Mündlich, schriftlich, multimedial, pp. 1–28. de Gryter, Berlin, Germany/Boston, USA (2023)

20. Laskar, S.R., Manna, R., Pakray, P., Bandyopadhyay, S.: Investigation of multilingual neural machine translation for Indian languages. In: Proceedings of the 9th Workshop on Asian Translation, Gyeongju, Republic of Korea, pp. 78–81 (2022)

21. Matzke, M., Mai, H., Nager, W., Rüsseler, J., Münte, T.: The costs of freedom: an ERP - study of non-canonical sentences. Clin. Neurophysiol. **113**(6), 844–852 (2002)

22. Memmesheimer, D., Harbusch, K.: Exploring the feasibility of accurate reconstruction of clausal coordinate ellipsis in German. In: Experimental and Corpus-based Approaches to Ellipsis, 5th edn. (ECBAE 2023). University of Massachusetts, Amherst, MA, USA (2023)

23. Mrini, K., Dernoncourt, F., Tran, Q.H., Bui, T., Chang, W., Nakashole, N.: Rethinking self-attention: towards interpretability in neural parsing. In: Findings of the Association for Computational Linguistics: EMNLP 2020, pp. 731–742 (2020)

24. Muhonen, K., Purtonen, T.: Rule-based detection of clausal coordinate ellipsis. In: Proceedings of the 8th LREC, Istanbul, Turkey, pp. 1955–1959 (2012)

25. Shiraïshi, A., Abeillé, A., Hemforth, B., Miller, P.: Verbal mismatch in right-node raising. Glossa: J. Gen. Linguist. **4**(1) (2019)
26. Stegmann, R., Telljohann, H., Hinrichs, E.W.: Stylebook for the German Treebank in VERB-MOBIL. Technical report, 239, DFKI, Saarbrücken, Germany (2000)
27. Telljohann, H., Hinrichs, E.W., Kübler, S., Zinsmeister, H., Beck, K.: Stylebook for the Tübingen Treebank of Written German (TüBa-D/Z). Seminar fur Sprachwissenschaft, Universitat Tübingen, Germany, Technical report (2017)
28. Tiedemann, J.: Parallel data, tools and interfaces in OPUS. In: Proceedings of the 8h LREC, Istanbul, Turkey, pp. 2214–2218 (2012)

Speech

Identifying Subjects Wearing a Mask from the Speech by Means of Encoded Speech Representations

José Vicente Egas-López[2(✉)] [iD] and Gábor Gosztolya[1,2] [iD]

[1] Institute of Informatics, University of Szeged, Szeged, Hungary
ggabor@inf.u-szeged.hu
[2] ELKH-SZTE Research Group on Artificial Intelligence, Szeged, Hungary
egasj@inf.u-szeged.hu

Abstract. In the current pandemic situation, one of the tools used to fight Covid-19 is wearing face masks in specific public spaces. As previous research on the Mask Augsburg Speech Corpus had verified, speech might be eligible to automatically determine whether the speaker is wearing a mask or not, but the performance of classification models is far from perfect at the moment. This paper employs seven transformer-based wav2vec2 models on this dataset, extracting the activations from the lower, convolutional blocks as well as from the higher, contextualized transformer blocks. We show that models obtained via the self-supervised pre-training phase lead to similar performances with both activation types. However, after fine-tuning the models for direct ASR purposes, the performance achieved by the contextualized representations dropped significantly. Here, we report the highest Unweighted Average Recall value on this corpus that was achieved by a standalone method.

Keywords: speech analysis · surgical mask · wav2vec2 · computational paralinguistics · transformers

1 Introduction

Although with the introduction of vaccines, the peak of the COVID-19 pandemic seems to be over, the virus is still widely spread worldwide. To reduce the number of new infection cases, besides social distancing, an effective tool was the compulsory wearing of masks. Automatic speech analysis might offer a solution to enforce and monitor whether this regulation is kept. Furthermore, forensics and *'live'* communication between surgeons may also benefit from a system that could determine whether a subject is wearing a mask based on their speech [20]. This task belongs to the area of computational paralinguistics, which focuses on information present in speech other than the actual words uttered.

This research was supported by the Hungarian Ministry of Innovation and Technology NRDI Office (grant TKP2021-NVA-09) and by the Artificial Intelligence National Laboratory (MILAB, RRF-2.3.1-21-2022-00004).

K. Ekštein et al. (Eds.): TSD 2023, LNAI 14102, pp. 131–140, 2023.
https://doi.org/10.1007/978-3-031-40498-6_12

It is well known that both Automatic Speech Recognition (ASR) and Speech Verification techniques can be applied to the field of computational paralinguistics and pathological speech processing. For instance, x-vectors [22] (a former SOTA for Speaker Recognition) have been successfully adapted to classify emotions [15] and for sleepiness detection [11]. Furthermore, ASR-based solutions have also been adapted to these fields, e.g. for detecting states of dementia [8] and for speech emotion recognition [7].

Nowadays, feature-encoder approaches are increasingly being applied by researchers in Speech Recognition. For instance, ASR has benefited from wav2vec 2.0 [3,6] and BERT [10,21], which are able to generate rich contextual representations from large amounts of unlabeled instances. Wav2vec 2.0 has been successfully applied in computational paralinguistics and pathological speech tasks, where pre-trained models were used to assess the emotions [16], to screen Alzheimer's Disease [17], or even to detect COVID-19 [4] from the speech and the coughing of subjects. The wav2vec 2.0 method is said to be a state-of-the-art method for Speech Recognition, as it has the lowest Phonetic Error Rate (8.3%) [3] and lowest Word Error Rate (WER) (1.4%) [24] on two of the most popular speech datasets, namely TIMIT and LibriSpeech, respectively[1].

In this paper, we utilize several (pre-trained) wav2vec 2.0 speech encoder models and extract two distinct types of embeddings from them. The basis of wav2vec relies on the goal of extracting new types of input vectors from raw (unlabeled) audio, which can be used to build an acoustic model [19]. Wav2vec 2.0 relies on the same self-supervised principle, but it encodes speech representations from masked audio-segments and passes them to a transformer network that builds contextualized representations. This self-supervised approach was able to outperform traditional ASR systems that are based on transcribed audio, using much less labeled training data [3].

Our main contributions are: (i) Exploring the sufficiency of wav2vec 2.0 encoder (pre-trained) models for a task specifically related to computational paralinguistics; (ii) Analyzing the difference in the quality of the embeddings produced by each of the encoders; (iii) Applying a more straightforward method in order to avoid the time-consuming and computationally expensive fusion or ensemble approaches; (iv) Investigating the robustness of both language-domain matching and cross-lingual pre-trained encoders for the original language of the corpus utilized. Our approach gives the highest Unweighted Average Recall (UAR) score achieved by a stand-alone method on the above-mentioned corpus, while our performance stays above most of earlier studies that utilized fusion of methods as well.

2   Data

The Mask Augsburg Speech Corpus (MASC) comprises recordings of 32 German native speakers. The subjects were asked to perform specific types of tasks and their speech was recorded while wearing and not wearing a surgical mask. It

---

[1] Source: https://paperswithcode.com/task/speech-recognition/latest, Oct 2022.

has a total duration of 10 h, 9 min and 14 s, segmented into chunks of 1 s. The recordings have a sampling rate of 16 kHz. The total number of utterances is 36,554: 10,895 for train, 14,647 for development, and 11,012 for test. This task was also included in the Computational Paralinguistics Challenge (ComParE) in 2020 [20].

3   Self-supervised Learning

Self-supervised learning makes it possible for models to learn from orders of magnitude more data, which is the key to process patterns of less common phenomena. Usually, speech recognition systems require massive amounts of transcribed (labeled) training data to perform well [1]. A good way to tackle this is to *pre-train* neural networks, which allows a model to learn general representations from massive amounts of (labeled or unlabeled) information, and then it can be used for downstream tasks where the number of samples is limited. Now, we shall discuss concepts concerning pre-training, wav2vec, and wav2vec 2.0 frameworks.

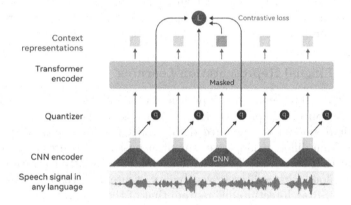

Fig. 1. Fine-tuned wav2vec 2.0 framework structure. Source: https://ai.facebook.com/blog

3.1   Pre-training and wav2vec

Pre-training consists of fitting a first neural network where huge amounts of data are available. The final weights from the training are then saved and this can be used to initialize a second neural network. This allows us to learn general representations from the large corpora; that is, representations that could be used for new tasks where the corpora size is limited.

wav2vec is basically a CNN that takes raw audio as input, and calculates a representation that can be fed into an ASR system. The wav2vec model is optimized to predict the next observations of a given speech sample. This would require us to accurately model the distribution of the data $p(x)$. To tackle this, the dimensions of the speech sample are first reduced by means of an encoder network; then a context network is used to predict the subsequent values [19].

3.2   wav2vec 2.0

This model, being the successor to wav2vec, also uses a self-supervised approach to learn representations from raw audio. Similar to wav2vec, it learns to predict the correct speech unit, but it does so for masked chunks of the audio. More specifically, wav2vec 2.0 encodes raw audio using a block of convolutional neural networks, then akin to masked language modeling, it masks small segments (shorter than phonemes) of the latent speech representations. These representations are fed to a quantizer as well as to a transformer network. The former selects a speech unit for the latent audio representation, while the latter appends data from the whole utterance. Afterwards, the transformer network is exposed to a contrastive loss function [3]. After pre-training has been finished, the model is fine-tuned using labeled data relying on a Connectionist Temporal Classification (CTC) loss, which is used for aligning sequences. After doing this, the model can be utilized for downstream speech recognition tasks. Figure 1 shows the layout of the (fine-tuned) wav2vec 2.0 structure described here.

3.3   Cross-Lingual Representation Learning

A multi-lingual representation approach based on wav2vec2 named XLSR (Cross-lingual Speech Representations) addresses the issue of languages even with a limited amount of *unlabeled* data. XLSR pre-trains a model on multiple corpora from different languages simultaneously. XLSR uses a similar DNN structure to that shown in Fig. 1, i.e. it is trained to jointly learn context representations along with a discrete vocabulary of latent speech audio representations. The XLSR architecture differs from that of the wav2vec2 in the quantization module: in XLRS it delivers multilingual quantized speech units, which are then fed to the transformer block as targets to learn via a contrastive task. This way, the model is capable of handling tokens across different languages [5].

3.4   wav2vec 2.0 for Feature Extraction

The outputs from the multi-layer convolutional block are the sequence of extracted feature vectors of the last convolutional layer, while the outputs from the second block comprise the sequence of the hidden states at the output of the last layer of the block. These two types of feature vectors, the *convolutional embeddings*, and the *contextualized representations* may carry relevant information related to speakers [13] and also other information encoded in the speech signal [6]. Due to this, they will be exploited for deriving features for our paralinguistic classification task (i.e. determining whether the speaker is wearing a mask). Of course, the actual classification step will be performed by another method, and wav2vec 2.0 will just be used for feature extraction. Also, since the number of wav2vec 2.0 embedding vectors is proportional to the length of the utterance, they have to be aggregated in some way, for which we simply took the mean of them over the time axis.

4   Experimental Setup

We extracted embeddings using seven different wav2vec 2.0 pre-trained models. The *first* is the so-called wav2vec2-base [3], which was pre-trained on 53k hours of unlabeled data of LibriSpeech, and it is not fine-tuned. The *second* is the wav2vec2-base-960h [3], pre-trained and fine-tuned using 960 h of labeled data. The *third* is a larger version of the previous one called wav2vec2-large-960h [3]. The main difference between these two is the number of parameters: *base* has 95 million, while *large* has 317 million parameters.

A cross-lingual wav2vec2 XLSR-53 model, trained on 53 different languages was our *fourth* model. Later, the successor of XLSR called XLS-R was introduced, which was pre-trained on about half million of hours of data in 128 languages [2]. Three different checkpoints of the model are available according to the number of parameters. Due to computational limitations, we just used the two smaller networks: wav2vec2-XLS-R-300M and wav2vec2-XLS-R-1B (300 million and 1 billion parameters, respectively). Lastly, to experiment with a model fine-tuned for the same language (i.e. German) as that in the MASC corpus, as the *seventh* model we employed the wav2vec2-XLSR-German-53 [9] encoder that was fine-tuned on the CommonVoice dataset.

We used a linear Support Vector Machine (SVM) for classification; the C complexity parameter was set in the range $10^{-5}, \ldots, 10^{1}$, based on the performance on the dev set. As for the metrics, since it is the standard on the MASC corpus, we relied on Unweighted Average Recall (UAR).

5   Results and Discussion

Table 1 shows the UAR scores for each of the pre-trained models with their corresponding type of embeddings. Every XLSR and XLS-R encoder surpassed the baseline scores from the ComParE challenge [20], except for the wav2vec2-base and -large models that gave slightly lower scores. This might be due to the size of the data and the language-domain of the pre-training process for these models. Also, fine-tuning itself relies on adjusting the inherited initialization weights to fit a function that performs well on a specific downstream task (i.e., speech recognition on a given language). While the adaptation to this new task is being performed, the fine-tuning process may drop some information that might not be relevant for ASR but may be crucial for applications unrelated to this field (such as pitch, speaking rate, irregularity and breathiness). This may be the reason for the superior performance scores of wav2vec2 models specifically fine-tuned for ASR.

Table 1. UAR (%) on the MASC dataset. Models marked with * denote fine-tuned models.

Model Type	Embedding Type	Dev	Test
wav2vec2-base	convolutional	67.6	70.1
	contextualized	63.3	69.6
wav2vec2-base-960h*	convolutional	67.6	69.1
	contextualized	53.0	54.6
wav2vec2-large-960h*	convolutional	65.0	70.8
	contextualized	52.1	53.7
Cross-Lingual Models			
XLSR-53	convolutional	67.9	71.9
	contextualized	68.2	72.1
XLS-R-300M	convolutional	69.0	71.9
	contextualized	**70.3**	**76.9**
XLS-R-1B	convolutional	68.2	73.0
	contextualized	66.1	74.6
XLSR-German-53*	convolutional	67.9	71.9
	contextualized	57.1	62.4

In the models and their representations, a trend can be seen: for the *base* and *fine-tuned* models (see Table 1), the convolutional embeddings had a better quality than their contextualized counterparts; but the opposite was the case for the other models. This is probably due to the convolutional embeddings being more sensitive to mono-lingual training than the contextualized representations. The two best UAR scores on the test set were achieved with the *XLS-R-300M* and *XLS-R-1B* models using the contextualized representations, while their convolutional features had slightly lower performances.

The baseline scores reported by the organizers of the ComParE Mask Sub-Challenge can be seen at the top of Table 2: a UAR of 70.8% that corresponds to a non-fused score, and a 71.8% score for the fusion of the best four configurations [20]. The same table shows the performances of the most competitive previous studies on the same task. Szep et al. [23] reported an UAR score of 80.1% on test, being the highest one on MASC at the time of writing, achieved by training multiple image classifiers, a K-fold cross-validation approach, along with an ensembling of both the CNN classifiers and distinct types of spectrograms. Similarly, Koike et al. [12] reported a UAR score of 77.5% by transfer learning, two kinds of augmentation techniques, and a fusion based on several snapshots taken during DNN training. Markitantov et al. [14] used ensembles of different CNN architectures along with raw data plus two types of frame-level audio representations. Lastly, Ristea et al. [18] made use of an ensemble of GANs with a cycle-consistency loss along with a data augmentation method based on those GANs.

Table 2. Results of former studies on the same MASC corpus. * denotes the scores achieved by a fusion of multiple models.

Features in the ComParE 2020 paper [20]	Dev	Test
ComParE functionals	62.6	66.9
Bag-of-Audio-Words (BoAW)	64.2	67.7
Deep Spectrum	63.4	70.8
AuDeep	64.4	66.6
Four-wise fusion*	–	71.8
Former Studies		
Szep et al.* [23]	70.5	80.1
Markitantov et al.* [14]	84.3	75.9
Ristea et al.* [18]	71.8	74.6
Koike et al.* [12]	–	77.5
This work		
XLS-R-300M	70.3	76.9

The above studies carried out late fusion or ensembling techniques in order to boost their configurations, which is a usual strategy for these kinds of challenges. Although these techniques might improve our performance scores as well, in this study we were interested in the results obtainable with wav2vec2 models alone. The method presented in our paper is more straightforward and led to competitive results while keeping the machine learning pipeline much simpler. Our best performance is competitive with [23] and [12], and it outperforms the other studies listed in Table 2.

Lastly, to investigate if there was any redundancy in the wav2vec 2.0 models, we further experimented with transforming the features obtained from the contextualized layer of the XLS-R-300M model by PCA and Gaussian random projection. We kept 90%, 95% and 99% of the information present in the original 512 attributes. The results (and the sizes of the transformed feature vectors) can be seen in Fig. 2. Clearly, features compressed by random projection produced lower scores than those using PCA (with the same feature vector lengths). Even by retaining 95% of the information, the resulting UAR values were relatively low (64.7–71.3%). When we kept most of the information (99%), the feature vectors became almost as large as those without compression (467–470 attributes out of the original 512). And although there was only a slight drop in performance on the development set (0.8% absolute in both cases), the test set UAR scores were significantly lower (74.26% and 73.46%, PCA and random projection, respectively). This, in our opinion, indicates that the feature vectors are redundant to such a low degree that even a slight compression (PCA 99%) leads to a notable drop in classification performance.

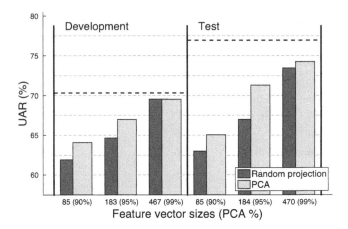

Fig. 2. UAR values after using PCA and random projection on the XLS-R-300M feature vectors. The dashed lines represent the scores obtained with all the attributes (i.e. Table 1)

6   Conclusions

Here, we investigated the effectiveness of employing wav-2-vec 2.0 embeddings for the identification of subjects wearing a mask based on their speech. We experimented with seven distinct pre-trained encoders for extracting convolutional and contextualized embeddings. It appears that the former were more sensitive to mono-lingual training than the latter, based on the quality difference of their corresponding feature vectors. The opposite occurred with the contextualized representations, which had lower performance scores when extracted using the fine-tuned models, which might discard information that is irrelevant for the ASR but important for computational paralinguistics. Based on the pre-trained cross-lingual encoders, both types of embeddings performed competitively and we demonstrated that the wav2vec2 architecture was capable of capturing speech and speaker traits that are relevant for paralinguistic approaches. Furthermore, we found that the number of training parameters is quite influential as models with 300 m provided better features than those with fewer (95 m) or more (1 billion) parameters both for pre-trained and fine-tuned encoders. Unlike earlier studies on the same dataset, we retained a simple yet effective and reproducible pipeline by dispensing with ensemble or fusion approaches while maintaining the competitiveness and even surpassing the performance score of most other studies. Overall, we achieved the highest UAR score (76.9%) reported on the MASC corpus obtained by a single (stand-alone) method.

References

1. Amodei, D., et al.: Deep speech 2: end-to-end speech recognition in English and mandarin. In: Proceedings of ICML, pp. 173–182 (2016)

2. Babu, A., et al.: XLS-R: self-supervised cross-lingual speech representation learning at scale. In: Proceedings of Interspeech, pp. 2278–2282 (2022)
3. Baevski, A., Zhou, Y., Mohamed, A., Auli, M.: wav2vec 2.0: a framework for self-supervised learning of speech representations. In: Advances in Neural Information Processing Systems, vol. 33, pp. 12449–12460 (2020)
4. Chen, X., Zhu, Q., Zhang, J., Dai, L.: Supervised and self-supervised pretraining based COVID-19 detection using acoustic breathing/cough/speech signals. In: Proceedings of ICASSP, pp. 561–565 (2022)
5. Conneau, A., Baevski, A., Collobert, R., Mohamed, A., Auli, M.: Unsupervised cross-lingual representation learning for speech recognition. In: Proceedings of Interspeech, pp. 2426–2430 (2021)
6. Fan, Z., Li, M., Zhou, S., Xu, B.: Exploring wav2vec 2.0 on speaker verification and language identification. In: Proceedings of Interspeech, pp. 1509–1513 (2021)
7. Feng, H., Ueno, S., Kawahara, T.: End-to-end speech emotion recognition combined with acoustic-to-word ASR model. In: Proceedings of Interspeech, pp. 501–505 (2020)
8. Fors, K., Fraser, K., Kokkinakis, D.: Automated syntactic analysis of language abilities in persons with mild and subjective cognitive impairment. In: Proceedings of MIE, pp. 705–709 (2018)
9. Grosman, J.: XLSR wav2vec2 German by Jonatas Grosman (2021)
10. Huang, W., Wu, C., Luo, S., Chen, K., Wang, H., Toda, T.: Speech recognition by simply fine-tuning BERT. In: Proceedings of ICASSP, pp. 7343–7347 (2021)
11. Huckvale, M., Beke, A., Ikushima, M.: Prediction of sleepiness ratings from voice by man and machine. In: Proceedings of Interspeech, pp. 4571–4575 (2020)
12. Koike, T., Qian, K., Schuller, B., Yamamoto, Y.: Learning higher representations from pre-trained deep models with data augmentation for the ComParE 2020 challenge mask task. In: Proceedings of Interspeech, pp. 2047–2051 (2020)
13. Lin, W.W., Mak, M.W.: Wav2Spk: a simple DNN architecture for learning speaker embeddings from waveforms. In: Proceedings of Interspeech, pp. 3211–3215 (2020)
14. Markitantov, M., Dresvyanskiy, D., Mamontov, D., Kaya, H., et al.: Ensembling end-to-end deep models for computational paralinguistics tasks: ComParE 2020 mask and breathing sub-challenges. In: Proceedings of Interspeech, pp. 2072–2076 (2020)
15. Pappagari, R., Wang, T., Villalba, J., Chen, N., Dehak, N.: X-vectors meet emotions: a study on dependencies between emotion and speaker verification. In: Proceedings of ICASSP, pp. 7169–7173 (2020)
16. Pepino, L., Riera, P., Ferrer, L.: Emotion recognition from speech using wav2vec 2.0 embeddings. In: Proceedings of Interspeech, pp. 3400–3404 (2021)
17. Qin, Y., et al.: Exploiting pre-trained ASR models for Alzheimer's disease recognition through spontaneous speech. arXiv preprint arXiv:2110.01493 (2021)
18. Ristea, N., Ionescu, R.: Are you wearing a mask? Improving mask detection from speech using augmentation by cycle-consistent GANs. In: Proceedings of Interspeech, pp. 2102–2106 (2020)
19. Schneider, S., Baevski, A., Collobert, R., Auli, M.: wav2vec: unsupervised pretraining for speech recognition. In: Proceedings of Interspeech, pp. 3465–3469 (2019)
20. Schuller, B.W., et al.: The INTERSPEECH 2020 computational paralinguistics challenge: elderly emotion, breathing & masks. In: Proceedings of Interspeech, Shanghai, China (2020)
21. Shin, J., Lee, Y., Jung, K.: Effective sentence scoring method using BERT for speech recognition. In: Proceedings of ACML, pp. 1081–1093 (2019)

22. Snyder, D., Garcia-Romero, D., Sell, G., Povey, D., Khudanpur, S.: X-vectors: robust DNN embeddings for speaker verification. In: Proceedings of ICASSP, pp. 5329–5333 (2018)
23. Szep, J., Hariri, S.: Paralinguistic classification of mask wearing by image classifiers and fusion. In: Proceedings of Interspeech, pp. 2087–2091 (2020)
24. Zhang, Y., et al.: Pushing the limits of semi-supervised learning for automatic speech recognition. arXiv preprint arXiv:2010.10504 (2020)

Impact of Including Pathological Speech in Pre-training on Pathology Detection

Tobias Weise[1,2(✉)], Andreas Maier[1], Kubilay Can Demir[2], Paula Andrea Pérez-Toro[1], Tomas Arias-Vergara[1], Björn Heismann[1], Elmar Nöth[1], Maria Schuster[3], and Seung Hee Yang[2]

[1] Pattern Recognition Lab, Friedrich-Alexander-Universität Erlangen-Nürnberg, Erlangen, Germany
tobias.weise@fau.de
[2] Speech and Language Processing Lab., Friedrich-Alexander-Universität Erlangen-Nürnberg, Erlangen, Germany
[3] Department of Otorhinolaryngology, Head and Neck Surgery, Ludwig-Maximilians University, Munich, Germany

Abstract. Transfer learning has achieved state-of-the-art performance across many different areas, requiring magnitudes less labeled data compared to traditional methods. Pre-trained weights are learned in a self-supervised way on large amounts of unlabeled data, which are fine-tuned for the desired downstream task using labeled data. An example of this in the speech domain is the wav2vec2.0 framework, which was originally designed for automatic speech recognition (ASR) but can also be fine-tuned for general sequence classification tasks.

This paper analyses the effects of including pathological speech during the pre-training of wav2vec2.0, where quantized speech representations are learned, on the performance of a fine-tuned pathology detection task. We show that this architecture can be successfully fine-tuned for cleft lip and palate (CLP) detection, where the best-performing model yields an F1-score of 82.3% when pre-trained on healthy speech only. Our experiments show, that including pathological speech during pre-training drastically degrades the performance on detection of the same pathology for which it was fine-tuned. The worst-performing model was pre-trained exclusively on CLP speech, resulting in an F1-score of 33.9%. Whilst performed experiments only focus on CLP, the magnitude of the results suggest, that other pathologies will also follow this trend.

Keywords: wav2vec2.0 · self-supervised learning · transformer · pathological speech

1 Introduction

Machine learning approaches for speech and language understanding have made great advances in recent years. OpenAI's generative pre-trained transformer (GPT), based on their GPT-3.5 model and called *ChatGPT*, has marked the most recent milestone for a very powerful large language model (LLM) that humans can interact with on a

© The Author(s), under exclusive license to Springer Nature Switzerland AG 2023
K. Ekštein et al. (Eds.): TSD 2023, LNAI 14102, pp. 141–153, 2023.
https://doi.org/10.1007/978-3-031-40498-6_13

chat basis, yielding stunning results when asked for answers to specific tasks. Tools like this can and are already a great assistant to humans in many different aspects and domains. An imagined and not-too-distant future, where similar tools form an essential and irreplaceable part of human everyday life is possible and even likely.

This raises an important question: how can people whose speech or language is impaired interact with such systems? According to the *Columbus Speech and Hearing* organization, communication disorders are among the most common disabilities in the US, with an estimated 7.6% of adults (ages 18 or older) reporting a problem with their voice/speech alone [5, 15]. It should be clear by now that solutions have to be developed in order to enable speech and language-based AI systems, and thus the underlying statistical models, to also deal with impaired inputs.

One of the two general paradigms employed to train such models (or in general in the machine learning domain) is called *supervised learning*. Here, the ground truth, i.e. typically human-created labels are available, enabling the training's optimization process to learn from information gained with these labels as a reference. It is common that labeled datasets contain relatively little amounts of data since labeling is typically a labor-intensive task, that can require human experts in the respective domains. This is especially true for pathological data, which is one of the reasons, next to data protection legislation, why these types of datasets are only scarcely available. Taking dysarthric speech data as an example: there are essentially only two English corpora used in this domain (*UA-Speech* and *TORGO*), which can lead to some problems, recently analyzed by Schu et al. [19].

On the other hand, there is the paradigm of *unsupervised* or more recently and accurately *self-supervised learning* (SSL). These are two names for the same principal idea, where the latter more accurately reflects how these types of statistical models have to learn from the available data alone: since supervised learning is often limited to small amounts of data, the contrasting idea for SSL is to utilize large amounts of unlabeled data. This implies that the only way for such models to learn is via a design that extracts underlying information from the data itself (i.e., self-supervised) and thus does not rely on ground truth labels. However, in the area of speech and language disorders, even relatively large unlabeled datasets, which would be required for self-supervised approaches, do not exist. A first step to remedy this problem was taken by Google in their *Project Euphonia* [13], where they aim at collecting all types of impaired or non-standard speech. Another problem arises in the evaluation of different SSL methods. For this reason, the authors of [7] introduced *LeBenchmark*, which introduces different wav2vec2.0 [2] models and contains spoken language understanding, speech translation, and emotion recognition in a reproducible framework.

Related or rather a combination of the two mentioned paradigms, is another very often utilized technique called *transfer learning*. It consists of taking features learned on one problem and utilizing them on another, but related problem. For instance, representations from a model that has learned quantized units of speech might be useful for a lot of possible tasks involving speech-relevant features. Furthermore, this concept contains two more terms that are commonly used: *pre-training* and *fine-tuning*. Both of these consequent training steps of a deep learning model typically use a similar network architecture, but pre-training is done on a large amount of unlabeled data, optimizing e.g. a contrastive objective in a self-supervised manner. Fine-tuning typically involves adding some new and trainable layers, as well as potentially freezing some of the previously learned layers (during pre-training). In combination with using a smaller and labeled dataset and e.g. a classification training objective, the fine-tuned model will adjust its weights accordingly for the desired downstream task.

Learning powerful representations that encode, for example, general features of human speech or language, has long been an area of research. Here, autoregressive models play an important role in capturing contextual information of a sequence, which is relevant for words in sentences and phonemes in speech respectively. Recently, *Transformers* utilizing the self-attention mechanism outperformed the previous state-of-the-art *Recurrent Neural Network* (RNN) architectures based on e.g. Long Short-Term Memory (LSTM) or Gated Recurrent Unit (GRU) cells. The two already mentioned architectures, GPT-3.5 and wav2vec2.0, also make use of Transformer blocks in their network design in order to encode context. The latter architecture is designed for learning speech representations during pre-training, which are then fine-tuned for ASR, however, other sequence classification tasks are also possible.

To our knowledge, this paper is the first to investigate the effects of including pathological speech during the pre-training step of wav2vec2.0. Evaluation is based on the performance of the downstream task of speech pathology detection, for which the individual models are fine-tuned. The data used in the five conducted experiments is a byproduct of a software called PEAKS [14], which was run by multiple institutions to aid speech therapists during the therapy of their patients. A subset of the overall recorded data from this software is used, containing children's speech that is impacted by CLP and healthy control speech of the same test that the children had to perform.

2   Related Works

Since the first introduction of wav2vec [18], and later its improved version wav2vec2.0, it has been applied to a wide range of speech-related tasks besides ASR, also in the pathological domain. In [4], Bayerl et al. investigate, which of the 12 Transformer layers of the wav2vec2.0 base model, combined with multi-task learning (MTL), yields the best representation in order to detect and differentiate six different types of stuttering in speech. Perez-Toro et al. [17] use the acoustic embeddings of wav2vec2.0 that were pre-trained on multi-lingual data, as well as linguistic embeddings from Bidirectional Encoder Representations from Transformers (BERT) [6] and a Robustly Optimized BERT Pretraining Approach (RoBERTa) [12], in order to investigate whether it is feasible to combine information from English and Spanish to discriminate Alzheimer's Disease (AD). Triantafyllopoulos et al. [20] compare eGeMAPS, ComParE, and multi-lingual wav2vec2-xlrs features for pre- and post-treatment detection of chronic obstructive pulmonary disease (COPD) patients. Here, the wav2vec embeddings, which can be seen as features, performed best when using speaker-level normalization of the data. The authors of [3] investigate how the different Transformer layer outputs of pre-trained wav2vec2.0 affect speech pathology detection results. They experiment with different datasets and pathologies (e.g. CLP, Parkinson's disease, oral squamous cell carcinoma), also in terms of cross-pathology and cross-healthy classification results.

Venugopalan et al. [21] compare the performance of three differently trained classifiers for predicting intelligibility labels, which is a common metric used in the therapy of patients with speech disorders. Their different classifiers are based on a convolutional network (CNN), non-semantic speech representations from CNNs trained with an unsupervised objective, and acoustic representations extracted from an ASR system trained on healthy speech. Lastly, the authors of [23] propose a novel method for the severity assessment of dysarthric speech by constructing a multi-task learning (MTL) objective during fine-tuning of a pre-trained wav2vec2.0. The main task during training is the severity assessment, which is jointly trained with an auxiliary ASR objective. Their proposed model outperforms baseline features like eGeMAPS, as well as the single-task learning model in the same scenario.

3 Framework: wav2vec2.0

The wav2vec2.0 architecture was introduced in 2020 as a significant improvement over the original wav2vec, taking raw audio as input in order to learn quantized speech representations that can be used for ASR. The authors were the first to show that pre-training on large amounts of (unlabeled) speech data, followed by fine-tuning on transcribed (labeled) speech can achieve state-of-the-art performance while using magnitudes less labeled data. After this general description, the remainder of this section will first go into more detail about the three core modules of the wav2vec2.0 architecture, before describing how these three parts are used for pre-training and fine-tuning. Differences between the *base* and *large* models will be highlighted during the relevant module descriptions.

Convolutional Local Encoder: The first part of the model involves encoding the raw audio waveform input, which is normalized to zero mean and unit variance, into vector representations on a discrete time scale. Its design does not change between the *base* and *large* model variants. In order to encode local features, this feature extractor consists of seven blocks, containing 1-dimensional temporal convolutions, followed by layer normalization and GELU activation [10].

The seven convolutional kernels have strides of $(5, 2, 2, 2, 2, 2, 2)$ and kernel widths of $(10, 3, 3, 3, 3, 2, 2)$, which equates to a frame hop of about 20 ms and a window size of 25 ms. This way, it is designed to mimic traditional audio signal processing methods in terms of feature computation (e.g. MFCCs). Assuming a raw waveform input to this encoder that was cropped to 3 s (i.e., 48 000 samples at 16 kHz sampling rate) of shape [B, 48 000], where B depends on the batch size. Then, the output shape of this encoder is [B, 147, 512] since the encoder has an output frequency 49 Hz, and the feature dimension consists of 512 channels.

Before the output of this feature extractor is fed to the contextualized feature encoder block, the feature dimension is linearly projected from 512 to 768 or 1024 respectively, dependent on whether the *base* or *large* model architecture is used. There is no activation function for this feature projection, but dropout ($p = 0.1$) is applied on its output.

Transformer Context Encoder: The motivation behind the second part of this framework is to encode a large context (i.e., capturing information from the entire sequence) with the local vector representations of a speech signal as its input.

In order to encode context, the first step is to compute a positional encoding. Here, wav2vec2.0 uses a convolutional layer, which acts as a relative positional embedding. This convolutional layer has a large kernel size of 128, a stride of 1, padding of 64, and 16 groups, followed by GELU activation. The receptive field of the original input to this convolution (i.e., local vector representations) is extended from 20 ms to $128 * 20\,\text{ms} = 2.5\,\text{s}$, by adding the computed relative positional embedding to it. Finally, layer normalization and dropout ($p = 0.1$) are again applied.

Next, the sequence of vectors with the larger receptive field is used as input for several consecutive transformer layers. The *base* wav2vec2.0 architecture utilizes 12 transformer blocks with 8 self-attention heads, whereas the *large* model uses 24 and 16 respectively. The output sequence of the final transformer layer, with each representation having both local and global information, is then used for a downstream task.

Vector Quantization Module: The last of the three parts of the wav2vec2.0 framework is trained during the pre-training of a model, in order to learn quantized speech representations in a self-supervised manner. For this, it takes the local encoder representations as input and consists of two codebooks with 320 entries each. Then, a linear mapping is applied to turn these vectors into logits, which are sampled from each codebook in a differentiable way via Gumbel-Softmax [11]. In order to arrive at the final discrete representation of the local encoder output, the two selected codes are concatenated in combination with a linear transformation. The purpose of this quantization module is to provide targets for the self-supervised learning objective during pre-training since there are in theory an infinite amount of possible embeddings output by the local encoder.

3.1   Pre-training

The goal of wav2vec2.0 pre-training is to learn representations of raw speech audio utilizing vector quantization into codebooks. This self-supervised approach is inspired by language models like BERT in the NLP domain. Here, next sentence prediction (NSP), as well as masked language modeling (MLM) are used on large amounts of text during pre-training. The principal idea behind the latter of these two techniques is applied by wav2vec2.0. A certain percentage of contiguous time steps from the local encoder representations are randomly masked and replaced with a trained feature vector. While pre-training the model, it learns to reproduce the quantized local encoder representations for the masked frames at the contextualized encoder's output. The overall pre-training objective is defined as

$$L = L_m + \alpha L_d \tag{1}$$

consisting of a contrastive (i.e., masking) and diversity loss term with a tuned hyperparameter α. The codebook diversity loss L_d is an augmentation for the vector quantization module in order to regularize the selection of codebook entries to be equal (see [2]). The contrastive loss is computed via

$$L_m = -\log \frac{\exp\left(\text{sim}\left(c_t, q_t\right)/\kappa\right)}{\sum_{\tilde{q}\in\tilde{Q}} \exp\left(\text{sim}\left(c_t, \tilde{q}\right)/\kappa\right)} \tag{2}$$

where $\mathrm{sim}(\mathbf{a}, \mathbf{b}) = \mathbf{a}^T\mathbf{b}/\|\mathbf{a}\|\|\mathbf{b}\|$ represents the cosine similarity between two vectors a, b. This contrastive task L_m, with masking at its core, requires identifying the original quantized latent audio representation (i.e., codebook entry) in a set of distractors for each masked time step. Equation 2 shows that this is implemented via cosine similarity $sim(c_t, q_t)$ between the contextualized encoder output vector c_t and the quantized local encoder vector q_t at time step t. Furthermore, $\tilde{q}$ represents a candidate representation $\in \tilde{Q}$, which is the union of a set of K distractors and q_t. These distractors are uniformly sampled from the other masked time steps belonging to the same utterance as q_t. The final contrastive loss is then the summation of L_m for all masked frames.

3.2 Fine-Tuning

Originally, wav2vec2.0 was fine-tuned for ASR based on the learned representations during pre-training. For this or for fine-tuning in general, **four** changes are made to the architecture compared to during pre-training:

First, discrete speech representations were learned during the pre-training step of the model, so the *vector quantization* module is not used. **Second**, the *local feature encoder*'s weights are frozen as a consequence of the previous statement. **Third**, masking is applied to the vector sequence after the *feature projection*. This masking is analogous to SpecAugment [16], where it is randomly applied in the time and/or frequency domain of the vector sequence, blanking the respective consecutive dimension values to zero. **Lastly**, a different objective function is optimized, by applying a random initialized linear projection to the *context encoder* output into C classes. Originally, with the ASR downstream task in mind, a CTC loss [9] is minimized with $C = 30$ (English character targets), including a word boundary token. However, wav2vec2.0 can be fine-tuned for a multitude of sequence classification tasks as well (see Sect. 2). For this, the same linear projection with e.g. $C = 2$ for a pathology detection task is added, in combination with optimizing a cross-entropy loss.

It should also be noted that recently, some works have analyzed using the output of intermediate transformer layers instead of the final output of the *context encoder* for certain downstream tasks since they seem to encode different types of relevant information (see Sect. 2).

4   Data

The data used for this work is a byproduct of a software called PEAKS. It is open-source and has been used by different institutions for scientific purposes across German-speaking regions since the year 2009. Therefore, its database contains a large number of recordings from patients with various pathologies or conditions. PEAKS can record and evaluate patients' speech during specific speaking tests. One of these tests is called *PLAKSS* [8], which is German and stands for "Psycholinguistische Analyse kindlicher Sprechstörungen", translating to "psycholinguistic analysis of childhood speech disorders". The name implies that this test is designed to evaluate children and it consists of slides that show pictograms, where the children have to name each of them, with an example slide being shown in Fig. 1b. Pictograms are chosen since it can not be

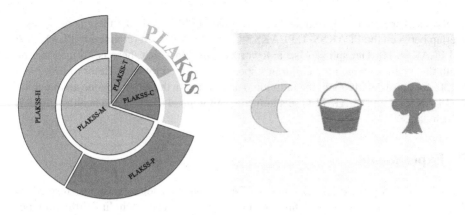

(a) PEAKS-PLAKSS data overview.

(b) PLAKSS picture example, taken from [14].

Fig. 1. The utilized data was recorded by the PEAKS software, containing children's speech performing the PLAKSS test.

assumed that all children are already able to read. Furthermore, this test is child appropriate since all objects are chosen such that children should already know them. In total, this test contains 97 words, which encompass all German phonemes in initial, medial, and final positions. Due to the possibility that children explain the pictograms with multiple words, or utter additional words in between the target words, PEAKS automatically segments the recordings at pauses longer than 1 s [14].

This test was performed by children with typical speech, as well as children suffering from CLP. This pathology is a congenital condition where an infant's lip or mouth does not form properly during fetal development, causing a split or opening in the lip or palate, alternating the child's speech. Children who are born with this pathology are typically operated in order to close the split(s) at ages ranging from 6 months to 2 years. CLP speech is typically evaluated holistically based on intelligibility via a five or seven point Likert scale. It should be noted, that it is technically not correct to state that CLP speech is being automatically detected or evaluated. Instead, and also true for this work, the impacts on the speech of a person, who was born with CLP but operated at an early age, can be automatically detected.

For the data used in this work, first, all PLAKSS data was extracted from the Server running the PEAKS software. In a second step, the data was scanned, analyzed, and pre-processed as described in [1]. This resulted in a total of 2557 children speakers (approximately 162 h), with 1666 being healthy controls and 891 children suffering from CLP (approximately 68 h and 44 h respectively). Audio recordings are labeled as either healthy speech or pathological speech and split into five different sets. PLAKSS-M is the union of the sets PLAKSS-H and PLAKSS-P, where the first contains all healthy speech and the latter all pathological speech. Furthermore, there are two more splits, called PLAKSS-C and PLAKSS-T, which are used for fine-tuning and testing of all five models respectively. For these two splits and PLAKSS-M, the percentage of pathological speech is approximately 35%. It should be noted, that there is no speaker overlap between the PLAKSS-T, PLAKSS-C, and PLAKSS-M (containing PLAKSS-P and PLAKSS-H) data splits. Also noteworthy is the fact that there is no information about the extent to which the children's speech is affected by CLP. Refer to Fig. 2 and Fig. 1a for more details about the individual data splits. In the latter, opaque areas behind the PLAKSS-T and PLAKSS-C sets indicate pathological (darker) and healthy (lighter) speech data.

5   Experiments

In total, five different experiments using different data split settings were performed for this work. The intention behind this is to analyze the effects of including different types of data (i.e., pathological vs. healthy) in the pre-training stage of wav2vec2.0 for the sequence classification task of pathology detection (i.e., CLP). An overall overview of the conducted experiment structure is depicted in Fig. 2.

In general, the structure of the experiments changes the data splits used during the pre-training stage and keeps the fine-tuning and testing data splits consistent. The only exception to this is BASELINE-1, where the idea is to explore if more data (i.e., PLAKSS-M in addition to the default PLAKSS-C split) used during fine-tuning will increase the performance in regard to pathology detection. The other baseline BASELINE-2 represents the default wav2vec2.0 sequence classification pipeline, where the model is pre-trained using librispeech-960h (read speech of English audio-books from volunteers) and fine-tuned with specific and labeled data from the intended downstream task. The other three experiments are intended to show the effects on pathology detection of pre-training wav2vec2.0 with a mixture of healthy and pathological, only healthy, and only pathological speech data.

It should be noted that there is a language difference between librispeech-960h (English) and the PEAKS-PLAKSS (German) data for the two baseline experiments. However, these two languages have a similar phonetic background, meaning that the learned speech representations during pre-training should still be relevant. There exists a multi-lingual (53 and 128 languages) version of wav2vec2.0, called *Cross-Lingual Speech Representations* (XLSR-53/128), which is based on the *large* version of wav2vec2.0. We did not use this version for the two baselines, since otherwise there would be an architectural difference between them and the other experiments, which would add an imbalance to the experiments. For these reasons, we decided to analyze the effects of including pathological speech during pre-training of the *basic* wav2vec2.0 architecture, which is used in all of our experiments.

In our experiments, we used the Transformer [22] implementation of this architecture for fine-tuning of all five models, as well as for the pre-trained model checkpoints on librispeech-960 for the two baselines. On the other hand, for pre-training of the PLAKSS-M, PLAKSS-H, and PLAKSS-P models, we used a repository[1] provided by the same authors of the Transformers library (Huggingface), specifically to pre-train wav2vec2.0 from scratch. All training was performed on a single NVIDIA RTX 3090 TI 24 GB GPU.

---

[1] https://github.com/huggingface/transformers/tree/main/examples/pytorch/speech-pretraining.

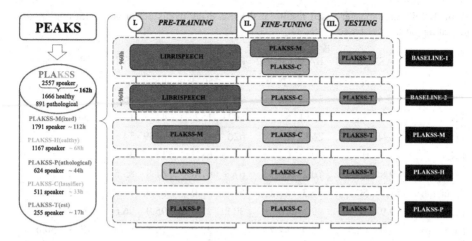

Fig. 2. The five experimental settings in this work, with the according data splits of the PEAKS-PLAKSS dataset, that were used in the respective stages of wav2vec2.0.

6 Results

After the five individual models were pre-trained and fine-tuned, their individual performance is evaluated based on the PEAKS-T data split of the PEAKS-PLAKSS dataset as shown in Fig. 2. To re-iterate, the downstream task that the wav2vec2.0 models are fine-tuned for is CLP detection (i.e., binary sequence classification). We report the confusion matrix, as well as the resulting accuracy, precision, recall, and F1-score for each experiment on a file- and speaker basis. Here, the speaker results are the average of the file-based results for all files of a given speaker in the PEAKS-T split. The detailed results can be found in Table 1. The most practical and balanced reported metric is the speaker-based F1-score. Based on this the best-performing model was PLAKSS-H with a score of 82.3%, and the worst-performing model was PLAKSS-P with 33.9%. The two baseline experiments performed very similarly with scores of 66.9% and 67.7% respectively, which is better than both the PLAKSS-M and PLAKSS-P, but worse than the PLAKSS-H model.

Table 1. File- and speaker-based results of the five experiments performed, with bold values indicating the speaker-based F1-Score.

Experiment	BASELINE-1		BASELINE-2		PLAKSS-P		PLAKSS-H		PLAKSS-M	
	file	speaker	file	speaker	file	speaker	file	speaker	file	speaker
TP	3284	89	3258	89	993	21	3154	86	1147	31
TN	2953	78	3014	81	5021	152	4158	132	5432	162
FP	2694	88	2633	85	626	14	1489	34	215	4
FN	4	0	30	0	2295	68	134	3	2141	58
Accuracy	69.8	65.5	70.2	66.7	67.3	67.8	81.8	85.5	73.6	75.7
Precision	54.9	50.3	55.3	51.2	61.3	60.0	67.9	71.7	84.2	88.6
Recall	99.9	100	99.1	100	30.2	23.6	95.9	96.6	34.9	34.8
F1-Score	70.9	**66.9**	71.0	**67.7**	40.5	**33.9**	79.5	**82.3**	49.3	**50.0**

7 Discussion

The results in Table 1 show, that it is possible to use wav2vec2.0 for CLP detection, confirming other research for different pathologies (see Sect. 2). However, the performance shows significant deviations across the five performed experiments.

Looking at the two baseline experiments first, it should be noted, that these models were pre-trained with librispeech-960h. This dataset contains recordings in English and no children's speech, whereas the fine-tuned downstream task is for German children's speech. However, a lot more speech was seen during pre-training compared to the PEAKS-PLAKSS-based models. Considering these facts, the performance is acceptable, with a notable high recall (i.e., almost no FN) for both baseline models. This could be explained by the fact that the model was able to learn typical speech representations during pre-training based on a different language (i.e., partially different phonemes) and the age of speakers. Especially the last factor could explain why the models are very sensitive to detecting CLP speech patterns during fine-tuning, leading to both models predicting a lot of healthy children's speech as CLP. In other words, the models might have learned, that as soon as it sees children's speech, it has a very high chance of being CLP, which stands in contrast with the fact that only approximately 35% of the PLAKSS-C data split (used for fine-tuning) is pathological speech. Comparing the results of the two baseline models reveals, that including more data in the fine-tuning stage of the two baseline models does not improve the performance significantly (66.9% versus 67.7%).

In contrast, the three PEAKS-PLAKSS-based experiments and resulting models saw only German children's speech during pre-training (healthy, pathological, and the union of both sets). The overall best performance across all five experiments was delivered in the PLAKSS-H setting, where pre-training is only performed on healthy speech from German-speaking children. The latter is likely the reason which gives it an edge over the two baseline models. Despite the fact that the final task is CLP detection, it is striking that including any form of pathological speech during pre-training degrades the downstream task's performance after fine-tuning significantly. This becomes evident when looking at PLAKSS-P and PLAKSS-M, the only two experiments that included pathological speech during pre-training, which yielded the worst overall performance across all experiments. Looking closer at the results of these two models, it seems that including pathological speech during pre-training leads to a higher FP, which could be due to the fact that the model learns pathologically distorted speech representations. This, in turn, might negatively influence the fine-tuning step of the wav2vec2.0 framework. Specifically, making it harder during this step to learn distinguishing and context-based features between healthy and pathological speech units within input audio sequences. This is highlighted by the fact that the PLAKSS-P experiment, where pre-training is solely based on CLP-impaired speech, yielded the overall worst performance, whereas PLAKSS-M had better performance, likely because healthy data was also present during its pre-training.

8   Conclusion

In general, we showed that fine-tuned wav2vec2.0 models can be used for CLP detection in the German language. We also confirmed, that fine-tuning wav2vec2.0 for sequence classification tasks (i.e., pathology detection) does not benefit greatly from including more labeled data during this step of the framework. However, results vary drastically based on what type of data is included during pre-training, where speech representations are learned in a contrastive way.

We showed, based on our experiments, that it is not advisable to include pathological speech during the pre-training step of wav2vec2.0 since it leads to significantly worse performance. For downstream tasks that revolve around pathology detection, our experiments indicate that it is best to pre-train only with healthy speech, ideally from the same domain. It should be noted, that our experiments only covered one specific pathology, but the magnitude of the results indicates that this is a trend, likely applicable to other pathologies as well.

For future works, it might be interesting to investigate changing the optimized pre-training objective in a way that could benefit from including pathological speech during this step of such a framework. For example, the contrastive optimization could be adjusted to the pathological domain by having the model learn to distinguish masked pathological time steps in a set of healthy distractors. However, as mentioned in the introduction, even in this scenario a basic problem remains: unlabeled, and thus ideally large, amounts of pathological speech data are not readily available, hampering potential progress.

Acknowledgements. We gratefully acknowledge funding for this study by Friedrich-Alexander-University Erlangen-Nuremberg, Medical Valley e.V. and Siemens Healthineers AG within the framework of d.hip campus.

References

1. Arasteh, S.T., Weise, T., Schuster, M., et al.: The effect of speech pathology on automatic speaker verification-a large-scale study. arXiv preprint arXiv:2204.06450 (2022)
2. Baevski, A., et al.: wav2vec 2.0: a framework for self-supervised learning of speech representations. In: Advances in Neural Information Processing Systems, vol. 33, pp. 12449–12460 (2020)
3. Baumann, I., Wagner, D., Braun, F., et al.: The importance of speech stimuli for pathologic speech classification. arXiv preprint arXiv:2210.15941 (2022)
4. Bayerl, S.P., Wagner, D., Nöth, E., Riedhammer, K.: Detecting dysfluencies in stuttering therapy using wav2vec 2.0. arXiv preprint arXiv:2204.03417 (2022)
5. Bhattacharyya, N.: The prevalence of voice problems among adults in the United States. Laryngoscope **124**(10), 2359–2362 (2014)
6. Devlin, J., Chang, M.W., Lee, K., Toutanova, K.: BERT: pre-training of deep bidirectional transformers for language understanding. arXiv preprint arXiv:1810.04805 (2018)
7. Evain, S., et al.: LeBenchmark: a reproducible framework for assessing self-supervised representation learning from speech. arXiv preprint arXiv:2104.11462 (2021)
8. Fox, A.: PLAKSS-psycholinguistische analyse kindlicher sprechstörungen. Swets & Zeitlinger, Frankfurt am Main (2002)
9. Graves, A., Fernández, S., Gomez, F., Schmidhuber, J.: Connectionist temporal classification: labelling unsegmented sequence data with recurrent neural networks. In: Proceedings of the 23rd International Conference on Machine Learning, pp. 369–376 (2006)
10. Hendrycks, D., Gimpel, K.: Gaussian error linear units (GELUs). arXiv preprint arXiv:1606.08415 (2016)
11. Jang, E., Gu, S., Poole, B.: Categorical reparameterization with gumbel-softmax. arXiv preprint arXiv:1611.01144 (2016)
12. Liu, Y., Ott, M., Goyal, N., Du, J., Joshi, M., et al.: RoBERTa: a robustly optimized BERT pretraining approach. arXiv preprint arXiv:1907.11692 (2019)
13. MacDonald, R.L., et al.: Disordered speech data collection: lessons learned at 1 million utterances from project euphonia. In: Proceedings of the Interspeech 2021, pp. 4833–4837 (2021). https://doi.org/10.21437/Interspeech.2021-697
14. Maier, A., Haderlein, T., et al.: PEAKS - a system for the automatic evaluation of voice and speech disorders. Speech Commun. **51**(5), 425–437 (2009)
15. Morris, M.A., Meier, S.K., Griffin, J.M., Branda, M.E., Phelan, S.M.: Prevalence and etiologies of adult communication disabilities in the United States: results from the 2012 National Health Interview Survey. Disabil. Health J. **9**(1), 140–144 (2016)
16. Park, D.S., Chan, W., et al.: SpecAugment: a simple data augmentation method for automatic speech recognition. arXiv preprint arXiv:1904.08779 (2019)
17. Pérez-Toro, P.A., et al.: Alzheimer's detection from English to Spanish using acoustic and linguistic embeddings. In: Proceedings of the Interspeech 2022, pp. 2483–2487 (2022)
18. Schneider, S., Baevski, A., Collobert, R., Auli, M.: wav2vec: unsupervised pre-training for speech recognition. arXiv preprint arXiv:1904.05862 (2019)
19. Schu, G., et al.: On using the UA-Speech and TORGO databases to validate automatic dysarthric speech classification approaches. arXiv preprint arXiv:2211.08833 (2022)
20. Triantafyllopoulos, A., et al.: Distinguishing between pre-and post-treatment in the speech of patients with chronic obstructive pulmonary disease. arXiv preprint arXiv:2207.12784 (2022)
21. Venugopalan, S., et al.: Comparing supervised models and learned speech representations for classifying intelligibility of disordered speech on selected phrases. arXiv preprint arXiv:2107.03985 (2021)

22. Wolf, T., Debut, L., et al.: Transformers: state-of-the-art natural language processing. In: Proceedings of the 2020 Conference on Empirical Methods in Natural Language Processing: System Demonstrations, pp. 38–45 (2020)
23. Yeo, E.J., Choi, K., Kim, S., Chung, M.: Automatic severity assessment of dysarthric speech by using self-supervised model with multi-task learning. arXiv preprint arXiv:2210.15387 (2022)

Morphological Tagging and Lemmatization of Spoken Corpora of Czech

Tomáš Jelínek[(⊠)]

Institute of the Czech National Corpus, Charles University, Prague, Czechia
tomas.jelinek@ff.cuni.cz

Abstract. We describe the annotation of corpora of spoken Czech according to a new annotation standard valid since the publication of the SYN2020 corpus of written Czech. The standard distinguishes lemmas and sublemmas, assigns a new attribute to verb forms, deals with multi-word tokens in an appropriate way. In order to annotate the corpora of spoken Czech by the same standard, new training data for the annotation of spoken text was created and experiments with using both written and spoken data for training a neural tagger were performed.

Keywords: corpus annotation · spoken corpora · Czech

1 Introduction

Corpora collecting informal spontaneous spoken Czech are an important part of the set of corpora that the Czech National Corpus (CNC) offers to its users. However, the corpora published so far either completely lack lemmatization and morphological annotation, or they are annotated using an annotation standard different from the one used for the corpora of written Czech. In this paper, we describe the work on automatic lemmatization and morphological annotation of spoken corpora based on the recently introduced annotation standard of the CNC corpora of Czech. We first describe the standard currently used for annotating the SYN2020 corpus [5] and other recent corpora of written Czech. We then describe the steps allowing for automatic annotation of spoken corpora with the same standard: creating a small amount of training data for spoken corpora, finding optimum parameters for the training of language models and tagging the corpora.

2 Corpus SYN2020 as the New Annotation Standard for Czech in the CNC

In 2020, the Czech National Corpus published a new representative corpus, SYN2020, with a new linguistic annotation that has become the new standard for annotating Czech corpora within CNC. This new annotation standard includes several important changes compared to earlier corpora aimed at providing users with tools for more accurate and easier corpus searches based on linguistic parameters. The new standard is described in detail in other papers (e.g. [2] or [6]), here we will only briefly mention some of its more important aspects: the introduction of the new attribute verbtag, the splitting of the original lemmas into lemma and sublemma attributes, and a new way of dealing with multiword tokens like *ses* 'himself+you are', *kdybych* 'if+I would'.

© The Author(s), under exclusive license to Springer Nature Switzerland AG 2023
K. Ekštein et al. (Eds.): TSD 2023, LNAI 14102, pp. 154–163, 2023.
https://doi.org/10.1007/978-3-031-40498-6_14

2.1   The Verbtag Attribute

For the SYN2020 corpus, a new attribute verbtag has been introduced, which is used to annotate morphological categories of verbs that can be expressed by auxiliary verbs. For example, grammatical person in Czech is in some cases expressed directly in the verb form (*čtu* 'I read', *čtěte* 'read_imper.2.pl.'), while in other forms it is expressed by an auxiliary verb, e.g. in the past indicative (*četla jsem* 'I read') or in the compound future (*bude číst* 'he/she will read'). In some older versions of the annotation of CNC written corpora (e.g. in the SYN2015 corpus), the person in the past participle (*četl* 'read') was not specified in morphological tags because the participle itself does not express person, in others (e.g. SYNv8) it was specified because users explicitly required this information. As Czech has a free word order, it can be difficult to differentiate between verbal modes or tenses using only simple corpus queries.

To address this problem, the verbtag attribute was created in the SYN2020 corpus grouping a number of verb categories in one place. The attribute is positional having six positions. The first position distinguishes whether the token is a main verb, an auxiliary verb, or no verb at all. The second position indicates the verb mode (e.g. indicative, conditional or imperative). The third position distinguishes active and passive verb forms. The fourth, fifth and sixth position expresses person, number and tense (pluperfect, past, present, future), respectively. Thus for the compound verb form of the future tense *budu číst* 'I will read', the form *budu* 'I will' is assigned the verbtag value "A——" (auxiliary verb) and the form *číst* 'read' (infinitive) gets the verbtag "VDA1SF" (main verb, indicative, active, 1st person, singular, future tense).

2.2   Lemma and Sublemma

The lemma attribute assigns the basic, dictionary form of a word to the token. However, the choice of a particular lemma for some word forms is not always clear; in case of stylistic or dialect variations, the lemma can be closer to the word form or more general. For example, we may assign to the non-standard variant *tejden* 'week' a standard lemma *týden* 'week' (where the vowel variation *ý/ej* in the middle of the word form is not manifested) or a more specific lemma *tejden*. Similarly, an archaic spelling, e.g. *theolog* 'theologian' may have the standard lemma *teolog* or the more specific lemma *theolog*. Both approaches have advantages and disadvantages, and in older CNC corpora annotations, different approaches were applied unsystematically for different words. To address this issue, a new sublemma attribute was introduced for the SYN2020 corpus. The sublemma is used for base forms as close as possible to a particular (sub)paradigm, distinguishing spelling or dialect variants, etc. A lemma is more general, it can contain several sublemmas. The choice of a lemma for a set of sublemmas corresponds to the standard sublemma; if there are more than one, it corresponds to the type that occurs most often in Czech. For example, the lemma *okénko* 'small window' thus encompasses the standard sublemma *okénko* and variant sublemmas *okýnko* and *vokýnko*.

2.3   Multiword Tokens

In many languages, there are cases where one text word represents several syntactic ones. In Romance languages, e.g., some combinations of a preposition and a definite article belong to this category, e.g. French *du* (*de+le*) 'of the' or Spanish *al* (*a+el*) 'to the'. In Czech, several such types of words exist. For example, the reflexive pronoun *se* 'herself' and a clitic form *s* of the auxiliary verb *být* 'to be' are frequently combined into a single text word *ses* (*se+jsi/s*) 'herself+you are'; some prepositions and pronouns can be combined into one text word, such as *na* 'to/on' and *co* 'what' into one text word *nač* (*na+co/č*) 'to+what'.

In Czech, syntactic word connected in this way can form syntactic relations with various words in a sentence, for example in the sentence *Jak ses chtěla bránit?* 'How did you want to defend yourself?' the reflexive *se* 'herself', part of the token *ses* belongs to the reflexive verb *bránit se* 'to defend oneself', whereas the syntactic word *s*, the short form of the auxiliary verb *být* 'to be', is an auxiliary verb forming a compound verb form with the past participle *chtěl* 'wanted'.

In older corpora, special morphological tags were used for words combining prepositions and pronouns (*nač*), or the clitic form of the verb *být* 'to be' with another word such as *přišels* (*přišel+jsi/s*) 'came + you are' or *ses* 'himself+you are'. For other types of multiword tokens, the presence of two syntactic words was not marked at all: *kdybych* 'if+I would' was marked only as the conjunction *kdyby* 'if'.

This problem has been solved for the SYN2020 corpus by continuing to treat these words as a single token, allowing them to be easily found in the corpus as a whole (one orthographic word), but assigning each part its own attributes (lemma, sublemma, tag, and verbtag). In the KonText search environment, these attributes are then displayed as multivalues, i.e. multiple attribute values for a single token separated by a vertical bar, so for example the word form *ses* 'herself+you are' is assigned the lemma *se|být* 'herself+to be'.

2.4   Uniform Tagging of Czech Corpora in CNC

After the publication of the SYN2020 corpus with the new annotation style, it was decided to use this new standard first for all newly published corpora of written Czech (SYN corpus, Online corpus, Net corpus), and then for the other corpora of Czech, first the corpora of spoken Czech and later the corpora of older Czech. The main advantage for the user will be a uniform annotation, and, moreover, the access to new attributes (sublemma, verbtag), which give the user wider possibilities of corpora search.

2.5   Universal Dependencies

Questions have been raised as to why CNC did not use Universal Dependencies (UD) [7] as its new markup standard, which would have made it easy to compare various phenomena studied in Czech with phenomena in other languages. This decision was made primarily because we consider it more appropriate for our users in the case of monolingual Czech corpora. For parallel corpora (InterCorp), there are already versions in the Universal Dependencies standard and future versions will probably use only this format.

For monolingual Czech corpora, however, we do not want to use this approach for several reasons. First of all, users are already used to the current system, augmented with sublemmas and verbtags, and according to our findings they are not interested in a radical change of the annotation system. With the current tagset, we are able to achieve a higher tagging success rate than the current tagging of Czech by the Universal Dependencies standard. The positional nature of the tagset currently used in CNC is better suited to work in the KonText search environment, as the (sometimes very long) UD morphological features are difficult to handle (both in queries and in working with frequencies). However, should users express their interest in corpora of written Czech in the UD standard, we could release such versions of these corpora in parallel.

3   Spoken Corpora of Czech in CNC

Since its very beginnings, CNC has published not only corpora of written Czech but also corpora of spoken Czech: transcribed audio recordings. It was first the Prague Spoken Corpus and the Brno Spoken Corpus, later the Oral Corpus and the Ortofon Corpus. Different standards of transcription from audio to written form were used for each corpus. The corpora either completely lack morphological annotation and lemmatization, or use morphological annotation based on older standards, different even from corpora of written Czech published at the same time (Ortofon).

3.1   The Ortofon Corpus

The Ortofon series of spoken Czech corpora ([4], see also [3]) offers the users two levels of transcription to search the corpus, in addition to the sound track: the phonetic transcription level and the "orthographic" level, where the phonetic transcription is converted into a Czech text more or less following Czech orthographic rules. Table 1 shows an example of two levels of transcription. However, even the orthographic level is noticeably different from the standard Czech written text: punctuation is missing (or used differently), capitalization is not used at the beginning of sentences/utterances, and, since the text faithfully corresponds to the recorded spoken utterances, it is often divided into shorter sections in which sometimes seemingly unrelated utterances of several speakers alternate. There is often a random repetition of words or phrases in the spoken texts.

Table 1. Orthographic and phonetic transcription

Ortographic	Phonetic	Quote
jsem	*sem*	'I am'
teď	*teǐ*	'now'
včera	*fčera*	'yesterday'
jsem	*səm*	'I am'
přijel	*přijel*	'come'
ze	*ze*	'from'
Skotska	*skocka*	'Scotland'
..	..	pause
a	*á*	'and'

The orthographic transcription is followed by morphological markup and lemmatization using the original PDT tagset (Prague Dependency Treebank 2.0, PDT 2.0, see [1]). This tagging was performed with the MorphoDita [10] tagger trained on PDT 2.0 data, with some changes made afterwards automatically (POS change for selected words, etc.). The annotation accuracy (correct identification of both lemma and tag) is approximately 94.1% (measured on a sample of 1000 tokens, not counting off-text tokens such as *(cinkání nádobí)* 'clinking dishes', which is only slightly lower than the annotation accuracy measured on PDT data with the same tagger (95.03%, see [10]). While the spoken data is significantly different from the written data, which reduces the success rate of the model, it has a relatively high proportion of unambiguous tokens (61.7%), which makes annotation easier (in written text, e.g. PDT, this ratio is much lower, just 41.2%). The average number of interpretations (lemmas and tag combinations) per token (again, counting only real words) is 2.26 (in PDT, it is 4.09 with the same tagset).

After the publication of the SYN2020 corpus, it was decided to tag the Ortofon series corpora by the same annotation standard. However, many words used in the Ortofon corpus were not contained in the lexicon used for annotating Czech text in CNC, training and test data for the annotation of spoken corpora was not available and the best practices for lemmatization and annotation of such corpora had not yet been found. These issues are addressed in the next section.

4   Annotating Spoken Corpora with the SYN2020 Standard

4.1   Extending the Lexicon to Improve the Coverage of the Spoken Corpora

Due to the complex and frequently homonymous nature of the Czech declension (e.g. case syncretism), we use a lexicon for the annotation process, because it significantly improves the results compared to the approach when a tagger (even based on neural networks) derives the properties of words from their spelling. First, all tokens are assigned all the possible combinations of lemmas and tags, then a tagger chooses one combination based on its language model.

However, the lexicon used for annotating written corpora is not sufficient for spoken corpora, since the spoken data include a large number of dialect variants; these need to be dealt with to improve the coverage of the text. Some of these dialect variants are formed by systematic substitutions of characters or character combinations in inflectional suffixes, e.g. *televiza* instead of *televize* 'television', *manželkó* instead of *manželkou* 'wife$_{instr.sg.}$', *jezdijou* instead of *jezdí* 'go$_{3.pl.}$'; or in the word stem, e.g. *Olomóc* instead of *Olomouc* 'Olomouc (town)', *mejvám* instead of *mívám* 'have$_{1.sg.}$'. We have developed a program which for each unknown word in the analyzed text checks whether the word, after removing dialect features, is already contained in the lexicon. If so, it puts this unknown word in a provisional dictionary and assigns it the same morphological categories as those assigned to the already known form. This provisional dictionary must then undergo a manual check. Thus ca. 3800 word forms were found in the Ortofon corpus data, of which 3500 were included in a special dictionary for spoken corpora after manual check.

4.2   Training Data for Spoken Corpus Annotation

To reliably annotate data with a machine learning-based tagger, it is best to train the tagger using data similar in nature to the data we want to annotate. If the training data differs too much from the target data, it reduces significantly the annotation accuracy. For example with the Morphodita neural tagger (see [9]), we achieve an accuracy of about 97.60% (percentage of correctly assigned lemmas, tags and verbtags) when annotating standard written data using a model trained on similar (standard written) data. When applying this model (i.e. trained on written data) on spoken data of the Ortofon corpus, we achieve a success rate of only 86.89%, which means that the tagger commits more than 5 times more errors. This is much lower than the accuracy of 94.10% (lemmas and tags) achieved with an older tagger trained on PDT 2.0. This is partly due to the fact that annotating with the SYN2020 corpus standard is a significantly more complex task than tagging with the PDT 2.0 standard: unambiguous tokens are only 27.6% in the newer annotation scheme, the average number of interpretations in the Ortofon data (combinations of lemma, tag and verbtag) per token is 5.11, i.e. more than twice as many as in the same data in the PDT annotation scheme.

Thus, it was decided to create training data for spoken corpora. However, as the manual annotation of large data is time consuming and expensive, we did not annotate a training corpus of the size comparable to the training corpus for the standard written language (which is a manually annotated corpus called Etalon with ca. 2.3 million word forms), but only less than 200,000 word forms that we wanted to supplement the written training data with to achieve better results.

Thus, 225 texts of similar length were chosen to create the training data for spoken Czech ("spoken Etalon"). From these texts, markup and tokens of non-linguistic nature were removed, mainly transcription annotations such as "(laugh)", "(clinking of dishes)", "(disturbing sound)". Words that were identified as multi-word tokens (i.e., text words containing multiple syntactic words) were split into tokens corresponding to syntactic words, since the tagger works with syntactic words in isolation, only merging them into a single token after annotation is complete.

An important step for the preparation of the training data for spoken Czech was the extension of the dictionary to include frequent word forms occurring in the spoken data that were not included in the existing dictionary. Thus, the original Morfflex dictionary (see [8]) was enriched, extended and adapted to the annotation needs of the SYN2020 corpus.

Furthermore, the spoken data was "manually" annotated in two phases. In the first phase, each token was assigned a set of lemma-tag combinations from which the annotators selected. Each text was annotated by two annotators, and differences between annotators were then decided by a third annotator. In the second phase, verbtags were assigned to unambiguous tags; where multiple possible verbtags were assigned (i.e., for verbs, especially for participles), again two annotators chose one verbtag from the menu; in case of disagreement, these verbtags were presented to a third annotator, who chose one of them.

This procedure resulted in 225 texts with an average length of approximately 800 tokens, for a total of 179,550 tokens, each token being assigned a lemma, a tag and a verbtag. We then work with this data to train and test models for the morphological annotation of spoken text.

4.3   Training Models for Lemmatization and Tagging of Spoken Text

As mentioned above, when a model trained only on written data is used to annotate spoken text, the annotation success rate is noticeably lower (86.89%) than when written data is annotated using the same model. On the other hand, if only spoken data is used, the result is also not satisfactory, although it is noticeably better (90.98%), because the newly created "etalon" for spoken data is too small for a reliable training. If we use both the written data and 90% of the newly created spoken data for training (10% remains for testing), the success rate increases to 92.25%. To make testing more reliable, every experiment is performed 5 times using different parts of the data and testing on the remaining parts (ideally, we would train 10 times, but every instance of the training requires 12–18 h and we lack computer time for all these experiments, even with parallel training). A success rate of 92.25% for non-standard language annotation is a good result, but we have tried to improve the success rate further. To do this, we took two routes (in addition to adjusting training settings which didn't yield any significant improvement): first, automatic adaptation of written training data to target spoken data, and second, experiments with the size of written training and development data. As we describe in the next two paragraphs, the experiments did lead to an increase in success rate, but less than we had hoped.

4.4   Written Data Adaptation

The differences between the written Etalon corpus and spoken data are significant. Sentences or rather speech sections in the spoken data do not begin with a capital letter, the text contains almost no punctuation, there are no numerals, words are often (more or less randomly) repeated etc. If it were possible to automatically modify the written training data to make it more similar to the data for which we want to train the model, the resulting model might be more successful. Therefore we developed a program that automatically alters written data removing some of the systematic differences. For example, the program removes capitalization at the beginning of a sentence and most of the punctuation (partly removing it entirely, partly replacing it with newlines marking the end of a speech segment), it replaces digits with numerals (where the correct form of the numeral can be unambiguously identified), and so on. In addition, a "bolder" version of the program mimics some other features of spoken language, such as occasional random repetition of words. A more conservative adaptation of the data improves the success rate of tagging spoken data by 0.4% (from 92.25% to 92.62%), a bolder adaptation improves the success rate less (92.38%): it seems that randomly adding irregularities to the input, even if similar to those in the target text, does not help the tagger.

4.5   Using Less Written Data

The second way to influence the success of the model we experimented with was the amount of written data used for training. Training of a neural tagger uses training data, on which the tagger repeatedly builds language models, and development data, on which the tagger continuously tests how correct the model is, adjusts the settings, and re-trains another model. Typically, about 80% of the data is used for training, 10%

for development data, and 10% is set aside for testing. In the case of using both written and spoken data, the amount of written data exceeds the spoken data available by more than ten times. However, we can set aside a random portion of the written data and not use it for training, development, or both, so that there is a better ratio of spoken to written data (but we will have less data overall). The table shows the results of experiments with both adapted data (see Sect. 4.4), with a reduced percentage (first column) of the written component in the training data (second column) or in the development data (third column). We always compute the accuracy of tagging lemmas, tags, and verbtags at the same time (Table 2).

Table 2. Experiments with using less written data

Percent	train	dev
100%	92.62%	92.62%
87.5%	92.69%	92.58%
75%	92.60%	92.68%
50%	92.26%	92.60%
25%	91.54%	92.41%
0%	91.06%	92.03%

The results presented in the table do not show a clear result on how to properly choose the size of the written data to train the model. The results for the proportion of written data between 100 and 75% for **train** and between 100 and 50% for **dev** are very similar, on the borderline of statistical error. The ideal proportion of data is probably somewhere between these boundaries, it would require more experiments to determine the best setting, and would probably not significantly affect the overall accuracy of the model anyway.

5   Outlook

The work on automatic tagging of spoken CNC corpora based on the SYN2020 corpus standard is not finished, there are still a number of steps to be taken. The newly created training data for the spoken corpora needs to be checked and errors removed. Frequent types of tagging errors can be addressed by specifically designed scripts. The annotation has to be finalized with sublemmas, multi-word tokens etc.

5.1   Correcting Errors in the Training Data

Our experience with manual annotation of written data shows that despite double manual tagging and subsequent adjudication by a third annotator in case of disagreement, many errors always remain in the data, which then decrease the reliability of the trained models and bias the measurement of their success. One method we use to correct this is to use several models trained with different settings and applied to the same text. Tokens for which several models agree on a reading which differs from the "gold" one (manually determined) need to be manually examined because they are more likely erroneous. Using 4 sets of models (in a 10-fold-cross-validation scheme) approx. 9000 such tokens were identified in our training data, out of which (measured on a small sample) approx. 15% are cases of errors in the gold data, 15% are limit cases requiring further investigation and approx. 30% are recurring tagging errors which could be corrected automatically (i.e. the gold data is correct).

5.2   Automatic Correction of Frequent Types of Tagging Errors

Some recurring errors in tagging are due to the nature of the spoken data, for example when a sentence is interrupted and an auxiliary verb finds itself in one segment and the rest of the compound verb form (e.g. a past participle) in another segment, the tagger frequently assigns an incorrect (from the global viewpoint) verbtag. This problem can be solved using simple programs (with some heuristics). This approach is able to remove several of the most frequent types of errors and increase the overall accuracy of the annotation.

5.3   Finalizing the Annotation

The annotation does not end with the tagging and lemmatization itself, we still need to automatically add additional information to the tokens. Sublemmas are assigned based on the lemma chosen by the tagger and the word form. Multi-word tokens (e.g. *ses* 'herself+to be', see Sect. 2.3), which are treated separately during the tagging phase, are merged into one token with two sets of attributes (lemma, tag, verbtag). Non-word tokens, e.g. *(cinkání nádobí)* 'cuttlery clinking' that has been removed to simplify the tagging has to be returned to the correct place. Only then will it be possible to publish the newly tagged spoken corpus.

6   Conclusion

This paper describes the process of annotating the Ortofon corpus, a corpus of spoken Czech, based on the SYN2020 annotation standard and the problems associated with annotating a transcription of spontaneous spoken language. The Ortofon corpus with the new markup will be published by September 2023. After that, other CNC spoken corpora may be published with the same standard. Eventually, written corpora of Czech from the first half of the twentieth century and Czech from the nineteenth century using the same annotation standard will be published. Uniform tagging of many corpora will make it easier for users to work with the corpora and to compare various phenomena across corpora.

Acknowledgements. This paper and the creation of the data have been supported by the Ministry of Education of the Czech Republic, through the project Czech National Corpus, no. LM2023044, and by Charles University through the Cooperatio programme (Linguistics).

References

1. Bejček, E., et al.: Prague Dependency Treebank 2.5-a revisited version of PDT 2.0. In: Proceedings of COLING 2012, pp. 231–246 (2012)
2. Jelínek, T., Křivan, J., Petkevič, V., Skoumalová, H., Šindlerová, J.: SYN2020: a new corpus of Czech with an innovated annotation. In: Ekštein, K., Pártl, F., Konopík, M. (eds.) TSD 2021. LNCS (LNAI), vol. 12848, pp. 48–59. Springer, Cham (2021). https://doi.org/10.1007/978-3-030-83527-9_4
3. Kopřivová, M., Goláňová, H., Klimešová, P., Lukeš, D.: Mapping diatopic and diachronic variation in spoken Czech: the ORTOFON and DIALEKT corpora. In: Proceedings of the Ninth International Conference on Language Resources and Evaluation (LREC 2014), pp. 376–382. European Language Resources Association (ELRA), Reykjavik (2014). http://www.lrec-conf.org/proceedings/lrec2014/pdf/252_Paper.pdf
4. Kopřivová, M., Laubeová, Z., Lukeš, D., Poukarová, P., škarpová, M.: ORTOFON: a corpus of informal spoken Czech with a multi-tier transcription, version 2. Czech National Corpus Institute, Prague, FF UK (2020). https://www.korpus.cz/
5. Křen, M., et al.: SYN2020: a representative corpus of written Czech. Czech National Corpus Institute, Prague, FF UK (2020). https://www.korpus.cz/
6. Křivan, J., šindlerová, J.: Změny v morfologické anotaci korpusáu řady syn: nové možnosti zkoumání české gramatiky a lexikonu. Slovo a slovesnost **83**(2), 122–145 (2022)
7. Nivre, J., et al.: Universal dependencies v2: an evergrowing multilingual treebank collection (2020)
8. Štěpánková, B., Mikulová, M., Hajič, J.: The MorfFlex dictionary of Czech as a source of linguistic data. In: Euralex XIX Proceedings Book: Lexicography for Inclusion, pp. 387–391 (2020)
9. Straka, M., Straková, J., Hajič, J.: Czech text processing with contextual embeddings: POS tagging, lemmatization, parsing and NER. In: Ekštein, K. (ed.) TSD 2019. LNCS (LNAI), vol. 11697, pp. 137–150. Springer, Cham (2019). https://doi.org/10.1007/978-3-030-27947-9_12
10. Straková, J., Straka, M., Hajič, J.: Open-source tools for morphology, lemmatization, POS tagging and named entity recognition. In: Proceedings of 52nd Annual Meeting of ACL: System Demonstrations, pp. 13–18 (2014)

HATS: An Open Data Set Integrating Human Perception Applied to the Evaluation of Automatic Speech Recognition Metrics

Thibault Bañeras-Roux[1]([✉]), Jane Wottawa[2], Mickael Rouvier[3], Teva Merlin[3], and Richard Dufour[1]

[1] LS2N, Nantes University, Nantes, France
{thibault.roux,richard.dufour}@univ-nantes.fr
[2] LIUM, Le Mans University, Le Mans, France
jane.wottawa@univ-lemans.fr
[3] LIA, Avignon University, Avignon, France
{mickael.rouvier,teva.merlin}@univ-avignon.fr

Abstract. Conventionally, Automatic Speech Recognition (ASR) systems are evaluated on their ability to correctly recognize each word contained in a speech signal. In this context, the word error rate (WER) metric is the reference for evaluating speech transcripts. Several studies have shown that this measure is too limited to correctly evaluate an ASR system, which has led to the proposal of other variants of metrics (weighted WER, BERTscore, semantic distance, etc.). However, they remain system-oriented, even when transcripts are intended for humans. In this paper, we firstly present **H**uman **A**ssessed **T**ranscription **S**ide-by-side (HATS), an original French manually annotated data set in terms of human perception of transcription errors produced by various ASR systems. 143 humans were asked to choose the best automatic transcription out of two hypotheses. We investigated the relationship between human preferences and various ASR evaluation metrics, including lexical and embedding-based ones, the latter being those that correlate supposedly the most with human perception.

Keywords: automatic speech recognition · evaluation metrics · human perception · manual annotation

1 Introduction

Automatic Speech Recognition (ASR) consists in transcribing speech into its textual form. Automatic transcriptions can for example be used by humans in the case of captioning, speech-to-text messages or by third systems such as virtual personal assistants. Since the emergence of hidden Markov model-based ASR systems [18] for processing continuous speech, the field has seen an important breakthrough with the use of deep neural networks and self-supervised methods

© The Author(s), under exclusive license to Springer Nature Switzerland AG 2023
K. Ekštein et al. (Eds.): TSD 2023, LNAI 14102, pp. 164–175, 2023.
https://doi.org/10.1007/978-3-031-40498-6_15

such as wav2vec [1] and HuBERT [16]. These approaches allow the extraction of meaningful information from speech without previously labeled data.

Faced with transcription errors, unlike a machine, a human is able to process the sentence anyway and extract its initial meaning if the latter was not fundamentally impacted by the errors. Errors in automatic transcriptions can arise due to various factors such as noise in the speech signal, speaker accents, or technical limitations. The question is to determine which errors are acceptable and which ones may cause comprehension difficulties for humans. Thus, it is crucial to evaluate the quality of automatic transcriptions based on their overall comprehensibility to humans.

Currently, the most commonly used metrics for evaluating ASR systems are the Word Error Rate (WER), which measures the number of incorrectly transcribed words, and the Character Error Rate (CER), which calculates the number of characters that differ from the reference transcription. However, many researchers [7,17,19,33] have pointed out issues with these metrics, such as the absence of error weighting or the lack of linguistic and semantic knowledge. Consequently, there has been a growing interest in developing new metrics to evaluate ASR systems. Some researchers [2,13,20,23,27] have therefore started exploring alternative metrics that can more accurately assess the quality and effectiveness of automatic transcriptions. Similarly, these issues have been observed in the field of machine translation. As a result, new metrics and data sets have been produced from multiple shared tasks [8,9,25,26]. Semantic-based metrics, such as BERTScore [34], have then been shown to be effective in evaluating the quality of machine-generated translations.

While these metrics are obtained automatically and are rather *machine-oriented*, human evaluations of ASR systems have been carried out in the past, which includes side-by-side experiments [13,19,21] where human subjects are asked to choose the best transcript among two options. These studies have also enabled assessing the quality of automatic metrics from a human perspective. The present study builds on these side-by-side experimental protocols, but instead of modifying the speech signal or text hypothesis with artificially generated errors, or using different outputs from the same ASR system to obtain two different hypotheses, our study utilizes the outputs of ten ASR systems with varying architectures applied on the same speech corpus. Furthermore, rigorous criteria were used to select the transcripts where choices are the harder in order to study metric and human behavior. The advantage of the side-by-side experiment is that the subject has to make a choice between two hypotheses, which does not allow for equality. In contrast to direct assessment, side-by-side experiments eliminate the potential bias of prior choices, allowing for consistent comparisons between transcriptions. By comparing human judgments to those of the metric, we can effectively evaluate its performance.

In this paper, we introduce HATS (Human-Assessed Transcription Side-by-Side), a new open data set of human preferences on erroneous transcriptions in French from various ASR architectures. As a second contribution, an original study is conducted using HATS to evaluate automatic metrics by analyzing their agreement with human assessments. Our objective is to identify the ASR evaluation metrics that most closely correlate with human perception. The HATS data set is freely released to the scientific community[1].

The paper is organized as follows: Sect. 2 describes the used ASR systems and the automatic metrics that will be evaluated based on their correlation with human perception. In Sect. 3, we present the implementation of the side-by-side human perception experiment, including the protocol for selecting the transcripts provided to human evaluators. Section 4 describes the HATS data set, while Sect. 5 presents a study on the quality of automatic metrics for evaluating transcription systems in relation to human perception. Finally, Sect. 6 provides the conclusion and future work.

2   Transcription Systems and ASR Evaluation Metrics

In Sect. 2.1, we present the different automatic speech recognition systems used to obtain the automatic transcriptions that constitute the HATS corpus. Then, in Sect. 2.2, we describe all the evaluation metrics applied to assess these transcriptions and evaluate them in relation to human perception.

2.1   Automatic Transcription Systems

In this study, we set up 8 end-to-end systems based on the Speechbrain toolkit [30] and 2 DNN-HMM-based systems using a state-of-the-art recipe[2] with the Kaldi toolkit [29]. The end-to-end ASR systems were trained using various self-supervised acoustic models. Seven of the systems used variants of the wav2vec2 models learned on French [6], and one system used the XLS-R-300m model. In the Kaldi pipeline systems, one of the systems included an extra rescoring step using a neural language model.

All ASR systems have been trained to process French using ESTER 1 and 2 [10,11], EPAC [5], ETAPE [15], REPERE [12] train corpora, as well as internal data. Taken together, the corpora represent approximately 940 h of audio comprised of radio and television broadcast data. The transcripts used to build our HATS corpus are extracted from the REPERE test set, which represents about 10 h of audio data.

2.2   Evaluation Metrics

We propose to focus on evaluation metrics for transcription systems that enable us to evaluate the systems at both lexical and semantic levels. First of all, we consider classical lexical metrics such as **Word Error Rate** and **Character Error Rate**.

Next, we examine three semantic metrics based on word embedding representations. The first one, **Embedding Error Rate (EmbER)** [2], is a WER

---

[1] https://github.com/thibault-roux/metric-evaluator.
[2] https://github.com/kaldi-asr/kaldi/blob/master/egs/librispeech/s5/.

where substitution errors are weighted according to the cosine distance between the reference and the substitute word embeddings obtained from fastText [3,14]. The second one, **SemDist** [20], involves calculating the cosine similarity between the reference and hypothesis using embeddings obtained at the sentence level. We compared different pre-trained word embedding models to evaluate their impact on the metric. Specifically, we compared using the embedding of the first token from CamemBERT [24] or FlauBERT [22] models, or using the output of a sentence embedding model (SentenceBERT [31]). Our last semantic metric is **BERTScore** [34], that computes a similarity score for each token in the candidate sentence with each token in the reference sentence using contextual embeddings. In our study, we use a multilingual BERT [4] and CamemBERT[3] [24] models (both CamemBERT-base and CamemBERT-large).

While text transcriptions are derived from speech, we also consider a **Phoneme Error Rate (PER)**, which involves computing the Levenshtein distance between reference and hypothesis sequences of phonemes obtained using a text-to-phoneme converter[4].

3   Side-by-Side Human Evaluation Protocol

This section describes the collection of the HATS corpus. The setup of the perceptual experiment is summarized in Sect. 3.1, while the protocol for selecting automatic transcripts for human evaluation is described in Sect. 3.2.

3.1   Perceptual Experiment

In our study, the side-by-side experiment involves presenting the subject with a manually transcribed reference to represent the speech, as well as two automatic transcripts, each produced by a different system. The automatic transcriptions always contained errors with respect to the reference. Each triplet comprised of a reference and two hypotheses is called a stimulus to which participants react in choosing their preferred hypothesis. In the following, *stimuli* refers to the different triplets to which each participant was confronted.

The experiment was made available online which allowed for participants to realize the task remotely and at their preferred time. They used a mouse to choose their preferred hypothesis according to the reference. The study utilized a minimal instruction protocol (See Fig. 1), which allowed participants to self-determine the criteria that were important in determining the quality of a transcript. Figure 1 illustrates the visual display presented to the subjects during the study. The reference was in written form only, in order to allow a comparison of ASR-oriented metrics and human perception within the same context [32].

To avoid possible biases, the stimuli were presented in a random order, both for the order of the triplet, and for the order of the two hypotheses (the same hypothesis can be A or B).

---

[3] https://camembert-model.fr.
[4] https://github.com/Remiphilius/PoemesProfonds.

Progress bar :

We call reference an exact transcription from audio to text.
We propose two hypotheses (called transcription) produced
by speech recognition systems. Choose the transcription
that seems to you the most acceptable.

Reference : how are you today patrick

Transcription 1 :

how are you two day patrick

Select transcription 1

Transcription 2 :

were you today patrick

Select transcription 2

Fig. 1. Screenshot from the side-by-side experiment.

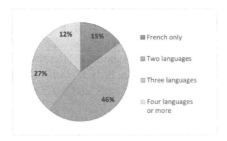

Fig. 2. Participant characterization in terms of number of spoken languages.

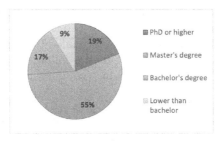

Fig. 3. Participant characterization in terms of level of education.

For this study, 143 online participants volunteered. Before starting with the
evaluation, they filled out a questionnaire helping to assess their age, spoken
languages, and level of education. All participants are fluent in French and have
an average age of 34 years with a standard deviation of 13.5 years. In Fig. 2 and
Fig. 3, we can see the distribution of number of spoken languages and educa-

tion level for our studied population. Each participant evaluated 50 triplets of transcripts in random order, for a total time of about 15 min per participant.

3.2 Protocol for Stimuli Selection

The transcription triplets coming from the REPERE test corpus were not selected randomly. In this study, we attach great importance to the selection of stimuli and we decided to study human behavior and metrics in complex situation, i.e. where humans have difficulties to choose the best transcription. In this context, the aim was to maximize the diversity of choices to be made: subjects had to choose among errors made by different systems (since it is unlikely that different systems produce identical errors). Also, it would be interesting to study the cases where the choice is easy for the automatic metrics, as well where ambiguous scores are obtained, or where two metrics disagree to determine which one of the two hypotheses is best.

Therefore, the following three criteria had to be respected: (1) both hypotheses must be different from each other and have at least one character that differs from the reference, (2) hypotheses from every system were contrasted with hypotheses from every other system, and (3) hypotheses pair selection was based on metric scores. The selection criteria (3) based on the metrics can be divided into three different categories: (A) each metric was compared to itself presenting either the same, a slightly different or a highly different score between the two hypotheses, (B) in both hypotheses the WER or CER were equal but WER or CER, EmbER, SemDist, BERTScore were different, (C) metrics were contrasted with opposing predictions of the better hypothesis (e.g. $WER_{(hypA)} > WER_{(hypB)}$ but $CER_{(hypA)} < CER_{(hypB)}$).

Table 1 illustrates how hypotheses were matched with concrete examples.

Table 1. Detail of some stimuli choice criteria with examples. The ϵ symbol represents a missing word.

Category	Metrics information	Reference	Hypothesis A	Hypothesis B
(A)	WER =	et on découvre les spectateurs / and they discover the spectators	ϵ on découvre les spectateurs / ϵ they discover the spectators	et on découvre les spectacles / and they discover the show
(A)	CER >	sur la vie politique / on the political life	ϵ la vie politique / ϵ the political life	c' la vie politique / t's the political life
(A)	SemDist >>	c' est á paris / it's at paris	ϵ est á paris / ϵ is at paris	c' est appau ϵ / it's atpau ϵ
(B)	WER = ; SemDist >	encore du rock / still rock	corps du rock / body of rock	encore du rok / still rok
(C)	WER ≠ BERTscore	où les passions sont si vives / where passions are so vivid	ϵ les patients sont si vive / ϵ the patients are so vivid	où les patients sont si vifs / where the patients are so lively

4   HATS Data Set

4.1   Corpus Description

The HATS data set includes 1,000 references, each with two different erroneous hypotheses generated by different ASR systems. The preferred choice of 143 human evaluators for each 50 reference-hypotheses triplets is recorded in this data set, resulting in a total of 7,150 annotations. Each triplet is evaluated by at least 7 participants.

To assess the level of agreement between raters, we calculate Fleiss' Kappa, which yields a value of 0.46. In 82% of the triplet cases, the agreement (See Eq. 1), is found to be at least 71.4%. Furthermore, in 60% of the triplet cases, the agreement reaches a minimum of 85.7%. This shows that the task is difficult, but that humans are still capable of determining a hypothesis as the best.

4.2   Methodology to Evaluate Metrics

Our method for evaluating metrics involved calculating the proportion of instances where both human annotators and the metric selected the same hypothesis as the best option. Subjects were not allowed to determine that the two hypotheses were equal. However, it is certain that there are cases where one hypothesis cannot be chosen and the subject chooses randomly. Since the number of annotators for each triplet is 90% of the time odd, there will still be a winning hypothesis due to chance. One strategy to overcome this problem may be to take into account only the cases where there is a consensus. In this study, we calculate a human agreement that corresponds to a percentage indicating consensus. This is calculated according to the following formula:

$$\frac{\max(A, B)}{A + B} \tag{1}$$

where A is the number of humans who select one hypothesis, and B is the number of humans who select the other one. When agreement is weak, agreement is close to 50%, and if all humans agree on the same hypothesis, agreement is 100%. A filter can be applied on the data set according to three values of agreement: **100%** (keep only triplets where all subjects agree), **70%**, or **0%** (no filter applied); which corresponds to 371, 819 and 1000 utterances respectively. The 70% threshold was chosen in order to have consistent annotator agreement even if not all participants answer in the same way [28]. Taking the predictions of the metrics as a starting point, we calculate the number of times that humans chose the best hypothesis based on the evaluated metric.

5   Evaluation of ASR Metrics from Human Perspective

Table 2 presents the results obtained by each metric according to the number of times they agree with human perception. Without surprise, the higher is the human agreement, the higher are the metrics performances. Unlike the results of previous studies [21], our study found that CER aligns more closely with human perception than WER. This divergence might be attributed to the use of written text as a reference in our perceptual experiment, rather than audio, or to intrinsic linguistic variations between French and English (French orthography contains a high number of silent letters compared to English).

Table 2. Performance of each metric according to their human agreement. **Full** means that no filter on agreement were applied on data set. The number in parentheses indicates the percentage of times the metric gave the same score to both hypotheses.

Agreement	100%	70%	0% (Full)
Word Error Rate	63% (23%)	53% (28%)	49% (28%)
Character Error Rate	77% (17%)	64% (21%)	60% (22%)
Embedding Error Rate	73% (12%)	62% (16%)	57% (17%)
BERTScore BERT-base-multilingual	84% (0%)	75% (1%)	70% (1%)
BERTScore CamemBERT-base	81% (0%)	72% (0%)	68% (0%)
BERTScore CamemBERT-large	80% (0%)	68% (0%)	65% (0%)
SemDist CamemBERT-base	86% (0%)	74% (0%)	70% (0%)
SemDist CamemBERT-large	80% (0%)	71% (0%)	67% (0%)
SemDist Sentence CamemBERT-base	86% (0%)	75% (0%)	71% (0%)
SemDist Sentence CamemBERT-large	90% (0%)	78% (0%)	73% (0%)
SemDist Sentence multilingual	76% (0%)	66% (0%)	62% (0%)
SemDist FlauBERT-base	65% (0%)	62% (0%)	59% (0%)
Phoneme Error Rate	80% (14%)	69% (16%)	64% (17%)

It is interesting to note that at phoneme level, PER performs well, better than WER and CER despite the fact that humans have made their choices based on text alone. It shows that humans seem to consider how sentences sound even while reading. This is especially true if sentences are contrasted with a reference.

Although hypotheses selected based on BERTScore using BERT-base-multilingual perform 8% better than those chosen with SemDist Sentence multilingual, it would be premature to conclude that the BERTScore strategy is superior for evaluating the quality of transcripts as both metrics use different embeddings. When comparing these metrics with the same embeddings, SemDist outperforms BERTScore using CamemBERT-base embeddings while SemDist has a similar performance with BERTScore using CamemBERT-large. This suggests that some embeddings are more optimized for specific metrics.

On the 70% and 0% agreement level, WER have performances close to a random choice. This is due to the fact that in our data set, many cases present hypotheses with the same WER, and equal predictions are considered as a failure of the metric since humans are able to faithfully select one hypothesis. Furthermore, we can observe that SemDist using FlauBERT-base embeddings performs

172 T. Bañeras-Roux et al.

worse than CER. This highlights the importance of carefully selecting embeddings and evaluating them on data sets like HATS before drawing conclusions about system performances at a semantic level. Based on our human-oriented data set, the best metric is SemDist using Sentence CamemBERT-large, which can be explained by the fact that this metric is based on embeddings specifically trained to maximize the similarity between sentences with similar meanings. It is worth noting that a large amount of annotated data is necessary to use these embedding-based metrics.

6   Conclusion and Perspectives

In this study, automatic evaluation metrics applied to transcriptions coming from different ASR systems were compared to human evaluation of different erroneous hypotheses according to one written reference. Our results show that SemDist with Sentence-BERT evaluates transcripts in a way that seems acceptable for human raters. If Sentence-BERT is not a possible option, BERTScore seems to be the second best option. This metric is more stable than SemDist on BERT embeddings. Nevertheless, if possible, metrics should be evaluated through data sets comprising also human annotations such as HATS.

Although these new evaluation methods are interesting in the context of ASR, the advantage of WER and CER metrics lies in their computational low-cost and interpretability of the score. Therefore, the next step could be to develop metrics that correlate with human perception while remaining interpretable.

As future work, an additional study could be conducted by replicating the current experiment using an audio reference instead of a textual reference, so that subjects do not have character information. This approach would enable us to examine any variations and if CER is still considered as better than the WER in a multimodal setting.

Limitations

The HATS data set is not necessarily representative of all kind of errors nor the most common because errors were selected applying strict criteria. In order to evaluate the representativeness of this data set, additional analyses with respect to the kind of errors that occur in each system's transcriptions have to be carried out.

Furthermore, conclusions drawn from this data set may be specific to the French language and may not generalize to other languages. Adding and comparing similar data sets in other languages would help to better understand the performance of metrics and human evaluations across different languages.

Ethics Statement. The aim of this paper is to propose a new method for evaluating speech-to-text systems that better aligns with human perception. However, the inherent subjectivity of transcription quality means that if we optimize systems to correlate only with the perception of the studied population, it could be inequitable if this perception does not generalize to the rest of the population.

References

1. Baevski, A., Zhou, Y., Mohamed, A., Auli, M.: wav2vec 2.0: a framework for self-supervised learning of speech representations. In: Advances in Neural Information Processing Systems, vol. 33, pp. 12449–12460 (2020)
2. Bañeras-Roux, T., Rouvier, M., Wottawa, J., Dufour, R.: Qualitative evaluation of language model rescoring in automatic speech recognition. In: Interspeech 2022 (2022)
3. Bojanowski, P., Grave, E., Joulin, A., Mikolov, T.: Enriching word vectors with subword information. Trans. Assoc. Comput. Linguist. **5**, 135–146 (2017)
4. Devlin, J., Chang, M.W., Lee, K., Toutanova, K.: Bert: pre-training of deep bidirectional transformers for language understanding. In: Proceedings of the 2019 Conference of the North American Chapter of the Association for Computational Linguistics: Human Language Technologies, Volume 1 (Long and Short Papers), pp. 4171–4186 (2019)
5. Esteve, Y., Bazillon, T., Antoine, J.Y., Béchet, F., Farinas, J.: The EPAC corpus: manual and automatic annotations of conversational speech in French broadcast news. In: International Conference on Language Resources and Evaluation (LREC) (2010)
6. Evain, S., et al.: Task agnostic and task specific self-supervised learning from speech with lebenchmark. In: Thirty-fifth Conference on Neural Information Processing Systems (NeurIPS 2021) (2021)
7. Favre, B., et al.: Automatic human utility evaluation of ASR systems: does WER really predict performance? In: INTERSPEECH, pp. 3463–3467 (2013)
8. Freitag, M., et al.: Results of WMT22 metrics shared task: stop using BLEU-neural metrics are better and more robust. In: Proceedings of the Seventh Conference on Machine Translation, Abu Dhabi. Association for Computational Linguistics (2022)
9. Freitag, M., et al.: Results of the WMT21 metrics shared task: evaluating metrics with expert-based human evaluations on TED and news domain. In: Proceedings of the Sixth Conference on Machine Translation, pp. 733–774 (2021)
10. Galliano, S., Geoffrois, E., Gravier, G., Bonastre, J.F., Mostefa, D., Choukri, K.: Corpus description of the ESTER evaluation campaign for the rich transcription of French broadcast news. In: International Conference on Language Resources and Evaluation (LREC), pp. 139–142 (2006)
11. Galliano, S., Gravier, G., Chaubard, L.: The ESTER 2 evaluation campaign for the rich transcription of French radio broadcasts. In: Tenth Annual Conference of the International Speech Communication Association (2009)
12. Giraudel, A., Carré, M., Mapelli, V., Kahn, J., Galibert, O., Quintard, L.: The REPERE corpus: a multimodal corpus for person recognition. In: International Conference on Language Resources and Evaluation (LREC), pp. 1102–1107 (2012)
13. Gordeeva, L., Ershov, V., Gulyaev, O., Kuralenok, I.: Meaning error rate: ASR domain-specific metric framework. In: Proceedings of the 27th ACM SIGKDD Conference on Knowledge Discovery & Data Mining, pp. 458–466 (2021)
14. Grave, É., Bojanowski, P., Gupta, P., Joulin, A., Mikolov, T.: Learning word vectors for 157 languages. In: Proceedings of the Eleventh International Conference on Language Resources and Evaluation (LREC 2018) (2018)
15. Gravier, G., Adda, G., Paulsson, N., Carré, M., Giraudel, A., Galibert, O.: The ETAPE corpus for the evaluation of speech-based TV content processing in the French language. In: International Conference on Language Resources and Evaluation (LREC), pp. 114–118 (2012)

16. Hsu, W.N., Bolte, B., Tsai, Y.H.H., Lakhotia, K., Salakhutdinov, R., Mohamed, A.: Hubert: self-supervised speech representation learning by masked prediction of hidden units. IEEE/ACM Trans. Audio Speech Lang. Process. **29**, 3451–3460 (2021)
17. Itoh, N., Kurata, G., Tachibana, R., Nishimura, M.: A metric for evaluating speech recognizer output based on human-perception model. In: Sixteenth Annual Conference of the International Speech Communication Association (2015)
18. Juang, B.H., Rabiner, L.R.: Hidden Markov models for speech recognition. Technometrics **33**(3), 251–272 (1991)
19. Kafle, S., Huenerfauth, M.: Evaluating the usability of automatically generated captions for people who are deaf or hard of hearing. In: Proceedings of the 19th International ACM SIGACCESS Conference on Computers and Accessibility, pp. 165–174 (2017)
20. Kim, S., et al.: Semantic distance: a new metric for ASR performance analysis towards spoken language understanding. In: Proceedings of the Interspeech 2021, pp. 1977–1981 (2021). https://doi.org/10.21437/Interspeech.2021-1929
21. Kim, S., et al.: Evaluating user perception of speech recognition system quality with semantic distance metric. In: Proceedings of the Interspeech 2022, pp. 3978–3982 (2022). https://doi.org/10.21437/Interspeech.2022-11144
22. Le, H., et al.: FlauBERT: unsupervised language model pre-training for French. In: Proceedings of the 12th Language Resources and Evaluation Conference, pp. 2479–2490 (2020)
23. Le, N.T., Servan, C., Lecouteux, B., Besacier, L.: Better evaluation of ASR in speech translation context using word embeddings. In: Proceedings of the Interspeech 2016, pp. 2538–2542 (2016). https://doi.org/10.21437/Interspeech.2016-464
24. Martin, L., et al.: CamemBERT: a tasty French language model. In: Proceedings of the 58th Annual Meeting of the Association for Computational Linguistics, pp. 7203–7219 (2020)
25. Mathur, N., Wei, J., Freitag, M., Ma, Q., Bojar, O.: Results of the WMT20 metrics shared task. In: Proceedings of the Fifth Conference on Machine Translation, pp. 688–725 (2020)
26. Mdhaffar, S., Estève, Y., Hernandez, N., Laurent, A., Dufour, R., Quiniou, S.: Qualitative evaluation of ASR adaptation in a lecture context: application to the pastel corpus. In: INTERSPEECH, pp. 569–573 (2019)
27. Nam, S., Fels, D.: Simulation of subjective closed captioning quality assessment using prediction models. Int. J. Semant. Comput. **13**(01), 45–65 (2019)
28. Nowak, S., Rüger, S.: How reliable are annotations via crowdsourcing: a study about inter-annotator agreement for multi-label image annotation. In: Proceedings of the International Conference on Multimedia Information Retrieval, pp. 557–566 (2010)
29. Povey, D., et al.: The Kaldi speech recognition toolkit. In: IEEE 2011 Workshop on Automatic Speech Recognition and Understanding (No. CONF). IEEE Signal Processing Society (2011)
30. Ravanelli, M., et al.: SpeechBrain: a general-purpose speech toolkit (2021). arXiv:2106.04624
31. Reimers, N., Gurevych, I.: Sentence-BERT: sentence embeddings using Siamese BERT-networks. In: Proceedings of the 2019 Conference on Empirical Methods in Natural Language Processing and the 9th International Joint Conference on Natural Language Processing (EMNLP-IJCNLP), pp. 3982–3992 (2019)

32. Vasilescu, I., Adda-Decker, M., Lamel, L.: Cross-lingual studies of ASR errors: paradigms for perceptual evaluations. In: Proceedings of the Eighth International Conference on Language Resources and Evaluation (LREC 2012), pp. 3511–3518 (2012)
33. Wang, Y.Y., Acero, A., Chelba, C.: Is word error rate a good indicator for spoken language understanding accuracy. In: 2003 IEEE Workshop on Automatic Speech Recognition and Understanding (IEEE Cat. No. 03EX721), pp. 577–582. IEEE (2003)
34. Zhang, T., Kishore, V., Wu, F., Weinberger, K.Q., Artzi, Y.: Bertscore: evaluating text generation with BERT. In: International Conference on Learning Representations (2020). https://openreview.net/forum?id=SkeHuCVFDr

Online Speaker Diarization Using Optimized SE-ResNet Architecture

Frantisek Kynych[✉], Jindrich Zdansky, Petr Cerva, and Lukas Mateju

Faculty of Mechatronics, Informatics and Interdisciplinary Studies,
Technical University of Liberec, Studentska 2, 461 17 Liberec, Czech Republic
`frantisek.kynych@tul.cz`

Abstract. A new approach to speaker diarization (SD) suitable for real-time processing of streamed data is presented in this work. It utilizes a modified residual network with squeeze-and-excitation blocks (SE-ResNet-34) for extraction of speaker embeddings. These speaker embeddings are calculated in an optimized way by using cached buffers and are subsequently used for voice activity detection (VAD) as well as for block-online k-means clustering with a look-ahead mechanism. All these processing steps are first evaluated separately on a development set compiled from recordings of Czech broadcast programs. The whole scheme is then compared to an offline reference approach on various speech databases that are publicly available and include data in various languages. On this data, our method yields results similar to the reference system while operating on a CPU with a low real-time factor (RTF) below 0.1 and a latency of around 5.5 s.

Keywords: Online speaker diarization · speaker embeddings · SE-ResNet · k-means clustering

1 Introduction

Speaker diarization (SD) is a process that answers the question "who spoke when" in a multi-speaker environment. Basically, two main possibilities exist for performing this task: in a) offline or b) streaming (online) mode. The input to the former (classic) scenario is usually formed by one speech recording. Its entire content can be processed without any strict limitations on computational demands, e.g., multiple passes through the data can be performed.

But today's world is accelerating; the data processing and information mining domains face a new challenge when their users ask for very quick results and analysis, ideally during the data flow. The increasing amount of data is organized into streams, which must be processed continuously.

Media monitoring is one of the typical applications where streamed data is processed. An example of such an application is our cloud platform for real-time transcription of TV and radio stations in several languages, including Czech, Slovak, Polish, and other predominantly Slavic languages.

K. Ekštein et al. (Eds.): TSD 2023, LNAI 14102, pp. 176–187, 2023.
https://doi.org/10.1007/978-3-031-40498-6_16

In this case, a diarization system allowing for real-time processing of the data streams must be employed. This system has to operate differently from its offline counterpart: it must be able to take in a sequence (stream) of frames on its input and provide a stream of speaker tags on its output. In consequence, there are additional limitations regarding namely the complexity of and computation demands on the used approach. Another important factor is latency: systems with a latency of around several seconds are considered to be online. In this case, there is an additional limitation on the context that can be processed in a given time step. Moreover, while offline SD can be improved by determining the number of speakers appearing in the data [2], this option is not available in most of our streamed scenarios (see Sect. 2).

In this work, we propose a new SD approach suitable for the above-mentioned real-time applications. Our approach processes the input data stream and produces a sequence of speaker embeddings on its output using SE-ResNet architecture optimized for online processing. These vectors are then filtered by a built-in voice activity detection module based on a single-layer binary classifier, and the remaining speech vectors are smoothed and clustered by the block-online k-means algorithm with a look-ahead mechanism.

At first, we evaluate and analyze the performance of individual phases of our method on a development set compiled from Czech TV/R recordings. Given all findings, this method is further evaluated on several publicly available datasets, including broadcast recordings in many languages.

2 Related Work

The early online SD approaches utilized hidden Markov models or Gaussian mixture models [11,34], and features such as the speaker factors [4]. More recently, the features used for online SD required a more robust speaker representation. Therefore, the i-vectors based on the total variability factor analysis began to be used [9,19,34].

These approaches were then surpassed by speaker embeddings produced by deep neural network architectures. These include d-vectors extracted mostly by long short-term memory recurrent neural networks [30,35] and x-vectors from the time-delay neural networks (TDNNs)[10].

The use of speaker embedding enables the option to perform diarization using various clustering algorithms. It is possible to use methods such as k-means [9,30], online naive clustering [30], or VBx algorithm with core samples selection [33]. Alternatively, a supervised model such as UIS-RNN [10,35] generating a sequence of speaker indices can be used instead of the conventional clustering. In addition to the aforementioned clustering-based diarization methods, recent work [31] has utilized a transformer transducer for detecting a change in speaker, extracting embeddings to represent speaker turns and clustering them using spectral clustering.

There has been a growing interest in end-to-end online diarization (EEND) approaches instead of the modular structure in recent years. Recent models are based on an x-vector extractor with incremental clustering [6], encoder-decoder-attractor-EEND architecture with either a speaker-tracing buffer [32] or an incremental transformer encoder [13]. These techniques can handle overlapped speech and have overcome the limitation of having a variable number of speakers. The EEND approach is currently limited by the amount of data from the target domain needed for training, and its performance gets significantly lower with a larger number of speakers.

3   Proposed Approach

Our method utilizes the optimized SE-ResNet-34 [14] architecture for the extraction of speaker embeddings. These embeddings are then used for VAD as well as for clustering. These three steps are all described in the following subsections.

3.1   Speaker Embedding Extraction

We introduce two key optimizations to the SE-ResNet-34 topology (see also Table 1). Firstly, the SE-blocks in the model incorporate buffers consisting of the last two vectors from the previously processed data. These buffers are concatenated to the input at the beginning of the subsequent time step. Secondly, we apply the stride operation even in the first set of SE-blocks, exclusively affecting the feature dimension while keeping the time dimension unchanged. A combination of both of these optimizations allows us to calculate one speaker embedding for every feature vector from the input stream with an RTF factor lower by an order of magnitude (see also Sect. 3.4). These embeddings are produced per block of the input signal, and their values are the same as if they were calculated within the conventional offline scenario.

The number of the SE-blocks is the same as in the ResNet-34 architecture, and their utilization adds global context information by weighting the channels of feature maps. Convolution layers are conventionally followed by batch normalization and ReLU activation function. In contrast to the SE-ResNet-34, we do not utilize the attention mechanism because it does not yield any performance gain on our development set.

After the optimized SE-blocks, local pooling is used to compute the means and variations of the frames, with a context of $t \pm 20$ frames. These features are fed to a fully connected layer from which the speaker embeddings are extracted. The model is trained using the AM-Softmax loss [29] to distinguish between N speakers. As input features, a 256-point log magnitude spectrogram is computed from every frame of the input signal. These spectrograms are locally mean-normalized (LFMN) over a sliding window with the context of $t \pm 40$ frames. The length of each frame is 25 ms with a shift of 12.5 ms.

Table 1. Structure of the proposed optimized SE-ResNet extractor. T stands for the input size ($2 \times 93 + 1$ in our case).

Stage	Kernel size	Stride	Output Size
LFMN	–	–	$256 \times T \times 1$
Cached Conv	$3 \times 3 \times 32$	1	$256 \times T \times 32$
Cached Res1	$3 \times 3 \times 32$	(4, 1)	$64 \times T \times 32$
Cached Res2	$3 \times 3 \times 64$	(4, 1)	$16 \times T \times 64$
Cached Res3	$3 \times 3 \times 128$	(4, 1)	$4 \times T \times 128$
Cached Res4	$3 \times 3 \times 256$	(4, 1)	$1 \times T \times 256$
Pooling	–	–	$T \times 512$
Linear	–	–	$T \times 512$

3.2   Voice Activity Detection

The proposed approach incorporates a computationally undemanding mechanism for voice activity detection. This method utilizes a simple binary classifier with one fully connected layer. This network is trained using the binary cross-entropy loss function. The input to the classifier is formed by a single speaker embedding without any additional context, and the output is smoothed with the aid of moving average smoothing.

The key point here is that we utilize one additional speaker representing a non-speech class during training of the above-mentioned embedding extractor. The embeddings representing the non-speech class then form one cluster, and the corresponding segments of the input signal can be filtered out using a single-layer classifier. Experimental evaluation of the described VAD module is presented in Sect. 5.3.

3.3   Block-Online K-Means Clustering with Look-Ahead

We apply a block-online k-means algorithm to cluster speakers using the speaker embeddings extracted by the optimized SE-ResNet architecture. We employ cosine distance in the clustering process as the AM-Softmax (used within the training of the embedding extractor) computes speaker probabilities based on the same distance measure.

To avoid high sensitivity of the clustering, first, the embeddings are smoothed with the aid of moving average within the context of $t \pm 40$. After smoothing, conventional k-means clustering is performed on a part of the input stream. Two parameters determine the size of this part: block size and look-ahead size. The block size corresponds to the number of vectors to which the speaker tags will be assigned in a given step of the diarization process, while look-ahead size states how many additional future (non-causal) vectors are used within the clustering process to improve its accuracy. The size of the data used for clustering is thus the block size plus look-ahead size. Note that each of the resulting clusters is represented by its centroid.

In the next step, we take into account only the resulting clusters whose numbers of associated vectors (embeddings) are higher than a defined threshold T_1. For each of these clusters, we compute its cosine distance from all of the existing centroids. If the distance to the closest existing centroid $c_{closest}$ is smaller than a threshold T_2 then the existing centroid is updated using linear interpolation with parameter α as $c_{closest} = (1 - \alpha)c_{closest} + \alpha c_{new}$. The remaining clusters with distances larger than T_2 represent new speakers.

The initial clusters are determined by a step size parameter. For example, if this value is set to 150, then every 150th embedding in the input sequence forms an initial cluster. Finally, all vectors within the given block (determined by the block size) are assigned the appropriate speaker tags according to their affiliations with individual existing clusters.

3.4   Latency and Real-Time Factor

The latency of the proposed clustering is mainly given by the block size and by the non-causal look-ahead mechanism. For example, the values of these two parameters that were established during the development process correspond to a latency value of 4.4 s. The next source of latency is the non-causal part of the context used by the embedding extractor. Its size is $t \pm 93$ frames, which creates an extraction latency of 1.17 s. The total latency of the proposed diarization scheme is thus around 5.5 s.

At the same time, it operates with an RTF value of around 0.06 on a CPU (measured on Intel® Core™ i7 CPU 9700K CPU @ 3.60 GHz using one thread) while the original SE-ResNet-34 achieves RTF around 1.1 on NVIDIA® GeForce GTX 1080 Ti. The RTF is computed as the ratio of processing time to real-time duration.

4   Experimental Setup

4.1   Development Data

A dataset covering 12.7 h of broadcast data in the Czech language is used for development purposes. It consists of 51 files with recordings containing a minimum of 2 speakers and a maximum of 15 speakers (4.2 speakers on average). These recordings contain both clean speech segments and segments with music, background noise, jingles, and advertisements.

4.2   Evaluation Metrics

The equal error rate (EER) is employed for a comparison of different speaker embedding extractors in the speaker verification task. The diarization accuracy of our system on the development data is measured by word-level diarization error rate (WDER). The motivation for using this metric stems from the fact that it is more important for our target application to assign the word to the correct speaker than to retrieve the exact time of the speaker change point. WDER represents the percentage of words with the correct speaker assigned.

Moreover, in Sect. 6, the standard diarization error rate (DER) is used for the comparison on other datasets that are publicly available. The DER consists of false alarm, missed speech, and speaker confusion and is computed using version 1.1.0 of the dscore[1] tool without any forgiveness collar. It also includes overlapped speech segments.

4.3 Reference System for Diarization

The diarization system is based on the Speechbrain (version 0.5.13) approach [7], which utilizes the ECAPA-TDNN [8] for embedding extraction, followed by spectral clustering. The embedding extractor uses 80-dimensional log Mel filterbank energies from the recording and mean normalizes them in the current segment. These features are extracted with a sliding window with a length of 1.5 s and a 0.5-second shift. After the embedding extraction, we use the unnormalized spectral clustering. The dataset used for training the ECAPA-TDNN model is the same as for our approach (see Sect. 5.1).

5 Experimental Evaluation

5.1 Speaker Embedding Extraction

In the first experiment, we compare the results on the speaker verification task of the original SE-ResNet-34 architecture, the proposed optimized SE-ResNet topology, and the ECAPA-TDNN reference system. All of these systems have been trained using the same data. This fact allows us to compare them directly.

The training data consists of VoxCeleb2 [5], "train-clean-360" subset of LibriSpeech [24], Czech microphone recordings, and part of CHiME-4 dataset [28] for the non-speech class. The LibriSpeech and Czech data have also been augmented with a combination of noise and reverberation, similar to that described in [21]. During training, the audio was randomly augmented with the MUSAN corpus [26] and with room impulse response simulations of small and medium rooms from [15]. A total number of 7,838 speakers have been used for training, where one additional class has represented noises.

The SE-ResNet model has been trained within 12 epochs using the AdamW optimizer with a learning rate of 0.003 and default torch parameters. We have employed the step learning rate decay with a 0.1 gamma value and lowered the learning rate every 5 epochs. The margin has been set to 0.3 and the scale factor to 15 in the AM-Softmax.

The datasets used for the evaluation represent the cleaned VoxCeleb1-E (extended), VoxCeleb1-H (hard) [23], TIMIT [12] and its augmented versions.

---
[1] https://github.com/nryant/dscore.

The applied augmentation strategies on TIMIT gradually increase the complexity of the speaker verification task. The original TIMIT version contains only noiseless signals. The Anechoic variant then includes anechoic and reverberated signals. These two augmentations are described in depth in [21]. The next Codecs version is described in [22], where the dataset is copied seven times, and different codecs are used for the augmentation of each copy. The last and most difficult Noisy version combines reverberation and noise for augmentation as proposed in [20].

The obtained results are compared in Table 2. The proposed online SE-ResNet architecture yields similar results as the original offline ResNet-34 topology and the reference ECAPA-TDNN system for the original TIMIT and its Anechoic version. At the same time, it has worse performance on both VoxCeleb datasets and TIMIT with more difficult augmentations, which is caused by its lower number of parameters.

Table 2. EER [%] for different architectures yielded in the speaker verification task on the VoxCeleb, TIMIT and its several augmented versions.

Datasets	SE-ResNet-34	proposed	ECAPA-TDNN
	offline	online	offline
VoxCeleb1-E	**1.61**	2.67	1.64
VoxCeleb1-H	3.14	4.34	**3.12**
orig. TIMIT	0.54	**0.16**	0.22
Anechoic	**0.19**	0.27	0.26
Codecs	0.58	1.53	**0.52**
Noisy	**1.48**	3.28	1.51

5.2   Block-Online Clustering

For the clustering, we have set α to 0.1 and T_1 to 149. The threshold T_2 for merging clusters has been 0.5. As mentioned in Sect. 3.3, the step size parameter for cluster initialization has been 150. All these parameters have been found on the development set in a series of experiments not presented in this paper.

Given these parameters, we have further investigated the effect of different block and look-ahead sizes as both of these parameters are important with regard to the latency. The block size has varied from 100 to 200 speaker embeddings and the look-ahead size from 150 to 250. We have also performed experiments with no look-ahead.

The obtained results (see Table 3) show that not using the look-ahead mechanism considerably worsens the performance of our system. The lowest WDER is achieved for the block size of 150 and the look-ahead size of 200. Both these values cause a latency of 4.4 s.

Table 3. WDER [%] on Czech broadcast recordings for different values of block size and look-ahead size.

Block size	Look-ahead size	WDER [%]
100	200	3.7
	250	4.1
150	0	12.3
	150	4.9
	200	**2.8**
	250	3.3
200	150	5.9
	200	3.7

5.3 Voice Activity Detection

The last experiment performed on the development set investigates the use of the VAD module with a binary classifier. For its training, 30 h of clean speech, 30 h of music, and 30 h of artificially mixed speech and music/noise recordings according to randomly chosen signal-to-noise ratio (SNR) have been used. All these recordings have also been concatenated in a random order to contain speech/non-speech transitions. Music recordings and the segments with SNR values smaller than 0 dB have been labeled as non-speech and the rest as speech.

The obtained results are presented in Table 4. Here, the VAD module without any smoothing slightly increases WDER from 2.8% to 2.9%. The reason is that the output decisions are too sensitive to noise in this case, and the module produces a lot of short speech segments. On the contrary, when VAD decisions are smoothed using the moving average filter with the context of 50 frames, the value of WDER is considerably decreased to 2.3%. Finally, it should also be noted that smoothing does not increase the latency of the whole diarization scheme. The reason is that it is not applied on the last 50 frames of the look-ahead data block during the clustering process.

Table 4. WDER [%] on Czech broadcast recordings with and without the VAD module.

Architecture	VAD	WDER [%]
SE-ResNet	none	2.8
	proposed	2.9
	proposed + MA	**2.3**

6 Results on other Datasets

The last section presents a comparison with the offline ECAPA-TDNN reference system. For this purpose, several broadcast datasets have been selected. The COST278 [27] database contains broadcast news in eleven European languages. The RTVE2018 [17] and RTVE2020 [18] databases contain recordings of various Spanish TV shows, including broadcast news, live magazines, quiz shows, or documentary series. Last, the RUNDKAST [1] is compiled from recordings of Norwegian broadcast news.

The results of the performed experiments recorded in Table 5 show that our optimized SE-ResNet system yields lower DER on the COST278, RUNDKAST, and RTVE2020 databases (e.g., 16.0% vs. 21.9% on RTVE2020 with VAD) and achieves slightly worse performance on the RTVE2018 dataset (i.e., 9.2% vs. 8.8% with applied VAD). These results show that our proposed architecture allows us to perform SD in streamed data with limited context while yielding performance comparable to the ECAPA-TDNN reference system.

Table 5. DER [%] results of the offline ECAPA-TDNN architecture and our proposed SE-ResNet online architecture on various datasets.

Dataset	VAD	ECAPA-TDNN offline	proposed online
COST278	proposed	14.2	13.4
	ground-truth	12.6	**10.7**
RTVE2018	proposed	11.0	11.7
	ground-truth	**8.8**	9.2
RTVE2020	proposed	24.0	18.8
	ground-truth	21.9	**16.0**
RUNDKAST	proposed	13.4	13.2
	ground-truth	10.1	**9.7**

Finally, we have evaluated the proposed system also on datasets that are a bit far from our target domain but widely used in the community: the AMI meeting corpus [3] and DIHARD II [25] dataset. In the former case, the AMI full Mix-Headset evaluation protocol proposed in [16] is employed. The AMI evaluation uses the same clustering parameters as the previous experiments. For DIHARD II, the clustering context is smaller with block size set to 100, look-ahead to 100, and T_2 threshold to 0.35. These values have been found on the development set, resulting in a smaller latency of around 3.6 s.

The results in Table 6 show that our method achieves results comparable to other existing methods, but there is room for further improvement. This holds, namely in the processing of segments containing overlapping speech, which were the source of most of the errors and do not occur to such a large extent in our target broadcast data. However, our diarization system has the advantage of requiring only one CPU core, while other systems require more computational resources, such as multiple CPU cores or GPUs. For example, the most powerful system [33] achieves an RTF of 0.1 using an NVIDIA® Geforce RTX 3090 GPU.

Table 6. DER [%] results on AMI and DIHARD II test sets.

Dataset	System				
	Proposed	[10]	[33]	[6]	[32]
AMI	21.2	–	**19.0**	27.5	–
DIHARD II	28.2	27.3	**23.1**	34.1	25.8

7   Conclusions

This work has focused on SD in streamed data. For this purpose, a new approach has been proposed. It consists of three consecutive phases. In the first one, speaker embeddings are extracted using SE-ResNet architecture, which is optimized by adding buffers and limited application of the stride. Then the VAD is applied, which utilizes the extracted embeddings and filters them using a single-layer binary classifier, whose output decisions are smoothed. The third (last) step makes use of block-online k-means clustering with a built-in look-ahead mechanism.

We compared our diarization scheme with a recent offline ECAPA-TDNN-based reference system on various broadcast datasets as well as with other online approaches on the out of domain but widely used AMI and DIHARD II datasets. All of the achieved results have demonstrated that the proposed method yields solid results. At the same time, it is capable of processing the streamed data just on a CPU with a low real-time factor below 0.1 and with a total latency of around 5.5 s.

Acknowledgements. The research leading to these results has received funding from the EEA / Norway Grants and the Technology Agency of the Czech Republic within the KAPPA Programme (project No. TO01000027) and from the Student Grant Competition of the Technical University of Liberec under project No. SGS-2022-3052.

References

1. Amdal, I., Strand, O.M., Almberg, J., Svendsen, T.: RUNDKAST: an annotated Norwegian broadcast news speech corpus. In: LREC (2008)
2. Aronowitz, H., Solewicz, Y.A., Toledo-Ronen, O.: Online two speaker diarization. In: Odyssey, pp. 122–129 (2012)

3. Carletta, J., Ashby, S., Bourban, S., Flynn, M., Guillemot, M., et al.: The AMI meeting corpus: a pre-announcement. In: MLMI, pp. 28–39 (2005)
4. Castaldo, F., Colibro, D., Dalmasso, E., Laface, P., Vair, C.: Stream-based speaker segmentation using speaker factors and eigenvoices. In: ICASSP, pp. 4133–4136 (2008)
5. Chung, J.S., Nagrani, A., Zisserman, A.: VoxCeleb2: deep speaker recognition. In: Interspeech, pp. 1086–1090 (2018)
6. Coria, J.M., Bredin, H., Ghannay, S., Rosset, S.: Overlap-aware low-latency online speaker diarization based on end-to-end local segmentation. In: ASRU, pp. 1139–1146 (2021)
7. Dawalatabad, N., Ravanelli, M., Grondin, F., Thienpondt, J., Desplanques, B., Na, H.: ECAPA-TDNN embeddings for speaker diarization. In: Interspeech, pp. 3560–3564 (2021)
8. Desplanques, B., Thienpondt, J., Demuynck, K.: ECAPA-TDNN: emphasized channel attention, propagation and aggregation in TDNN based speaker verification. In: Interspeech, pp. 3830–3834 (2020)
9. Dimitriadis, D., Fousek, P.: Developing on-line speaker diarization system. In: Interspeech, pp. 2739–2743 (2017)
10. Fini, E., Brutti, A.: Supervised online diarization with sample mean loss for multi-domain data. In: ICASSP, pp. 7134–7138 (2020)
11. Friedland, G., Janin, A., Imseng, D., Miro, X.A., Gottlieb, L.R., et al.: The ICSI RT-09 speaker diarization system. IEEE Trans. Speech Audio Process. **20**(2), 371–381 (2012)
12. Garofolo, J.S.: TIMIT acoustic-phonetic continuous speech corpus. Linguistic Data Consortium (1993)
13. Han, E., Lee, C., Stolcke, A.: BW-EDA-EEND: streaming END-TO-END neural speaker diarization for a variable number of speakers. In: ICASSP, pp. 7193–7197 (2021)
14. Heo, H.S., Lee, B., Huh, J., Chung, J.S.: Clova baseline system for the VoxCeleb speaker recognition challenge 2020. CoRR abs/2009.14153 (2020)
15. Ko, T., Peddinti, V., Povey, D., Seltzer, M.L., Khudanpur, S.: A study on data augmentation of reverberant speech for robust speech recognition. In: ICASSP, pp. 5220–5224 (2017)
16. Landini, F., Profant, J., Diez, M., Burget, L.: Bayesian HMM clustering of x-vector sequences (VBx) in speaker diarization: theory, implementation and analysis on standard tasks. Comput. Speech Lang. **71**, 101254 (2022)
17. Lleida, E., Ortega, A., Miguel, A., Bazan, V., Perez, C., et al.: RTVE2018 database description (2018)
18. Lleida, E., Ortega, A., Miguel, A., Bazan-Gil, V., Perez, C., et al.: RTVE2020 database description (2020)
19. Madikeri, S.R., Himawan, I., Motlicek, P., Ferras, M.: Integrating online i-vector extractor with information bottleneck based speaker diarization system. In: Interspeech, pp. 3105–3109 (2015)
20. Malek, J., Jansky, J., Kounovsky, T., Koldovsky, Z., Zdansky, J.: Blind extraction of moving audio source in a challenging environment supported by speaker identification via x-vectors. In: ICASSP, pp. 226–230 (2021)
21. Malek, J., Zdansky, J.: Voice-activity and overlapped speech detection using x-vectors. In: TSD, pp. 366–376 (2020)
22. Malek, J., Zdansky, J., Cerva, P.: Robust recognition of conversational telephone speech via multi-condition training and data augmentation. In: TSD, pp. 324–333 (2018)

23. Nagrani, A., Chung, J.S., Zisserman, A.: VoxCeleb: a large-scale speaker identification dataset. In: Interspeech, pp. 2616–2620 (2017)
24. Panayotov, V., Chen, G., Povey, D., Khudanpur, S.: LibriSpeech: an ASR corpus based on public domain audio books. In: ICASSP, pp. 5206–5210 (2015)
25. Ryant, N., Church, K., Cieri, C., Cristia, A., Du, J., et al.: The second DIHARD diarization challenge: dataset, task, and baselines. In: Interspeech, pp. 978–982 (2019)
26. Snyder, D., Chen, G., Povey, D.: MUSAN: a music, speech, and noise corpus. CoRR abs/1510.08484 (2015)
27. Vandecatseye, A., Martens, J., Neto, J.P., Meinedo, H., Garcia-Mateo, C., et al.: The COST278 pan-European broadcast news database. In: LREC (2004)
28. Vincent, E., Watanabe, S., Nugraha, A.A., Barker, J., Marxer, R.: An analysis of environment, microphone and data simulation mismatches in robust speech recognition. Comput. Speech Lang. **46**, 535–557 (2017)
29. Wang, F., Cheng, J., Liu, W., Liu, H.: Additive margin softmax for face verification. IEEE Signal Process. Lett. **25**(7), 926–930 (2018)
30. Wang, Q., Downey, C., Wan, L., Mansfield, P.A., Lopez-Moreno, I.: Speaker diarization with LSTM. In: ICASSP, pp. 5239–5243 (2018)
31. Xia, W., et al.: Turn-to-diarize: online speaker diarization constrained by transformer transducer speaker turn detection. In: ICASSP, pp. 8077–8081 (2022)
32. Xue, Y., Horiguchi, S., Fujita, Y., Takashima, Y., Watanabe, S., et al.: Online streaming end-to-end neural diarization handling overlapping speech and flexible numbers of speakers. In: Interspeech, pp. 3116–3120 (2021)
33. Yue, Y., Du, J., He, M., Yeung, Y.T., Wang, R.: Online speaker diarization with core samples selection. In: Interspeech, pp. 1466–1470 (2022)
34. Zelenak, M., Schulz, H., Hernando, J.: Speaker diarization of broadcast news in Albayzin 2010 evaluation campaign. EURASIP J. Audio Speech Music Process. **2012**(19) (2012)
35. Zhang, A., Wang, Q., Zhu, Z., Paisley, J.W., Wang, C.: Fully supervised speaker diarization. In: ICASSP, pp. 6301–6305 (2019)

CML-TTS: A Multilingual Dataset for Speech Synthesis in Low-Resource Languages

Frederico S. Oliveira[✉], Edresson Casanova[✉], Arnaldo Candido Junior[✉],
Anderson S. Soares[✉], and Arlindo R. Galvão Filho[✉]

UFG, Goiás, GO, Brazil
frederico.oliveira@ufmt.br, edresson@coqui.ai,
arnaldo.candido@unesp.br, {andersonsoares,arlindogalvao}@ufg.br

Abstract. In this paper, we present CML-TTS, a recursive acronym for CML-Multi-Lingual-TTS, a new Text-to-Speech (TTS) dataset developed at the Center of Excellence in Artificial Intelligence (CEIA) of the Federal University of Goias (UFG). CML-TTS is based on Multilingual LibriSpeech (MLS) and adapted for training TTS models, consisting of audiobooks in seven languages: Dutch, French, German, Italian, Portuguese, Polish, and Spanish. Additionally, we provide the YourTTS model, a multi-lingual TTS model, trained using 3,176.13 h from CML-TTS and also with 245.07 h from LibriTTS, in English. Our purpose in creating this dataset is to open up new research possibilities in the TTS area for multi-lingual models. The dataset is publicly available under the CC-BY 4.0 license (https://freds0.github.io/CML-TTS-Dataset).

Keywords: text-to-speech · dataset · multilingual

1 Introduction

Text-To-Speech (TTS) systems have received a lot of attention in recent years due to the great advance provided by the use of Deep Learning, which allowed the popularization of virtual assistants, such as Apple Siri [10], Amazon Alexa [28] and Google Home [8]. Traditional TTS systems, according to [32], were composed of several specific modules, which are difficult to develop, such as a text analyzer, a grapheme-to-phoneme converter, a duration estimator, and an acoustic model [37]. Deep learning [9] allows the integration of all these modules into a single model, producing spectrograms from texts, with good performance and quality [2]. As examples, check [12,16,17,26,30–33,35].

The difficulty in training models based on Deep Learning is that these models, such as [26,30–32,35], require a greater amount of data for training. For this reason, most current TTS models are designed for the English language [12,16,17,26,30,33], which is a language with many open resources. The main datasets available for training TTS models in the English language are Voice Cloning Toolkit (VCTK) [36], LJSpeech [13] and LibriTTS corpus [38]. VCTK [36] is a dataset comprising a total of 44 h of recordings, with 109 native English speakers, in which each speaker reads approximately 400 sentences. In VCTK, recordings were made in a studio, with high quality, and a sampling rate equal to 48 kHz. LJSpeech is a single-speaker reading dataset in English,

K. Ekštein et al. (Eds.): TSD 2023, LNAI 14102, pp. 188–199, 2023.
https://doi.org/10.1007/978-3-031-40498-6_17

which contains 24 h of audiobook reading with a sampling rate equal to 22 kHz, whose recordings come from the LibriVox project. LibriTTS is a dataset adapted from the LibriSpeech [25] corpus, which contains 585 h of speech at 24 kHz, and is composed of 2,456 speakers.

With the increasing availability of datasets in languages other than English, several [19, 20, 23, 39] researches are focusing on multi-lingual TTS models, which can be trained concurrently in different languages, or that are easily adapted to other languages. Lux and Vu [20] present techniques to transfer learning from high-resource languages to low-resource languages, using articulatory and phonological features. Zhang et al. [39] make modifications to the architecture of Tacotron-2 [30], incorporating a speaker and a language embedding, to develop a model capable of synthesizing audio of different speakers in different languages. Nekvinda and Dusek [23] also adapt Tacotron-2 to produce a multi-lingual model, which uses different levels of sharing encoder parameters.

Unlike Speech-to-Text (STT) datasets, TTS datasets require good quality audio, preferably recorded in studio with a sample rate of at least 22 kHz, and transcripts containing punctuation. Therefore, multilingual datasets for STT systems, such as the Multilingual LibriSpeech (MLS) [27], Common Voice [1] or TedX [29], cannot be directly applied in training TTS models. In view of this, the aim of this work is to create a multilingual dataset for training TTS models. For that, we present the CML-Multi-Lingual-TTS (CML-TTS) dataset, a version based on MLS dataset, adapted for training TTS models. CML-TTS is derived from readings from LibriVox and consists of audiobooks in seven languages, with a total of 3,233.43 h and 613 speakers with a sampling rate equal to 24 kHz.

This work is organized as follows. Section 2 presents information about CML-TTS, describing its creation process. Section 3 presents details about the YourTTS model. Section 4 shows the results of the experiments performed. The conclusions are presented in the final Section.

2 CML-TTS

CML-TTS is a dataset composed of reading audiobooks from the LibriVox[1] project, which uses books from Project Gutenberg[2], released in the public domain. In this way, it is possible to make CML-TTS available also in the public domain. It consists of recordings in Dutch, German, French, Italian, Polish, Portuguese, and Spanish, with a sampling rate of 24 kHz. The following are details about the CML-TTS creation process.

2.1 Data Processing Pipeline

The CML-TTS data processing pipeline consists of four steps. The first step is to download the original audios in mp3, using the LibriVox API, referring to the audiobooks present in the target languages. These languages were selected because they are the

---

[1] https://librivox.org/.

[2] https://www.gutenberg.org/.

same ones present in the MLS dataset, with the exception of English, which was not selected because there is already a large number of datasets available. After the audio files are downloaded, they are converted to wav format with a sample rate of 24 kHz, and those with a lower sample rate are discarded.

The second step is to retrieve punctuation for each sentences in the MLS, which have no punctuation. For this, the textbooks with punctuation are downloaded. For each sentence $S = \{w_1, w_2, ..., w_n\}$ formed by a sequence of n words w, a search is performed for the equivalent sentence $P = \{wp_1, wp_2, ..., wp_m\}$ formed by a sequence of m words/punctuations wp, where $m \geq n$. This is done by defining a search window of length len, for each sentence S, which is slided through the textbook, word-by-word, in order to find the equivalent sentence P. Due to differences in spelling, spaces, hyphenation, etc., it was defined len equal to 90% of the length of S. For sentences comparison, a similarity metric based on Levenshtein's distance is used, normalized between 0 and 1, disregarding punctuation and blank spaces. When finding a segment with similarity >0.5 the length of the search window is incrementally increased, word-by-word, until reaching the maximum similarity value. Otherwise, the search window is slided by the rest of the text, and the process is repeated. This entire step is presented in Algorithm 1.

Algorithm 1. Algorithm Search Punctuated Sentence

$P \leftarrow$ sentence of the Textbook defined by the search window
if P has minimal similarity with S **then**
    Iteratively increase the length of the sentence
else
    Slide the Textbook search window to define a new sentence P
    Repeat the search algorithm for the new sentence P
end if

Analyzing the LibriTTS dataset, it was verified that the segments have durations between 1 and 20 s. However, MLS segments have durations between 10 and 20 s, that is, it does not have segments with a duration of fewer than 10 s. Therefore, in the third step, segments longer than 15 s were divided according to the text punctuation, that is, an audio segment, formed by two text sentences separated by a dot, is divided into two audio segments. This step was performed using Aeneas[3] an audio-text alignment tool.

In this process, the sentence with the greatest similarity may not be the correct sentence spoken in the audio. Or, there may be failures in the audio-text alignment of the segmented sentences, causing an error in the cutting of the audio segments. Therefore, in the last step, validation of the texts is carried out using an STT model to transcribe audio segments and calculate the similarity between the text of the segment and its transcription. The transcription is performed using the Wav2Vec 2.0 XLSR Large [7], without any language model, trained originally in 53 languages and fine-tuned individually in each of the languages present in CML-TTS, using the Common Voice dataset [1] version 6.1.

---

[3] https://www.readbeyond.it/aeneas/docs/index.html.

Finally, a similarity metric based on Levenshtein distance is calculated between the transcript and the sentence. The value of this similarity is normalized between 0 and 1, and if the value is less than 0.9, the sentence and the audio are discarded. In this way, a minimum quality of the CML-TTS is guaranteed. The entire Data Processing Pipeline can be seen in Fig. 1.

Data Processing Pipeline

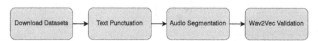

Fig. 1. The data processing pipeline is divided into four steps: (1) downloading the original audio; (2) text normalization, adding punctuation; (3) segmentation of the audio in smaller parts; (4) validation of texts through audio transcription.

2.2   CML-TTS Statistics

Table 1 presents the total duration in hours of each language subsets present in the CML-TTS dataset, and also of the *Train*, *Test* and *Dev* sets. The same *Train*, *Test*, and *Dev* sets of the MLS dataset was kept. In this table, you can also check the duration of the sets in relation to the speaker's gender. A model trained in VoxCeleb 2 [6] dataset was used for gender classification.

Table 1. Total hours and total speakers of Train, Test and Dev sets present in the CML-TTS dataset.

Language	Duration						Speakers					
	Train		Test		Dev		Train		Test		Dev	
	M	F	M	F	M	F	M	F	M	F	M	F
Dutch	482.82	162.17	2.46	1.29	2.24	1.67	8	27	3	3	2	4
French	260.08	24.04	2.48	3.55	3.31	2.72	25	20	8	9	10	8
German	1128.96	436.64	3.75	5.27	4.31	5.03	78	90	13	17	13	15
Italian	73.78	57.51	1.47	0.85	0.40	1.52	23	38	5	5	4	6
Polish	30.61	8.32	0.70	0.90	0.56	0.80	4	4	2	2	2	2
Portuguese	23.14	44.81	0.28	0.24	0.68	0.20	20	10	5	4	6	3
Spanish	279.15	164.08	2.77	2.06	3.40	2.34	35	42	10	8	11	9
Total	3,176.13		28.11		29.19		424		94		95	

In Fig. 2 pie charts can be checked indicating the percentage considering the duration of each language (on the left), the percentage of quality of the samples (at center), and the percentage in relation to the gender of the speakers (on the right). The quality of the samples was verified by calculating the SNR using Waveform Amplitude Distribution Analysis (WADA) [15], and samples with WADA ≥ 40 dB, 10 dB < WADA < 40, and WADA ≤ 10 dB are indicated respectively as high, medium and low quality. In the CML-TTS dataset, there are 613 speakers, of which 325 are female and 288 are male. However, when checking the total hours of each gender, the dataset is unbalanced, presenting 2.278 h for the male gender and 897 h for the female gender.

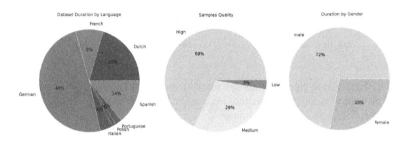

Fig. 2. CML-TTS analysis: on the left, the percentage of the duration of each language in the CML-TTS; in the center, the percentage of samples quality using the WADA; on the right, the percentage of duration in relation to the speaker's gender.

Figure 3 shows the violin plot of the number of words per sentence of each of the sub-datasets present in CML-TTS. It can be seen that the sub-datasets are similar in terms of distribution, with an average number of words close to 20. Some differences were caused by the sentence segmentation process and also by the validation process, detailed in Sect. (2.1), which discarded some segments. In this figure, it is also noticed that there is a slight difference when analyzing the gender of the speakers, but it does not affect the quality of the dataset.

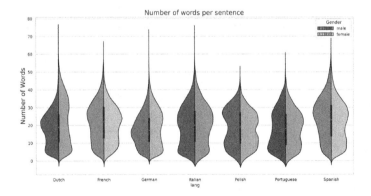

Fig. 3. CML-TTS number of words violin plot per language.

Figure 4 shows the violin plot of the duration per sentence of each of the sub-datasets present in CML-TTS. It can be seen that the segmentation step was effective, making the segments last between 1 and 22 s. Each of the sub-datasets has an average sentence length of between 8 and 12 s. However, a disadvantage of the segmentation and validation process is that it made the dataset unbalanced in terms of the duration of the segments, with a greater number of segments with durations close to 12 s. In this figure, it is also verified that there is a slight difference in relation to the gender of the speakers.

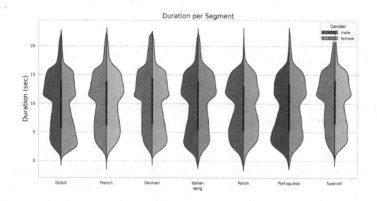

Fig. 4. CML-TTS segments duration violin plot per language.

Duration diversity is required for training successfully most TTS models. For this reason, it is interesting to analyze how our dataset is near or far from LibriTTS. Therefore, Fig. 5, on the left, shows a comparison of the duration of the segments between the CML-TTS, LibriTTS, and MLS datasets. It can be seen that most of the LibriTTS segments have a duration of less than 10 s, while the MLS segments are distributed between 10 and 20 s. The CML-TTS segments are distributed between 0 and 20 s. There was a decrease in the average duration of the segments, which was originally 18 s in MLS, decreasing to 12 s in CML-TTS, while the average in LibriTTS is closer to 2 s. Due to the sentence validation process, there was a drastic reduction in the total number of segments with duration close to 10 s.

Also looking at LibriTTS, very long sentences with a large number of words are not desired. Figure 5, on the right, shows a comparison of the number of words in sentences between the CML-TTS, LibriTTS, and MLS datasets. With the segmentation process, similar to the length of the audio segments, there was also a reduction in the average number of words in the sentences, falling from 35 in the MLS to 20 in the CML-TTS. Therefore, the segmentation process made CML-TTS closer to LibriTTS, which averages 10 words per sentence.

3   YourTTS Model

YourTTS [4] is a multilingual zero-shot multi-speaker TTS model, that was built upon VITS [17] architecture. The goal of zero-shot multi-speaker TTS models is to generate

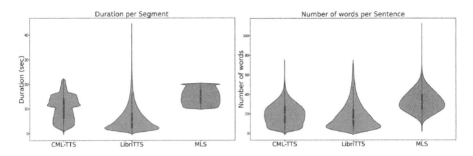

Fig. 5. Comparison among CML-TTS, LibriTTS, and MLS. On the left: durations of segments; right: number of words per sentence.

speech of speakers not seen during training, employing only a few seconds of the target speaker's voice. Although the YourTTS model was proposed on the zero-shot multi-speaker scenario and the main objective of the multilingual training was to reduce the number of speakers needed to develop a zero-shot multi-speaker TTS model in a target language. YourTTS multilingual results are very good and it can do cross-lingual speaker transfer with good quality as well. In addition, the model can generate high-quality speech in the 3 languages that the model was trained in. Although the authors did not explore code-switching [23], YourTTS can do code-switching with great quality producing the word of the other language with naturality and great speaker similarity even for speakers not seen in training.

YourTTS architecture is composed of a Text-Encoder, Posterior-Encoder, Duration Predictor, Flow-Based Decoder, Vocoder, and a pre-trained Speaker-Encoder.

Text-Encoder has Transformer-based architecture, as used in [3,16,17] consisting of 10 transformer blocks and 196 hidden channels. For multilingual training, the authors concatenated 4-dimensional trainable language embeddings into the embeddings of each input character.

The Posterior-Encoder, proposed by [17], is responsible for connecting the Flow-Based to the Vocoder during the training or voice conversion mode. Its architecture is composed of 16 non-causal residual blocks, as per [24]. The Posterior-Encode receives as input a linear spectrogram and speaker embedding and produces latent variable z, which is an intermediate representation, similar to a mel-spectrogram, however, here this representation is learned by the model. During inference, the Posterior-Encoder is not used and the latent variable z is predicted by the Flow-Based Decoder.

As Vocoder it uses the HiFi-GAN model [18] with the discriminator modifications introduced by [17].

The pre-trained Speaker-Encoder is based on the H/ASP [11] architecture and was trained with the Prototypical Angular [5] plus Softmax loss functions in the VoxCeleb 2 [6] dataset. The Speaker-Encoder was used to extract speaker embeddings that were conditioned on the Duration Predictor, Flow-Based Decoder, and Vocoder.

4   Experiments

This section describes the experiments performed using the YourTTS model with CML-TTS and LibriTTS. The LibriTTS dataset was included in order to improve the generalization of the model for speakers not seen during training because LibriTTS has a large number of speakers, which is approximately 1100 speakers. Thus, the model was trained in eight languages: Dutch, English, French, German, Italian, Polish, Portuguese, and Spanish.

4.1   Training

YourTTS was trained using the Train subset of the CML-TTS and LibriTTS datasets (clean-100 and clean-360). To speed up the training, we carry out transfer learning from the official checkpoints, trained in three languages: English, Portuguese and French, using the VCTK [36], TTS-Portuguese [2] and M-AILABS datasets [21]. The training was performed on a DGX-A100, with 82G of memory, for a maximum period of two weeks, using the AdamW optimizer, with a learning rate equal to 0.001, betas equal to 0.8 and 0.99, and batch size equal to 60.

As Speaker-Encoder, we followed the YourTTS paper and uses the H/ASP [11] pre-trained using the VoxCeleb2 [6] dataset with Prototypical Angular [5] together with Softmax as loss function. The embeddings were previously extracted to save computational resources.

4.2   Results

The objective of these experiments is to evaluate whether the CML-TTS has sufficient quality for training TTS models, therefore, we only evaluate the languages present in the CML-TTS dataset, since the use of LibriTTS was only to increase the generalization power of the model due to a large number of different speakers.

To evaluate the similarity between the synthesized speech and the ground truth, we calculate the Speaker Encoder Cosine Similarity (SECS) [4] between the embeddings extracted from the generated audios and from the ground truth audios. In SECS, the closer to 1, the greater the similarity, while the closer to -1 indicates low speaker similarity.

The embeddings were extracted using the model proposed by [34] trained on the VoxCeleb 1, 2 datasets [6,22]. The implementation is available in the Resemblyzer package [14], which is the same one used in the YourTTS paper, in order to allow a fair comparison.

A total of 1,000 sentences for each language were synthesized using different speakers. Since some languages in the CML-TTS have a Test set with fewer than a thousand samples, the sentences were randomly extracted from the Dev and Test sets, which were not used during the training phase. Ten speakers were selected from the Train set and another ten from the Test and Dev sets, or all speakers when the total was less than ten. The evaluation process using unseen speakers is named the zero-shot way.

Table 2 shows the results of the SECS metric of seen and unseen speakers during training for each of the languages present in CML-TTS. The worst result was obtained in the Portuguese language, however, in the original paper YourTTS presented SECS values for the Portuguese language equal to 0.740, in the worst experiment, and 0.798 in the best experiment. Our experiment for the Portuguese language presented a result of the SECS metric equal to 0.777.

Table 2. Speaker Encoder Cosine Similarity (SECS)

Language	SECS	
	Seen	Unseen
Dutch	0.8181 ± 0.0050	0.8010 ± 0.0042
French	0.8299 ± 0.0044	0.8205 ± 0.0044
German	0.8366 ± 0.0046	0.8453 ± 0.0032
Italian	0.7904 ± 0.0069	0.7906 ± 0.0059
Polish	0.8280 ± 0.0039	0.8041 ± 0.0043
Portuguese	0.7772 ± 0.0063	0.7717 ± 0.0079
Spanish	0.8536 ± 0.0048	0.8180 ± 0.0050

To verify if the synthesized sentences were in agreement with the input text, we performed the transcription of the synthesized audios using a Speech-to-Text model. The model chosen was Wav2Vec 2.0 XLSR Large [7], the same used for validation during the data processing pipeline in the Sect. (2.1). Using the transcripts and the ground truth text, we calculated the Word Error Rate (WER) and Character Error Rate (CER) metrics. CER metric is calculated according to the equation $CER = \frac{S+D+I}{N}$ where S is the number of substitutions, D deletions, I insertions, and N is the total characters of the ground truth text. WER metric operates is similar, but operating at the word level instead.

Table 3 shows the results of the WER and CER metrics of seen and unseen speakers during training for each of the languages present in CML-TTS. In both metrics, the language that presented the best results was Spanish, while Portuguese had the worst results. However, this is explained because in Portuguese there was a significant change in orthographic rules due to an Orthographic Agreement[4] carried out in 1990, to unify orthography among Portuguese-speaking countries. Therefore, this influenced the results, given that the books present in LibriVox were published prior to this agreement. It should also be considered that a language model was not used to transcribe the audios.

---

[4] https://www.instituto-camoes.pt/en/activity-camoes/what-we-do/teach-portuguese/ orthographic-agreement.

Table 3. WER and CER metrics between ground truth sentences and transcriptions using Wav2Vec.

Language	WER		CER	
	Seen	Unseen	Seen	Unseen
Dutch	0.3223	0.3062	0.1192	0.0941
French	0.2909	0.1636	0.1330	0.0490
German	0.2305	0.1737	0.0830	0.0407
Italian	0.2956	0.2002	0.1260	0.0574
Polish	0.3133	0.3285	0.0955	0.0970
Portuguese	0.4134	0.4548	0.1985	0.2098
Spanish	0.1862	0.1039	0.07947	0.0243

5 Conclusions

We have presented the CML-Multi-Lingual-TTS dataset, a dataset composed of Librivox recordings, comprising audiobooks in seven languages: Dutch, German, French, Italian, Polish, Portuguese and Spanish. This dataset was created from the MLS dataset, performing a data processing step in order to make it more suitable for training TTS models. Statistical data of the dataset were presented, comparing it with the main dataset for training TTS models, LibriTTS. Experiments were also performed using the YourTTS model, training it with the CML-TTS and LibriTTS datasets, demonstrating that the dataset is suitable for training TTS models.

Acknowledgements. The authors are grateful to CEIA at UFG for their support and to Coqui and CyberLabs for their valuable assistance. We also thank the LibriVox volunteers for making this project possible.

References

1. Ardila, R., et al.: Common voice: a massively-multilingual speech corpus. In: Proceedings of the Twelfth Language Resources and Evaluation Conference, pp. 4218–4222. European Language Resources Association, Marseille, France, May 2020. https://aclanthology.org/2020.lrec-1.520
2. Casanova, E., et al.: TTS-Portuguese Corpus: a corpus for speech synthesis in Brazilian Portuguese. Lang. Resour. Eval. 1–13 (2022)
3. Casanova, E., et al.: SC-GlowTTS: an efficient zero-shot multi-speaker text-to-speech model (2021). https://doi.org/10.48550/ARXIV.2104.05557, https://arxiv.org/abs/2104.05557
4. Casanova, E., Weber, J., Shulby, C.D., Junior, A.C., Gölge, E., Ponti, M.A.: YourTTS: towards zero-shot multi-speaker TTS and zero-shot voice conversion for everyone. In: International Conference on Machine Learning, pp. 2709–2720. PMLR (2022)
5. Chung, J.S., et al.: In defence of metric learning for speaker recognition. arXiv preprint arXiv:2003.11982 (2020)
6. Chung, J.S., Nagrani, A., Zisserman, A.: VoxCeleb2: deep speaker recognition. CoRR abs/1806.05622 (2018). http://arxiv.org/abs/1806.05622

7. Conneau, A., Baevski, A., Collobert, R., Mohamed, A., Auli, M.: Unsupervised cross-lingual representation learning for speech recognition. In: Hermansky, H., Cernocký, H., Burget, L., Lamel, L., Scharenborg, O., Motlícek, P. (eds.) Interspeech 2021, 22nd Annual Conference of the International Speech Communication Association, Brno, Czechia, 30 August–3 September 2021, pp. 2426–2430. ISCA (2021). https://doi.org/10.21437/Interspeech.2021-329

8. Dempsey, P.: The teardown: google home personal assistant. Eng. Technol. **12**(3), 80–81 (2017)

9. Goodfellow, I., Bengio, Y., Courville, A., Bengio, Y.: Deep Learning, vol. 1. MIT press, Cambridge (2016)

10. Gruber, T.R.: Siri, a virtual personal assistant-bringing intelligence to the interface. In: Semantic Technologies Conference (2009)

11. Heo, H.S., Lee, B.J., Huh, J., Chung, J.S.: Clova Baseline System for the VoxCeleb Speaker Recognition Challenge 2020 (2020). https://doi.org/10.48550/ARXIV.2009.14153, https://arxiv.org/abs/2009.14153

12. Huang, R., Zhao, Z., Liu, H., Liu, J., Cui, C., Ren, Y.: ProDiff: progressive fast diffusion model for high-quality text-to-speech. In: Proceedings of the 30th ACM International Conference on Multimedia, pp. 2595–2605 (2022)

13. Ito, K., Johnson, L.: The LJSpeech Dataset (2017). https://keithito.com/LJ-Speech-Dataset/

14. Jemine, C.: Master Thesis: Real-time voice cloning. Master's thesis, Faculté des Sciences Appliquèes (2019)

15. Kim, C., Stern, R.M.: Robust signal-to-noise ratio estimation based on waveform amplitude distribution analysis. In: Ninth Annual Conference of the International Speech Communication Association (2008)

16. Kim, J., Kim, S., Kong, J., Yoon, S.: Glow-TTS: a generative flow for text-to-speech via monotonic alignment search. Adv. Neural Inf. Process. Syst. **33**, 8067–8077 (2020)

17. Kim, J., Kong, J., Son, J.: Conditional variational autoencoder with adversarial learning for end-to-end text-to-speech. In: International Conference on Machine Learning, pp. 5530–5540. PMLR (2021)

18. Kong, J., Kim, J., Bae, J.: HiFi-GAN: generative adversarial networks for efficient and high fidelity speech synthesis (2020)

19. Li, B., Zhang, Y., Sainath, T., Wu, Y., Chan, W.: Bytes are all you need: end-to-end multilingual speech recognition and synthesis with bytes. In: ICASSP 2019–2019 IEEE International Conference on Acoustics, Speech and Signal Processing (ICASSP), pp. 5621–5625. IEEE (2019)

20. Lux, F., Vu, N.T.: Language-agnostic meta-learning for low-resource text-to-speech with articulatory features. arXiv preprint arXiv:2203.03191 (2022)

21. Munich Artificial Intelligence Laboratories GmbH: The M-AILABS Speech Dataset (2017). https://www.caito.de/2019/01/03/the-m-ailabs-speech-dataset/feld.de/content/bworld-robot-control-software/. Accessed 05 Nov 2022

22. Nagrani, A., Chung, J.S., Zisserman, A.: Voxceleb: a large-scale speaker identification dataset. In: INTERSPEECH (2017)

23. Nekvinda, T., Dušek, O.: One model, many languages: meta-learning for multilingual text-to-speech. arXiv preprint arXiv:2008.00768 (2020)

24. van den Oord, A., et al: WaveNet: a generative model for raw audio. CoRR abs/1609.03499 (2016). http://arxiv.org/abs/1609.03499

25. Panayotov, V., Chen, G., Povey, D., Khudanpur, S.: Librispeech: an ASR corpus based on public domain audio books. In: 2015 IEEE International Conference on Acoustics, Speech and Signal Processing (ICASSP), pp. 5206–5210 (2015)

26. Ping, W., et al.: Deep voice 3: 2000-speaker neural text-to-speech. arXiv preprint arXiv:1710.07654 (2017)

27. Pratap, V., Xu, Q., Sriram, A., Synnaeve, G., Collobert, R.: MLS: a large-scale multilingual dataset for speech research. In: Interspeech 2020. ISCA, October 2020. https://doi.org/10.21437/interspeech.2020-2826, https://doi.org/10.21437%2Finterspeech.2020-2826

28. Purington, A., Taft, J.G., Sannon, S., Bazarova, N.N., Taylor, S.H.: Alexa is my new BFF social roles, user satisfaction, and personification of the Amazon Echo. In: Proceedings of the 2017 CHI Conference Extended Abstracts on Human Factors in Computing Systems, pp. 2853–2859 (2017)

29. Salesky, E., et al.: The multilingual TEDx corpus for speech recognition and translation. CoRR abs/2102.01757 (2021). https://arxiv.org/abs/2102.01757

30. Shen, J., et al.: Natural TTS synthesis by conditioning WaveNet on Mel spectrogram predictions. In: 2018 IEEE International Conference on Acoustics, Speech and Signal Processing (ICASSP), pp. 4779–4783. IEEE (2018)

31. Sotelo, J., et al.: Char2Wav: end-to-end speech synthesis. In: International Conference on Learning Representations, Workshop (2017)

32. Tachibana, H., Uenoyama, K., Aihara, S.: Efficiently trainable text-to-speech system based on deep convolutional networks with guided attention. arXiv preprint arXiv:1710.08969 (2017)

33. Valle, R., Shih, K.J., Prenger, R., Catanzaro, B.: Flowtron: an autoregressive flow-based generative network for text-to-speech synthesis. In: International Conference on Learning Representations (2020)

34. Wan, L., Wang, Q., Papir, A., Moreno, I.L.: Generalized end-to-end loss for speaker verification. In: 2018 IEEE International Conference on Acoustics, Speech and Signal Processing (ICASSP), pp. 4879–4883. IEEE (2018)

35. Wang, Y., et al.: Tacotron: a fully end-to-end text-to-speech synthesis model. arXiv preprint arXiv:1703.10135 (2017)

36. Yamagishi, J., Veaux, C., MacDonald, K.: CSTR VCTK corpus: English multi-speaker corpus for CSTR voice cloning toolkit (2019). https://datashare.ed.ac.uk/handle/10283/3443. Accessed 05 Nov 2022

37. Ze, H., Senior, A., Schuster, M.: Statistical parametric speech synthesis using deep neural networks. In: 2013 IEEE International Conference on Acoustics, Speech and Signal Processing, pp. 7962–7966. IEEE (2013)

38. Zen, H., et al.: LibriTTS: a corpus derived from LibriSpeech for text-to-speech. arXiv preprint arXiv:1904.02882 (2019)

39. Zhang, Y., et al.: Learning to speak fluently in a foreign language: multilingual speech synthesis and cross-language voice cloning. arXiv preprint arXiv:1907.04448 (2019)

Developing State-of-the-Art End-to-End ASR for Norwegian

Jan Nouza$^{(\boxtimes)}$, Lukas Mateju, Petr Cerva, and Jindrich Zdansky

Faculty of Mechatronics, Informatics and Interdisciplinary Studies, Technical University of Liberec, Studentska 2, 461 17 Liberec, Czech Republic
jan.nouza@tul.cz

Abstract. We present the process of developing a modern end-to-end (E2E) automatic speech recognition (ASR) system for Norwegian (NO), which is a challenging language with many dialects and two written standards (Bokmål and Nynorsk). Since the existing speech corpora for this language are severely limited, we have had to acquire large amounts of additional data. This acquisition has been done by automatic processing of publicly accessible broadcast and parliament archives, YouTube and podcast channels, and also audiobooks. The data-harvesting process has been controlled by the ASR system, whose model has continuously been updated on the extracted chunks of speech. The final model has been trained on 1,246 h of Norwegian and further enhanced by transfer learning from an existing Swedish model. The performance of the ASR system has been evaluated on an 18-h collection of test sets (most of them publicly available) representing different application areas. Our best word error rate (WER) achieved on this collection is 7.6%, which is better than the results obtained from Google and Microsoft cloud services.

Keywords: speech recognition · end-to-end system · Norwegian · transfer learning

1 Introduction

Norwegian is a European language, which is very specific in terms of automatic speech recognition. It is used by 5.3 million people who speak many local dialects and use two different written standards (Bokmål and Nynorsk) in official communication. This reflects both the rugged nature of the country as well as its historical development, in which the periods of Danish and Swedish rule played an important role.

Earlier, when developing a traditional ASR system based on a lexicon, a language model (LM), and an acoustic model (AM), one had to take into account all the spelling, phonetic, grammatical, and morphological variants and compile an extensive vocabulary with many alternative pronunciations [15]. All of these variations also had to be captured in the AM and LM, which was a challenge for a language of that size with limited spoken and written resources.

K. Ekštein et al. (Eds.): TSD 2023, LNAI 14102, pp. 200–213, 2023.
https://doi.org/10.1007/978-3-031-40498-6_18

The advent of modern end-to-end systems [21] has greatly facilitated development, because extensive dictionaries with explicit pronunciations have become unnecessary. These systems can encapsulate the lexical, syntactic, and phonetic features within their complex architectures based on neural networks (NN). Since many of the existing E2E platforms are available as open-source frameworks, one of the main tasks in the ASR research is now to effectively gather data suitable for training these systems.

To support and encourage research in the Norwegian speech/language processing area, the National Library of Norway has created a web portal called Språkbanken[1] where language corpora collected by other (primarily academic) institutions are stored and made freely available. Spoken data represents mainly read or dictated passages but also includes collections of talks in local dialects. In 2021, more than 100 h of recordings from the Norwegian parliament were added together with their official transcripts [20]. Recently, several works have been published that utilize this data for investigating various NN-based ASR approaches, such as Google's DeepSpeech2 platform [16,20], or ESPNet framework [15]. Results reported in these works look promising, but they were achieved mainly on test sets that matched the data used in training.

Our research aims to develop a general-purpose ASR system that could be deployed in real applications. This goal requires much larger amounts of training material in which various types of speech (read, planned, emotional or spontaneous) and acoustic conditions (clean, noisy, studio, or outdoor) prevail, and diverse topics are covered. We propose and implement procedures that can identify sources of speech in the public domain and convert that speech into data suitable for training E2E systems. Since resources in Norwegian are limited, we also investigate several possibilities to combine them with those from other languages.

2   Overview of End-to-End Systems

End-to-end ASR systems have become the subject of intensive scientific efforts in the most recent decade. Their popularity stems from utilizing a single (yet complex) NN-based architecture that learns to convert an input speech signal directly to the corresponding written text. They have become possible after the introduction of several key concepts; namely, the connectionist temporal classification (CTC) [8] and its successful application to speech [9], attention-based encoder-decoder (AED) design [4] and sequence transduction with recurrent neural networks (RNN-T) [7].

The first scheme (CTC) utilizes a dynamic programming strategy (similar to that used in hidden Markov models) to map speech frames to the output symbols, which may be characters, words, or word fragments. The second one (AED) tries to solve the same task via the encoder-decoder NN structure supported by an attention mechanism that identifies regions belonging to individual parts of the

---

[1] https://nb.no/sprakbanken/.

text. The RNN-T solves the forced segmentation alignment problem in ASR using three subnetworks: the transcription, prediction, and joint networks.

What is common to all of these systems is the fact that they require large amounts of annotated speech to reach the state-of-the-art performance level. For major world languages, e.g., English or Chinese, the requirement is for tens of thousands of hours [21]. A thousand-hour training set is considered a minimum. For low-resource languages, multilingual techniques such as transfer learning [3] or multilingual training [6] are almost necessary to improve performance. They have been tested for various language groups [18], including the Nordic one (Norwegian, Swedish, and Danish) [24]. Another way to address the lack of training data is to use a concept known as wav2vec [2]. Such a system is first pre-trained on large amounts of unlabeled audio data (which can represent different languages) and then fine-tuned using a much smaller set of annotated speech in the target language. However, if gathering at least 1,000 h in the given language is possible, a monolingual system built from scratch can outperform the multilingual ones.

3   Our ASR System

In this work, we employ the ESPNet platform [23] to enable an E2E architecture combining CTC and AED techniques. Our model is thus composed of three parts: a shared encoder represented by a conformer [10] and two decoders – CTC-based and attention-based – using a CTC weighting factor of 0.3.

The shared encoder is composed of 12 blocks, each with eight attention heads, and is preceded by two sub-sampling convolutional layers (kernel size 3×3 and stride 2). The CTC decoder uses a linear layer to transform the encoder output to the CTC activation, while the attention decoder is a transformer with six blocks, each containing eight attention heads. In each block, the attention dimension is set to 512, and the position-wise feed-forward layer has 2,048 units. The entire model consists of 136M parameters.

To parameterize the input speech, we use 80-dimensional Mel-spectral filter banks (25 ms), and we apply SpecAugment [17] to augment the training data on the fly. The duration of each training recording is limited to 25 s. We train the model for 120 epochs using the Adam optimizer with a batch size of 20. The final model is obtained by averaging 30 epochs with the lowest loss values on a 10-h development set. For decoding, we use the CTC prefix beam search algorithm and have implemented our own decoder that can transcribe streamed audio signals with a latency value lower than 2 s. The basic text units used in the decoding are the 5,000 most frequent word fragments derived from the training corpus by the SentencePiece toolkit [12].

Since we have previously adopted this architecture for several other languages, we can combine the already developed models with the new ones; this approach can mainly be beneficial in the initial (bootstrapping) phase.

4   Development and Experimental Work

4.1   Test Data Used for Performance Evaluation

As the development has been carried out in several phases and iterative steps, we need an extensive set of test data to evaluate the results and optimize the subsequent procedures continuously. We have thus created a large test collection to cover various application areas and operating conditions. Where possible, we include official test parts of public datasets so that anybody could use them for comparison. The collection is presented in Table 1, where we show the relevant statistics (hours of speech and numbers of words), the written standard used in the reference transcripts (Bokmål or Nynorsk), and the basic speech and channel characteristics.

The first three sets represent data publicly available in Språkbanken (described in more detail in Sect. 4.2). The NST5h and NPSC5h sets are 5-h subsets randomly chosen from the official test parts of the NST (read speech) and NPSC (parliament speech) datasets. We have decided to make this reduction because the complete test sets would be too large (125 h for NST and 12 h for NPSC) compared to the rest of the collection. The TALE set is created from recordings in Part3 of the NB TALE data that consists of 2-min spontaneous talks, oriented mainly on personal hobby activities, given by speakers in 12 Norwegian dialects.

The next two sets represent broadcast speech occurring in news programs of Norwegian major TV Company NRK. The RUNDKAST dataset [1] contains recordings from the early 2000s, and the test set is made of 3 complete news shows. The NRK set is focused on more recent broadcast TV programs (from 2022) and was prepared by the partner team at the NTNU in Trondheim.

The FLEURS set [5] is a test subset of the eponymous multi-lingual data collected by Google. It has been frequently used in the speech and language community recently. The abbreviation CV stands for Mozilla's Common Voice data[2]. Its Norwegian test part is tiny but has a unique role in the collection because it is the only set with Nynorsk-only transcripts. The last set is an audio-book titled Kampen on Norden (The Battle of the North in English). We have chosen this documentary text dealing with events in Nordic countries during WWII because it contains many non-Norwegian names, foreign locations, and professional terms that never occurred in the training data. This feature allows us to investigate how the models learn to generalize.

---

[2] https://commonvoice.mozilla.org/.

Table 1. Norwegian test set collection (Bk – Bokmål, Nn – Nynorsk).

Test set	Hours	Words	Transcript	Speech style	Environment
NST5h	5.0	28,809	Bk	read	office
NPSC5h	5.0	45,919	Bk/Nn	planned/spontaneous	large hall
TALE	0.4	3,366	Bk	spontaneous	office
RUNDKAST	1.0	9,305	Bk/Nn	read/planned/spontaneous	studio/outdoor/phone
NRK	1.1	10.456	Bk/Nn	read/planned/spontaneous	studio/outdoor/phone
FLEURS	1.2	7,615	Bk	read/spontaneous	home
CV	0.3	1,728	Nn	read	home
Abook	4.0	36,427	Bk	read	studio
Total	18.0	142,005			

4.2   Model Bootstrapping Phase

In the first phase, we needed to create an initial Norwegian model. For that purpose, we have utilized mainly the freely available data from the Språkbanken portal. There are four major sources of annotated speech there. The largest is the NST dataset, created in the early 2000s by Nordisk Språkteknology Company to support the development of ASR (dictation) programs. The set comprises read utterances that cover lexical and phonetic features relevant to Norwegian. Its training part contains 450 h of recordings from about 1,040 speakers. Since many sentences are repeated, we have limited each unique one to 3 occurrences. This has reduced the size of the NST training set to 348 h.

The next resources are the NB TALE and TUVA sets. Both are made of mainly read passages, too, but their content is more natural compared to the NST set. The primary goal of the former is to capture multiple Norwegian dialects (Part1) and also speech from non-native speakers living in Norway (Part2). We have used 28 h for training. The latter (TUVA) was created by Max Manus AS company and contains mainly read speech based on newspaper articles. Because a part of these texts is the same for all 40 speakers, we have made a similar reduction as in the NST case, which has resulted in 14 h of (mostly unique) training data.

The Norwegian Parliamentary Speech Corpus (NPSC) represents speech from plenary sessions in the Norwegian parliament recorded in 2017–2018. Its latest (extended) version comes from 2021 [20]. The corpus is split into the training, evaluation, and test parts, with 100, 13, and 12 h of speech, respectively. The NPSC set is the only one in this collection that contains natural (not prompted) speech, and its correct transcription is crucial for the training. Therefore, we performed an automated checking procedure before adopting this set: We have trained a model on the remaining three sets and used it to transcribe the NPSC training part. By comparing the ASR output to the reference annotations, we have identified the files with a significantly large mismatch. A brief check unveils that some contain non-Norwegian utterances, and the others are probably wrongly annotated. Hence, the data used for the training has a size of 97 h.

Finally, we have added the training parts of the already mentioned datasets FLEURS and CommonVoice, although their sizes are tiny compared to the others.

The following text will refer to all these freely available speech resources as collection F. Its constituents and their relevant statistics are listed in Table 2.

Table 2. Train collection F – freely available Norwegian data.

Train set	Hours	Speakers	Transcript	Speech style	Environment
NST	348	1040	Bk	read	office
TALE	28	380	Bk	read	office
TUVA	14	40	Bk/Nn	read	office
NPSC	97	267	Bk/Nn	planned/spontaneous	large hall
FLEURS	8	3	Bk	read	home
CV	1	26	Nn	read	home
Total	496				

We have trained the first model using all the currently available data (496 h) and evaluated it on the complete test collection. The results in the form of word error rate values are presented in the first row of Table 3. We can see that the WER value gets below 10% only for two sets (NST5h and NPSC5h), which is obvious because this type of data is well represented in the training set.

The performance can be further improved if we utilize one of the transfer learning methods presented, e.g., in [22]. The simplest yet efficient one is a parameter initialization from an existing model. It can be a model of another language, provided that the architectures match. In our case, we initialize all the parameters of the shared encoder of our hybrid CTC/AED model. We have conducted experiments with a German model (trained on some 3,000 h) and a Swedish one (1,226 h [14]).

We add the results to Table 3. It is evident that the method has helped in both cases. Unsurprisingly, the more significant improvement has been achieved with Swedish because it belongs to the same branch of North-Germanic languages. Let us also note that the initialized model yields significant WER reduction, mainly in the domains not so well represented in the training set. We have utilized this fact in the iterative data harvesting scheme (described in the next section) and used the Swedish-initialized models in all iteration steps to boost the data collection process.

Table 3. WER [%] for various models in bootstrapping. NO(F) means trained on Norwegian collection F, 'init' means initialized by German (DE) or Swedish (SWE) model. WAvg is the weighted average over all of the test sets.

Model	NST5h	NPSC5h	TALE	RUNDKAST	NRK	FLEURS	CV	Abook	WAvg
NO(F)	5.7	7.8	16.4	24.8	21.5	10.0	26.9	20.2	**13.2**
NO(F) init DE	5.4	7.6	17.1	22.6	21.4	9.0	21.2	19.6	**12.6**
NO(F) init SWE	4.2	6.2	15.2	21.2	19.6	7.8	20.3	16.2	**10.7**

4.3 Automatic Data Harvesting from Public and other Sources

The main goal of this phase is to enlarge the training set by utilizing public sources containing speech. There are two main ones that provide both spoken and text content. One is the Norwegian parliament, whose archives include videos taken during all plenary sessions and their official transcriptions[3]. The other is the Norwegian public TV and radio company NRK. According to European Union law, it must broadcast a specific part of its programs (particularly news) with subtitles. These programs are available on the NRK's webpage[4]. Both sources could be used for semi-supervised training because audio data is accompanied by some text. Unfortunately, the relation between the speech records and the provided text is rather loose. This is especially true for the TV subtitles, which need to be shorter and condensed versions of what is actually said. The parliament transcriptions are usually closer to the actual spoken content, but they are always more or less modified to meet the official standards. This means we must carefully process both the speech and text files to get reliable data for the ASR training.

In our harvesting scheme, the data is processed as follows: First, if the source is made up of video files, these are converted to audio ones. Usually, they are very long (up to several hours) and must be split into chunks shorter than 25 s. This is performed by the available ASR system, which also employs a voice activity detector [13] to determine suitable split points. The ASR output is aligned (using the Levenshtein distance method) with the provided reference text, which is then split into fragments assigned to the chunks. (During the alignment, numbers and abbreviations are converted into words with respect to what was spoken.) The second phase runs in iterations. In each iteration, we use the ASR system with an updated model to transcribe the chunks and compare the ASR outputs to the reference fragments. Those with a character mismatch rate below 2% are added to the training set. After processing all of the available chunks, a new model is trained. This procedure is repeated until the amount of newly acquired training data drops below a reasonable level. This process can be fully automated. However, we have found it helpful to introduce minor human assistance after each iteration step. A special tool identifies the most frequent

---

[3] https://stortinget.no/no/Hva-skjer-pa-Stortinget/Videoarkiv/.
[4] https://tv.nrk.no/programmer/nyheter/.

errors (typically foreign names) and prepares a selection of files that contain them for easy auditory check and manual editing.

We have applied this iterative scheme to all the data that could be downloaded from the two sources. In the parliament case, we have used archive data from 2016–2022, excluding those already present in the NPSC set. From the NRK web, we have processed mainly the TV news programs broadcasted during the last five years. Note that we must process several thousands of hours to get the final 309-h set, as only a tiny fraction passes the given criteria.

The same approach has also been applied to the RUNDKAST dataset [1]. It contains about 70 h from NRK programs broadcasted in the early 2000s. In this case, the provided transcriptions are almost verbatim because human annotators had made them. However, the above-described automatic scheme is also beneficial because it removes non-speech parts (mostly music), makes the splits and alignment, and eventually selects those chunks (35 h) that safely meet the criteria.

There are also several other sources with spoken content that are accompanied by text, such as podcasts with published transcripts or YouTube videos with subtitles, although their number is still quite limited. We have found some and processed them in the way described above, resulting in an additional 50 h.

The basic facts on the harvested data (collection H) are summarized in Table 4.

Table 4. Train collection H – data harvested from public sources.

Train set	Hours	Speakers	Transcript	Speech style	Environment
Parliament	208	hundreds	Bk/Nn	planned/spontaneous	large hall
NRK	101	hundreds	Bk/Nn	read/planned/spont	studio/outdoor/phone
RUNDKAST	35	hundreds	Bk/Nn	read/planned/spont	studio/outdoor/phone
Podcasts	36	tens	Bk/Nn	read/planned	office/home
YouTube	14	tens	Bk/Nn	planned/spontaneous	home/outdoor
Total	394				

In order to further expand the volume and scope of the training corpus, we have also considered other resources: audiobooks and ebooks. While there is the possibility of free access to some texts in electronic form (e.g., project Gutenberg[5]), the books available in this way are mostly old (copyright-free) and without access to audio. Therefore, we have decided on a provider with paid access[6]. We have chosen 30 pairs of audio and ebooks (with respect to their topic, genre, narrator, and size) and purchased them in a downloadable format. The books include the biography genre (e.g., Jens Stoltenberg, Michelle Obama, or Elon Musk), novels and fiction books (to introduce various topics and emotional narration style), and texts on health, media, philosophy, and traveling. Table 5

---

[5] https://www.gutenberg.org/.
[6] https://ebok.no/.

provides a brief overview of this collection (denoted A). The same harvesting approach has been used here because a) it is necessary to make the splits into audio chunks and text fragments, and b) there is no guarantee that the written and spoken text match precisely. In the case of the books, it is possible to harvest about 95% of their content.

Table 5. Train collection A – data harvested from audiobooks.

Train set	Hours	Genre	Transcript	Speech style	Environment
Abooks1	111	biography	Bk	read	studio
Abooks2	193	novel/fiction/crime	Bk	read/emotional	studio
Abooks3	52	lifestyle	Bk	read	studio
Total	356				

In Table 6, we present the results obtained after training the E2E models using the additional data and compare them to the model trained on the free resources. Note that both types of automatically harvested data (collections H and A) contribute to a noticeable reduction in the WER values.

Table 6. WER [%] of models trained on collections F, H and A.

Model	NST5h	NPSC5h	TALE	RUNDKAST	NRK	FLEURS	CV	Abook	WAvg
NO(F)	5.7	7.8	16.4	24.8	21.5	10.0	26.9	20.2	**13.2**
NO(FH)	4.7	5.9	15.1	12.0	14.0	7.8	20.8	15.6	**9.6**
NO(FHA)	3.9	5.6	13.7	11.5	13.0	6.9	21.1	11.6	**8.1**

4.4   Models Combining Norwegian with Swedish

In Sect. 4.2, we demonstrate that initializing the parameters of the shared encoder in the Norwegian model by those of a previously developed Swedish model is very helpful during the bootstrapping step and, namely, within the iterative harvesting phase. It is also reasonable to experiment with some multilingual data/model-combining approaches when we have exploited most of the publicly available Norwegian sources and collected a total of 1,246 h. The natural idea is to use Swedish for these experiments as well because it is a closely related language, and we already have both speech data (1,226 h) and an E2E model.

Overall, we have explored three different multilingual techniques. The first is the already utilized parameter initialization via transfer learning. The other two represent multilingual training, i.e., they directly use the Norwegian and Swedish data to train a joint model. The more straightforward of the two simply merges the data and trains the final model as a monolingual one [18]. Alternatively, the ASR system can be provided with language identity (LID) information, usually in the form of a one-hot vector [11] that is appended to the input features during both the training and decoding. This information should guide the system to provide better transcriptions of the target language. Only in this case, the language of the decoded utterances must be known beforehand.

A comparison of our best monolingual model with the three multilingual techniques is summarized in Table 7. The results show that the two multilingual training approaches (see the last two rows of Table 7) fall short of expectations as they do not perform better than the monolingual model. This is most likely due to the confusion caused by the additional Swedish data, especially when the amount of collected Norwegian speech exceeds 1,200 h. Surprisingly, the second method, which utilizes auxiliary LID information, is even slightly worse. It is known that multilingual training is generally much better when dealing with severely limited data, as shown in [14]. On the other hand, initializing the Norwegian model from a Swedish one has, to a great extent, been beneficial even with more than 1,200 h of training data and has significantly improved the overall results (see the second row in Table 7). Moreover, this is computationally much less expensive than the other investigated multilingual techniques.

Table 7. WER [%] of models combining Norwegian (FHA) with Swedish.

Model	NST5h	NPSC5h	TALE	RUNDKAST	NRK	FLEURS	CV	Abook	WAvg
NO	3.9	5.6	13.7	11.5	13.0	6.9	21.1	11.6	**8.1**
NO init SWE	3.4	5.1	13.8	11.4	12.9	6.3	18.4	10.9	**7.6**
joint NO+SWE	3.9	5.7	13.8	10.7	12.7	7.0	44.4	11.5	**8.4**
LID NO+SWE	4.0	5.9	12.9	10.7	12.5	6.4	44.5	12.5	**8.6**

4.5   Performance Comparison to other Systems

There are only a few published works on Norwegian ASR, and we have found a single paper whose authors used the same or similar test data. In [20], the NST and NPSC sets are utilized in experiments with Google's DeepSpeech2 platform adapted to Norwegian. The authors train their system on the two sets and test it on the NST, NPSC, and TALE sets. Their best WER values are 2.9%, 17.1% and 37.3%, respectively (compared to ours 3.4%, 5.1%, and 13.8%).

To provide a broader perspective of our results, we have submitted all of the test sets to two available ASR commercial cloud services that have Norwegian in their portfolio: Microsoft Azure's Speech to Text[7] (version 03/2023) and Google Cloud's Speech-to-Text[8] (version 03/2023). The received transcriptions have been evaluated and scored in the same way as the outputs from our best E2E system (with the Norwegian model initialized from the Swedish one).

Table 8 compares the WER values of the three systems. It is evident that Google's service performs significantly worse than the other two. Since there is no public information about their system's architecture and training data

---

[7] https://azure.microsoft.com/en-us/products/cognitive-services/speech-to-text.
[8] https://cloud.google.com/speech-to-text.

used, we cannot comment on what the reason may be. The service provided by Microsoft yields results that are similar to ours. Again, we have no information about their system. However, we can notice that their results are slightly better for those sets that have been publicly available for a long time. The extremely low WER value (1.2%) achieved for the NST data may suggest that this resource (including its test subset) might have been used in training, which could also happen to other publicly available test sets. When evaluated on the complete test collection, our system yields 0.5% lower weighted averaged WER value.

Table 8. WER [%] comparison of our best Norwegian system with commercial cloud services.

Model	NST5h	NPSC5h	TALE	RUNDKAST	NRK	FLEURS	CV	Abook	WAvg
our best	3.4	5.1	13.8	11.4	12.9	6.3	18.4	10.9	**7.6**
Microsoft	1.2	7.6	10.3	10.0	10.3	9.4	42.4	11.2	**8.1**
Google	17.7	30.6	30.1	27.2	29.0	19.5	50.4	36.2	**28.7**

4.6   Analysis of the Most Frequent Errors and Mismatches

All the presented results have been determined using the standard evaluation procedure that takes the ASR output, aligns it to the provided text reference, and counts the number of substitutions, insertions, and deletions. The WER value is computed as a sum of these three errors normalized by the number of reference words. If we analyze the aligned ASR and reference text sequences over all of the test data, we can get more detailed information on the most frequent errors and investigate their primary causes. We have made such an analysis, and here are the major findings:

1. The primary source of errors in Norwegian ASR is the confusion between the two written standards, Bokmål and Nynorsk. In real life, their choice depends on a personal or regional/institutional preference. As any utterance can be transcribed in two (sometimes quite different) ways, the ASR system must decide which standard to use. Its decision depends on several factors learned during the training, namely, which word variant was seen more often in training, in which context, and also with respect to the similarity between the spoken and orthographic form.

   Since most of the training data is annotated in Bokmål (used by more than 85% Norwegians), there is a much higher probability that test data annotated in Nynorsk will have higher WER values. (This is why the worst results were obtained for the CV set with Nynorsk-only transcriptions). Moreover, the two written standards are more or less related to major regional dialects. So, if the ASR has to decide whether it should output one of the Bk/Nn word alternatives, such as *'ikke/ikkje'* (the equivalent of English 'not'), *'Norge/Noreg'* ('Norway'), *'hvordan/korleis'* ('how'), or *'se/sjå'* ('see'), it considers both the word context and which of the variants is closer to the actual pronunciation and selects the more likely alternative.

2. Another source of mismatch is spelling variants. They exist in both standards. Many words have two (sometimes even more) spelling forms that differ in one or two characters, and both are considered correct. Here are several examples in Bokmål: *'bro/bru'* ('bridge'), *'aleine/alene'* ('alone'), *'bred/brei'* ('wide'), *'teateret/teatret'* ('theater'), *'forskning/forsking'* ('research'). Also, many foreign words and names occur with an alternative spelling, e.g., *'Zelenskyj/Zelensky'* or *'Aalborg/Ålborg'*.

3. Word compounding (a linguistic phenomenon typical for Germanic languages) also contributes to frequent mismatches. A compound word consists of several words or lemmas merged into a single long text string. In the case of less frequent compounds, the system may recognize them as separate words, which is then evaluated as multiple errors. Also, many multi-word terms can appear either as compounds, words separated by spaces, or joined by a hyphen, e.g., *'playoff/play off/play-off'*.

4. Another frequent type of error is confusion between different word forms of the same lemma, especially when their pronunciation is very similar or even identical, e.g., *'arbeide/arbeider'* ('work(er)'), *'regjering/regjeringen'* ('government'), or *'tema/temaet'* ('theme').

5. The above-mentioned types of errors/mismatches make up about one-third of the total amount, and, in general, they are not critical for understanding. However, the current ASR system still produces a certain number of fully misrecognized words. This happens mainly when a speaker uses a minor dialect or unusual pronunciation or when speech is spontaneous, highly emotional, or recorded in heavy noise. In general, it can be said that most Norwegian words not seen in the training are recognized correctly now. Foreign words and names depend on whether they (or words similar to them) are included in the training set. Adding various types of audiobooks to the corpus has significantly helped to reduce this type of error.

Our analysis demonstrates that the WER, even though widely used, is not always the best metric when evaluating the readability of a Norwegian ASR output. It gives the same weight to minor errors (or quasi-errors) as well as to really confusing mistakes. That is why ongoing research also focuses on defining a more appropriate metric that considers semantic relations between words, phrases, and sentences. One example is the so-called Aligned Semantic Distance proposed recently in [19] and tested on Norwegian.

5   Conclusions

Developing an ASR system for Norwegian is more challenging than for most of the other European languages. The main reasons are many dialects, two written standards, and relatively limited resources for training a modern end-to-end recognition system. We have utilized the available resources for bootstrapping an E2E model, which has allowed us to launch an iterative process of harvesting additional speech data from public Internet sources, such as broadcast and parliament archives, some YouTube and podcast channels, and eventually, also audiobooks. During the fully automated process, the ASR system with a continuously updated model has been employed to identify, extract and annotate those parts of the collected speech files that can safely be added to the training corpus. In this way, we have acquired 1,246 h of training data representing various speaking styles, most Norwegian dialects, and different recording environments.

The system's performance has been tested regularly using an 18-h test collection covering various types of speech and application domains. We have also investigated the possibility of combining Norwegian and Swedish resources and found that initializing Norwegian model parameters with the Swedish ones is the most beneficial technique. It boosts the performance of the models utilized in the iterative harvesting and training process and also improves the final model. We compare the developed system to two major commercial services available for Norwegian; we have found that our results (averaged over all the test sets) are superior. Note that most data used in the performance evaluation is publicly accessible so that anybody interested in Norwegian ASR can make use of such data in comparative experiments.

Acknowledgements. The research leading to these results has received funding from the EEA/Norway Grants and the Technology Agency of the Czech Republic within the KAPPA Programme (project No. TO01000027). Computational resources were provided by the e-INFRA CZ project (ID:90140), supported by the Ministry of Education, Youth and Sports of the Czech Republic. We also want to thank Torbjørn Svendsen and his team at the NTNU Trondheim for preparing the NRK test set.

References

1. Amdal, I., Strand, O.M., Almberg, J., Svendsen, T.: RUNDKAST: an annotated Norwegian broadcast news speech corpus. In: LREC 2008, Marrakech, Morocco. ELRA (2008)
2. Baevski, A., Zhou, Y., Mohamed, A., Auli, M.: Wav2vec 2.0: a framework for self-supervised learning of speech representations. In: NeurIPS 2020, virtual event (2020)
3. Cho, J., et al.: Multilingual sequence-to-sequence speech recognition: architecture, transfer learning, and language modeling. In: SLT 2018, Athens, Greece, pp. 521–527. IEEE (2018)
4. Chorowski, J., Bahdanau, D., Serdyuk, D., Cho, K., Bengio, Y.: Attention-based models for speech recognition. In: NeurIPS 2015, Montreal, Canada, pp. 577–585 (2015)
5. Conneau, A., et al.: FLEURS: few-shot learning evaluation of universal representations of speech. In: SLT 2022, Doha, Qatar, pp. 798–805. IEEE (2022)
6. Dalmia, S., Sanabria, R., Metze, F., Black, A.W.: Sequence-based multi-lingual low resource speech recognition. In: ICASSP 2018, Calgary, Canada, pp. 4909–4913. IEEE (2018)
7. Graves, A.: Sequence transduction with recurrent neural networks. In: ICML 2012 (2012)

8. Graves, A., Fernandez, S., Gomez, F.J., Schmidhuber, J.: Connectionist temporal classification: labelling unsegmented sequence data with recurrent neural networks. In: ICML 2006, Pittsburgh, USA, pp. 369–376. ACM (2006)
9. Graves, A., Jaitly, N.: Towards end-to-end speech recognition with recurrent neural networks. In: ICML 2014, Beijing, China, pp. 1764–1772. JMLR.org (2014)
10. Gulati, A., et al.: Conformer: Convolution-augmented transformer for speech recognition. In: Interspeech 2020, Shanghai, China, pp. 5036–5040. ISCA (2020)
11. Kannan, A., et al.: Large-scale multilingual speech recognition with a streaming end-to-end model. In: Interspeech 2019, Graz, Austria, pp. 2130–2134. ISCA (2019)
12. Kudo, T., Richardson, J.: Sentencepiece: a simple and language independent subword tokenizer and detokenizer for neural text processing. In: EMNLP 2018, Brussels, Belgium, pp. 66–71. ACL (2018)
13. Mateju, L., Kynych, F., Cerva, P., Zdansky, J., Malek, J.: Using x-vectors for speech activity detection in broadcast streams. In: Interspeech 2021, Brno, Czechia, pp. 1474–1478. ISCA (2021)
14. Mateju, L., Nouza, J., Cerva, P., Zdansky, J., Kynych, F.: Combining multilingual resources and models to develop state-of-the-art E2E ASR for Swedish. In: Interspeech 2023, Dublin, Ireland. ISCA (2023)
15. Nouza, J., Cerva, P., Zdansky, J.: Lexicon-based vs. lexicon-free ASR for Norwegian parliament speech transcription. In: Sojka, P., Horak, A., Kopecek, I., Pala, K. (eds.) Text, Speech, and Dialogue. TSD 2022. LNCS, vol. 13502, pp. 401–409. Springer, Cham (2022). https://doi.org/10.1007/978-3-031-16270-1_33
16. Ortiz, P., Burud, S.: BERT attends the conversation: improving low-resource conversational ASR (2021). preprint arXiv:2110.02267
17. Park, D.S., et al.: Specaugment: a simple data augmentation method for automatic speech recognition. In: Interspeech 2019, Graz, Austria, pp. 2613–2617. ISCA (2019)
18. Pratap, V., et al.: Massively multilingual ASR: 50 languages, 1 model, 1 billion parameters. In: Interspeech 2020, Shanghai, China, pp. 4751–4755. ISCA (2020)
19. Rugayan, J., Svendsen, T., Salvi, G.: Semantically meaningful metrics for Norwegian ASR systems. In: Interspeech 2022, Incheon, Korea, pp. 2283–2287. ISCA (2022)
20. Solberg, P.E., Ortiz, P.: The Norwegian parliamentary speech corpus. In: LREC 2022, Marseille, France, pp. 1003–1008. ELRA (2022)
21. Wang, D., Wang, X., Lv, S.: An overview of end-to-end automatic speech recognition. Symmetry 11, 1018 (2019)
22. Wang, D., Zheng, T.F.: Transfer learning for speech and language processing. In: APSIPA 2015, Hong Kong, pp. 1225–1237. IEEE (2015)
23. Watanabe, S., et al.: ESPnet: end-to-end speech processing toolkit. In: Interspeech 2018, Hyderabad, India, pp. 2207–2211. ISCA (2018)
24. Zhu, Y., et al.: Multilingual speech recognition with self-attention structured parameterization. In: Interspeech 2020, Shanghai, China, pp. 4741–4745 (2020)

VITS: Quality Vs. Speed Analysis

Jindřich Matoušek[1,2][✉] and Daniel Tihelka[2]

[1] Department of Cybernetics, Faculty of Applied Sciences,
University of West Bohemia, Plzeň, Czech Republic
`jmatouse@kky.zcu.cz`
[2] New Technology for the Information Society (NTIS), Faculty of Applied Sciences,
University of West Bohemia, Plzeň, Czech Republic
`dtihelka@ntis.zcu.cz`

Abstract. In this paper, we analyze the performance of a modern end-to-end speech synthesis model called Variational Inference with adversarial learning for end-to-end Text-to-Speech (VITS). We build on the original VITS model and examine how different modifications to its architecture affect synthetic speech quality and computational complexity. Experiments with two Czech voices, a male and a female, were carried out. To assess the quality of speech synthesized by the different modified models, MUSHRA listening tests were performed. The computational complexity was measured in terms of synthesis speed over real time. While the original VITS model is still preferred regarding speech quality, we present a modification of the original structure with a significantly better response yet providing acceptable output quality. Such a configuration can be used when system response latency is critical.

Keywords: Neural speech synthesis · End-to-end modeling · Variational autoencoder · VITS · Speed optimization

1 Introduction

Modern text-to-speech (TTS) systems are based on deep neural network (DNN) architectures [31]. While the quality of synthetic speech generated by these systems has improved dramatically compared to the previous generation of concatenation-based synthesis systems, the computational complexity of the DNN-based models has also increased significantly, limiting them from deploying on less powerful devices.

Most of the current TTS systems use a *cascade architecture* of two separate models (also called *two-staged* models) – an *acoustic model* that generates acoustic features (typically mel-spectrograms) from the input text (or, more specifically, from its phonetic representation, often just a sequence of phonemes) [2,10,11,25,34] and a *vocoder* that synthesizes the output waveform from the acoustic features [4,15,17,22,24]. The disadvantage of two-staged models is that

---

This research was supported by the Technology Agency of the Czech Republic (TA CR), project No. TL05000546.

K. Ekštein et al. (Eds.): TSD 2023, LNAI 14102, pp. 214–225, 2023.
https://doi.org/10.1007/978-3-031-40498-6_19

they are trained and optimized separately for the two independent models and are connected with pre-defined acoustic features (mel-spectrograms), which are not necessarily the best acoustic representation. Moreover, a mismatch between acoustic features used in training and inference (synthesis) is introduced. While in training both models use acoustic features from natural speech recordings; in inference, the vocoder utilizes acoustic features predicted by the acoustic model. Sequential training, in which the vocoder also uses acoustic features predicted by the acoustic model, can mitigate these problems. However, the training procedure is even more time-consuming and thus impractical [28].

To avoid the problems mentioned above, the current trend is to use a *one-staged* model, i.e., *end-to-end* model that jointly optimizes the acoustic and vocoding models [6,12,23,25]. On the other hand, this approach leads to even more complex models with a vast number of parameters making their run in real-time even more challenging.

Among the end-to-end models, *Variational Inference with adversarial learning for end-to-end Text-to-Speech* (VITS) is very popular, achieving very good output speech quality. Recently, several extensions to the original model and the *variational autoencoder* (VAE) approach behind VITS have emerged, trying to improve the quality and/or reduce the computational complexity [5,27–30]. In this study, we build on the original VITS model and analyze how different modifications to its architecture affect synthetic speech quality and computational complexity, i.e., inference speed.

The paper is organized as follows. In Section 2, we describe the original architecture of the VITS model. In Section 3, modifications to the VITS architecture are presented. Speech data used for our experiments are described in Section 4. In Sects. 5 and 6, we present and discuss the results of our experiments. Finally, conclusions are drawn in Section 7.

2 VITS

Variational Inference with adversarial learning for end-to-end Text-to-Speech (VITS) is a successful end-to-end model proposed for text-to-speech by Kim et al. [12]. VITS employs different deep-learning techniques together (adversarial learning [15], normalizing flows [26], and variational autoencoder (VAE) [13]) to achieve high-quality natural-sounding output. VAE internally links the two modules of TTS systems corresponding to the acoustic model and the vocoder through latent variables z, thus enabling a one-stage training.

Formally, the objective of conditional VAE is to maximize the variational lower bound, also called the evidence lower bound (ELBO), of the intractable marginal log-likelihood of data $\log p_\theta(x|c)$

$$\log p_\theta(x|c) \geq \mathbb{E}_{q_\phi(z|x)} \left[\log p_\theta(x|z) - \log \frac{q_\phi(z|x)}{p_\theta(z|c)} \right] \tag{1}$$

where $p_\theta(z|c)$ denotes a prior distribution of the latent variables z given condition c, $p_\theta(x|z)$ is the likelihood function of a data point x, and $q_\phi(z|x)$ is an approximate posterior distribution [12].

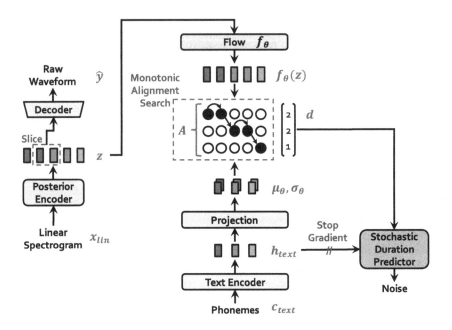

Fig. 1. The original VITS training scheme [12].

Less formally, VAE is composed of a posterior encoder $q_\phi(z|x_{lin})$ used to acquire the trainable latent acoustic features z from waveforms represented by linear spectrograms x_{lin}, and a decoder responsible for reconstructing waveforms $\hat{y}$ from the learned latent features. The original VITS training and inference schemes are shown in Fig. 1 and Fig. 2, respectively.

For the posterior encoder, non-causal WaveNet residual blocks [11,24] consisting of dilated convolutions with a gated activation unit and skip connection were used.

The prior distribution of VAE $p_\theta(z|c_{text})$ is conditioned on input text (or phonemes) c_{text} and is modeled by a prior encoder. The prior encoder consists of a transformer-based text encoder [32] that processes the input text c_{text} and a normalizing flow f_θ (consisting of a stack of WaveNet residual blocks) that improves the flexibility of the prior distribution [12].

HiFi-GAN V1 [15] generator was employed as the decoder. It comprises a stack of transposed convolutions and residual connections, each followed by a multi-receptive field fusion module (MRF).

To capture speech variations behind the input text and to synthesize speech with diverse rhythms, a flow-based *stochastic duration predictor* (SDP) that estimates the distribution of phoneme duration d (with the mean μ_θ and standard deviation σ_θ) from a conditional input h_{text} was proposed. Monotonic alignment search (MAS) [11] was adopted to align input text and target speech and to obtain ground-truth phoneme durations during training.

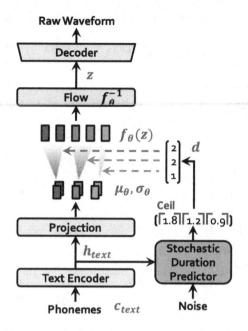

Fig. 2. The original VITS inference scheme [12].

In our experiments, VITS models were trained using the AdamW optimizer [18] with $\beta_1 = 0.8$, $\beta_2 = 0.99$, and weight decay $\lambda = 0.01$. The learning rate decay was scheduled by a $0.999^{1/8}$ factor in every epoch with an initial learning rate of 2×10^{-4}. The batch size was set to 32, and the models were trained up to 1M steps (2640 epochs) with mixed precision using the Coqui-TTS framework[1].

3   Modifications to the VITS Architecture

In this section, we describe the modifications to the original VITS architecture. As described in Section 2, VITS uses a flow-based stochastic duration predictor (SDP) that better models the rhythm variability in speech. To avoid further uncertainty in our experiments, and because some studies point out that SDP could in some cases generate unnatural duration causing unclear pronunciation [3,5], a *deterministic duration predictor* (DDP) from Glow-TTS [11] was used in *all* VITS versions.

3.1   Waveform Decoder Modifications

Most of the modifications concerned the waveform decoder. The original VITS model employs HiFi-GAN version 1 (V1) [15]. Henceforth, the original VITS model will be referred to as VITS1.

---

[1] https://github.com/coqui-ai/TTS.

Table 1. Summary of modifications to the VITS architecture.

Desc.		VITS1	VITS2	VITS3	VITS4	VITS5
Wav. decoder	DRBT	I	I	II	II	II
	DUHC	512	128	256	128	128
	DRKS	$[16, 16, 4, 4]$	$[16, 16, 4, 4]$	$[16, 16, 8]$	$[16, 16, 8]$	$[16, 16, 8]$
		$[1, 1]$	$[1, 1]$	$[1, 2]$	$[1, 2]$	$[1, 3]$
	DRDS	$[3, 1] \times 3$	$[3, 1] \times 3$	$[2, 6]$	$[2, 6]$	$[2, 8]$
		$[5, 1]$	$[5, 1]$	$[3, 12]$	$[3, 12]$	$[3, 15]$
Encoder	TEHC	768	768	768	768	512
	TETL	6	6	6	6	4
	PEKS	5	5	5	5	3
	PEL	16	16	16	16	8
	FNKS	5	5	5	5	3
	FNRL	4	4	4	4	2
MHC		192	192	192	192	128
# params.		82M	69M	69M	68M	52M

Kong et al. [15] introduced three variants of the waveform generator. HiFi-GAN V2 is simply a smaller version of V1 with fewer hidden channels of the first upsampling convolution layer (DUHC, 128 vs. 512) but with precisely the same receptive fields. To further reduce the number of layers while maintaining receptive fields wide, a different type of residual block (denoted as "II" as opposed to "I" in VITS1 and VITS2) with different kernel sizes (DRKS) and dilation rates (DRDS) was proposed in V3 [15]. We have incorporated versions V2 and V3 into the VITS model and named them VITS2 and VITS3, respectively.

To simplify the generator structure further, we introduced an "unofficial" version V4, an even more reduced version of V3 with a smaller hidden dimension of the first upsampling convolution layer DUHC (128 vs. 256) and denoted it as VITS4.

All modifications to the waveform generator are summarized in the "waveform decoder" section of Table 1.

3.2   Encoder Modifications

To make even bigger changes to the original VITS model architecture, we also experimented with the encoder part of the VITS model. These modifications further significantly reduce the complexity of the model (see the number of parameters of each model in Table 1) and thus have a great potential to speed up speech synthesis. On the other hand, we expect a significant drop in the quality of synthetic speech as well.

We simplified the text encoder, posterior encoder, and the flow network itself. As for the text encoder, the number of hidden channels of the transformer feed-forward layers (TEHC) was reduced from 768 to 512, and the number of transformer layers (TETL) from 6 to 4.

In the posterior encoder, the kernel size (PEKS) of WaveNet layers decreased from 5 to 3, and the number of the posterior encoder's WaveNet layers (PEL) from 16 to 8.

Similarly, we reduced the kernel size (FNKS) and the number of residual coupling WaveNet layers (FNRL) of the flow network from 5 to 3 and from 4 to 2, respectively.

Modifications made to the encoder part were used together with the HiFi-GAN V4 waveform generator, forming the most reduced VITS5 model, and are summarized in the "Encoder" section of the Table 1. Note that we also further increased the dilation rates of waveform generator residual blocks. In VITS5, we also reduced the number of hidden channels in the whole model (MHC), i.e., the dimension of the latent acoustic features z, from 192 to 128.

4 Speech Data

For our experiments, we used two large corpora of Czech news-reading speech recorded by a professional male (**speaker M**) and female (**speaker F**) speaker. The corpora were primarily designed for the use with *unit-selection* speech synthesis [20], but Vít et al. [33] showed that the corpora are also suitable for neural speech synthesis. They contain paired text-audio data with approximately 14 h of audio (including pauses) distributed over 12,240 (speaker M) and 12,151 (speaker F) utterances. For our purposes, the audio has been downsampled to 24 kHz, carefully annotated, and the resulting text has been normalized to expand out numbers, dates, ordinals, monetary amounts, etc. Finally, the text of each audio was transcribed into a sequence of phones using a set of carefully designed Czech phonetic rules and a pronunciation dictionary with words that do not obey Czech pronunciation rules [35]. Since Matoušek & Tihelka [19] showed that it is advantageous to explicitly include pauses and punctuation marks in the phonetic representation when training a synthesizer, each phonetic transcript was supplemented by pauses using an external speech segmentation tool [7,8].

5 Results

In this paper, two evaluation types of the proposed modifications to the baseline VITS algorithm were carried out – evaluation of the quality of synthetic speech and measurement of synthesis speed. Objective evaluation of synthetic speech quality is presented in Section 5.1 whereas subjective evaluation is described in Section 5.2. In Section 5.3, the synthesis speed of each modified model is analyzed.

Table 2. Mel cepstral distortion (MCD) results (lower is better) with 95% confidence intervals.

Speaker	VITS1	VITS2	VITS3	VITS4	VITS5
M	5.880 ± 0.310	5.889 ± 0.253	5.845 ± 0.261	5.870 ± 0.249	6.075 ± 0.255
F	5.683 ± 0.296	5.974 ± 0.353	5.984 ± 0.295	5.882 ± 0.322	6.291 ± 0.289

5.1   Objective Evaluation

Among objective measures, mel cepstral distortion (MCD) [14,16] is often used to measure differences between two speech segments represented by mel-cepstral coefficients (MCEPs)

$$MCD(x, \hat{x}) = \frac{10\sqrt{2}}{\ln 10} \frac{1}{T} \sqrt{\sum_{t=1}^{T} ||x_t - \hat{x}_t||} \qquad (2)$$

where x is a ground-truth segment (computed from natural speech) and $\hat{x}$ is its synthesized version. T denotes the number of frames, and t is the index of a particular frame.

Comparing results of the objective evaluation in Table 2 with the following subjective evaluation by MUSHRA tests in Table 3 and Fig. 3 (and particularly for Speaker F), it can be seen that the tendencies are correlated. Especially the VITS5 model obtained a measurably worse score than the other systems, while the difference among the remaining systems is lower than the difference to VITS5.

5.2   Subjective Evaluation

We used Multiple Stimuli with Hidden Reference and Anchor (MUSHRA) listening tests to compare speech quality generated by the various VITS models. Listening tests followed the ITU-R recommendation BS.1534-2 [1]. Two listening tests were performed, the first for speaker M and the second for speaker F.

Each listening test consisted of a set of the same 20 sentences that were synthesized by the baseline VITS1 and the different modified VITS models described in Section 3: VITS2, VITS4, VITS5. In addition, a natural version of each sentence was hidden in each set and used as a reference (upper anchor). The sentences were 3–10 words long and contained both single and compound/complex sentences. Of course, we used sentences not included in the training data. The longer sentences were compound/complex sentences that contained internal pauses. Versions of every sentence were compared with respect to naturalness. Since it is unclear how to interpret a lower hidden anchor when rating synthetic speech [9,21] and it is not possible to assume a priori that the VITS5 model will be worse, no lower anchor was included in the tests. Due to the higher elaborateness of the listening tests, we decided not to include the VITS3

Table 3. MUSHRA test evaluation results (higher is better) with 95% confidence intervals.

Speaker	Natural	VITS1	VITS2	VITS4	VITS5
M	98.41 ± 0.410	92.33 ± 0.901	83.52 ± 1.287	87.55 ± 1.128	69.34 ± 1.989
F	98.31 ± 0.443	94.30 ± 0.805	90.52 ± 1.187	91.52 ± 0.849	71.45 ± 2.070

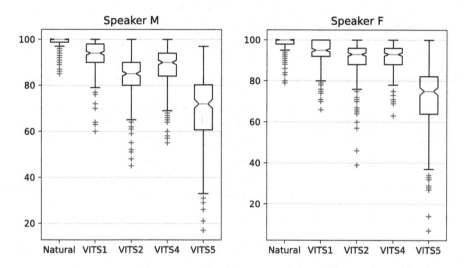

Fig. 3. Boxplot of the MUSHRA evaluations for both speakers.

model, particularly as the impact of HiFi-GAN V3 on the quality has already been studied in [15], and compared to V3, V4 has a higher inference speed-up potential, containing slightly fewer parameters.

The listener was required to rate the versions between 0 (completely unnatural) and 100 (completely natural). Due to the presence of the reference version in each set, the listener was instructed to give at least one of the versions a rating of 100. 12 listeners participated in each test, and each of them evaluated all the sentences. The ordering of sentences was randomized within each test query, but the same ordering was presented to all the listeners. All the listeners were native Czech speakers, some of them had very little knowledge of speech synthesis, and none of them reported any hearing problems. The results of the listening tests are shown in Tables 3 and 4, and in Fig. 3.

5.3 Speed Analysis

To measure the runtime speed of the individual VITS modifications, we synthesized 2,000 sentences by the different VITS models on 12-core Intel® Core™ i7-6850K CPU, running at 3.60 GHz with 256 GB of RAM. The GPU was NVIDIA GeForce RTX 3090 Ti with 24 GB memory. The raw time of the synthesis run (excluding the time of the model initialization) was measured by a testing script.

Table 4. The rankings of the models in MUSHRA test for speaker M / F. *Natural* represents the reference.

	Natural	VITS1	VITS2	VITS4	VITS5
1st	**219 / 207**	57 / 84	9 / 40	19 / 39	2 / 2
2nd	12 / 16	**122 / 96**	26 / 42	55 / 56	1 / 1
3rd	5 / 8	37 / 41	77 / **84**	116 / 59	8 / 6
4th	4 / 8	23 / 15	**114** / 64	42 / **79**	30 / 19
5th	0 / 1	1 / 4	14 / 10	8 / 7	**199 / 212**

Table 5. Computational complexity when running on CPU or GPU, regarding inference speed over real-time.

	Speaker	VITS1	VITS2	VITS3	VITS4	VITS5
CPU	M	3.79	18.57	20.83	39.00	50.13
	F	3.76	20.49	20.87	39.23	50.91
GPU	M	118.58	160.52	201.49	220.67	282.67
	F	125.76	169.98	220.04	237.14	322.70

The result in Table 5 is the ratio between the length of the audio and the synthesis runtime (real-time factor 2.0 means that audio playback took twice the synthesis time). The synthesis was carried out first exclusively on the CPU, followed by the run on GPU. It was ensured that no other processes, except the fundamental low-level system services, were running on the computer.

The results show that running on GPU is, naturally, significantly faster than on the 12-core CPU, but the differences between the slowest VITS1 and the fastest VITS5 are far less significant on GPU.

6   Discussion

To no surprise, the results clearly confirmed that the full VITS1 model provides the most natural-sounding speech as well as the lowest (or one of the lowest) MCD, at the cost of relatively low inference speed, though. Especially in applications where the minimal latency (the time lag between a request for synthesis and speech availability) is a crucial factor, such as dialogue systems, the VITS4 variant may be considered. Although its speech quality is still subjectively perceived as worse than the VITS1, the VITS4 variant has a lower MCD than VITS2 and is also subjectively perceived as better or similar to VITS2 for speaker M and speaker F, respectively. And on top of that, its inference speed is better than that of VITS2, being approximately 10 times faster than VITS1 (almost 40 times faster than real-time) when running on a CPU.

7   Conclusion

In this paper, we analyzed the performance of a modern end-to-end speech synthesis model VITS. Since VITS is a complex model with approximately 82 M parameters, we proposed different modifications that simplified its architecture and, on two Czech voices, a male and a female, investigated how these modifications affect both the quality and speed of resulting synthetic speech. We found that while the original (and the most complex) VITS model is still preferred in terms of speech quality, a modification denoted as VITS4, which significantly simplifies the original architecture (from 82 M to 68 M parameters), leads to acceptable synthetic speech quality, being approximately 10 times faster than VITS1 (almost 40 times faster than real-time) when running on a CPU. Such a configuration can be used when system response latency is critical.

Since the most drastic simplification (VITS5) revealed the potential for even more significant system speedup, our future work in this area will focus on more fine-grained exploration of encoder parameters to reveal if there is a possibility of additional speedup while not lowering quality below the VITS4 modification.

Acknowledgements. Computational resources were provided by the e-INFRA CZ project (ID:90140), supported by the Ministry of Education, Youth and Sports of the Czech Republic.

References

1. Method for the subjective assessment of intermediate quality level of coding systems. Technical report BS.1534-2, International Telecommunication Union (2014)
2. Arik, S., et al.: Deep voice: real-time neural text-to-speech. In: International Conference on Machine Learning (2017)
3. Casanova, E., Weber, J., Shulby, C., Junior, A.C., Gölge, E., Ponti, M.A.: YourTTS: towards zero-shot multi-speaker TTS and zero-shot voice conversion for everyone. In: International Conference on Machine Learning. Baltimore, USA (2022)
4. Chen, M., et al.: MultiSpeech: Multi-Speaker text to speech with transformer. In: INTERSPEECH, pp. 4024–4028. International Speech Communication Association, Shanghai, China (2020). https://doi.org/10.21437/Interspeech.2020-3139
5. Cho, H., Jung, W., Lee, J., Woo, S.H.: SANE-TTS: stable and natural end-to-end multilingual text-to-speech. In: INTERSPEECH, pp. 1–5. Incheon, Korea (2022). https://doi.org/10.21437/Interspeech.2022-46
6. Donahue, J., Dieleman, S., Binkowski, M., Elsen, E., Simonyan, K.: End-to-end adversarial text-to-speech. In: International Conference on Learning Representations (2021)
7. Hanzlíček, Z., Matoušek, J.: Phonetic speech segmentation of audiobooks by using adapted LSTM-based acoustic models. In: Garcia, A.C.B., Ferro, M., Ribón, J.C.R. (eds.) IBERAMIA 2022. Lecture Notes in Computer Science, vol. 13788, pp. 317–327. Springer, Cham (2022). https://doi.org/10.1007/978-3-031-22419-5_27
8. Hanzlíček, Z., Vít, J.: LSTM-based speech segmentation trained on different foreign languages. In: Sojka, P., Kopeček, I., Pala, K., Horák, A. (eds.) TSD 2020. LNCS (LNAI), vol. 12284, pp. 456–464. Springer, Cham (2020). https://doi.org/10.1007/978-3-030-58323-1_49

9. Henter, G.E., Merritt, T., Shannon, M., Mayo, C., King, S.: Measuring the perceptual effects of modelling assumptions in speech synthesis using stimuli constructed from repeated natural speech. In: INTERSPEECH, pp. 1504–1508. Singapore (2014)

10. Jeong, M., Kim, H., Cheon, S.J., Choi, B.J., Kim, N.S.: Diff-TTS: a denoising diffusion model for text-to-speech. In: INTERSPEECH, pp. 3605–3609. Brno, Czechia (2021). https://doi.org/10.21437/Interspeech.2021-469

11. Kim, J., Kim, S., Kong, J., Yoon, S.: Glow-TTS: a generative flow for text-to-speech via monotonic alignment search. In: Neural Information Processing Systems. Vancouver, Canada (2020)

12. Kim, J., Kong, J., Son, J.: Conditional variational autoencoder with adversarial learning for end-to-end text-to-speech. In: International Conference on Machine Learning, pp. 5530–5540 (2021)

13. Kingma, D.P., Welling, M.: Auto-encoding variational Bayes. In: International Conference on Learning Representations, pp. 1–14. No. Ml, Banff, Canada (2014)

14. Kominek, J., Schultz, T., Black, A.W.: Synthesizer voice quality of new languages calibrated with mean cepstral distortion. In: Speech Technology for Under-Resourced Languages, pp. 63–68. Hanoi, Vietnam (2008)

15. Kong, J., Kim, J., Bae, J.: HiFi-GAN: generative adversarial networks for efficient and high fidelity speech synthesis. In: Conference on Neural Information Processing Systems. Vancouver, Canada (2020)

16. Kubichek, R.F.: Mel-cepstral distance measure for objective speech quality assessment. In: IEEE Pacific Rim Conference on Communications Computers and Signal Processing, pp. 125–128. Victoria, Canada (1993). https://doi.org/10.1109/pacrim.1993.407206

17. Kumar, K., et al.: MelGAN: generative adversarial networks for conditional waveform synthesis. In: Advances in Neural Information Processing Systems (2019)

18. Loshchilov, I., Hutter, F.: Decoupled weight decay regularization. In: International Conference on Learning Representations. New Orleans, USA (2019)

19. Matoušek, J., Tihelka, D.: On comparison of phonetic representations for Czech neural speech synthesis. In: Sojka, P., Horák, A., Kopeček, I., Pala, K. (eds.) Text, Speech, and Dialogue, TSD 2022. Lecture Notes in Computer Science, vol. 13502, pp. 410–422. Springer, Cham (2022). https://doi.org/10.1007/978-3-031-16270-1_34

20. Matoušek, J., Tihelka, D., Romportl, J.: Building of a speech corpus optimised for unit selection TTS synthesis. In: Language Resources and Evaluation Conference, pp. 1296–1299. Marrakech, Morocco (2008)

21. Merritt, T., Clark, R.A.J., Wu, Z., Yamagishi, J., King, S.: Deep neural network-guided unit selection synthesis. In: IEEE International Conference on Acoustics Speech and Signal Processing, pp. 5145–5149. Shanghai, China (2016)

22. van den Oord, A., et al.: Parallel WaveNet: fast high-fidelity speech synthesis. CoRR (2017). arxiv.org/abs/1711.10433

23. Ping, W., Peng, K., Chen, J.: Clarinet: parallel wave generation in end-to-end text-to-speech. In: International Conference on Learning Representations. New Orleans, USA (2019)

24. Prenger, R., Valle, R., Catanzaro, B.: WaveGlow: a flow-based generative network for speech synthesis. In: IEEE International Conference on Acoustics Speech and Signal Processing, pp. 3617–3621. Brighton, United Kingdom (2019). https://doi.org/10.1109/ICASSP.2019.8683143

25. Ren, Y., et al.: FastSpeech 2: fast and high-quality end-to-end text to speech. In: International Conference on Learning Representations (2021)

26. Rezende, D.J., Mohamed, S.: Variational inference with normalizing flows. In: International Conference on Machine Learning. Lille, France (2015)

27. Shang, Z., Shi, P., Zhang, P., Wang, L., Zhao, G.: HierTTS?: expressive end-to-end text-to-waveform using a multi-scale hierarchical variational auto-encoder. Appl. Sci. (Switzerland) **13**(2), 868 (2023)

28. Shirahata, Y., Yamamoto, R., Song, E., Terashima, R., Kim, J.M., Tachibana, K.: Period VITS: variational inference with explicit pitch modeling for end-to-end emotional speech synthesis. In: IEEE International Conference on Acoustics Speech and Signal Processing. Rhodes Island, Greece (2023). https://doi.org/10.1109/ICASSP49357.2023.10096480

29. Song, K., et al.: AdaVITS: Tiny VITS for low computing resource speaker adaptation. In: International Symposium on Chinese Language Processing. Singapore (2022). https://doi.org/10.1109/ISCSLP57327.2022.10037585

30. Tan, X., et al.: NaturalSpeech: end-to-end text to speech synthesis with human-level quality. CoRR, pp. 1–19 (2022). arxiv.org/abs/2205.04421

31. Tan, X., Qin, T., Soong, F.K., Liu, T.Y.: A Survey on neural speech synthesis. CoRR abs/2106.1 (2021). https://doi.org/10.48550/arXiv.2106.15561

32. Vaswani, A., et al.: Attention is all you need. In: Advances in Neural Information Processing Systems, pp. 6000–6010. Long Beach, CA, USA (2017)

33. Vít, J., Hanzlíček, Z., Matoušek, J.: On the analysis of training data for WaveNet-based speech synthesis. In: IEEE International Conference on Acoustics Speech and Signal Processing, pp. 5684–5688. Calgary, Canada (2018). https://doi.org/10.1109/ICASSP.2018.8461960

34. Wang, Y., et al.: Tacotron: towards end-to-end speech synthesis. In: INTER-SPEECH, pp. 4006–4010. Stockholm, Sweden (2017). https://doi.org/10.21437/Interspeech.2017-1452

35. Řezáčková, M., Švec, J., Tihelka, D.: T5G2P: using text-to-text transfer transformer for grapheme-to-phoneme conversion. In: INTERSPEECH, pp. 6–10. Brno, Czechia (2021). https://doi.org/10.21437/Interspeech.2021-546

When Whisper Meets TTS: Domain Adaptation Using only Synthetic Speech Data

Juan Camilo Vásquez-Correa[1]([✉]), Haritz Arzelus[1], Juan M. Martin-Doñas[1], Joaquin Arellano[1], Ander Gonzalez-Docasal[1,2], and Aitor Álvarez[1]

[1] Fundacion Vicomtech, Basque Research and Technology Alliance (BRTA), Mikeletegi 57, 20009 Donostia - San Sebastian, Spain
`jcvasquez@vicomtech.org`
[2] University of Zaragoza, Department of Electronics, Engineering and Communications, Pedro Cerbuna 12, 50009 Zaragoza, Spain

Abstract. Automatic Speech Recognition is among the most important areas of Artificial Intelligence research today. One of the most notable advances in this area is the development of end-to-end models, which have shown state-of-the-art performance in many benchmark scenarios. In spite of the recent improvements, these architectures still require large amounts of transcribed speech data to be trained, which can be challenging in low resource languages, or in specific domains due to privacy concerns. This study proposes a methodology to fine-tune Whisper-based models using only synthetic speech. The aim is to enable training robust systems for specific domains and low resource languages, where large labeled corpora are difficult to collect. Our approach is based on a language model adaptation by fine-tuning only the decoder of the model, thus the network is able to learn specific vocabulary that is not initially available. The proposed methodology is evaluated with data from different languages and domains. In addition, Parameter Efficient Fine-Tuning strategies were used to efficiently adapt the large pre-trained Whisper models. This is one of the first studies that considers the effect of using only synthetic speech for domain adaption of speech recognition systems in non-English data, providing word error rate reductions in low resource languages between 2 and 30 points, depending on the Whisper version.

Keywords: Speech Recognition · Whisper · Text to Speech · Domain Adaptation · Parameter Efficient Fine-Tuning

1 Introduction

In recent years, there have been significant advances in Automatic Speech Recognition (ASR) using End-to-End (E2E) models [1]. One of the most notable outcomes in this area is the development of Transformer-based architectures, such as Wav2Vec2.0 [2], the Conformer networks [3], and more recently, fully supervised models like Whisper [4]. These models have achieved state-of-the-art performance on a variety of speech recognition benchmarks, including those that involve noisy or accented speech. Although the results observed to date are impressive, several challenges still remain for the research community. For instance, these E2E architectures still require large amounts of transcribed speech data to be trained and to reach good performance. Furthermore, specific domains such as health care, forensics, multimedia, or government, among others, may face limited data availability due to privacy concerns or difficulties in data collection. These scenarios pose challenges due to non-controlled acoustic conditions and domain-specific vocabulary. Addressing these problems is particularly challenging for low-resource languages where large labeled corpora are scarce for training ASR systems. Therefore, training robust ASR models for specific domains, low resource languages, and in non-controlled acoustic conditions becomes a difficult task.

One strategy to adapt ASR systems to specific domains, especially under low resource settings, is to use data augmentation strategies to artificially increase the size of the training data. Methods like SpecAugment [5] or those based on speed perturbation and noise injection have shown to be helpful in adapting ASR models to specific domains. However, these methods only focus on adapting the ASR system to the specific acoustic conditions of the target domain, overlooking the challenge of domain-specific vocabulary.

Recent studies have demonstrated that it is possible to perform data augmentation, or even full training of ASR systems, using synthetic data obtained from Text-To-Speech (TTS) systems [6–9]. Given the improvements in neural TTS models, such as Tacotron-2 with Global State Tokens [10] and more recently VALL-E [11], it is possible to generate high quality speech with varying prosody that can be used also to train and adapt E2E ASR models. The use of synthetic speech to fine-tune ASR systems can be particularly helpful to deal with the issue of out-of-vocabulary words and to expand the vocabulary of E2E systems during training [6,12,13]. In [14], the authors use synthetic speech to teach medication names to an E2E ASR system based on a Recurrent Neural Networks Transducer (RNN-T). The training process involved mixing real and synthetic samples. The fine-tuned model reduced relatively the word error rate (WER) by up to 65% when recognizing out-of-vocabulary words related to medication names. Additional studies have shown that combining real and synthetic speech data during training and fine-tuning can reduce the WER of an ASR system [6–9,15,16]. However, there are important considerations to address in those cases to achieve accurate results. For instance, when using synthetic speech for ASR training, it is important to deal with the mismatch in acoustic characteristics between real and synthetic audio. Synthetic speech may contain artifacts that do not exist in real data, such as unrealistic speaking styles and the absence of background noise. Some studies have mitigated this issue by implementing regularization strategies [13,17] and freezing the encoder of the E2E model during fine-tuning [12,13]. The process of fine-tuning only the decoder of the network is similar to adapting a language model. Therefore, the model only learns the token representation of out-of-vocabulary words, rather than the acoustic properties of synthetic speech [18].

These previous works have proven the benefits of increased acoustic and lexical diversity in synthetic data for ASR training. Nevertheless, most of them are evaluated using standard benchmark corpora, such as Librispeech [19]. Moreover, in the majority of cases, TTS-derived data is used only for data augmentation, rather than to adapt the model to new, unseen domains, particularly in low resource languages, where there is the real need to adapt E2E ASR models. Finally, most of the previous studies have focused on mixing real and synthetic audio data, and have not shown reliable results using only synthetic speech [7,17].

This study extends all previous research by using only synthetic data for domain adaptation of E2E ASR models. Our approach is motivated by the recent release of Whisper [4], which was pre-trained with large amounts of labeled data from the Internet (up to 680k h). This leads us to believe that it is now possible to fine-tune models using only synthetic speech, making the domain adaptation tasks more feasible, especially in low resource languages. We considered a state-of-the-art TTS system to create realistic speech signals in order to create adapted Whisper models for a variety of domains, including forensics, broadcast media, and parliamentary. Our proposed methodology was also evaluated in different languages to test the effect of using synthetic speech to adapt pre-trained models with large, intermediate, and low resource languages such as English, Spanish, and Basque, respectively. To the best of our knowledge, this is one of the first studies to consider the effect of using only synthetic speech in ASR model adaptation for non-English data. An additional contribution of this paper relies on the evaluation and comparison of different Parameter Efficient Fine-Tuning (PEFT) methods [20] when training large Transformer-based models. PEFT-based approaches focus on fine-tuning only a small number of model parameters, thereby greatly decreasing the computational and storage costs. The use of these strategies have not been extensively explored for speech-based models. However, this is an important aspect to be considered when training large models such as Whisper.

The rest of the paper is distributed as follows. Section 2 describes the methods and strategies considered to adapt an ASR system based on Whisper to new unknown domains in different languages. Section 3 describes the different corpora considered in this study to train and evaluate the proposed approach. Section 4 shows the main results obtained and discusses the main insights derived from the performed experiments. Finally, Sect. 5 draws the main conclusions and presents further perspectives to be addressed.

2 Methods

2.1 Whisper

Whisper is an encoder-decoder Transformer network recently introduced by OpenAI [4]. The model is trained in a fully supervised manner, using up to 680k h of labeled speech data from multiple sources. The encoder is fed by 80-channel

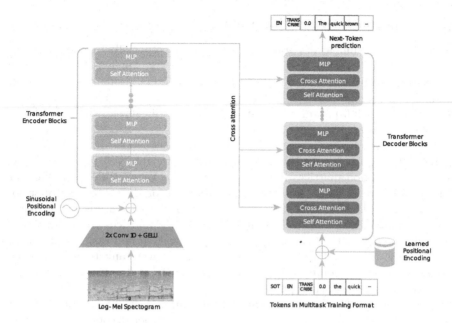

Fig. 1. Whisper architecture representation. The log Mel-spectrograms are encoded by a Transformer network. Encoded representations are transformed into character outputs and non-speech tokens via the Transformer decoder. Figure inspired from [4].

log-Mel spectrograms and it consists of two convolution layers (kernel size of 3), followed by sinusoidal positional encoding, and a stacked set of Transformer blocks. The decoder uses the learned positional embeddings and the same number of Transformer blocks as the encoder (see Fig. 1).

Five pre-trained versions of Whisper are available, with variations in the number of layers (ranging from 4 to 32) and attention heads (ranging from 6 to 20). These configurations yield models with 39 M to 1550 M parameters. The conducted experiments involved fine-tuning the five versions of the model to evaluate their capability to be adapted to the target domain. The process is performed freezing the weights of the encoder network, similar to previous studies [13,18]. Freezing the encoder aims to mitigate the mismatch in acoustic characteristics between real and synthetic audio, which can be problematic for model training and fine-tuning. Hence, the learning process focuses only on adapting the vocabulary to the E2E system, similar to a language model adaptation.

The hyper parameters for fine-tuning included a learning rate of 5×10^{-5}, warmed up during the initial 10% of the training, and batch size of 16 (using gradient accumulation steps due to memory constraints). The decoding was performed using a beam search strategy with 5 beams, an array of temperature weights of $[0.2, 0.4, 0.6, 0.8, 1]$, and a no repeat 3-gram strategy to avoid loops [4].

2.2 Parameter Efficient Fine-Tuning

Due to the large number of parameters to fine-tune, especially for the Large version of Whisper (1550 M), a set of PEFT strategies were applied. These methods aimed to fine-tune a small number of model parameters, decreasing the computational and storage costs [20]. In general, PEFT methods have shown to be comparable to a full parameter fine-tuning despite the substantial reduction of tunable parameters [20].

We compared three different PEFT methods: (1) the Low-Rank Adaptation (LoRA) [21], which freezes the pretrained model weights and injects trainable rank decomposition matrices into each layer of the Whisper decoder. We consider a rank $r = 32$ and a re-scaling factor $\alpha = 64$ for the matrix factorization in LoRA [21]. (2) AdaLoRA [22], where the rank decomposition of the weight matrices is performed adaptively. Critical incremental matrices are assigned with high rank such that they can capture more fine-grained and task-specific information. Less important ones are pruned to have lower rank to prevent overfitting and save the computational budget [22]. (3) Finally, in addition to the rank decomposition-based approaches, we considered the Bias-terms Fine-tuning (BitFit) strategy [23]. BitFit updates the bias terms in the pre-trained model, while freezing the remaining parameters of the Whisper decoder. The authors in [23] showed that fine-tuning only a subset of bias parameters in a Transformer network is comparable to a full fine-tuning of the model.

2.3 Text to Speech Models

The generation of realistic synthetic speech data was performed through a state-of-the-art TTS system composed by a Tacotron-2 [24] acoustic model followed by a HiFi-GAN [25] neural vocoder. Tacotron-2 consists of a sequence-to-sequence model, which includes an encoder, a decoder, and a final post-processing convolutional neural network. The encoder is fed with embedding representations of the input characters, generated by a 1D convolutional-recurrent network, and which is simultaneously trained with the whole TTS system. The Tacotron-2 models for English, Spanish and Basque were trained on pairs of text and its corresponding acoustic information, represented by audios sampled at $22,050\,\text{Hz}$, using 80-channel Mel-spectrograms, a frame length of 1024, a time-shift of 256 samples, and a 1024-resolution Fourier transform. During training, this network learned to generalize and generate new spectrograms from unseen texts using the examples given for training. The model was trained using an Adam optimizer [26], and a learning rate of 10^{-3} that exponentially decays to 10^{-5} after 50k steps. We also applied L_2 regularization with a weight of 10^{-7} and a batch-size of 32. The final training steps were slightly different for each model, although they were established between 170k and 190k steps. The English model was trained with the LJ Speech Dataset [27] composed of $13,100$ short audio clips from a single speaker (23 h and 54 min). The Spanish and Basque models were trained using mono-speaker proprietary datasets, containing $11,650$ (20 h and 46 min) and $11,640$ (19 h and 4 min) short audio clips for Spanish and Basque, respectively.

The Tacotron-2 model is combined with a HiFi-GAN [25] neural vocoder that receives the spectrograms generated by the acoustic model, and produce the final waveform. Each model was trained and adapted to each target voice by using a set of ground-truth aligned Mel spectrograms, compatible with the Tacotron-2 model. The vocoder was trained using a learning rate of 2×10^{-4} with a decaying factor of 0.999, whilst the batch-size was set to 16.

2.4   Methodology

The proposed methodology is shown in Fig. 2. The text data for each domain was crawled from the Internet to obtain the target vocabulary for recognition. The crawled corpora were then preprocessed and used as input for the TTS system. After generating the synthetic speech data, different versions of Whisper were fine-tuned to obtain domain-specific ASRs. Only the decoder of Whisper was adapted to learn the target vocabulary and not the acoustic characteristics of synthetic speech. The evaluation was performed using real acoustic data from the specific domains.

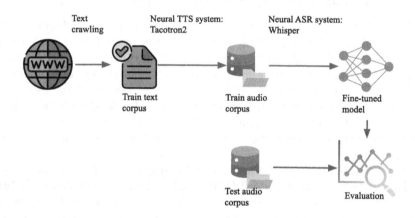

Fig. 2. Methodology to fine-tune Whisper ASR systems using synthetic data.

Three scenarios were considered to cover specific domains in forensics, broadcast media, and parliamentary. These scenarios often include specialized terminology that a general-purpose ASR system may not be able to recognize accurately. At the same time, each domain contains data in a different language. The considered languages were selected to cover large, intermediate, and low resource scenarios [4].

3   Data Description

We considered data in English, Spanish, and Basque with the aim to cover different scenarios where the original Whisper model was trained with large,

Table 1. Data distribution for each corpus.

	English	Spanish	Basque
Domain	Forensics	Broadcast media	Parliament
Hours for pre training [4]	438,200	11,100	21
Hours for fine-tuning	11.7	20.4	26.7
Hours for test	10	54	7.2
Tokens for fine-tuning	99,470	141,236	187,975
Unique tokens for fine-tuning	7,473	18,393	30,471

intermediate, and low resource data. For each language, the data used were specific to a particular domain of application, which included forensics, broadcast media, and parliament. Table 1 summarizes the main characteristics for each corpus. Further details about each scenario are found in the following sections.

3.1 English Data. Forensic Child Abuse Analysis Domain

The experiments for this scenario were performed with the GRACE corpus [28]. This is a multilingual dataset that comprises audio recordings from multiple sources from the research community. Audios from different public databases were compiled and filtered according to the presence of 86 keywords related to child abuse. This study considered only the English version of the dataset, which comprises 9.2 h of audio recordings from the Spoken Wikipedia corpus [29], the Debating technology corpus [30], and TEDLIUMv2 [31]. This corpus is available online[1] to be used as a benchmark corpus for speech recognition under forensic domains.

The text data used for synthesis and fine-tuning of the Whisper model included crawled documents from EUROPOL[2], UNICEF[3], and Wikipedia articles related to child abuse. The crawled corpus is composed of 55,059 words (without stop words) from which 4,571 audio utterances were created (11.7 h).

3.2 Spanish Data. Broadcast Media Domain

The data for this experiment considered the test set of the IberSPEECH-RTVE 2022 Speech to Text Transcription Challenge [32][4]. The database is a collection of 54 h of audio materials from the Spanish national TV (RTVE) archive in various genres. The corpus covers a wide variety of scenarios of read and spontaneous speech, including material from scripted content to live broadcasts. The

---

[1] https://shorturl.at/dfjx2.
[2] https://www.europol.europa.eu/media-press/newsroom?q=child%20abuse.
[3] https://www.unicef.org/search?force=0&query=child+abuse&created%5Bmin%5D=&created%5Bmax%5D=.
[4] http://catedrartve.unizar.es/rtvedatabase.html.

corpus incorporates a diverse range of content, such as fiction series, contest shows, social and cultural documentaries, unedited live interviews, and newscasts, among others. This corpus is not directly segmented and contains challenging acoustic conditions (e.g. background music and noise). Therefore, we first applied a Voice Activity Detection (VAD) module based on the GPVAD convolutional-recurrent architecture [33] trained with 5k h from the Google AudioSet database [34]. The GPVAD raw output is further processed by joining small speech regions separated by less than two seconds of non-speech, thus generating speech segments longer than five seconds when possible.

The training text material to generate synthetic data for this domain covered TV subtitles from the *RTVE Play* web portal[5] and news crawled from the RTVE website[6] [35]. We also collected news gathered from digital newspapers in the Internet in order to generalize to other news formats and improve generalization. A total of 17,524 sentences covering different news topics were synthesized, forming a corpus with 20.4 h duration.

3.3   Basque Data. Parliament Domain

The Mintzai corpus[7] was considered for this scenario. This dataset consists of parliamentary sessions of the Basque government between 2011 and 2018. The corpus was originally designed for speech translation studies, and contains parallel utterances in Basque and Spanish [36]. The considered experiments cover only Basque data. The test includes audio from 127 speakers (7.2 h).

The training corpus to be synthesized for this domain was obtained by crawling the web sites where the official plenary sessions of the parliament are available[8]. Texts from the sessions between 2012 and 2020 were downloaded as PDF files, and converted to plain text using the PDFtoText Linux tool. A set of 13,910 sentences were generated, forming a training corpus with 26.7 h duration.

4   Results and Discussion

Table 2 shows the results obtained by fine-tuning the different Whisper models using synthetic speech. The results include those obtained for large (English), intermediate (Spanish), and low (Basque) resource languages. The fine-tuning process in this case was performed using LoRA as the PEFT method.

The experiments confirm the reliability of the proposed methodology to adapt the Whisper domain using synthetic data, especially when the amount of pre-training data is intermediate or low, as is the case for Spanish and Basque. For Spanish, the fine-tuning process reduces the WER between 0.4 and 6.2 points compared to the original models, depending on the Whisper version. For the case of Basque, the fine-tuning process has a greater impact on the WER, reducing

---

[5] https://www.rtve.es/play/.
[6] https://www.rtve.es/noticias.
[7] https://github.com/Vicomtech/mintzai-ST.
[8] http://www.legebiltzarra.eus.

Table 2. Results obtained by fine-tuning each Whisper version using synthetic speech in English, Spanish, and Basque. The performance is measured in terms of total WER.

Model version	Fine-tuning (Yes/No)	WER English	Spanish	Basque
tiny	No	21.8	38.6	94.8
tiny	Yes	22.4	34.2	69.8
base	No	20.0	30.7	91.5
base	Yes	21.7	24.5	60.4
small	No	18.6	24.3	73.3
small	Yes	19.4	23.9	55.4
medium	No	18.0	22.1	61.3
medium	Yes	17.9	20.5	53.8
large	No	17.6	16.1	59.7
large	Yes	17.8	14.9	50.9

between 6.2 and 31 points depending on the model size. For both languages, the WER reduction is more evident for the case of the smallest models (tiny and base). For the English language, the fine-tuning process using synthetic speech does not result in a reduction in WER with respect to the original models, which is contrary to the results obtained for Spanish and Basque. In some cases, the fine-tuned version even produces a higher WER than the original one (base and large). This behavior can be explained by two reasons: (1) the amount of data used to train the original Whisper models for English is much greater than the amount considered for Spanish and Basque (see Table 1). (2) The test data used in English is a compilation of several corpora from the literature, including TEDLIUMv2 and the Spoken Wikipedia corpus. Information from such corpora may already be available within the original Whisper weights. Therefore, the information added to the model via synthetic speech does not contribute to new knowledge, as in the case of Spanish and Basque.

With the aim to compare different PEFT methods when fine-tuning Whisper, Table 3 shows results comparing LoRA [21], AdaLoRA [22], and BitFit [23]. The comparison is performed fine-tuning the medium Whisper model (769 M parameters). The fine-tuning process for all methods is performed under the same conditions and using the same hyperparameters for training.

Similar results are observed when using either LoRA or AdaLoRA. Both approaches are able to reduce the WER compared to the original Whisper model, especially for Spanish and Basque. This is explained considering that both approaches rely on the same principle of weight decomposition into low rank matrices. The main difference is that AdaLoRA is able to achieve the same results, but fine-tuning less than half the parameters fine-tuned by LoRA. This leads less memory consumption (see Fig. 3). BitFit helps to reduce the train-

Table 3. Comparison between different PEFT methods for fine-tuning the medium version of Whisper. Results are presented in terms of WER and the normalized WER (nWER) with respect to the original Whisper model.

PEFT Method	Trainable params.	Trainable %	English		Spanish		Basque	
			WER	nWER	WER	nWER	WER	nWER
Not fine-tuned	-	-	18.0	100.0	22.1	100.0	61.3	100.0
LoRA [21]	9.4M	1.22	17.9	99.4	20.5	92.8	53.8	87.8
AdaLoRA [22]	3.5M	0.46	17.8	98.9	20.1	91.0	52.9	86.6
BitFit [23]	0.6M	0.08	17.9	99.4	21.8	98.6	59.8	97.6

ing time and the memory costs even further, by fine-tuning only 0.08% of the weights, but at the cost of sacrificing performance, especially in Basque.

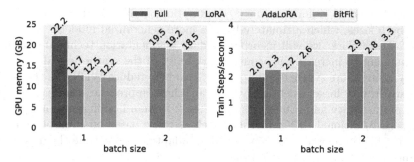

Fig. 3. GPU memory and train speed for the different PEFT methods. All evaluations are conducted on a NVIDIA GeForce RTX-3090 GPU (24GB VRAM). Full fine-tuning is not possible for batch sizes larger than 1 due to memory constraints.

Training speed for BitFit is significantly higher than for the other two methods (p-value $\ll 0.005$ in all cases). The differences between the training speed for LoRA, AdaLoRA, and the full fine-tuning is not significant (p-value > 0.005 in all cases). The statistical comparisons were performed using an ANOVA with a Tukey Post-Hoc test. Although there is not significant differences for the training speed between LoRA, AdaLoRA, and the full fine-tuning, the memory consumption of the PEFT methods is much lower than the observed for the full fine-tuning. This makes possible the use of larger batch sizes (either directly or using training accumulation steps for the gradient computation), which at the end will be translated in a significant improvement of training speed [20].

5 Conclusion

This paper proposes a methodology for adapting the vocabulary of Whisper-based speech recognizers to new domains in different languages using only TTS-derived data. The proposed approach was tested on data from large, intermediate, and low resource scenarios in English, Spanish, and Basque languages, respectively. In addition, we compared different PEFT-based methods to perform the fine-tuning process due to the large number of parameters to train. This study demonstrated that it is possible to improve the performance of an E2E ASR system using only synthetic data, which is a novel approach. Previous studies relied on the combination of synthetic and real speech, which still requires data annotation procedures that can slow down the training process. Using only synthetic speech data can be a more efficient and cost-effective approach, especially when there is limited time or resources available for data collection.

The results indicated that using only synthetic data for domain adaptation of Whisper-based ASRs leads to performance improvements, particularly in low-resource scenarios. The proposed methodology was successful in reducing the WER between 6.2 and 31 points, depending on the language and model version. In addition, we confirm the utility of using PEFT methods to train large models, which would be difficult to achieve under limited hardware resources. PEFT methods helped to reduce memory consumption, giving the possibility to use larger bath sizes, which ultimately lead to more generalized models.

For future work, we will incorporate data augmentation techniques such as SpecAugment to increase the acoustic variability of the synthetic audios. Additionally, using more synthetic samples can also help reduce WERs, as the model can learn from a larger vocabulary. Overall, these approaches can lead to even better performance and robustness of the ASR system in different domains and languages. Additional PEFT methods such as those based on Prompt and Prefix tuning [37,38] can also be considered an adapted to fine-tune the decoder of large acoustic models such as Whisper.

References

1. Li, J., et al.: Recent advances in end-to-end automatic speech recognition. APSIPA Trans. Sign. Inf. Proc. **11**(1) (2022)
2. Baevski, A., et al.: Wav2Vec 2.0: a framework for self-supervised learning of speech representations. In: NEURIPS, vol. 33, pp. 12449–12460 (2020)
3. Gulati, A., et al.: Conformer: convolution-augmented transformer for speech recognition. In: Proceedings of the INTERSPEECH, pp. 5036–5040 (2020)
4. Radford, A., et al.: Robust speech recognition via large-scale weak supervision. Technical report, OpenAI (2022)
5. Park, D.S., et al.: SpecAugment: a simple data augmentation method for automatic speech recognition. In: Proceedings of the INTERSPEECH, pp. 2613–2617 (2019)
6. Li, J., et al.: Training neural speech recognition systems with synthetic speech augmentation. arXiv preprint arXiv:1811.00707 (2018)
7. Rosenberg, A., et al.: Speech recognition with augmented synthesized speech. In: Proceedings of the ASRU, pp. 996–1002. IEEE (2019)
8. Laptev, A., et al.: You do not need more data: improving end-to-end speech recognition by text-to-speech data augmentation. In: Proceedings of the CISP-BMEI, pp. 439–444. IEEE (2020)

9. Rossenbach, N., et al.: Generating synthetic audio data for attention-based speech recognition systems. In: Proceedings of the ICASSP, pp. 7069–7073. IEEE (2020)
10. Wang, Y., et al.: Style tokens: unsupervised style modeling, control and transfer in end-to-end speech synthesis. In Proceedings of the ICML, pp. 5180–5189. PMLR (2018)
11. Wang, C., et al.: Neural codec language models are zero-shot text to speech synthesizers. arXiv preprint arXiv:2301.02111 (2023)
12. Ueno, S., et al.: Multi-speaker sequence-to-sequence speech synthesis for data augmentation in acoustic-to-word speech recognition. In Proceedings of the ICASSP, pp. 6161–6165. IEEE (2019)
13. Zheng, X., Liu, Y., Gunceler, D., Willett, D.: Using synthetic audio to improve the recognition of out-of-vocabulary words in end-to-end ASR systems. In: Proceedings of the ICASSP, pp. 5674–5678. IEEE (2021)
14. Fazel, A., et al.: SynthASR: unlocking synthetic data for speech recognition. arXiv preprint arXiv:2106.07803 (2021)
15. Ueno, S., et al.: Data augmentation for ASR using TTS via a discrete representation. In: Proceedings of the ASRU, pp. 68–75. IEEE (2021)
16. Qu, L., Weber, C., Wermter, S.: Emphasizing unseen words: new vocabulary acquisition for end-to-end speech recognition. Neural Netw. **161**, 494–504 (2023)
17. Hu, T.Y., et al.: Synt++: utilizing imperfect synthetic data to improve speech recognition. In: Proceedings of the ICASSP, pp. 7682–7686. IEEE (2022)
18. Mimura, M., et al.: Leveraging sequence-to-sequence speech synthesis for enhancing acoustic-to-word speech recognition. In: Proceedings of the SLT, pp. 477–484. IEEE (2018)
19. Panayotov, V., et al.: LibriSpeech: an ASR corpus based on public domain audio books. In: Proceedings of the ICASSP, pp. 5206–5210 (2015)
20. Ding, N., et al.: Parameter-efficient fine-tuning of large-scale pre-trained language models. Nature Mach. Intell. **5**, 1–16 (2023)
21. Hu, E.J., Shen, Y., et al.: LoRA: low-rank adaptation of large language models. arXiv preprint arXiv:2106.09685 (2021)
22. Zhang, Q., et al.: Adaptive budget allocation for parameter-efficient fine-tuning. arXiv preprint arXiv:2303.10512 (2023)
23. Zaken, E.B., et al.: BitFit: simple parameter-efficient fine-tuning for transformer-based masked language-models. arXiv preprint arXiv:2106.10199 (2021)
24. Shen, et al.: Natural TTS synthesis by conditioning WaveNet on MEL spectrogram predictions. In: Proceedings of the ICASSP, pp. 4779–4783. IEEE (2018)
25. Kong, J., et al.: Hifi-gan: Generative adversarial networks for efficient and high fidelity speech synthesis. Proceedings of the NEURIPS, vol. 33, pp. 17022–17033 (2020)
26. Kingma, D.P., Ba, J.: Adam: a method for stochastic optimization. 2015 ICLR. arXiv preprint arXiv:1412.6980 (2015)
27. Ito, K., Johnson, L.: The LJ speech dataset (2017). www.http://keithito.com/LJ-Speech-Dataset/
28. Vásquez-Correa, J.C., Álvarez Muniain, A.: Novel speech recognition systems applied to forensics within child exploitation: Wav2Vec 2. 0 vs. whisper. Sensors **23**(4), 1843 (2023)
29. Baumann, T., et al.: The spoken Wikipedia corpus collection: harvesting, alignment and an application to hyperlistening. Lang. Resour. Eval. **53**(2), 303–329 (2019)
30. Mirkin, S., et al.: A recorded debating dataset. In: Proceedings of the LREC, pp. 250–254 (2017)

31. Rousseau, A., et al.: Enhancing the TED-LIUM corpus with selected data for language modeling and more ted talks. In: Proceedings of the LREC, pp. 3935–3939 (2014)
32. Lleida, E., et al.: Albayzin evaluation: IberSPEECH-RTVE 2022 speech to text transcription challenge (2022)
33. Dinkel, H., et al.: Voice activity detection in the wild: a data-driven approach using teacher-student training. IEEE/ACM Trans. Audio, Speech Lang. Process. **29**, 1542–1555 (2021)
34. Gemmeke, J., et al.: Audio set: an ontology and human-labeled dataset for audio events. In: Proceedings of the ICASSP, pp. 776–780 (2017)
35. Arzelus, H., et al.: The Vicomtech-UPM speech transcription systems for the albayzın-rtve 2022 speech to text transcription challenge. In: Proceedings of the IberSPEECH, pp. 266–270 (2022)
36. T. Etchegoyhen et al. mintzai-st: Corpus and baselines for basque-spanish speech translation. In: Proceedings of the IberSPEECH, pp. 1–5 (2021)
37. Liu, X., et al.: P-tuning v2: prompt tuning can be comparable to fine-tuning universally across scales and tasks. arXiv preprint arXiv:2110.07602 (2021)
38. Li, X.L., Liang, P.: Prefix-tuning: optimizing continuous prompts for generation. In: Proceedings of the ACL, pp. 4582–4597 (2021)

Unsupervised Learning for Automatic Speech Recognition in Air Traffic Control Environment

Lars Formoe[1], Dan Bruun Mygind[1], Espen Løkke[2], and Hasan Ogul[1(✉)]

[1] Department of Computer Science and Communication, Østfold University College,
B R A Veien 4, 1757 Halden, Norway
{lars.formoe,dan.b.mygind,hasan.ogul}@hiof.no
[2] Kongsberg Defence & Aerospace, Drammen, Viken, Norway
espen.lokke@kongsberg.com

Abstract. This paper addresses the enduring challenge of domain-specific automatic speech recognition (ASR) with limited training data, particularly in air traffic control (ATC) communications involving highly accented speakers. While state-of-the-art models like wav2vec have achieved significant progress when fine-tuned on smaller, specialized datasets, the issue of having little or no transcribed data for specific domains like ATC remains unresolved. We present our findings using the wav2vec-U 2.0 model, an advanced self-supervised ASR framework that learns from raw audio and unpaired text without the need for transcriptions. By fine-tuning wav2vec-U 2.0 on the domain-specific ATCOSIM dataset, we explore its effectiveness in handling domain-specific ASR tasks with scarce or non-existent transcribed data. Our results demonstrate promising speech recognition accuracy, suggesting that wav2vec-U 2.0 can effectively address the problem with small amounts of transcribed data posed by highly specific ASR-domains such as ATC communications. Furthermore, we discuss the implications of our findings for the broader ASR research community and provide suggestions into potential future directions for improving ASR accuracy in ATC communications and other specialized domains with limited training data.

Keywords: Automatic speech recognition · wav2vec 2.0 · wav2vec unsupervised · unsupervised learning · generative adversarial network · air traffic control communications

1 Introduction

Automatic Speech Recognition (ASR) has been a topic of interest in the air traffic control (ATC) domain for several decades, with the potential to enhance safety and efficiency by reducing controllers' workload and improving communication accuracy between pilots and controllers [14,30]. However, the unique challenges associated with the ATC domain have made developing effective ASR systems particularly difficult.

K. Ekštein et al. (Eds.): TSD 2023, LNAI 14102, pp. 239–248, 2023.
https://doi.org/10.1007/978-3-031-40498-6_21

ATC communications is a highly specialized domain that requires precise and accurate communication between pilots and controllers to ensure the safety and efficiency of air travel. Unlike other speech recognition applications, ATC communications often involve technical terminology and specific communication protocols unique to the aviation industry [6]. Furthermore, ATC communications typically occur in high-noise environments, such as airports and control towers, which can significantly degrade speech signal quality and increase speech recognition tasks' complexity [9].

One key challenge in developing ASR systems for domain-specific applications is the limited availability of training data. Recently, an innovative ASR system, called Wav2vec-U 2.0, was released to address this challenge by learning from raw audio and unpaired text without the need for transcriptions [22]. It employs a self-supervised learning model and a generative adversarial network [13] to recognize words in audio recordings.

To the best of our knowledge, the promise of Wav2vec-U 2.0 in the ATC domain has not been explored yet. This paper presents our findings on implementing the wav2vec-U framework in the ATC domain using the publicly available dataset ATCOSIM [15]. Our experiments are geared towards assessing the efficacy of this ASR system in handling domain-specific challenges and evaluating its performance. By employing unlabeled data and the aforementioned framework, we have achieved word error rates below 30%.

2   Related Work

2.1   ASR in ATC Domain

The development of robust solutions for ATC involves addressing several challenges that are specific to this domain. For instance, noisy radio channels, a wide range of accents, and high speech rates are all individual challenges that coincide in the ATC domain. Recently, a study on methods to extract operational information from ATC audio yielded a Word Error Rate (WER) of 17% using a Recurrent Neural Network (RNN) model trained on a combination of ATC datasets that contained a total of 84 h of transcribed speech data [7].

However, a key challenge in ATC is the limited available data. A recent study addressed this challenge by employing transfer learning techniques and leveraging multiple Chinese speech datasets. The study showed promising results, with an overall reduction of Character Error Rate (CER) of 2% when compared to the supervised learning approach [21].

2.2   Self-supervised Representations for Speech

Learning vector representations from high amount of labeled or unlabeled data is a recent trend to leverage the learned representations to improve performance on a local task for which a relatively small dataset is available. Wav2vec is an attempt to provide a learning representations of raw audio for speech recognition by unsupervised pre-training [26]. It is trained on large amounts of unlabeled audio data and the resulting representations are then used to improve acoustic model training. The model is a convolutional neural network that takes raw audio as input and computes a general representation that can be input to a speech recognition system.

Wav2vec 2.0 presents an improved version of the original wav2vec model. Wav2vec 2.0 employs a self-supervised learning framework that utilizes a contrastive loss to learn speech representations from raw audio without labeled data [8]. In addition, the model learns to predict future audio samples by employing a transformer-based architecture and a masked language modeling objective. Experiments demonstrate that wav2vec 2.0 outperforms previous approaches, achieving state-of-the-art results on the LibriSpeech and Switchboard-300 datasets, even with limited labeled data for fine-tuning.

Wav2vec-U 2.0 is an unsupervised model designed to learn and understand audio representations, especially when labeled data is scarce [22]. It uses raw audio and unrelated text data, removing the need for transcriptions. The model combines the self-supervised wav2vec 2.0, pre-trained on raw audio, with a generative adversarial network (GAN) [13] to improve audio representations. Using contrastive learning, it aligns speech representations with text embeddings, allowing effective word recognition without labeled data.

2.3   Use of Learned Representations in ATC

Wav2vec 2.0 Fine-Tuning. A recent study conducted experiments on pre-trained Wav2Vec 2.0 models' robustness in downstream ASR tasks, explicitly targeting the air traffic control domain [31]. Using domain-specific datasets, a range of corpora has been utilized to ascertain the effectiveness of fine-tuning these pre-trained models, which have been exposed to substantial amounts of generic English audio. The results highlight the potential of implementing pre-trained Wav2Vec 2.0 models for ASR tasks within specialized domains.

While this study does not present explicit results concerning ASR performance on the ATCOSIM dataset [15], their experimental framework resembles the approach we have undertaken in our work. Using pre-trained Wav2Vec 2.0 models for ASR tasks in the air traffic control domain underscores the value of transfer learning and domain-specific fine-tuning. Furthermore, the study suggests that the versatility and adaptability of Wav2Vec 2.0 models make them ideal candidates for a wide range of specialized ASR tasks, including those in the air traffic control domain. Furthermore, the end-to-end nature of these models, as evidenced by their superior performance compared to hybrid-based ASR systems, emphasizes the importance of investigating and developing more streamlined and efficient ASR architectures.

Wav2vec-U 2.0. A study investigated ASR for use with Uyghur, Kazakh, and Kyrgyz audio, employing unsupervised learning by implementing the wav2vec-U 2.0 framework [11]. With only 1.8 h of Kyrgyz audio data from the Common

Voice dataset [4], their approach achieved a 14.9% Character Error Rate (CER), demonstrating the potential of unsupervised learning for ASR in languages with scarce resources.

Another study into the robustness of unsupervised speech recognition investigated the utilization of unrelated text data within the same language across common datasets used in ASR research [20]. The findings of this research suggest a correlation between the nature of the text supplied for the GAN and the overall performance. It was observed that out-of-domain text data generally yielded inferior results, reinforcing the necessity of ATC-specific text data to achieve optimal performance.

3   Methods

The primary objective of ASR research is to generate the most accurate textual representation of audio possible. Here, we conducted an experimental study to assess the performance of recent end-to-end speech recognition technology in the ATC domain. To this end, we employed a rigorous preprocessing procedure on the text data to ensure consistency and a uniform input representation. All corpus transcriptions were filtered, transforming all letters to lowercase and removing special characters not part of the alphabet. The process reduces the number of tokens used in both models by 49%, impacting training cost and the output probability distribution in the output layer. However, the preprocessing of the models differentiates from this point. While fine-tuning the wav2vec 2.0 model can be initiated with the raw audio files and the paired transcripts. The wav2vec 2.0 Unsupervised preprocessing is more circumstantial. Although various representations of sentences, words, and phones were mapped accordingly, given the domain-specific nature of air traffic control communications, we elected to use the actual text data from the same dataset to maintain relevance and accuracy. This decision was based on the understanding that air traffic control communication data exhibits unique characteristics that may not be present in generic text data, thus requiring specialized treatment. Furthermore, the audio was files trimmed to remove silence [27] and a Mel-frequency cepstral coefficients (MFCCs) [16] representations of the trimmed audio was created for training purposes.

Subsequently, the ATCOSIM dataset of 9538 samples was partitioned into training, validation, and testing subsets at 70%, 20%, and 10% distributions, respectively. The distribution resulted in a split key of 6677/1907/954. The samples were selected randomly to ensure a fair representation of the data. This partitioning strategy allowed us to establish a robust evaluation framework, minimizing the risk of overfitting and ensuring that the model's performance could be assessed on unseen data.

wav2vec 2.0: The experiment's first phase was conducted with the wav2vec 2.0 framework and weights from four pre-trained models to evaluate the downstream infusion of the ATCOSIM dataset. Wav2vec 2.0 results are based on the following weight pipelines. Wav2vec2-base (95 m param.) pre-trained on 53000 h with no fine-tuning, wav2vec2-large-960h-lv60-self (317 m param.) pre-trained on

53.000 h of unlabeled data from the LibriVox subset Librilight [19] and fine-tuned on 960 h of LibriSpeech [23]. Wav2vec2-xls-r-300m (300 m param.) pre-trained on 436.000 h of unlabeled multilingual data from multiple corpora Common-Voice [5], VoxPopuli [29], Multilingual LibriSpeech (MLS) [24], VoxLingua107 [28] and the Babel project. Wav2vec2-large-robust-ft-swbd-300h pre-trained on Libri-light, CommonVoice, Switchboard [12] and Fisher [10], then fine-tuned on 300 h of noisy telephone data from the Switchboard corpus. All pre-trained pipelines provide a diverse and comprehensive source of training data for ASR systems, adding a robust context baseline for downstream tasks.

We implemented the pre-trained pipelines using the Huggingface platform [2], adapting the code for custom fine-tuning of the ATCOSIM corpus. Further-more, we added a hyper-parameter loop to examine different training arguments' impacts on the results. The parameters used were warmup steps, epochs, batch size, and learning rate. All results are based on the 954 unseen samples from the ATCOSIM corpus.

wav2vec 2.0 Unsupervised: The experiment's second phase was conducted using the Wav2vec Unsupervised 2.0. To implement the wav2vec Unsupervised 2.0 framework, we followed the guidelines in the Fairseq GitHub repo [1]. In addi-tion, we created an additional layer on the framework to execute the many steps involved in the process seamlessly and efficiently. For preparing the input to the Generative Adversarial Network (GAN), we used the pre-trained wav2vec2-large model with no fine-tuning of the model, extracting the contextual representations in latent space from the raw audio files. The wav2vec2-large model is equivalent to the Wav2vec2-base described in the above section but has a feature dimen-sion of 1024 instead of 768. Clustering it with the recommended 64 centroids for the K-means training. For the language identification model, we used fastText lid176.bin model [17,18] instead of the proposed model.

We then conducted several training runs with minor configuration adjust-ments to the training parameters, including learning rate, batch size, and the number of training epochs. This iterative approach allowed us to refine the model based on the results of each training run and facilitated the identification of opti-mal parameter settings for our specific task. The results have also been generated utilizing 954 unseen samples derived from the ATCOSIM corpus.

OpenAI Whisper: In addition to the first and second phases and for compar-ison purposes, we used the Whisper models [25] from OpenAi's GitHub reposi-tory [3] to conduct zero-shot predictions on our ATCOSIM test-set audio files. Using the small (244M. param.), medium (769M param.), and large (1550M. param.) architectures. Each model was pre-trained on 680.000 h of labeled mul-tilingual data. The integrated pre-processing within the framework allows for the simple input of an audio file as the sole requirement to receive a prediction. Subsequently, we developed a module for post-prediction analysis to evaluate the WER against outcomes from earlier phases while excluding upper- and lower-case letters and special characters from the output.

By comparing the performance of the unsupervised wav2vec 2.0 framework with that of self-supervised and supervised approaches using pre-trained models,

Table 1. Pre-trained models data foundation. Models containing unlabeled and labeled data are pre-trained and fine-tuned before the experiments.

Model	Unlabeled data (hours)	Labeled data (Hours)
wav2vec2-base	53.000	–
wav2vec2-xls-r-300m	436.000	–
wav2vec2-large-960h-lv60-self	53.000	960
wav2vec2-large-robust-ft-swbd-300h	NA	300
openai whisper (small, medium, large)	–	680.000

we aimed to gain insight into the relative effectiveness of these methodologies in the context of air traffic control communications.

4   Results

4.1   Wav2vec 2.0 Downstream

The wav2vec2-large-960h-lv60-self pipeline described in Sect. 3 had the best overall performance of the pre-trained models. Figure 1 show the loss across the 50-epoch training sequence. The model was used to predict text outputs from the unseen test subset. Using the jiwer package for Python[1], each prediction was given an individual *WER* score, yielding an average *WER* of 0.97%.

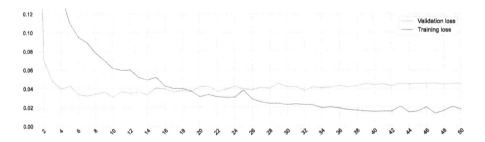

Fig. 1. Results from large-960h-lvl60-self model training.

4.2   Wav2vec Unsupervised

In terms of accuracy metrics, there appears to be some ambiguity within the framework itself. During training, there is a validation run performed every n-th epoch where one of the metrics is *valid_uer*. When running the script for generating phone labels - w2vu_generate.py - the metric used is *WER*. As both valid_uer and WER appear to be the same, for consistency, we have elected only to use the term WER.

---

[1] https://github.com/jitsi/jiwer.

The two different perspectives in Fig. 2a and 2b shows the progress of the *WER* throughout the training phase. The lowest *WER* achieved on the validation subset was 23.79% and 25.37% on the unseen test subset.

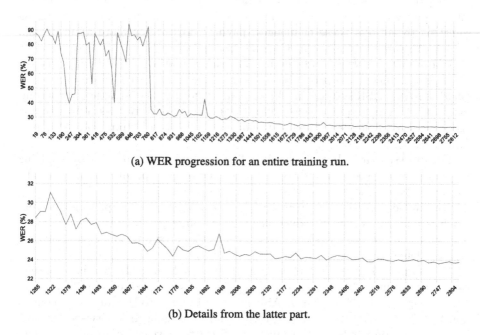

(a) WER progression for an entire training run.

(b) Details from the latter part.

Fig. 2. wav2vec 2.0 Unsupervised on ATCOSIM dataset.

4.3   Whisper

Table 2 presents the performance metrics of the Whisper architectures on the test subset. Original WER results are based on the output with full token representation, and the corrected output is post-processed to match the token set used in 4.1 and 4.2. The best *WER* achieved by Whisper was 29.54%.

Table 2. Whisper model performance.

model	original WER	corrected WER
small	91.13%	46.95%
medium	84.22%	31.32%
large	82.94%	29.54%

5   Conclusion

While ASR technology has the potential to significantly benefit the ATC domain, its development and implementation face unique challenges. Recent advancements, such as transfer learning and the wav2vec-U framework, offer promising solutions to address these challenges, paving the way for more accurate and reliable ASR systems in the ATC domain.

The findings of this study underscore the potential of using unsupervised learning and fine-tuning pre-trained Wav2Vec 2.0 models to advance research in creating robust ASR systems for the specialized domain of air traffic control communications. Furthermore, the results highlight the effectiveness of fine-tuning these models on smaller, domain-specific datasets to yield improved ASR performance.

Future research endeavors should refine the fine-tuning process by applying the experimental setup to larger corpora of audio data specific to the air traffic control domain. This process would involve using small transcribed datasets for fine-tuning across multiple airports within the same region. Exploring this approach is crucial, as it may reduce dependency on large volumes of transcribed data and facilitate ASR system development in low-resource languages and specialized domains.

In summary, this study has provided some insight into the potential of fine-tuning pre-trained Wav2Vec 2.0 models using unsupervised learning techniques for advancing research in robust ASR systems tailored to the air traffic control domain. Refining the fine-tuning process and leveraging unsupervised learning benefits can contribute to the ongoing efforts to develop more accurate and versatile ASR systems.

References

1. Fairseq facebookresearch. https://github.com/facebookresearch/fairseq. Accessed 30 Jan 2022
2. Huggingface platform. https://huggingface.co. Accessed 30 Nov 2021
3. Whisper openai. https://github.com/openai/whisper. Accessed 10 Feb 2022
4. Ardila, R., et al.: Common voice: A massively-multilingual speech corpus. arXiv preprint arXiv:1912.06670 (2019)
5. Ardila, R., et al.: Common voice: A massively-multilingual speech corpus (2020)
6. Authority, C.A.: Cap 413: Radiotelephony manual. Civil Aviation Authority (2020)
7. Badrinath, S., Balakrishnan, H.: Automatic speech recognition for air traffic control communications. Transp. Res. Rec. **2676**(1), 798–810 (2022)
8. Baevski, A., Zhou, Y., Mohamed, A., Auli, M.: wav2vec 2.0: a framework for self-supervised learning of speech representations. In: Advances in Neural Information Processing Systems, vol. 33, pp. 12449–12460 (2020)
9. Benzeghiba, M., et al.: Automatic speech recognition and speech variability: a review. Speech Commun. **49**(10–11), 763–786 (2007)
10. Cieri, C., Miller, D., Walker, K.: The fisher corpus: a resource for the next generations of speech-to-text. In: International Conference on Language Resources and Evaluation (2004)

11. Du, W., Maimaitiyiming, Y., Nijat, M., Li, L., Hamdulla, A., Wang, D.: Automatic speech recognition for uyghur, kazakh, and kyrgyz: an overview. Appl. Sci. **13**(1), 326 (2022)

12. Godfrey, J., Holliman, E., McDaniel, J.: SWITCHBOARD: telephone speech corpus for research and development. In: [Proceedings] ICASSP-92: 1992 IEEE International Conference on Acoustics, Speech, and Signal Processing, vol. 1, pp. 517–520 (1992). https://doi.org/10.1109/ICASSP.1992.225858

13. Goodfellow, I., et al.: Generative adversarial networks. Commun. ACM **63**(11), 139–144 (2020)

14. Helmke, H., Ohneiser, O., Mühlhausen, T., Wies, M.: Reducing controller workload with automatic speech recognition. In: 2016 IEEE/AIAA 35th Digital Avionics Systems Conference (DASC), pp. 1–10. IEEE (2016)

15. Hofbauer, K., Petrik, S., Hering, H.: The ATCOSIM corpus of non-prompted clean air traffic control speech. In: LREC. Citeseer (2008)

16. Hossan, M.A., Memon, S., Gregory, M.A.: A novel approach for MFCC feature extraction. In: 2010 4th International Conference on Signal Processing and Communication Systems, pp. 1–5 (2010). https://doi.org/10.1109/ICSPCS.2010.5709752

17. Joulin, A., Grave, E., Bojanowski, P., Douze, M., Jégou, H., Mikolov, T.: Fasttext.zip: Compressing text classification models. arXiv preprint arXiv:1612.03651 (2016)

18. Joulin, A., Grave, E., Bojanowski, P., Mikolov, T.: Bag of tricks for efficient text classification. arXiv preprint arXiv:1607.01759 (2016)

19. Kahn, J., et al.: Libri-light: A benchmark for ASR with limited or no supervision. In: ICASSP 2020–2020 IEEE International Conference on Acoustics, Speech and Signal Processing (ICASSP). IEEE (2020). https://doi.org/10.1109/icassp40776.2020.9052942,https://doi.org/10.1109%2Ficassp40776.2020.9052942

20. Lin, G.T., Hsu, C.J., Liu, D.R., Lee, H.Y., Tsao, Y.: Analyzing the robustness of unsupervised speech recognition. In: ICASSP 2022–2022 IEEE International Conference on Acoustics, Speech and Signal Processing (ICASSP), pp. 8202–8206. IEEE (2022)

21. Lin, Y., Li, Q., Yang, B., Yan, Z., Tan, H., Chen, Z.: Improving speech recognition models with small samples for air traffic control systems. Neurocomputing **445**, 287–297 (2021)

22. Liu, A.H., Hsu, W.N., Auli, M., Baevski, A.: Towards end-to-end unsupervised speech recognition. In: 2022 IEEE Spoken Language Technology Workshop (SLT), pp. 221–228. IEEE (2023)

23. Panayotov, V., Chen, G., Povey, D., Khudanpur, S.: Librispeech: an ASR corpus based on public domain audio books. In: 2015 IEEE international conference on acoustics, speech and signal processing (ICASSP), pp. 5206–5210. IEEE (2015)

24. Pratap, V., Xu, Q., Sriram, A., Synnaeve, G., Collobert, R.: MLS: a large-scale multilingual dataset for speech research. In: Interspeech 2020. ISCA (2020). https://doi.org/10.21437/interspeech.2020-2826, https://doi.org/10.21437%2Finterspeech.2020-2826

25. Radford, A., Kim, J.W., Xu, T., Brockman, G., McLeavey, C., Sutskever, I.: Robust speech recognition via large-scale weak supervision (2022)

26. Schneider, S., Baevski, A., Collobert, R., Auli, M.: wav2vec: Unsupervised pre-training for speech recognition. arXiv preprint arXiv:1904.05862 (2019)

27. Tan, Z.H., kr. Sarkar, A., Dehak, N.: rVAD: an unsupervised segment-based robust voice activity detection method (2022)

28. Valk, J., Alumäe, T.: Voxlingua107: a dataset for spoken language recognition (2020)
29. Wang, C., et al.: Voxpopuli: a large-scale multilingual speech corpus for representation learning, semi-supervised learning and interpretation (2021)
30. Yi, L., et al.: Identifying and managing risks of AI-driven operations: a case study of automatic speech recognition for improving air traffic safety. Chin. J. Aeronaut. **36**(4), 366–386 (2022)
31. Zuluaga-Gomez, J., et al.: How does pre-trained wav2vec 2.0 perform on domain-shifted asr? an extensive benchmark on air traffic control communications. In: 2022 IEEE Spoken Language Technology Workshop (SLT), pp. 205–212. IEEE (2023)

The Effect of Human-Likeliness in French Robot-Directed Speech: A Study of Speech Rate and Fluency

Natalia Kalashnikova[1](✉), Mathilde Hutin[1,2], Ioana Vasilescu[1], and Laurence Devillers[1,3]

[1] Université Paris-Saclay, CNRS, Laboratoire Interdisciplinaire des Sciences du Numérique, 91400 Orsay, France
{natalia.kalashnikova,hutin,ioana,devil}@lisn.upsaclay.fr
[2] Institut Langage & Communication, Université Catholique de Louvain, 1348 Louvain-la-Neuve, Belgium
[3] Sorbonne Université, Paris, France

Abstract. Robot-directed speech refers to speech to a robotic device, ranging from small home smart speakers to full-size humanoid robots. Studies have investigated the phonetic and linguistic properties of this type of speech or the effect of anthropomorphism of the devices on the social aspect of interaction. However, none have investigated the effect of the device's human-likeliness on linguistic realizations. This preliminary study proposes to fill this gap by investigating one phonetic parameter (speech rate) and one linguistic parameter (use of filled pauses) in speech directed at a home speaker *vs* a humanoid robot *vs* a human. The data from 71 native speakers of French indicate that human-directed speech shows longer utterances at a faster speech rate and more filled pauses than speech directed at a home speaker and a robot. Speaker- and robot-directed speech is significantly different from human-directed speech, but not from each other, indicating a unique device-directed type of speech.

Keywords: human-computer interaction · speech rate · filled pauses

1 Introduction

So-called "robot-directed speech" (RDS) refers to language productions uttered by a (generally grown-up) human to a robotic device, ranging from small home speakers to full-size humanoid robots. It can be compared to computer-directed speech in that it belongs to the category of device-directed speech, itself a category of special speech registers such as infant-, child-, foreigner- or even pet-directed speech. The exploration of such speech styles holds promise for a better understanding of human-computer interaction (HCI) or more broadly of dialogical adjustment and audience accommodation, which in turn may help develop concrete tools such as addressee detection.

Several studies have investigated specifically the acoustic properties of computer- or robot- *vs* adult-directed speech. They have shown that, when talking to a computer, humans tend to produce more utterances [1] and to hyperarticulate their vowels (in

K. Ekštein et al. (Eds.): TSD 2023, LNAI 14102, pp. 249–257, 2023.
https://doi.org/10.1007/978-3-031-40498-6_22

terms of formants and duration) but not to display a higher pitch (F0) [2]. When talking to a robot, however, pitch and intensity are usually higher [7,9], vowels hyperarticulated [7], but speech rate shows fewer differences [9]. Regarding linguistic characteristics, when talking to a computer, humans tend to control and simplify their use of language (fewer fillers, incomplete sentences or discourse markers, limited information load per sentence...): In particular, speakers display less filled pauses (such as *uh* or *um*) [1]. To the best of our knowledge, the correlation between the addressee and the presence of disfluencies has not yet been tested in robot-directed speech. All these studies also indicate that the differences between device- and human-directed speech subside overtime [1] and that adults show more intra-speaker variation in the device- than in child-directed speech [3,6].

These differences between computer- and robot-directed speech imply that all devices are not equal to the eyes of humans. However, all these studies are binary, in the sense that they explore device- *vs* human-directed speech but fail to take into account the diversity of devices and in particular the effect of human-likeliness of the device. Only two studies that we know of investigate the effect of the device's anthropomorphism on the human-robot interaction [4,5]. Gong [4] shows that, on a scale of four levels of anthropomorphism, the more anthropomorphic the agent is, the more social responses it receives from users. Krach et al. [5] confirm these results from a neurological perspective since increased human-likeliness of the device correlates with higher cortical activity in regions of the brain linked to reasoning about others' intention (Theory-of-Mind).

None of these studies investigates the acoustic properties correlating with the degree of anthropomorphism of the device.

We propose to fill this gap by presenting the preliminary results of a larger study opposing participants dialoguing with a Google Home speaker *vs* a human-like Pepper robot *vs* another human. In particular, we investigate:

- **phonetic factors:** whether participants produce (i) longer utterances (duration of speech turns) (ii) with slower speech rate in the speaker *vs* human condition;
- **linguistic factors:** whether participants produce (iii) less filled pauses ("*heu*", "*hem*"...) in the speaker *vs* human condition;
- **variation:** (iv) whether these measures differ more intra-speaker in speaker- than in human-directed speech and (v) evolve overtime;
- **the effect of anthropomorphism:** (vi) whether the Pepper-directed speech patterns with the speaker- or with the human-directed speech (or lies somewhere inbetween).

In the remainder of this paper, we first present our methodology and resulting data in Sect. 2, then our results in Sect. 3 and finally we conclude and discuss the results in Sect. 4.

2   Method

2.1   Experimental Design

Procedure. First, members of our team explain the flow of the experiment and the consent notice to each participant and participants fill out a written form of baseline questions, where they note their level of willingness to adopt a series of 8 ecological habits. After that, they follow volunteers to one of the 3 rooms (corresponding to each conversational agent), where two team members control the setup of the experiment. At the end of the recording, participants are thanked by the experimenters and invited to go back to the organizers where they are offered a snack and can ask their questions. The whole procedure was vetted by our research center's ethics committee and took place according to covid-19 safety protocols.

Recordings. During the recording, a conversational agent (smart speaker, robot or human) asks questions about environmental habits. The conditions of the smart speaker and the Pepper robot are realized in the form of a Wizard-of-Oz setting which was inspired by [8]. The synthesized voice of a child is provided by the default settings of the Pepper robot and is used for both robot and smart-speaker agents. The human agent is a member of our team who reads aloud the devices' script. The oral exchange consists of 4 steps.

- S0: The agent establishes common ground with the subject by doing small talk.
- S1: The agent presents hypothetical situations in which participants should choose between the option by default and the eco-friendly option which demands more investment (of money or time).
- S2: The agent provides information presenting the negative consequences of each habit on the environment and asks the same questions as in the written form of baseline questions.
- S3: The agent replicates S1 with similar yet slightly different hypothetical situations.

Audio data are recorded using unidirectional headset microphones (AKG45) and Audacity at 44.1 kHz.

Participants. In April and June 2022, our research team recruited attendants and visitors of Collège des Bernardins, the research center and faculty of theology in Paris, France. We enrolled 71 native speakers of French (46 women, 25 men) over 18 and up to 65+ years old (globally equally distributed across age-ranges).[1]

Among them, 21 (16 women, 5 men) participated in the human-directed speech condition, 28 (18 women, 10 men) in the robot-directed speech condition, and 22 (12 women, 10 men) in the smart speaker-directed speech condition. A total of more than 16 h of speech were recorded.

2.2 Methodology

The audio files were manually transcribed in the orthography of French by two interns. Filled pauses were also manually annotated in the transcription. The resulting transcription files contain timestamps of speech turns. All calculations are made using Python 3 [12].

For the duration of utterances, we use these files to calculate the total duration (in seconds) of each subject's speech turn in the conversation.

---

[1] To ensure the privacy of participants, their exact age was not required in the form. They only had to specify their age range between 18–30, 30–45, 45–65 and 65+.

For speech rate, we divide the transcription file using the spaces between words, resulting in a series of smaller "tokens".[2] We then compute the sum of tokens for each experiment step, and divide this sum by the duration of the step, thus resulting in a number of tokens-per-second ratio.

For filled pauses, we calculate the total number of filled pauses and divide this number by the duration of the step, thus providing a ratio of the number of filled pauses per second.

For the analysis of intra-speaker variation, we calculate the standard deviation of each parameter for every participant and then the mean value for each condition.

The significance of our results is tested using a t-test for two independent samples applied with SciPy [13]. The obtained p-values are Bonferroni-corrected with threshold alpha = 0.5 using Statsmodels [10]. Thus, in Sect. 3 we report corrected p-values.

3 Results

3.1 Length of Utterance and Speech Rate

In general, participants tend to produce insignificantly longer utterances when talking to a human (mean = 372 s) than when talking to a smart speaker (mean = 191 s, $\Delta = 181$ s, $t = 2.19$, p = 0.09), and significantly longer than when speaking with a humanoid robot (mean = 147 s, $\Delta = 225$ s, $t = 2.87$, p = 0.01). The length of utterances in a speech addressed to a robot and a smart-speaker is not significantly different ($\Delta = 44$ s, $t = -1.08$, p = 0.85).

When looking at each step separately, as in Fig. 1, the only significant differences in average duration are to be found between human- and robot-directed speech in Step S2 ($\Delta = 181.15$ s, p = 0.01) and in Step S3 ($\Delta = 28.14$ s, p = 0.02).

Contrary to the literature comparing device- with child-directed speech [3,6], participants displayed more intra-speaker variation in the human-directed speech condition, with a mean standard deviation across participants of 137.54 s, than in the speaker- (mean sd = 69.57 s, $\Delta = 67.97$ s, $t = 2.47$, p = 0.06). This parameter is significantly different between human- and robot-directed speech (mean sd = 53.18 s, $\Delta = 84.36$ s, $t = 3.24$, p = 0.004). However, the differences are not significant between smart-speaker- and robot-directed speech ($\Delta = 16.39$ s, $t = -1.3$, p = 0.2).

Regarding speech rate, human-directed speech is slower at first but quickens around S1, i.e., when substancial conversation actually starts (Fig. 2). In general, participants address the human at a rate of 2.96 tokens/second, the robot at a rate of 2.63 tokens/second, and the speaker at a rate of 2.5 tokens/second. As expected, the difference between human- and speaker-directed speech is significant ($\Delta = 0.46$ tokens/s, $t = 3.43$, p = 0.004). Contrary to [9], the difference between human- and robot-directed speech is also significant ($\Delta = 0.32$ tokens/s, $t = 2.8$, p = 0.009), but not the one between robot- and speaker-directed speech ($\Delta = 0.14$ tokens/s, $t = 1.32$, p = 0.58).

---

[2] We call these units "tokens" as they can refer to only one word, or sometimes to two in cases of elision which are frequent in French (e.g., *l'ami* (le + ami), "the friend", is two words, but only one token.).

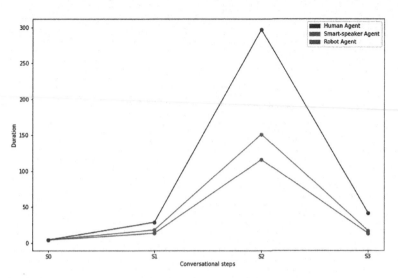

Fig. 1. Mean duration of utterances in speech directed at the human (blue), at the smart speaker (red) and at the humanoid robot (green). (Color figure online)

The analysis of each step shows that the two significant differences in speech rate are observed at step "S2" in conditions between human- and speaker-directed speech ($\Delta = 0.4$ token/s, p = 0.002), and between human- and robot-directed speech at the same step ($\Delta = 0.36$ token/s, p = 0.003). However, no significant difference is to be found in robot- *vs* speaker-directed speech at any step.

Contrary to what has been expected, less intra-speaker variation is observed in smart-speaker directed speech, with a mean standard deviation across participants of 0.6 token/s, against 0.68 ($\Delta = -0.08$ token/s, $t = 0.92$, p>1.) in robot-directed speech and 0.62 ($\Delta = -0.02$ token/s, $t = 0.19$, p>1.) in human-directed speech. The difference between robot and human is not significant either ($\Delta = 0.06$ token/s, $t = -0.7$, p>1.).

These results indicate that the human-likeliness of the device moderately impacts the length of utterances and speech rate. Participants tend to speak much longer to humans than to robots, but not to smart speakers. Parties speak faster to humans than to robots and especially to smart-speakers. However, when comparing robot and smart-speaker, no differences in the length of utterance rapidly nor in speech rate were observed.

3.2 Filled Pauses

Filled pauses are instances of disfluencies, accidents in speech production that are extremely natural and frequent in human-human interaction [11]. In general, participants produce significantly fewer filled pauses when talking to a smart speaker than when talking to a human ($\Delta = -0.4$, $t = 2.92$, p = 0.01) and to a robot ($\Delta = -0.29$,

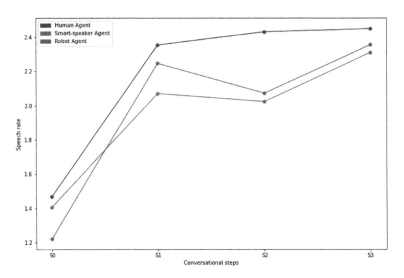

Fig. 2. Mean speech rate in speech directed at the human (blue), at the smart speaker (red) and at the humanoid robot (green). (Color figure online)

$t = 2.62$, $p = 0.03$). The amount of filled pauses between the human- and the robot-directed speech, however, is not significant ($\Delta = 0.11$, $t = 0.8$, $p > 1$.).

The situation evolves over time (Fig. 3). At the beginning of the conversation, especially in S0 (small talk), participants produce more filled pauses when talking to a human (0.35 filled pauses per second) than to a robot (0.19, $\Delta = 0.16$, $p = 0.4$) and especially to a speaker (0.09, $\Delta = 0.26$, $p = 0.04$). At the end of the interaction, for instance, at S3, participants produce almost as many filled pauses when talking to humans (0.27) than to robots (0.28, $\Delta = 0.01$, $p > 1$.) but still more than when talking to speakers (0.19, $\Delta = 0.08$, $p = 0.4$).

Intra-speaker variation is similar in all three conditions, with a standard deviation of 0.17, 0.17 ($\Delta = 0$, $t = 0.004$, $p = 1$) and 0.12 ($\Delta = 0.05$, $t = 1.1$, $p = 0.28$) filled pauses per second in human-, robot- and speaker-directed speech respectively.

These results indicate that in line with previous research [1], participants produce more dysfluencies in human-directed speech than in device-directed speech, but the discrepancy shrinks over time. However, robot-directed speech does not differ significantly either from human- nor speaker-directed speech.

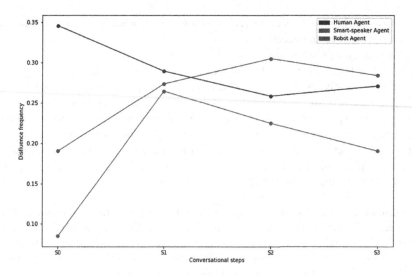

Fig. 3. Mean disfluency frequency in speech directed at the human (blue), at the smart speaker (red) and at the humanoid robot (green). (Color figure online)

4   Conclusion and Discussion

In the present study, we analyze 16 h of speech by 71 native speakers of French to investigate speech rate and use of filled pauses in speech directed at a human, a humanoid robot, or a smart speaker. Our study partially shows the same findings as in previous research [1]: participants produce less filled pauses when addressing a speaker than a human. Nevertheless, contrary to [1], parties in our research speak faster to a human than to a robot or a speaker. Regarding the humanoid robot, building on studies advocating for an effect of anthropomorphism on spoken interaction [4,5], we hypothesized that speech addressed to the robot would share characteristics with human-directed speech rather than with speaker-directed speech. Participants produced indeed longer utterances and faster with more filled pauses in human- than in robot-directed speech. Moreover, robot- and speaker-directed speech does not differ in length of utterance, nor in speech rate, or frequency of disfluencies. We also expected more intra-speaker variation in device- than in human-directed speech. We find the reverse tendency for the length of utterances, and no difference for the use of filled pauses and speech rate. In general, human-directed speech is opposed to smart-speaker- and robot-directed speech.

The similarity between robot- and speaker-directed speech could be due to the fact that both devices communicated with a child's voice, while the human conversational agents were adults. It is possible that participants aligned with child-directed speech rather than with device-directed speech. However, the robot and speaker conditions were comparable but displayed no significant difference, indicating that the behavior of participants quickly converges towards a unique device-directed type of speech. Another caveat is that, while the robot and the speaker always used the same voice, there were four human agents, among which 1 man and 3 women. It is possible that the data from the human-directed speech condition is impacted by a difference between women- *vs* men-directed speech.

Further analyses should also focus on the age of the participants and their daily usage of each robotic device to establish the effect of familiarity and habit in our results. In future steps of this research, we intend to investigate more phonetic characteristics, mainly pitch and acoustic characteristics of the vowels and consonants (formants, duration, etc.), more types of disfluencies, such as unfinished sentences, repetitions (stutter), etc. and finally linguistic properties of discourse, such as discourse markers, the complexity of syntax, etc. We also plan to analyze the similarity of phonetic characteristics between the speech of agents and the speech of subjects in order to study the mechanisms of linguistic alignment during the conversation.

Acknowledgments. This research was supported by Chair AI HUMAAINE (ANR-19-CHIA-0019) directed by Laurence Devillers. The authors sincerely acknowledge all the participants for this experience. We highly appreciate the help of our colleagues from Collège des Bernardins and LISN lab during the recordings, and especially the technical support from Alban Petit during the analysis. We would also like to thank the reviewers for their valuable comments.

References

1. Amalberti, R., Carbonell, N., Falzon, P.: User representations of computer systems in human-computer speech interaction. Int. J. Man-Mach. Stud. **38**(4), 547–566 (1993). https://doi.org/10.1006/imms.1993.1026, https://www.sciencedirect.com/science/article/pii/S0020737383710266

2. Burnham, D., Joeffry, S., Rice, L.: Computer-and human-directed speech before and after correction. In: Proceedings Of The 13Th Australasian International Conference On Speech Science and Technology, vol. 6, pp. 13–17 (2010)

3. Fischer, K., Foth, K., Rohlfing, K.J., Wrede, B.: Mindful tutors: linguistic choice and action demonstration in speech to infants and a simulated robot. Interact. Stud. **12**, 134–161 (2011). https://doi.org/10.1075/is.12.1.06fis

4. Gong, L.: How social is social responses to computers? The function of the degree of anthropomorphism in computer representations. Comput. Hum. Behav. **24**(4), 1494–1509 (2008). https://doi.org/10.1016/j.chb.2007.05.007, https://www.sciencedirect.com/science/article/pii/S0747563207000945, including the Special Issue: Integration of Human Factors in Networked Computing

5. Krach, S., Hegel, F., Wrede, B., Sagerer, G., Binkofski, F., Kircher, T.: Can machines think? Interaction and perspective taking with robots investigated via fMRI. PLoS ONE **3**(7), 1494–1509 (2008). https://doi.org/10.1371/journal.pone.0002597, including the Special Issue: Integration of Human Factors in Networked Computing

6. Kriz, S., Anderson, G., Bugajska, M., Trafton, J.G.: Robot-directed speech as a means of exploring conceptualizations of robots. In: Proceedings of the 4th ACM/IEEE International Conference on Human Robot Interaction, pp. 271–272. HRI 2009, Association for Computing Machinery, New York, NY, USA (2009). https://doi.org/10.1145/1514095.1514171

7. Kriz, S., Anderson, G., Trafton, J.G.: Robot-directed speech: Using language to assess first-time users' conceptualizations of a robot. In: 2010 5th ACM/IEEE International Conference on Human-Robot Interaction (HRI), pp. 267–274 (2010). https://doi.org/10.1109/HRI.2010.5453187

8. Mehenni, H.A., Kobylyanskaya, S., Vasilescu, I., Devillers, L.: Nudges with conversational agents and social robots: a first experiment with children at a primary school. In: 11th International Workshop on Spoken Dialog System Technology, Madrid, Spain (2020). https://hal.science/hal-03083526

9. Raveh, E., Steiner, I., Siegert, I., Gessinger, I., Möbius, B.: Comparing phonetic changes in computer-directed and human-directed speech. In: Birkholz, P., Stone, S. (eds.) Studientexte zur Sprachkommunikation: Elektronische Sprachsignalverarbeitung 2019, pp. 42–49. TUDpress, Dresden (2019)

10. Seabold, S., Perktold, J.: Statsmodels: econometric and statistical modeling with Python. In: 9th Python in Science Conference (2010)

11. Shriberg, E.: Preliminaries to a Theory of Speech Disfluencies. Ph.D. thesis, University of California, Berkeley (1994)

12. Van Rossum, G., Drake, F.L.: Python 3 Reference Manual. CreateSpace, Scotts Valley, CA (2009)

13. Virtanen, P., et al.: SciPy 1.0 contributors: SciPy 1.0: fundamental algorithms for scientific computing in Python. Nat. Meth. **17**, 261–272 (2020). https://doi.org/10.1038/s41592-019-0686-2

An Online Diarization Approach for Streaming Applications Based on Tree-Clustering and Bayesian Resegmentation

Juan M. Martín-Doñas$^{(\boxtimes)}$, Haritz Arzelus, Aitor Álvarez, and Joaquín Arellano

Fundación Vicomtech, Basque Research and Technology Alliance (BRTA), Mikeletegi 57, 20009 Donostia - San Sebastian, Spain
{jmmartin,harzelus,aalvarez,jarellano}@vicomtech.org

Abstract. This paper describes our proposed system for online speaker diarization suitable for streaming applications. Assuming the availability of an audio segment before the partial result is required, our method exploits this information by combining online clustering and resegmentation. First, the speaker embeddings extracted from an x-vector neural network are labeled using tree-based clustering. Then, when a complete batch of x-vectors is available, a Bayesian resegmentation is applied to refine the clusters further. Moreover, we exploit the fact that both methods share the same statistical framework, adapting the resegmentation step to use the history of the decision tree to avoid permutation label issues. Our approach is evaluated with broadcast TV content from the Albayzin Diarization Challenges. The results show that our system is able to outperform online tree-based clustering and obtain comparable performance with state-of-the-art offline approaches while allowing low-latency requirements for practical streaming services.

Keywords: Speaker Diarization · Batch-online processing · X-vector extractor · Tree-based clustering · Variational Bayes resegmentation

1 Introduction

Speaker diarization aims to solve the problem of "who spoke when", that is, segmenting a given audio over the active speaker and clustering the segments belonging to each speaker by assigning the same label to each one [1]. Unlike speaker recognition technologies, no prior knowledge about the speakers' identity or the total number of speakers in the audio is required for the diarization task. These characteristics make speaker diarization useful for speaker-index audio data in domains such as broadcast media, telephonic conversations, or meetings, among others. Moreover, it can be employed with other technologies like automatic speech recognition.

Thanks to its powerful modeling capabilities, the deep learning paradigm has centralized research in this area in recent years. In this sense, the most

K. Ekštein et al. (Eds.): TSD 2023, LNAI 14102, pp. 258–269, 2023.
https://doi.org/10.1007/978-3-031-40498-6_23

common methodology in the literature focuses on a multistage approach, in which different submodules are involved acting as a pipeline. As an example of this pipeline, firstly, an initial speech activity detection module is applied to detect active speaker regions; these speaker regions are then divided into short overlapped segments to extract representative speaker embeddings, using neural networks such as x-vectors [2]. Finally, these embeddings are clustered in same speaker groups given a similarity metric [3, 4] and, optionally, a resegmentation step further refine these clusters [5]. More recently, this paradigm is progressively evolving to end-to-end (E2E) approaches [6–9] where a single neural network is trained to output diarization labels. Nevertheless, this alternative is not mature yet and finds difficulties in complex scenarios involving several speakers.

The approaches above work offline, assuming all the audio is available during the diarization process. On the other hand, online alternatives can be employed when speaker labels have to be assigned on-the-fly as the audio recording feeds the system, as in the case of streaming applications. This is a challenging diarization task, where an incorrect detection and (or) clustering can degrade future decisions' accuracy. Online speaker diarization systems based on deep learning are usually developed as adaptations of offline systems, including clustering-based approaches [10–13] or E2E methods [14–16]. Despite the improvements in the last years, online systems still underperform compared to offline ones. The main drawback is the trade-off between the accuracy of the system and the required low latency for the decisions. However, there are scenarios where a certain delay is allowed between the input audio and the results broadcast, including the diarization decisions. This is common in broadcast streaming, where a buffer time is required for other services to be accommodated, such as speech transcription or translation. In those cases, the availability of longer audio segments can be exploited for developing batch-online diarization systems that can reduce the performance gap with offline methods.

In this paper, we describe our proposed approach for batch-online speaker diarization. Our method efficiently combines offline and online clustering-based techniques. Firstly, the speaker embeddings computed from the x-vector extractor are labeled using an online tree-clustering approach, and the clustered embeddings are used to characterize the corresponding speaker. Then, after a number of accumulated embeddings, a Variational Bayes resegmentation (VBx) [5] is applied to refine the label assignments on the current batch. The resegmentation is also adapted to consider the history of the previous clustering in past batches. Moreover, both models share the same underlying statistical framework, which allows to reduce the operational computations for low-latency applications. Our method is evaluated using broadcast domain corpus available in the community. The experimental results show that our proposed approach is able to reduce the performance gap and achieve close or comparable results with state-of-the-art offline approaches by allowing batch processing. In addition, we analyze the latency requirements of our system to ensure its practical applicability.

The remainder of this paper is structured as follows. Section 2 briefly reviews related works for speaker diarization and their features compared to our approach. Our proposed method is described in Sect. 3, including the tree-clustering and resegmentation modules and its jointly processing. Then, in Sect. 4 the experimental framework and results are presented and analyzed. Finally, the conclusions are summarized in Sect. 5.

2   Related Work

Our proposed approach follows the clustering-based approach, where the embeddings extracted from a deep neural network are processed to be assigned to the corresponding speaker. An online statistical tree-based clustering framework was proposed by [10] and further described in [17]. A similar approach is also explored for the UIS-RNN method [11,18], using a recurrent neural network that tracks the hidden state of the speaker. The authors of [19] used a transformer transducer to detect speaker turns. These turns are thus represented by speaker embeddings, which are then clustered. A low-latency graph-based label generation is described in [12]. This approach modifies an offline agglomerative hierarchical clustering (AHC) algorithm to operate online. The work in [20] combines a clustering-guided training of the recurrent embedding extractor with a truncated-beam searching clustering algorithm. Recently, the authors of [13] explored using VBx for online diarization. For the clustering of the current embedding, core samples are selected from each speaker and concatenated with the new embedding to perform VBx, Then, global constrained clustering is applied to decide if the embedding belongs to a new speaker.

The E2E-based approaches have also been adapted to operate in an online framework. For example, a speaker-tracing buffer is considered in [14] to adapt E2E neural diarization (EEND) network to perform online diarization. The same authors also incorporated the ability to handle a flexible number of speakers in [15]. An online version of the target-speaker voice activity detection (TSVAD) system was proposed in [16]. On the other hand, some approaches have explored a joint approximation of E2E systems for local segmentation and global clustering of extracted embeddings. This is the case of the system proposed in [21]. A similar approach is followed in [22], where the EEND system with speaker-tracing buffer computes the local embeddings, which are then clustered. Despite the progress, the performance of these methods still degrades when the number of speakers is higher than those considered during training.

Our approach is directly related to the tree-based clustering proposed in [10,17] and the VBx technique presented in [5]. We explored a joint combination of both approaches, allowing for pipeline optimization. Our system fully exploits the online behaviour of the decision tree as an initialization for the VBx algorithm. Moreover, we adapted the VBx resegmentation to take advantage of the previous clustering, avoiding the permutation label problem among batches. Compared to [13], our method exploits the speaker clusters' complete statistics and reduces the computational time (the resegmentation is performed in a batch-wise setting). To the best of our knowledge, this is the first work to explore the combination of online tree-based clustering with VBx resegmentation.

3   VBtree-Based Clustering for Batch-Online Diarization

Let us consider the speech signal to be diarized as a sequence of feature vectors $\mathbf{X} = [\mathbf{x}_1, \cdots, \mathbf{x}_T]$, with $\mathbf{Z} = [z_1, \cdots, z_T]$ as the set of discrete variables indicating the corresponding speaker label of each vector. The diarization clustering problem can be formulated as the solution of the following maximization procedure,

$$\mathbf{Z}^* = \underset{\mathbf{Z}}{\operatorname{argmax}} P\left(\mathbf{X} \,|\, \mathbf{Z}\right) P\left(\mathbf{Z}\right), \tag{1}$$

where $P\left(\mathbf{X} \,|\, \mathbf{Z}\right)$ is the likelihood of a given clustering solution, and $P\left(\mathbf{Z}\right)$ represents the a priori distribution of the speaker assignments. We will further assume that $\mathbf{X}$ are x-vectors processed by a Probabilistic Linear Discriminant Analysis (PLDA) model, such as they can be described by speaker-dependent distributions $P\left(\mathbf{x}_t \,|\, \mathbf{y}_s\right) = \mathcal{N}\left(\mathbf{x}_t; \mathbf{V}\mathbf{y}_s, \mathbf{I}\right)$, where $\mathbf{y}_s \sim \mathcal{N}\left(\mathbf{0}, \mathbf{I}\right)$ are the latent speaker vectors $(z_t = s)$, $\mathbf{V}$ is a diagonal matrix, and $\mathbf{I}$ is the identity matrix.

The previous maximization problem only applies in an offline scenario where the entire sequence $\mathbf{X}$ is available. On the contrary, we are interested in a batch-online diarization approach that can exploit the current batch of feature vectors and the assigned clustering in the previous batches. In the following subsections, we first introduce a tree-based online algorithm and the VBx offline resegmentation approaches, and then we describe our proposed system for batch-online diarization.

3.1   Tree-Based Online Clustering

The tree-based model proposed in [10,17] is intended to assign the most probable speaker for the current vector $\mathbf{x}_{t'}$ given the previous set of vectors and computed assignments, $\mathbf{X}^{t'-1}$ and $\mathbf{Z}^{t'-1}$, respectively. First, the likelihood for the current vector given a speaker can be obtained as

$$\begin{aligned} P\left(\mathbf{x}_{t'} \,\Big|\, z_t = s, \mathbf{X}^{t'-1}, \mathbf{Z}^{t'-1}\right) &= \int P\left(\mathbf{x}_{t'} \,|\, \mathbf{y}_{s,t'}\right) P\left(\mathbf{y}_{s,t'} \,\Big|\, \mathbf{X}^{t'-1}, \mathbf{Z}^{t'-1}\right) d\mathbf{y}_{s,t'} \\ &= \mathcal{N}\left(\mathbf{x}_{t'}; \mathbf{V}\boldsymbol{\mu}_{s,t'}, \mathbf{I} + \mathbf{V}\boldsymbol{\Sigma}_{s,t'}\mathbf{V}^\top\right), \end{aligned} \tag{2}$$

where $\boldsymbol{\mu}_{s,t'}$ and $\boldsymbol{\Sigma}_{s,t'}$ are the conditional first- and second-order statistical moments of $\mathbf{y}_{s,t'}$, respectively, which can be computed as

$$\boldsymbol{\mu}_{s,t'} = \boldsymbol{\Sigma}_{s,t'} V^\top \sum_{t=1}^{t'-1} \theta_{s,t} \mathbf{x}_t, \tag{3}$$

$$\boldsymbol{\Sigma}_{s,t'}^{-1} = \mathbf{I} + \mathbf{V}^\top \mathbf{V} \sum_{t=1}^{t'-1} \theta_{s,t}, \tag{4}$$

where $\theta_{s,t}$ is a binary variable equals one when $z_t = s$, zero otherwise.

On the other hand, the speaker priors are modeled by a Distance-dependent Chinese Restaurant (DDCR) process [23], which assigns probabilities to keep in the same speaker, select an existing speaker, or add a new one,

$$P\left(z_{t'} = s \,\Big|\, \mathbf{Z}^{t'-1}\right) = \begin{cases} p_0 & \text{if } z_{t'-1} = s \\ (1-p_0)N_s/B_s & \text{if } z_{t'-1} \neq s \text{ and } s \leq S \\ (1-p_0)\alpha/B_s & \text{if } z_{t'-1} \neq s \text{ and } s = S+1 \end{cases} \tag{5}$$

where p_0 is the probability of keeping in the same speaker, N_s is the number of consecutive blocks of vectors for speaker s, α is a factor proportional to the probability of a new speaker, and $B_s = \sum_{i \neq s} N_i + \alpha$ is a normalization factor.

The model above takes the shape of a decision tree, where the log probability of a given path can be computed as the cumulative log probabilities at each time step. As the decision tree is conditioned to previous assignments, the Markov assumption does not hold. Thus, the M algorithm [24] is used to search for the best path in the tree, propagating a number of surviving paths along all possible branches and ranking them in terms of their likelihood.

3.2 Variational Bayes Resegmentation

The VBx approach proposed in [5] is an offline resegmentation algorithm that uses a Bayesian hidden Markov model (HMM) to find the sequence of speakers. The speaker-specific distributions are derived from the PLDA model, while the transition between speakers follows the next HMM topology,

$$P\left(z_t = s \,|\, z_{t-1} = s'\right) = (1 - p_{\text{loop}}) \pi_s + \delta\left(s, s'\right) p_{\text{loop}}, \tag{6}$$

where p_{loop} is the loop probability of a state, π_s represents the initial probabilities of each speaker, and $\delta\left(s, s'\right)$ is the delta function ($\delta\left(s, s'\right) = 1$ when $s = s'$, otherwise zero). The diarization problem is addressed using a Variational Bayes (VB) approximation of the posterior distribution $P\left(\mathbf{Z}, \mathbf{Y} \,|\, \mathbf{X}\right) \approx q\left(\mathbf{Y}\right) q\left(\mathbf{Z}\right)$, where $\mathbf{Y} = [\mathbf{y}_1, \cdots, \mathbf{y}_S]$. The approximate posterior is found by maximizing the following Evidence Lower Bound Objective (ELBO),

$$\mathcal{L}_{\text{ELBO}} = E_{q(\mathbf{Y})q(\mathbf{Z})} \left[\ln \left(\frac{P\left(\mathbf{X}, \mathbf{Y}, \mathbf{Z}\right)}{q\left(\mathbf{Y}\right) q\left(\mathbf{Z}\right)} \right) \right]. \tag{7}$$

This is an iterative procedure where we find the $q\left(\mathbf{Y}\right)$ that maximizes the ELBO given fixed $q\left(\mathbf{Z}\right)$ and vice versa.

The speaker-specific posteriors are updated as $q^*\left(\mathbf{y}_s\right) = \mathcal{N}\left(\mathbf{y}_s; \boldsymbol{\mu}_s, \boldsymbol{\Sigma}_s\right)$,

$$\boldsymbol{\mu}_s = F_A \boldsymbol{\Sigma}_s V^\top \sum_t \gamma_{s,t} \mathbf{x}_t, \tag{8}$$

$$\boldsymbol{\Sigma}_s^{-1} = \mathbf{I} + F_A V^\top V \sum_t \gamma_{s,t}, \tag{9}$$

where F_A is an empirical acoustic factor and $\gamma_{s,t} = q\,(z_t = s)$. Ignoring the F_A factor, these equations are similar to the ones used in the tree-based algorithm except for two differences: 1) the use of posterior probabilities $\gamma_{s,t}$ for the speakers instead of absolute decisions $\theta_{s,t}$, and 2) the computation is performed for the whole time sequence. Given the updated $q\,(\mathbf{Y})$, the $q^*\,(\mathbf{Z})$ that maximizes the ELBO can be calculated using a forward-backward algorithm. Finally, the initial priors π_s are updated, and the ELBO is evaluated.

The VBx algorithm acts as a resegmentation approach, requiring an initialization for $\gamma_{s,t}$. Thus, it is used along with another offline diarization method. A common approach uses PLDA scoring to compute the similarity matrix between the x-vectors and AHC clustering to obtain a first speaker assignment for the VBx procedure.

3.3   Proposed Approach

In the previous sections, we described tree-based clustering and the VBx resegmentation. The former is appropriate for online diarization but is error-prone due to the absolute decisions at each time step. On the other hand, the VBx approach is not feasible in an online scenario. Moreover, we are interested in a batch-online algorithm that allows a number of accumulated time steps to be diarized before outputting a final decision.

Therefore, we propose a VBtree-based batch-online diarization approach that performs as follows. We consider batches of L x-vectors. For example, we consider the case where $k - 1$ batches have been already diarized, and a new k batch is starting. First, tree-based clustering is applied to each x-vector sequentially to initialize the speaker assignments. Then, the VBx resegmentation is applied to the batch to refine the diarization. To use the previous information from the past batches, we modify the computation of the expected moments of $\mathbf{y}_s$ as follows,

$$\boldsymbol{\mu}_s(k) = F_A \boldsymbol{\Sigma}_s(k) V^\top \left(\sum_{t=1}^{(k-1)L} \theta_{s,t} \mathbf{x}_t + \sum_{t=(k-1)L+1}^{kL} \gamma_{s,t} \mathbf{x}_t \right), \tag{10}$$

$$\boldsymbol{\Sigma}_s^{-1}(k) = \mathbf{I} + F_A \mathbf{V}^\top \mathbf{V} \left(\sum_{t=1}^{(k-1)L} \theta_{s,t} + \sum_{t=(k-1)L+1}^{kL} \gamma_{s,t} \right). \tag{11}$$

The first sum is fixed for the iterative procedure and can be pre-computed for the current batch. The forward-backward algorithm is then applied on the L x-vectors of the batch, but the forward probabilities for the first time step are modified to keep the temporal consistency with the previous batch. After the resegmentation, the new assignments are used to update the tree path.

A diagram of our proposed approach is depicted in Fig. 1. The speech signal is first segmented using voice activity detection (VAD), and the x-vector embeddings are extracted from subsegments of the speech-active segments. These embeddings are clustered in an online manner using the aforementioned decision

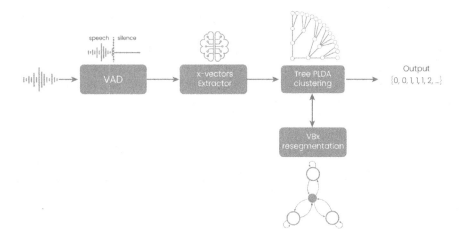

Fig. 1. Scheme of the proposed VBtree-based batch-online diarization approach.

tree. After a batch is completed, VBx resegmentation is applied to correct the assigned labels and output the final decisions to the streaming service.

The advantage of this approach is that it allows a robust batch diarization with low latency. The tree-based clustering gives a good-enough initialization with few computations, while the resegmentation is only performed for the current batch taking advantage of the previously diarized batches. Moreover, both methodologies share a similar statistical framework, which helps the integration of both approaches and merges computations that are common for both methods. Again, this makes the approach better optimized for streaming applications with low latency.

4   Experimental Results

In this section, we first describe the experimental framework of this work, including the datasets used to train and evaluate our method, the x-vector architecture and PLDA, and the diarization pipeline for the batch-online procedure. Then, we present and discuss the evaluation results obtained.

4.1   Experimental Framework

Training and Evaluation Data. In-domain training data is only used to train the PLDA model. It comprises two different corpora. The first corresponds to the data from the Albayzin (ABZ) 2016 diarization corpus [25]. This is a Spanish dataset including broadcast news and radio programs. Besides, additional data from Spanish broadcast TV with speaker labels are considered. The data include the available SAVAS corpus and the commercial IDAZLE corpus (described in more detail in [26]). Table 1 indicates the total number of training hours.

Table 1. Total amount of hours and minutes used for training, development and testing, split by the corresponding dataset.

	Broadcast	ABZ16	ABZ18	ABZ20	ABZ22
Train	162:21	97:22	-	-	-
Development	-	-	15:09	-	-
Test	-	-	21:08	33:21	24:59

Different approaches are evaluated using the test data from the three last Albayzin Diarization Challenges[1] (2018, 2020 and 2022). These datasets include Spanish broadcast contents from different TV programs with diverse conditions: news and talk shows, social and cultural documentaries, and fictional series. In addition, the difficulty increases as new editions are organized. We chose these datasets for a three-fold reason: (1) they are freely available for the research community, (2) the broadcast content is a scenario of great interest for the application of streaming technologies for the market and the scientific community, and (3) we can evaluate our algorithms in challenging data with different acoustic conditions compared to the ones considered from the training of the deep learning systems involved (Spanish language, broadcast content). The total amount of hours for development and testing in each edition is also shown in Table 1.

X-Vector Extractor and PLDA. The x-vector extractor network is the one used in [5] for the 16 kHz evaluation data, and it is based on the ResNet101 architecture [27]. The architecture input consists of 64 log Mel-filterbank features extracted using 25 ms windows, each 10 ms, and the x-vector dimension is 256. The network is trained using VoxCeleb 1 and 2 databases [28] as well as the CN-Celeb dataset [29]. To this end, 4-second segments are used, and data augmentation is performed by adding noise, music, and reverberation. On the other hand, the PLDA is trained with the Kaldi toolkit[2] as in [3] using the training data previously defined. To this end, x-vectors are computed for 3-second segments from the audio. To reduce the domain mismatch, a whitening transformation based on principal component analysis (PCA) is computed from the development data of the Albayzin 2018 dataset and applied to the x-vectors.

Diarization Pipeline. During the inference, audio signals are first segmented to detect speech regions using a voice activity detection module based on GPVAD [30]. An x-vector is extracted from the speech signal each 0.75 seconds using a window length of 1.5 seconds. The x-vectors are centered, whitened using the PCA transformation, and length-normalized. After that, the x-vectors are further processed (mean subtraction and matrix transformation) using the PLDA

---

[1] http://catedrartve.unizar.es/albayzin.html.
[2] https://github.com/kaldi-asr/kaldi/tree/master/egs/dihard_2018.

Table 2. Experimental results obtained from our proposed approach and compared diarization systems for the Albayzin Diarization Challenges from 2018 to 2022. The results are indicated in terms of DER and speaker-confusion error (in parentheses).

System	ABZ18	ABZ20	ABZ22
Chinese whispers	11.40 (6.6)	-	-
Fully-bayesian PLDA	-	15.24 (9.6)	-
PyAnnote	-	16.00 (7.6)	**18.47** (11.0)
VBx	9.83 (4.6)	**13.59** (6.9)	25.52 (14.1)
tree-PLDA	21.82 (16.6)	26.33 (19.7)	33.25 (21.8)
VBtree ($L = 30$, $I = 10$)	9.11 (3.9)	14.28 (7.6)	28.62 (17.2)
VBtree ($L = 15$, $I = 10$)	**8.94** (3.7)	15.60 (8.9)	30.04 (18.6)
VBtree ($L = 15$, $I = 2$)	9.10 (3.9)	13.97 (7.3)	27.75 (16.3)
VBtree ($L = 15$, $I = 1$)	10.47 (5.2)	*13.71* (7.0)	*27.20* (15.8)

parameters to follow the standardized model. Moreover, the dimension of the x-vectors is reduced to 128. The tree-based clustering is used for each L number of x-vectors, and the resegmentation is performed afterward over the whole batch. The fixed hyperparameters used during our experiments are $\alpha = 1$, $p_0 = 0.975$, $F_A = 0.1$, and $p_{\text{loop}} = 0.5$. The beam size for the decision tree is equals to one.

4.2 Evaluation Results

Our proposed approach is evaluated using the test data from the three different Albayzin Diarization Challenges. The accuracy of the diarization systems is measured using the diarization error rate (DER) metric, which considers three different error types: false alarm, missed speech, and confusion among speaker labels. The DER is the rate between the sum of the duration of these errors and the total duration of the audio. While false alarms and missed speech are related to the VAD module (and possibly missed overlapped speech), speaker confusion is caused directly by the error produced during clustering.

Table 2 shows the experimental results obtained from this evaluation in terms of DER and speaker confusion error. We compared our system with the tree-based clustering (tree-PLDA), the offline system using VBx, and the three best systems from each challenge: the GTM-VIGO system based on Chinese whispers [31], the Vivolab system based on Fully-bayesian PLDA [17], and the offline PyAnnote system[3] [32]. Moreover, we report results with our system using different batch sizes (L) and maximum iterations for the resegmentation (I).

The results demonstrate that our approach can effectively improve the online tree-clustering process using batch resegmentation, closing the gap with offline systems and even outperforming them in some cases. For example, our VBtree

---

[3] Results for the Albayzin 2022 Diarization challenge can be found in http://catedrartve.unizar.es/albayzin2022results.html.

Table 3. Average computational time (in seconds) for $L = 15$ batch processing. The times are broken down for processing module and number of iterations.

X-vector & tree-clustering	VBx ($I = 1$)	VBx ($I = 2$)
0.60	3.06	3.82

approach obtains comparable results with VBx in the different datasets. It even gives better results in Albayzin 2018 with some configurations, outperforming the best system in this challenge. Similarly, our approach outperforms the Fully-bayesian PLDA in Albayzin 2020 and achieves close results with VBx using only one iteration for the resegmentation. Regarding Albayzin 2022, the performance gap between PyAnnote and VBx is partly due to different speech segmentation, a better adaptation to this domain, and overlap-aware approaches. Nevertheless, VBtree still achieves competitive results, especially in terms of speaker-confusion error, yielding close results with VBx just using one resegmentation step. Moreover, we show that our approach can perform well when reducing the batch size and the number of iterations. This means that the tree-clustering procedure can provide good initialization for batch-online processing while the resegmentation ensures robustness and decision tree correction. Reducing the batch size can help the resegmentation to correct tree-clustering decisions better, while a low number of iterations prevents resegmentation from diverging during initial clustering. Furthermore, reducing the batch size and iterations allows low-latency computation for streaming applications.

Finally, in Table 3, we show our evaluation of the average computational time to process a batch ($L = 15$), breaking down the tree-clustering step (including x-vector extraction) and the VBx resegmentation (for $I = 1, 2$). We evaluated a subset of audio files in the Albayzin 2018 test data. The experiment was run in a server with Intel Xeon CPU E5-2683 v4 at 2.1 GHz using 32 cores and a Nvidia GeForce GTX 1080Ti GPU with 12 GB of memory. The GPU is used for the inference of the neural network models. The resulting averaged times show that our system is feasible for batch-online computations with low delay and can be applied to a streaming service scenario.

5 Conclusions

In this work, we have presented a batch-online diarization approach suitable for streaming applications. Our system integrates an online tree-clustering diarization approach based on x-vector and PLDA with a VBx resegmentation over the current batch. Moreover, the VBx algorithm is adapted to take into account the history of the decision tree, thus increasing the robustness and accuracy of the diarization output. Our approach is evaluated using the test data from the last editions of the Albayzin Diarization Challenge, which contains diverse TV content with complex conditions. We compared our method with state-of-the-art systems in these challenges as well as related offline and online approaches.

The results showed that our system can outperform the online tree-clustering and achieve comparable results with offline systems while accomplishing streaming service requirements. Furthermore, we were able to reduce the batch size and the number of iterations for the resegmentation algorithm without losing performance, which shows the robustness of the proposed method. Finally, we evaluated the average computational time needed during processing, and the findings further support the use of our system in the streaming scenario. As future work, we will explore adapting the neural modules with in-domain data and additional optimizations for integrating our system into streaming services.

References

1. Park, T., Kanda, N., Dimitriadis, D., Han, K., Watanabe, S., Narayanan, S.: A review of speaker diarization: recent advances with deep learning. Comput. Speech Lang. **72**, 101317 (2022)
2. Snyder, D., Garcia-Romero, D., Sell, G., Povey, D., Khudanpur, S.: X-vectors: Robust DNN embeddings for speaker recognition. In: Proceedings of the ICASSP, pp. 5329–5333 (2018)
3. Ryant, N., et al.: The second DIHARD diarization challenge: dataset, task, and baselines. In: Proceedings of the InterSpeech, pp. 978–982 (2019)
4. Park, T., Han, K., Kumar, M., Narayanan, S.: Auto-tuning spectral clustering for speaker diarization using normalized maximum eigengap. IEEE Sign. Process. Lett. **27**, 381–385 (2019)
5. Landini, F., Profant, J., Diez, M., Burget, L.: Bayesian HMM clustering of x-vector sequences (VBx) in speaker diarization: theory, implementation and analysis on standard tasks. Comput. Speech Lang. **71**, 101254 (2022)
6. Medennikov, I., et al.: Target-speaker voice activity detection: a novel approach for multi-speaker diarization in a dinner party scenario. In: Proceedings of the Interspeech, pp. 274–278 (2020)
7. Maiti, S., Erdogan, H., Wilson, K., Wisdom, S., Watanabe, S., Hershey, J.R.: End-to-end diarization for variable number of speakers with local-global networks and discriminative speaker embeddings. In: Proceedings of the ICASSP, pp. 7183–7187 (2021)
8. Kinoshita, K., Delcroix, M., Tawara, N.: Integrating end-to-end neural and clustering-based diarization: getting the best of both worlds. In: Proceedings of the ICASSP, pp. 7198–7202 (2021)
9. Horiguchi, S., Fujita, Y., Watanabe, S., Xue, Y., Garcia, P.: Encoder-decoder based attractors for end-to-end neural diarization. IEEE/ACM Trans. Audio, Speech, Lang. Process. **30**, 1493–1507 (2022)
10. Viñals, I., Gimeno, P., Ortega, A., Miguel, A., Lleida, E.: ViVoLAB speaker diarization system for the DIHARD 2019 Challenge. In: Proceedings of the InterSpeech, pp. 988–992 (2019)
11. Zhang, A., Wang, Q., Zhu, Z., Paisley, J., Wang, C.: Fully supervised speaker diarization. In: Proceedings of the ICASSP, pp. 6301–6305 (2019)
12. Zhang, Y., et al.: Low-latency online speaker diarization with graph-based label generation. In: Proceedings of the Odyssey, pp. 162–169 (2022)
13. Yue, Y., Du, J., He, M., Yang, Y., Wang, R.: Online speaker diarization with core samples selection. In: Proceedings of the InterSpeech, pp. 1466–1470 (2022)

14. Xue, Y., Horiguchi, S., Fujita, Y., Watanabe, S., García, P., Nagamatsu, K.: Online end-to-end neural diarization with speaker-tracing buffer. In: Proceedings of the IEEE SLT, pp. 841–848 (2021)
15. Xue, Y., et al.: Online streaming end-to-end neural diarization handling overlapping speech and flexible numbers of speakers. In: Proceedings of the InterSpeech, pp. 3116–3120 (2021)
16. Wang, W., Lin, Q., Li, M.: Online target speaker voice activity detection for speaker diarization. In: Proceedings of the InterSpeech, pp. 1441–1445 (2022)
17. Viñals, I., Ortega, A., Miguel, A., Lleida, E.: The domain mismatch problem in the broadcast speaker attribution task. Appl. Sci. 11(18), 8521 (2021)
18. Fini, E., Brutti, A.: Supervised online diarization with sample mean loss for multi-domain data. In: Proceedings of the ICASSP, pp. 7134–7138 (2020)
19. Xia, W., et al.: Turn-to-diarize: online speaker diarization constrained by transformer transducer speaker turn detection. In: Proceedings of the ICASSP, pp. 8077–8081 (2022)
20. Chen, Y., Guo, Y., Li, Q., Cheng, G., Zhang, P., Yan, Y.: Interrelate training and searching: a unified online clustering framework for speaker diarization. In: Proceedings of the InterSpeech, pp. 1456–1460 (2022)
21. Coria, J., Bredin, H., Ghannay, S., Rosset, S.: Overlap-aware low-latency online speaker diarization based on end-to-end local segmentation. In: Proceedings of the IEEE ASRU, pp. 1139–1146 (2021)
22. Horiguchi, S., Watanabe, S., García, P., Takashima, Y., Kawaguchi, Y.: Online neural diarization of unlimited numbers of speakers using global and local attractors. IEEE/ACM Trans. Audio, Speech, Lang. Process. 31, 706–720 (2023)
23. Blei, D., Frazier, P.: Distance dependent Chinese restaurant processes. J. Mach. Learn. Res. 12(8), 2461–2488 (2011)
24. Jelinek, F., Anderson, J.: Instrumentable tree encoding of information sources. IEEE Trans. Inf. Theory 17(1), 118–119 (1971)
25. Ortega, A., Vinals, I., Miguel, A., Lleida, E.: The Albayzin 2016 speaker diarization evaluation. Proc. IberSpeech (2016)
26. Álvarez, A., Arzelus, H., Torre, I., González-Docasal, A.: Evaluating novel speech transcription architectures on the Spanish RTVE2020 database. Appl. Sci. 12(4), 1889 (2022)
27. He, K., Zhang, X., Ren, S., Sun, J.: Deep residual learning for image recognition. In: Proceedings of the IEEE CVPR, pp. 770–778 (2016)
28. Nagrani, A., Chung, J., Xie, W., Zisserman, A.: VoxCeleb: large-scale speaker verification in the wild. Comput. Speech Lang. 60, 101027 (2020)
29. Fan, Y., et al.: CN-Celeb: a challenging Chinese speaker recognition dataset. In: Proceedings of the ICASSP, pp. 7604–7608 (2020)
30. Dinkel, H., Wang, S., Xu, X., Wu, M., Yu, K.: Voice activity detection in the wild: a data-driven approach using teacher-student training. IEEE/ACM Trans. Audio, Speech, Lang. Process. 29, 1542–1555 (2021)
31. Lleida, E., et al.: Albayzin 2018 evaluation: the IberSpeech-RTVE challenge on speech technologies for Spanish broadcast media. Appl. Sci. 9(24), 5412 (2019)
32. Bredin, H., et al.: Pyannote. audio: neural building blocks for speaker diarization. In: Proceedings of the ICASSP, pp. 7124–7128 (2020)

Evaluation of Speech Representations for MOS Prediction

Frederico S. Oliveira[(⊠)], Edresson Casanova[(⊠)], Arnaldo Candido Junior[(⊠)],
Lucas R. S. Gris[(⊠)], Anderson S. Soares[(⊠)], and Arlindo R. Galvão Filho[(⊠)]

UFG, Goiás, GO, Brazil
frederico.oliveira@ufmt.br, edresson@coqui.ai, arnaldo.candido@unesp.br,
lucas.gris@discente.ufg.br, {andersonsoares,arlindogalvao}@ufg.br

Abstract. In this paper, we evaluate feature extraction models for predicting speech quality. We also propose a model architecture to compare embeddings of supervised learning and self-supervised learning models with embeddings of speaker verification models to predict the metric
MOS. Our experiments were performed on the VCC2018 dataset and a
Brazilian-Portuguese dataset called BRSpeechMOS, which was created for
this work. The results show that the Whisper model is appropriate in all
scenarios: with both the VCC2018 and BRSpeechMOS datasets. Among
the supervised and self-supervised learning models using BRSpeechMOS,
Whisper-Small achieved the best linear correlation of 0.6980, and the
speaker verification model, SpeakerNet, had linear correlation of 0.6963.
Using VCC2018, the best supervised and self-supervised learning model,
Whisper-Large, achieved linear correlation of 0.7274, and the best model
speaker verification, TitaNet, achieved a linear correlation of 0.6933.
Although the results of the speaker verification models are slightly lower,
the SpeakerNet model has only 5M parameters, making it suitable for real-
time applications, and the TitaNet model produces an embedding of size
192, the smallest among all the evaluated models. The experiment results
are reproducible with publicly available source-code.

Keywords: speech assessment · speech evaluation · mos prediction

1 Introduction

The[1] development of speech synthesis and voice conversion models has increased
the need for automatic methods to evaluate the quality of generated speech. The
most reliable methods among the available options rely on manual evaluation,
where human evaluators are chosen to assess signal quality using a predefined
numerical scale. In recent work, self-supervised learning (SSL) models have been
used to predict the quality of synthesized speech. Representations obtained from
models such as Wav2Vec 2.0 [3], HuBERT [12], WavLM [4], and TERA [18] have
been used. These models produce high quality representations and their training
requires a large amount of data.

---

[1] https://github.com/freds0/BSpeech-MOS-Prediction.

© The Author(s), under exclusive license to Springer Nature Switzerland AG 2023
K. Ekštein et al. (Eds.): TSD 2023, LNAI 14102, pp. 270–282, 2023.
https://doi.org/10.1007/978-3-031-40498-6_24

Whisper [24], in the other hand is a for general-purpose speech recognition model based on supervised learning (SL), and it was developed with the goal of creating a robust system that generalizes well across domains, tasks and languages without relying on fine-tuning to achieve high accuracy. Whisper embeddings can be used to speech recognition, speech translation, language identification and other tasks. The authors demonstrated that training on a large and diverse supervised dataset alone can significantly enhance the robustness of speech systems. However, to date, the embeddings generated by the Whisper model have not been evaluated for their effectiveness in the task of speech quality prediction.

Speaker embeddings generated by speaker verification models (SV) offer an alternative to high-quality embeddings. Unlike the latter, speaker embeddings have a fixed size that remains constant regardless of the length of the utterance. Earlier studies, such as [31], have examined the properties that are captured by speaker embeddings, such as the spoken content, speaker's gender, speaking rate and audio channel information. These studies have demonstrated satisfactory performance on various tasks, which has motivated further exploration of these features for predicting the quality of synthesized speech. Also, so far, the representations of SV models have not been evaluated in the speech quality prediction task.

In this paper, we propose to evaluate high-quality representations from both SL and SSL models, as well as SV representations, for the purpose of predicting the quality of synthesized speech in text-to-speech (TTS) systems. In addition, we investigate the use of these models to evaluate speech samples in a low resource dataset, in Brazilian Portuguese. Models based on SV can be an alternative to generate high quality embeddings with low computational cost, allowing the evaluation of speech quality in real time.

This paper is organized as follows: Sect. 2 presents some prior research on automatically predicting the quality of synthesized speech. Section 3 outlines the proposed model architecture developed in this study and Sect. 4 details the experiments proposed. Then, Sect. 5 discusses the obtained results, and finally, Sect. 7 presents the conclusions of this work.

2   Related Works

Several studies have addressed the development of automatic methods for evaluating the quality of synthesized speech and have obtained results that correlate with human evaluation methods. The first pioneering work that used Deep Learning to predict quality was proposed in 2016 with the AutoMOS model by Patton et al. [23]. Fu et al. [9] proposed the Quality-Net model to predict the PESQ [26], a metric which compares a degraded speech signal with a reference speech signal to provide an objective measure of the perceived voice quality by the human listener. Lo et al. [19] developed MOSNet, a improved version of Quality-Net for the MOS prediction task.

Cooper et al. [7] investigate the ability of SSL models to predict speech quality in out-of-domain scenarios. With the aim of achieving this goal, the researchers conducted experiments on embedding extraction models, such as Wav2Vec 2.0 [3] and HuBERT [12], and compare them to the MOSNet model. The models were trained on datasets such as the Blizzard Challenge [13] and the Voice Conversion Challenge [8], and then evaluated on the ASVSpoof 2019 [27] and Blizzard Challenge 2019 [32] datasets. The findings reveal that the Wav2Vec model outperforms the other evaluated models. However, evaluating without fine-tuning in a zero-shot setting proved to be challenging and resulted in a notable decrease in performance.

MOSA-Net [34] is a cross-domain model that uses inputs from multiple domains, including spectrograms, waveforms and SSL features. According to the authors, using features from multiple domains contributes to more accurate results, and training for predicting multiple metrics outperforms the task of predicting a single one. Although the model can be adjusted to predict subjective metrics, no comparative experiments have been conducted with other models.

Tseng et al. [28] compared models for predicting MOS using embeddings generated by Wav2Vec 2.0 [3], TERA [17], CAC [22], and APC [5]. The authors proposed an architecture where the human's identification is the input and defines the human bias. The experiments show that the Wav2Vec model achieves the best results at the sentence and system levels. Similarly, Tseng, Kao and Lee [29] proposed DDOS, a model for MOS prediction that uses Wav2Vec 2.0 for feature extraction in conjunction with a representation of the evaluator, in order to specify the human bias. The model consists of two submodules, the regression head and the distribution head, which uses attentive pooling and DNNs to predict the score and distribution of the data. The results of the submodules are then combined to predict the MOS.

Yang et al. [33] developed an framework for improving speech quality prediction by combining various SSL models, such as Wav2Vec 2.0, WavLM, HuBERT, and Data2Vec [2]. The framework consists of two parts: the first involves training the SSL models individually, while the second involves fusing the results of each model. The goal of the framework is to fine-tune the SSL models and enhance the accuracy of MOS prediction, treating model fusion as a technique similar to ensemble. Ragano et al. [25] presented experiments comparing combining Wav2Vec 2.0 model representations with features extracted from convolutional layers, exploring different architectural combinations. Ultimately, the authors found that incorporating features extracted from convolutional layers did not improve the results.

3   Model Proposal

The proposed model for evaluating the quality of synthesized speech consists of two modules: the Feature Extractor, which is responsible for extracting speech features, and the MOS Predictor, which predicts speech quality based on the extracted features. The architecture of the MOS Predictor consists of two dense blocks, ReLU activation function, and dropout. Several models are evaluated as the Feature Extractor, including SV, SL, and SSL models. The architecture of the proposed model can be seen in Fig. 1. Details of the selected models are given below.

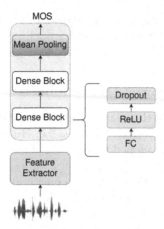

Fig. 1. The proposed model consists of two modules: Feature Extractor (in blue) and MOS Predictor (in yellow). (Color figure online)

3.1 Speaker Verification Models

The GE2E, Clova, TitaNet, and SpeakerNet models, originally proposed for SV, were selected for speech feature extraction and are discussed in more detail below:

GE2E [30] is a model that uses the Generalized End-to-End loss function for training and consists of LSTM layers and a fully connected layer with softmax activation. It extracts the vector of embeddings from the log-mel filterbank energies of each speaker's sentences and computes the centroid of each speaker. The similarity matrix is determined from the centroid of each speaker and the parameters learned during training.

Clova [11] is a model based on the ResNet architecture [10] proposed in 2020 for speaker recognition. There are two versions: Q/SAP, lighter and with fewer parameters, and H/ASP, which focuses on the quality of the results. Both versions take log-mel-filterbanks as input and use residual blocks and attentive pooling layers. Version Q/ SAP uses self-attentive pooling. The model was trained with a combination of prototypical and softmax angular loss functions. Version H/ ASP achieved higher accuracy and was selected for use in this work.

SpeakerNet [14] is a model with encoder-decoder architecture proposed in 2020 for speaker recognition and verification. It is based on the QuartzNet [16] model and has a statistics pooling layer for intermediate feature extraction. The model is trained with the loss functions cross-entropy and additive angular margin. There are two versions, SpeakerNet-L and SpeakerNet-M, with 7M and 5M trainable parameters, respectively. The SpeakerNet-M version showed better results and is used in this work.

TitaNet [15] is a model with an encoder-decoder architecture proposed in 2022 for speaker verification tasks. It is based on the ContextNet model and has an initial block, a final block, and intermediate blocks that use time-channel separable convolutional layers and residual connections with squeeze and excitation layers. The model uses an attentive statistics pooling layer to extract temporal-independent intermediate features and a decoder consisting of two linear layers.

3.2   Self-Supervised Learning Based Models

SSL models are trained with thousands of hours of unlabeled audio. In this work, the following models were selected: Wav2vec 2.0, HuBERT, and WavLM.

Wav2vec 2.0 [3] was developed for the task of automatic speech recognition, which learns latent representations through a process of masking parts of the audio. A new version, XLSR [6], was trained on a multilingual dataset consisting of 50,000 h of recordings in 53 languages. The XLS-R [1] version is the latest and has been trained using over 400,000 h of recordings in 128 languages.

HuBERT [12] learns latent representations of speech through training similar to that of Wav2Vec, along with the K-means algorithm used to discretize the input Mel spectrogram. In this work, two versions of the HuBERT model are used, called Large and xLarge, trained with 60,000 h of English audio data.

WavLM [4] is a more general version of the HuBERT model that can be used for tasks such as speech separation, speaker diarization, speaker verification, and speech recognition. In this work, two versions were selected for evaluation: Large and Base-Plus.

3.3   Supervised Learning Based Model

Radford et al. proposed *Web-scale Supervised Pretraining for Speech Recognition* (Whisper) [24], an encoder-decoder model based on Transformer, which maps the audio spectrogram to a sequence of text tokens. Whisper was trained through supervised training with approximately 680,000 h of labeled audio data in English and other 96 languages, including Brazilian Portuguese. Results show that the Whisper model is robust in different scenarios and outperforms SSL-based models when evaluated on different datasets. In this work, five versions were selected for evaluation: Tiny, Base, Small, Medium, and Large.

4   Experiments

This study evaluates a total of 16 models for predicting speech quality. Four of them are based on SV; seven are based on SSL (versions of Wav2vec 2.0 [3], WavLM [4] and HuBERT [12]); and five based on SL (versions of Whisper). Table 1 summarizes the models evaluated in this study. This table shows the dimensions of the output embedding and the total parameters of each model, in order to better compare the models.

We used two datasets for the experiments in this study: the VCC2018 dataset [20] and a Brazilian-Portuguese dataset, which was exclusively created for this present study and is known as BRSpeechMOS. The VCC2018 dataset consists of a total of 28,292 audio samples in English with a sampling rate of 16kHz, each

Table 1. The MOSNet model is in the *Baseline* category; in the SV category, models based on speaker verification; in the SSL category, models based on self-supervised training; in the SL category, models based on supervised training. The "Output dim" column shows the size of *embeddings* generated by the *Feature Extractor* module. The "Total param" column shows the total set of training parameters for the Feature Extractor module.

Category	Model	Version	Output dim	Total param
Baseline	MOSNet [19]	–	–	1,1M
SV	TitaNet [15]	Large	[192]	25,3M
	SpeakerNet [14]	Medium	[256]	5M
	GE2E [30]	–	[256]	1,4M
	CLOVA [11]	H/ASP	[512]	8M
SSL	Wav2Vec 2.0 [1]	xls-r-300m	[1024, T]	300M
		xls-r-1b	[1280, T]	1B
		xls-r-2b	[1920, T]	2B
	WavLM [4]	Base-Plus	[768, T]	94M
		Large	[1024, T]	316M
	HuBERT [12]	Large	[768, T]	300M
		xLarge	[1024, T]	1B
SL	Whisper [24]	Tiny	[384, T]	39M
		Base	[512, T]	74M
		Small	[768, T]	244M
		Medium	[1024, T]	769M
		Large	[1280, T]	1,5B

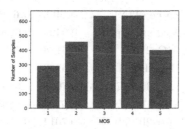

Fig. 2. Distributions of scores for BRSpeechMOS dataset.

sample being evaluated by 4 evaluators. The BRSpeechMOS dataset contains 2,428 audio samples at 16kHz, and each of these samples has been evaluated by an average of two evaluators. The distribution of scores for the dataset can be seen in Fig. 2. This dataset has been utilized to assess the model's performance on a dataset with limited resources.

All evaluated models were first trained with the VCC2018 dataset and then fine-tuned with BRSpeechMOS. Model training was stopped early when no more improvements were observed in a test set, with Spearman correlation analysis. Then, the weights of the best models were selected to be evaluated in a validation set. The experiments were performed on a DGX-1 server running the Linux Ubuntu 18.04 operating system. The server was equipped with a Dual 20-Core Intel Xeon processor E5-2698 v4 2.2 GH, 256 GB RAM, and an NVIDIA® Tesla® V100 GPU.

5   Results

The results are presented below, grouping the models according to the following categories: speaker verification (SV), self-supervised learning (SSL) and supervised learning (SL). The evaluation metrics used in this study include Pearson correlation (LCC), Spearman rank correlation coefficient (SRCC), Kendall-Tau rank correlation (KTAU), and mean square error (MSE).

5.1   VCC2018 Experiments

Table 2 shows the results of all performed experiments using the VCC2018 dataset. For comparison purposes, the results of the experiments using the MOSNet [19] model are also presented. Among the SV models, TitaNet obtained the best results in all metrics, with LCC = 0.6933, SRCC = 0.6667, KTAU =

Table 2. Results of experiments using the VCC2018 dataset.

Category	Model	Version	LCC ↑	SRCC ↑	KTAU ↑	MSE ↓
SV	MOSNet	–	0.5588	0.5159	0.3765	0.5166
	TitaNet	Large (TtN)	**0.6933**	**0.6667**	**0.5005**	**0.0160**
	SpeakerNet	Medium (SpN)	0.6428	0,6210	0.4598	0.0202
	GE2E	- (Ge2)	0.6118	0.5846	0,4306	0.0193
	CLOVA	H/ASP (CLO)	0.6903	0.6623	0,4966	0.0162
SSL	Wav2Vec 2.0	xls-r-300m (Wv3)	0.7090	0.6866	0.5190	0.0153
		xls-r-1b (Wv1)	**0.7140**	0.6893	0.5210	0.0268
		xls-r-2b (Wv2)	0.7014	0.6757	0.5096	0.0159
	WavLM	Base-Plus (WlB)	0.6917	0.6816	0.5122	0.0163
		Large (WlL)	0.7120	**0.7036**	**0.5316**	**0.0151**
	HuBERT	Large (HbL)	0.6692	0.6441	0.4800	0.0170
		xLarge (HbX)	0.6871	0.6684	0.5012	0.0170
SL	Whisper	Tiny (WpT)	0.7072	0.6881	0.5187	0.0281
		Base (WpB)	0.7178	0.6951	0.5249	0.0225
		Small (WpS)	0.7136	0.6906	0.5218	0.0212
		Medium (WpM)	0.7205	0.6957	0.5267	0.0195
		Large (WpM)	**0.7274**	**0.7061**	**0.5365**	**0.0194**

0.5005 and MSE = 0.0160. However, the SpeakerNet, GE2E, and CLOVA models show similar results, all superior to the MOSNet model.

Among the SSL models, Table 2 shows that the Wav2Vec 2.0 xls-r-1b model presented the best LCC value, with a value equal to 0.7140. However, in the other metrics, the WavLM-Large model performs best, with SRCC = 0.7036, KTAU = 0.5316 and MSE = 0.0151. On the other hand, HuBERT presented the worst results among the SSL models evaluated. And among the SL models, it appears that the Whisper Large model presented the best results, with LCC = 0.727, SRCC = 0.7061, KTAU=0.5365 and MSE = 0.0194. It is worth mentioning that the Whisper Large model presented the best results among all the models using the VCC2018 dataset.

5.2 BRSpeechMOS Experiments

Table 3 shows the results of all experiments using the BRSpeechMOS dataset. The following experiments using the MOSNet model are also presented: *MOSNet ZeroShot* (MZS), which was trained using only the VCC2018 dataset and follows the methodology and hyperparameters used by the original authors; *MOSNet From Scratch* (MFS), which was trained exclusively with the BRSpeechMOS dataset; and *MOSNet Fine Tuning* (MFT), which was pre-trained with the VCC2018 dataset and fine-tuned with the BRSpeechMOS dataset.

The results of the experiments using the BRSpeechMOS dataset showed that not all models generalize well in a low-resource dataset. Among the SV models, the SpeakerNet model performed best in all metrics evaluated, with LCC = 0.6963, SRCC = 0.6772, KTAU = 0.5173 and MSE = 0.0311, followed by the CLOVA model. The TitaNet model was the one that presented the worst results. We believe that the poor performance on the BRSpeechMOS dataset is due to the small dimension of the output embedding, equal to 192 as shown in Table 1, which likely causes the embeddings to specialize in the features that differentiate the speakers. Therefore, more training data would be needed for the MOS Prediction module to accurately map the features to the MOS score.

Among the SSL models using the BRSpeechMOS, the Whisper Large model stood out, with LCC = 0.6858, SRCC = 0.6831, KTAU = 0.5275 and MSE = 0.0322. This table also confirms that the HuBERT model has lower performance compared to the other models. And among the SL models, it can be seen that the Whisper Small model had the best performance, with LCC = 0.6980, SRCC = 0.6968, KTAU = 0.5400 and MSE = 0.0440, followed by the Whisper Large model.

Table 3. Results of experiments using the BRSpeechMOS dataset.

Category	Model	Version	LCC ↑	SRCC ↑	KTAU ↑	MSE ↓
Baseline	MOSNet	Zero Shot (MZS)	0.2196	0.2107	0.1520	0.0611
	MOSNet	From Scratch (MFS)	0.5090	**0.3677**	**0.2693**	0.0452
	MOSNet	Fine Tuning (MFT)	**0.5118**	0.3603	0.2612	**0.0445**
SV	TitaNet	(TtN)	0.1012	0.1177	0.0849	0.0623
	SpeakerNet	(SpN)	**0.6963**	**0.6772**	**0.5173**	**0.0311**
	GE2E	(Ge2)	0.2655	0.2584	0.1791	0.0704
	CLOVA	(CLO)	0.6860	0.6755	0.5123	0.0359
SSL	Wav2Vec 2.0	xls-r-300m (Wv3)	0.6739	0.6593	0.5073	0.0335
		xls-r-1b (Wv1)	0.6539	0.6451	0.4937	0.0477
		xls-r-2b (Wv2)	0.6667	0.6439	0.4959	0.0341
	WavLM	Base-Plus (WlB)	0.6082	0.5936	0.4463	0.0382
		Large (WlL)	**0.6858**	**0.6831**	**0.5275**	**0.0322**
	HuBERT	Large (HbL)	0.5959	0.5863	0.4407	0.0482
		xLarge (HbX)	0.6262	0.6214	0.4669	0.0368
SL	Whisper	Tiny (WpT)	0.6587	0.6240	0.4753	0.0564
		Base (WpB)	0.6460	0.6083	0.4645	0.0486
		Small (WpS)	**0.6980**	**0.6968**	**0.5400**	**0.0440**
		Medium (WpM)	0.6904	0.6696	0.5161	0.0534
		Large (WpL)	0.6956	0.6852	0.5277	0.0777

6   Discussion

When evaluating SV models using the VCC2018 dataset, all models presented good results. That is, using a dataset with a large number of samples, all models proved to be adequate to predict speech quality, with TitaNet presenting the best results. However, when conducting the same experiments with the BRSpeech-MOS dataset, which has 2,428 samples, the results showed that the SpeakerNet model can extract more adequate features to evaluate samples quality even when using a much smaller dataset compared to VCC2018.

The representations of the BSpeechMOS using the SpeakerNet model were extracted and projected to 2D space using t-SNE [21]. Figure 3 illustrates the relationship between sample representations and their MOS score. It can be observed that the samples with score 5 (blue), 4 (cyan), and 3 (green) are in clusters. On the other hand, there are also clusters formed by samples with grades 1 (red), 2 (yellow), and 3 (green). Probably, if the BRSpeechMOS samples were evaluated by a larger number of evaluators, the clusters would be more homogeneous. The projections using the VCC2018 are not shown since all the models performed relatively well in the quality prediction task.

Experiments with the SSL models, Wav2Vec 2.0 [1], WavLM [4], HuBERT [12], and with SL model Whisper [24], using both datasets showed very similar results. The Whisper model showed the best results, which can be justified by

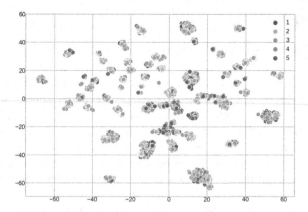

Fig. 3. T-SNE projection of embeddings from SpeakerNet extracted from BRspeech-MOS.

a large amount of training data in different languages, including Brazilian Portuguese. In contrast, the HuBERT model showed slightly worse results compared to the other SSL models. This is evidenced by the correlation metrics, as shown in Tables 2 and 3.

When comparing all models, it is noticeable that the SL and SSL models are superior to the SV models. However, it is worth noting that the SL model with the best results, SpeakerNet, has only 5M parameters, while the smallest SL-SSL model, Whisper-Tiny, has 39M parameters, almost 8 *times* the number of parameters of the SpeakerNet model. To better compare the models, Fig. 4 shows the ranking of the models with the best results, with the models sorted on the x axis by the number of parameters of the Feature Extractor module.

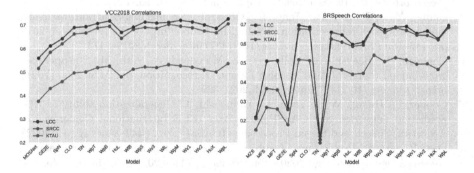

Fig. 4. On the left, there are graphs displaying the correlation metrics results from the VCC2018 dataset. On the right, there are graphs displaying the results from the BRSpeechMOS dataset. On the x-axis, the models are ordered according to the number of parameters.

7   Conclusions

Our results indicate that the Whisper model, particularly the Large version, is the most effective for the task of speech quality prediction, as demonstrated through its superior performance on the VCC2018 dataset. Additionally, when applied to the BRSpeechMOS dataset, the Whisper model, specifically the Small version, continued to exhibit the highest predictive accuracy, highlighting its ability to generalize well. Furthermore, our study suggests that models designed for speaker verification can also be suitable for predicting speech quality, with the SpeakerNet model performing particularly well, even when using the BRSpeech dataset, which has limited resources and was created exclusively for this study.

Acknowledgements. The authors are grateful to the Center of Excellence in Artificial Intelligence (https://ceia.ufg.br/) (CEIA) at the Federal University of Goias (UFG) for their support and to CyberLabs (https://cyberlabs.ai) and Coqui (https://coqui.ai/) for their valuable assistance.

References

1. Babu, A., et al.: XLS-R: self-supervised cross-lingual speech representation learning at scale. CoRR abs/2111.09296 (2021). https://arxiv.org/abs/2111.09296
2. Baevski, A., Hsu, W.N., Xu, Q., Babu, A., Gu, J., Auli, M.: Data2vec: a general framework for self-supervised learning in speech, vision and language. In: International Conference on Machine Learning, pp. 1298–1312. PMLR (2022)
3. Baevski, A., Zhou, H., Mohamed, A., Auli, M.: Wav2vec 2.0: a framework for self-supervised learning of speech representations. In: Proceedings of the 34th International Conference on Neural Information Processing Systems, NIPS 2020, Curran Associates Inc., Red Hook, NY, USA (2020)
4. Chen, S., et al.: WavLM: large-scale self-supervised pre-training for full stack speech processing. IEEE J. Select. Top. Signal Process. **16**, 1505–1518 (2021)
5. Chung, Y.A., Hsu, W.N., Tang, H., Glass, J.: An unsupervised autoregressive model for speech representation learning. In: Proceedings of the Interspeech 2019, pp. 146–150 (2019). https://doi.org/10.21437/Interspeech.2019-1473
6. Conneau, A., Baevski, A., Collobert, R., Mohamed, A., Auli, M.: Unsupervised cross-lingual representation learning for speech recognition, pp. 2426–2430 (2021). https://doi.org/10.21437/Interspeech.2021-329
7. Cooper, E., Huang, W.C., Toda, T., Yamagishi, J.: Generalization ability of MOS prediction networks. In: ICASSP 2022–2022 IEEE International Conference on Acoustics, Speech and Signal Processing (ICASSP), pp. 8442–8446. IEEE (2022)
8. Das, R., et al.: Predictions of subjective ratings and spoofing assessments of voice conversion challenge 2020 submissions, pp. 99–120 (2020). https://doi.org/10.21437/VCC_BC.2020-15
9. Fu, S.W., Tsao, Y., Hwang, H.T., Wang, H.M.: Quality-net: an end-to-end non-intrusive speech quality assessment model based on BLSTM (2018)
10. He, K., Zhang, X., Ren, S., Sun, J.: Deep residual learning for image recognition. In: 2016 IEEE Conference on Computer Vision and Pattern Recognition (CVPR), pp. 770–778 (2016). https://doi.org/10.1109/CVPR.2016.90

11. Heo, H.S., Lee, B.J., Huh, J., Chung, J.S.: Clova baseline system for the voxceleb speaker recognition challenge 2020. arXiv preprint arXiv:2009.14153 (2020)

12. Hsu, W.N., Bolte, B., Tsai, Y.H.H., Lakhotia, K., Salakhutdinov, R., Mohamed, A.: HuBERT: self-supervised speech representation learning by masked prediction of hidden units. IEEE/ACM Trans. Audio, Speech Lang. Proc. **29**, 3451–3460 (2021). https://doi.org/10.1109/TASLP.2021.3122291

13. King, S., Karaiskos, V.: The blizzard challenge 2016 (2016)

14. Koluguri, N.R., Li, J., Lavrukhin, V., Ginsburg, B.: Speakernet: 1d depth-wise separable convolutional network for text-independent speaker recognition and verification (2020). https://doi.org/10.48550/ARXIV.2010.12653,https://arxiv.org/abs/2010.12653

15. Koluguri, N.R., Park, T., Ginsburg, B.: Titanet: neural model for speaker representation with 1d depth-wise separable convolutions and global context. In: ICASSP 2022–2022 IEEE International Conference on Acoustics, Speech and Signal Processing (ICASSP), pp. 8102–8106. IEEE (2022)

16. Kriman, S., et al.: Quartznet: deep automatic speech recognition with 1d time-channel separable convolutions. In: ICASSP 2020–2020 IEEE International Conference on Acoustics, Speech and Signal Processing (ICASSP), pp. 6124–6128 (2020). https://doi.org/10.1109/ICASSP40776.2020.9053889

17. Liu, A.T., Li, S.W., Lee, H.Y.: Tera: self-supervised learning of transformer encoder representation for speech. IEEE/ACM Trans. Audio Speech Lang. Process. **29**, 2351–2366 (2020)

18. Liu, A.T., Li, S.W., Lee, H.Y.: Tera: self-supervised learning of transformer encoder representation for speech. IEEE/ACM Trans. Audio Speech Lang. Process. **29**, 2351–2366 (2021)

19. Lo, C.C., et al.: MOSNet: deep learning-based objective assessment for voice conversion. In: Interspeech 2019. ISCA (2019). https://doi.org/10.21437/interspeech.2019-2003, https://doi.org/10.21437%2Finterspeech.2019-2003

20. Lorenzo-Trueba, J., et al.: The voice conversion challenge 2018: promoting development of parallel and nonparallel methods (2018)

21. Van der Maaten, L., Hinton, G.: Visualizing data using t-SNE. J. Mach. Learn. Res. **9**(11) (2008)

22. Oord, A.v.d., Li, Y., Vinyals, O.: Representation learning with contrastive predictive coding (2018). https://doi.org/10.48550/ARXIV.1807.03748, https://arxiv.org/abs/1807.03748

23. Patton, B., Agiomyrgiannakis, Y., Terry, M., Wilson, K.W., Saurous, R.A., Sculley, D.: AutoMOS: learning a non-intrusive assessor of naturalness-of-speech. CoRR abs/1611.09207 (2016). https://arxiv.org/abs/1611.09207

24. Radford, A., Kim, J.W., Xu, T., Brockman, G., McLeavey, C., Sutskever, I.: Robust speech recognition via large-scale weak supervision (2022). https://doi.org/10.48550/ARXIV.2212.04356,https://arxiv.org/abs/2212.04356

25. Ragano, A., et al.: A comparison of deep learning MOS predictors for speech synthesis quality (2022)

26. Rix, A., Beerends, J., Hollier, M., Hekstra, A.: Perceptual evaluation of speech quality (PESQ) - a new method for speech quality assessment of telephone networks and codecs. In: Proceedings 2001 IEEE International Conference on Acoustics, Speech, and Signal Processing, vol. 2, pp. 749–752. (Cat. No.01CH37221) (2001). https://doi.org/10.1109/ICASSP.2001.941023

27. Todisco, M., et al.: ASVspoof 2019: Future horizons in spoofed and fake audio detection. arXiv preprint arXiv:1904.05441 (2019)

28. Tseng, W.C., Huang, C.Y., Kao, W.T., Lin, Y.Y., Lee, H.Y.: Utilizing self-supervised representations for MOS prediction. In: Interspeech (2021)

29. Tseng, W.C., Kao, W.T., Lee, H.Y.: DDOS: a MOS prediction framework utilizing domain adaptive pre-training and distribution of opinion scores. In: Interspeech (2022)

30. Wan, L., Wang, Q., Papir, A., Moreno, I.L.: Generalized end-to-end loss for speaker verification. In: 2018 IEEE International Conference on Acoustics, Speech and Signal Processing (ICASSP), pp. 4879–4883. IEEE (2018)

31. Wang, S., Qian, Y., Yu, K.: What does the speaker embedding encode? In: Interspeech, pp. 1497–1501 (2017)

32. Wu, Z., Xie, Z., King, S.: The blizzard challenge 2019 (2019)

33. Yang, Z., et al.: Fusion of self-supervised learned models for MOS prediction. In: Proceedings of the Interspeech 2022, pp. 5443–5447 (2022). https://doi.org/10.21437/Interspeech.2022-10262

34. Zezario, R.E., Fu, S.W., Chen, F., Fuh, C.S., Wang, H.M., Tsao, Y.: Deep learning-based non-intrusive multi-objective speech assessment model with cross-domain features. IEEE/ACM Trans. Audio Speech Lang. Process. **31**, 54–70 (2022)

Unified Modeling of Multi-Domain Multi-Device ASR Systems

Soumyajit Mitra[1]([✉]), Swayambhu Nath Ray[1], Bharat Padi[1],
Raghavendra Bilgi[1], Harish Arsikere[1], Shalini Ghosh[2], Ajay Srinivasamurthy[1],
and Sri Garimella[1]

[1] Amazon Alexa, Bangalore, India
{ssomit,swayar}@amazon.com
[2] Amazon, San Francisco, USA

Abstract. Modern Automatic Speech Recognition (ASR) technology is typically fine-tuned for a targeted domain or application to obtain the best recognition results. This requires training and maintaining a dedicated ASR model for each domain, which increases the overall cost. Moreover, fine-tuned model might not be the most optimal way of sharing knowledge across domains. To address this, we propose a novel unified RNN-T based ASR technology that leverages domain embeddings and attention based mixture of experts architecture. Further, the proposed unified neural architecture allows for sharing of data and parameters seamlessly across domains. Our experiments show that the proposed approach outperforms a carefully fine-tuned domain-specific ASR model, yielding up to 10% relative word error rate (WER) improvement and 30% reduction in overall training cost.

Keywords: End-to-end speech recognition · multi-domain ASR models · mixture of experts · DAT · RNN-T

1 Introduction

Commercial ASR systems often have to support multiple domains and a variety of acoustic conditions. For example, a conversational assistant like Alexa has to run on different devices such as Echo devices, FireTV remotes and mobile phones.

Type of queries provided by users to the assistant can vary across devices as well, e.g. shopping queries on the shopping assistant on mobile phones can be different from content-only queries related to movies on the video assistant. To handle variations in usage patterns and acoustic conditions better, a dedicated ASR system is often trained and deployed for each device-type corresponding to a particular *domain*. Such a domain-specific ASR model is typically obtained by first training a general ASR model on data from all devices and then fine-tuning it on data from targeted domain.

S. Mitra and S. N. Ray—Equal Contribution.

K. Ekštein et al. (Eds.): TSD 2023, LNAI 14102, pp. 283–292, 2023.
https://doi.org/10.1007/978-3-031-40498-6_25

Although the per-domain ASR model improves speech recognition accuracy for the relevant subset of user queries, it becomes cumbersome to maintain multiple per-domain models as each change (technology advancement, bug-fix, etc.) needs to be deployed to all the device-types. Further, the two stage training mechanism of the per-domain models turns out be costly in terms of compute requirement. Therefore, there is renewed interest in unifying per-domain models without regressing on accuracy.

In this paper, we explore variety of novel approaches to address the challenge of *unifying multiple per-domain ASR models*, for the RNN-T [6] model architecture. We start with a simple approach of using domain embedding to bias the unified ASR model during run-time. Our next approach explores the use of the *mixture-of-experts* (MOE) architecture [15], where each domain is represented by an expert. We also aim to combine the knowledge from multiple experts, without constraining any single expert to capture domain-specific knowledge. Accordingly, we developed a variant of the MOE framework by introducing an *attention* formulation into the model [17].

We show that our proposed unified model outperforms the individual domain-specific fine-tuned models by 10%. We also establish that our model performs 6% better than standard domain adaptation technique of Domain Adversarial Training (DAT).

2   Related Work

Domain specific models have been used to improve ASR performance in previous work [11]. Recent approaches have studied how domain knowledge can be incorporated as context in universal contextual model [2,10,19] and language model [7]. Another aspect of unified modeling has explored combining language-specific models into a unified multilingual model [5], using semi-supervised learning [1] or code switching [20] approaches. Adapter [8] and attention [12,18] modeling have also been studied in different contexts earlier, specifically in the domain of natural language processing. Our proposed approach (attentive mixture of experts) of unifying domain-specific ASR models into a universal model is novel and significantly outperforms the per-domain models. Similar techniques of model unification, having such significant gains over per-domain models, to best of our knowledge have not been tried earlier in ASR systems.

3   Multi-device Unification

In this section, we present the motivation and different approaches explored for unifying RNN-T ASR model. In an ASR system, we use device-types to address domain-specific models – so *for the rest of the paper, we will use the terms domain and device-type interchangeably.* For our experiments we consider three device-types, based on three distinct acoustic and domain variations in the data. Far-field device-type (P1) caters to multiple top domains e.g. music, home-automation, knowledge, shopping. The push-to-talk device-type (P2) primarily caters to video and music domains, while close-talk device-type (P3) primarily caters to the shopping domain.

3.1 Baseline Model Analysis

We begin with training a pooled RNN-T ASR model where we use data from all device-types. To get some idea about how the encoder tries to capture the device specific characteristics in pooled training, we generated t-SNE plot of the final representation of encoder by randomly selecting 1000 utterances from each device-types.

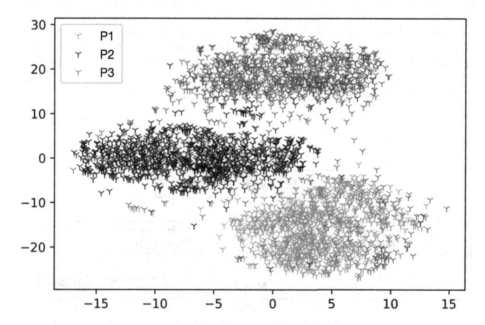

Fig. 1. t-SNE plot of Baseline Pooled model.

Figure 1 shows that the RNN-T encoder try to segregate features across device-types which form loose clusters in space, while still having some overlap among them. The overlap is due to the limited device specific representation capacity of LSTM based encoder. We hypothesise that reducing the overlap or having tight-knit device-specific clusters should provide better recognition across devices for a pooled model. Based on the above analysis we outline our RNN-T ASR model unification strategies in the following sections.

3.2 Device-Type Embedding

In this approach, each device-type is encoded as a one-hot vector and provided as input to the model to learn device specific bias component. We experimented with introducing the device-type embedding to different layers of RNN-T encoder and decoder, results of which are discussed in Sect. 5.

3.3   Mixture of Device Experts (MoDE)

The standard approach to train a device-specific model is to first pool data from multiple devices, followed by fine-tuning using device-specific data to help it adapt and match the device characteristics, thereby improving the model performance. We are proposing to capture the essence of this approach in the universal model by introducing a *Mixture of Device Experts* (MoDE) during pooled model training. Each device-type has its own expert, the parameters of which are learned only using device-specific data.

Figure 2 shows an encoder layer with expert blocks introduced between layers of the network. We use adapter modules [8] as device experts, which helps to limit the increase in parameters. MoDE uses a hard-gating mechanism, where only one device expert block (corresponding to the device-type of the corresponding utterance) is active during run-time for an utterance.

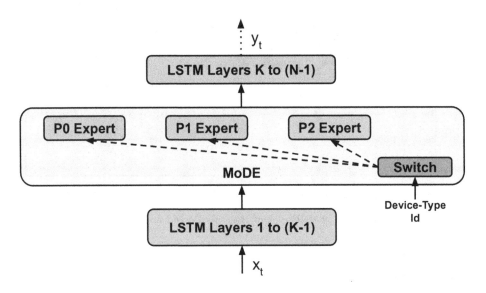

Fig. 2. Schematic diagram of Mixture of Device Experts.

We experimented with having unique device experts per layers of encoder and decoder of RNN-T and also with sharing the device experts across multiple layers (details in Sect. 5). It is important to note that experts are not shared across devices – they are only shared across layers.

3.4 Attentive Mixture of Experts (AMoE)

MoDE, discussed in Sect. 3.3, restricts the experts to learn device specific characteristics only and doesn't enable sharing of information across the experts which
might not be ideal. Motivated by this, we propose to remove the restriction on
the experts and let each expert get trained with all device data and then introduce an attention module to learn the optimal contribution from each expert on
the fly. This module is trained along with the rest of the model in an end-to-end
fashion. We call this the Attentive Mixture of Experts (AMoE) approach, where
we learn attention weights over experts, trained using data from all device-types.

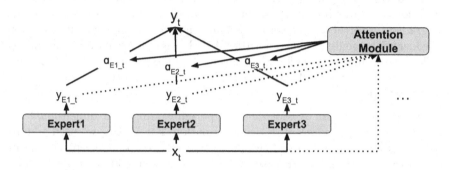

Fig. 3. Attentive Mixture of Experts.

Figure 3 outlines the details of AMoE. The attention weights in AMoE regu-
late the gradients while learning the expert parameters – this facilitates sharing
of information across experts. The attention variables α in AMoE model are
computed as:

$$\alpha_{Ei\_t} = \text{Softmax}(A_{Ei\_t}), \forall i \in 1, 2, 3 \tag{1}$$

$$\text{where,} \ A_{Ei\_t} = W_a(sigmoid(W_b[x_t : y_{Ei\_t}])), \tag{2}$$

$$W_b \in \mathrm{R}^{m*n}, W_a \in \mathrm{R}^{n*1}, \tag{3}$$

$$m = len(x_t) + len(y_{Ei\_t}). \tag{4}$$

W_a and W_b are trainable parameters which are trained along with RNN-T.

4 Data and Experimental Setup

4.1 Datasets

For our experiments, we used de-identified speech data collected from queries
to voice-controlled devices. We used 15K hours of human labelled data and
45K hours of machine transcribed data for model training. The data consists of
Indian-English queries to a voice-controlled device. The distribution of training
data per device is 2:1:1 for P1:P2:P3 (defined in Sect. 3). The evaluation set
consists of 58 h, 7 h and 4 h of de-identified data corresponding to devices P1,
P2 and P3 respectively.

4.2   Experimental Setup

Baselines: Our RNN-T baseline model consists of 40.6M parameters – 5 unidirectional LSTM encoder layers and 2 unidirectional LSTM decoder layers, each with 832 hidden units followed by a final 512 dimensional output projection layer. The joint network is a feed forward network of 512 hidden units and output dimension of 4001, which corresponds to the number of subword tokens [16]. The feature front end and optimizer used is similar to the one used in [13,14].

We also set up a stronger second baseline to compare with our proposed method. We used one of the state-of-the-art domain adaptation techniques: domain adversarial training (DAT) [3,4,9] to learn device agnostic encoder representations by reversing the gradients from a device-type prediction task. We used gradient reversal co-efficient of 0.03 and shared first 2 layers out of 5 layers of encoder with the device classifier (decided through hyper-parameter tuning). The device classifier is a single LSTM layer (128 units), output of which is combined through attention and passed through a softmax layer to perform utterance level classification.

Proposed Models: In case of device-type embedding, a 3 dimensional one hot vector is used to represent device information. For MoDE, we used adapter as device experts and restricted the projection size to 256 to keep the parameter increase to minimum. In case of MoDE, the device id information for a particular utterance is used as a switch to allow forward-pass and gradient backpropagation only through the corresponding device expert. We also experimented extensively with the position of the experts across different layers of encoder and decoder. For AMoE we used 64 dimensional learn-able attention weights, i.e. n in Eq. 3 is 64.

Table 1. WERR(%) for all devices with our experimental models with respect to individually finetuned device specific baselines. Encoder and Decoder One-Hot refers to the encoder and decoder layers to which device-type-embedding has been added as input. Encoder and decoder layers after which device experts have been added is indicated by the Encoder and Decoder Experts column All results are obtained after averaging checkpoints from last 5 epochs.

Exp.	Device One-Hot	Encoder One-Hot	Decoder One-Hot	Device Experts	Attentive Experts	Encoder Experts	Decoder Experts	Shared	Dataset P1	P2	P3	Model Params
Baseline	No	N/A	N/A	No	No	N/A	N/A	N/A	–	–	–	40.6M
DAT	No	N/A	N/A	No	No	N/A	N/A	N/A	3.9	2.5	1.4	+0M
L. Baseline	No	N/A	N/A	No	No	N/A	N/A	N/A	3.8	3.1	3.5	+5.55M
Device-type Embedding	Yes	0	0	No	No	N/A	N/A	N/A	2.4	0.7	−0.5	+0.02M
	Yes	0,1,2,3,4	None	No	No	N/A	N/A	N/A	2.5	−1.1	0.1	+0.05M
	Yes	None	0,1	No	No	N/A	N/A	N/A	−0.5	−3.7	−2.1	+0.02M
	Yes	0,1,2,3,4	0,1	No	No	N/A	N/A	N/A	**3.6**	**0.8**	**−0.6**	+0.09M
MoDE	No	N/A	N/A	Yes	No	0,1,2,3,4	0,1	No	5.4	1.5	2.2	+2.97M
	No	N/A	N/A	Yes	No	2,3,4	0,1	No	**7.6**	**5.0**	**5.7**	+2.14M
	No	N/A	N/A	Yes	No	2,3,4	None	No	6.0	3.6	5.0	+1.28M
	No	N/A	N/A	Yes	No	2,3,4	0,1	Yes	**7.9**	**4.2**	**2.9**	+0.85M
	Yes	0,1,2,3,4	0,1	Yes	No	2,3,4	0,1	Yes	5.8	2.2	2.4	+0.88M
AMoE	Yes	0,1,2,3,4	0,1	No	Yes	2,3,4	0,1	Yes	**10.3**	**5.8**	**4.5**	+2.86M
	Yes	0,1,2,3,4	0,1	No	Yes	2,3,4	0,1	No	**10.0**	**5.7**	**7.3**	+7.03M

5   Results and Analysis

In Table 1 we list results on baseline and experimental models. Our first baseline model is three individual fine-tuned models for the three devices. Our second baseline model (DAT) is a single unified RNN-T model trained with pooled data from all devices but trained in device adversarial setup. All our experimental models only has a single stage of pooled training, similar to DAT baseline. This provides us with a single unified model that can serve all three devices without any two-stage training process. The WER improvements shown for all other experiments are relative to the first baseline model. *Due to company policy, we are not able to report the absolute WER numbers. However, the baseline is a competitive state-of-the-art model.*

Large Baseline: We also trained a Large Baseline model wherein an additional encoder layer is added resulting in 5.55M additional parameters over the Baseline model. From Table 1 we see that, Large Baseline model in-spite of having 2x-5x additional model parameters compared to some of the experimental candidates, doesn't perform as well as the respective candidates.

Device Embedding: In this setup, we get the best results when we append the embedding to all encoder and decoder layers, where we saw some gains over Baseline for P1 and P2 but for P3 we observed some regression.

Mixture of Device Experts: With MoDE, we saw consistent improvements across all the devices for all the candidates. The results from Table 1 show that device experts were more helpful in the top half of the encoder compared to all the layers (Row 1 vs Row 2 of MoDE section in Table 1). From this observation, all other experiments were tried out only with experts in the top half of the encoder. Moreover, we saw that – experts in encoder are more effective than in decoder. However, when combined together, it delivered additional incremental gain in performance for all devices (Row 2 & Row 3). We also performed an experiment where we shared the experts across layers in both encoder and decoder instead of having unique expert in each layer which resulted in 67% less additional trainable model parameters. Although we saw some regression for P3, we were still able to get similar results for P1 and P2 (Row 4) as compared to having unique experts. Also, since we had device specific experts in this setup, providing device embedding to encoder and decoder (Row 5 in MoDE block) didn't boost the performance.

Attentive Mixture of Experts: Unlike MoDE, in AMoE, we enabled sharing of information across experts through attention. From the results we see that this gives much superior performance compared to MoDE across devices. Also, similar to MoDE, we see that even in AMoE, sharing of expert block across layers gives similar performance as compared to having unique experts.

Cost Savings: The baseline model has two stages of training - pooled training followed by three device specific fine-tuning. Contrary to this, our proposed model has a single stage of pooled training, which reduces the number of epochs of model training by 30%, thereby reducing overall training time and compute cost. Thus, our proposed unified model, in addition to providing better performance, has significantly less carbon footprint and uses 30% less compute resources.

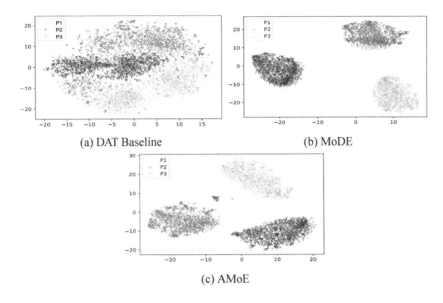

(a) DAT Baseline   (b) MoDE

(c) AMoE

Fig. 4. t-SNE plots for different models.

Encoder Analysis: In order to visualise the representation learned by encoder, we generated t-SNE plots using encoder features from last layer and using the same setup mentioned in Sect. 3.1. In case of DAT (Fig. 4a), since we are enforcing the model to learn device agnostic characteristics, we see that the learned features across devices are more distributed. For MoDE model (Fig. 4b), we observe an interesting fact that, even though the encoder LSTM layers are shared, each expert learns features in such a way that the final encoder features from different devices form distinct tight-knit clusters that are disjoint and distant from each other. In case of AMoE (Fig. 4c), even though we did not impose any restriction on the experts to be device specific, the experts learned to segregate the utterances across device-types implicitly.

Decoder Analysis: To understand the role of the experts in the decoder, we analyzed the attention weights given to each expert across word pieces in an utterance, for the AMoE model. We observed an interesting trend wherein we saw that one of the expert is mostly active during decoding of the head word-pieces and the other experts pitch in only during the recognition of slot content and rare words. Since P2 and P3 are dominated by slot contents, the experts catering to slot content recognition remains mostly active for these devices. Hence the

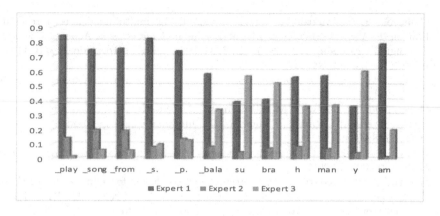

Fig. 5. Attention weights for AMoE across word pieces.

experts in the decoder also captured some device specific characteristics without any explicit device information. We picked one example to demonstrate the above phenomenon in Fig. 5. In this particular utterance, while decoding frequent word pieces like 'play', 'song', 'from' - the expert 1 is mostly active and only while decoding the artist name 'balasubrahmanyam', the expert 3 gets more weight.

6   Conclusion

This paper proposed to build a unified RNN-T based ASR model that generalized for various domains and acoustic conditions. The paper conducted a detailed ablation study involving domain embedding, mixture of experts, and attention to identify an optimal unified neural ASR architecture, which gave up to 10% relative WER reduction over simple fine-tuning approach. In addition, we simplified the overall training process and kept the number of model parameters in check compared to baseline, which resulted in up to 30% savings in compute cost. Both MoDE and AMoE yielded significant WER improvements, and offered options to trade-off WER and latency to cater to various applications.

References

1. Biswas, A., Yilmaz, E., de Wet, F., van der Westhuizen, E., Niesler, T.: Semi-supervised acoustic model training for five-lingual code-switched ASR. CoRR arXiv:1906.08647 (2019)
2. Chen, Z., Jain, M., Wang, Y., Seltzer, M.L., Fuegen, C.: Joint grapheme and phoneme embeddings for contextual end-to-end ASR (2019)
3. Ganin, Y., Lempitsky, V.S.: Unsupervised domain adaptation by backpropagation. ArXiv: abs/1409.7495 (2015)
4. Ganin, Y., et al.: Domain-adversarial training of neural networks (2016)

5. Gaur, N., et al.: Mixture of informed experts for multilingual speech recognition. In: ICASSP 2021–2021 IEEE International Conference on Acoustics, Speech and Signal Processing (ICASSP), pp. 6234–6238 (2021). https://doi.org/10.1109/ICASSP39728.2021.9414379

6. Graves, A.: Sequence transduction with recurrent neural networks. CoRR arXiv:1211.3711 (2012)

7. Gururangan, S., Lewis, M., Holtzman, A., Smith, N.A., Zettlemoyer, L.: Demix layers: disentangling domains for modular language modeling. CoRR arXiv:2108.05036 (2021)

8. Houlsby, N., et al.: Parameter-efficient transfer learning for NLP. CoRR arXiv:1902.00751 (2019)

9. Hu, H., et al.: Redat: accent-invariant representation for end-to-end ASR by domain adversarial training with relabeling. In: ICASSP 2021–2021 IEEE International Conference on Acoustics, Speech and Signal Processing (ICASSP), pp. 6408–6412 (2021). https://doi.org/10.1109/ICASSP39728.2021.9414291

10. Jain, M., Keren, G., Mahadeokar, J., Zweig, G., Metze, F., Saraf, Y.: Contextual RNN-T for open domain ASR. arXiv preprint arXiv:2006.03411 (2020)

11. Kim, K., et al.: Attention based on-device streaming speech recognition with large speech corpus. In: 2019 IEEE Automatic Speech Recognition and Understanding Workshop (ASRU), pp. 956–963. IEEE (2019)

12. Ray, S.N., Dasgupta, S.S., Talukdar, P.P.: AD3: attentive deep document dater. CoRR arXiv:1902.02161 (2019)

13. Ray, S.N., Mitra, S., Bilgi, R., Garimella, S.: Improving RNN-T ASR performance with date-time and location awareness. In: Ekštein, K., Pártl, F., Konopík, M. (eds.) TSD 2021. LNCS (LNAI), vol. 12848, pp. 394–404. Springer, Cham (2021). https://doi.org/10.1007/978-3-030-83527-9_33

14. Ray, S.N., et al.: Listen with intent: Improving speech recognition with audio-to-intent front-end. arXiv preprint arXiv:2105.07071 (2021)

15. Shazeer, N., et al.: Outrageously large neural networks: The sparsely-gated mixture-of-experts layer. CoRR arXiv:1701.06538 (2017)

16. Shibata, Y., et al.: Byte pair encoding: a text compression scheme that accelerates pattern matching (1999)

17. Singh, V.P., Rath, S.P., Pandey, A.: A mixture of expert based deep neural network for improved ASR. arXiv preprint arXiv:2112.01025 (2021)

18. Vaswani, A., et al.: Attention is all you need. CoRR arXiv:1706.03762 (2017)

19. Wu, Z., Li, B., Zhang, Y., Aleksic, P.S., Sainath, T.N.: Multistate encoding with end-to-end speech RNN transducer network. In: ICASSP 2020, pp. 7819–7823 (2020)

20. Yilmaz, E., Biswas, A., van der Westhuizen, E., de Wet, F., Niesler, T.: Building a unified code-switching ASR system for south African languages. CoRR arXiv:1807.10949 (2018)

Voice Cloning for Voice Disorders: Impact of Phonetic Content

Lily Wadoux, Nelly Barbot, Jonathan Chevelu[(✉)], and Damien Lolive

Univ Rennes, CNRS, IRISA, 22300 Lannion, France
{lily.wadoux,nelly.barbot,jonathan.chevelu,
damien.lolive}@irisa.fr

Abstract. Organic dysphonia can lead to vocal impairments. Recording patients' impaired voice could allow them to use voice cloning systems. Voice cloning, being the process of producing speech matching a target speaker voice, given textual input and an audio sample from the speaker, can be used in such a context. However, dysphonic patients may only produce speech with specific or limited phonetic content.

Considering a complete voice cloning process, we investigate the relation between the phonetic content, the length of samples and their impact on the output quality and speaker similarity through the use of phonetically limited artificial voices.

The analysis of the speakers embedding which are used to capture voices shows an impact of the phonetic content. However, we were not able to observe those variations in the final generated speech.

Keywords: voice cloning · speaker encoder · speech synthesis · x-vector · voice disorders

1 Introduction

Organic dysphonia can lead to serious vocal damage [7], deteriorating communication and causing social isolation. Besides, as the voice is a personal way of expression, it can be considered as part of a person's identity. This is why it would be an interesting possibility to use speech synthesis devices, fed by patients' vocal data, to improve their speech intelligibility. However, patients' health condition presents constraints which can impact voice recording. Long recording sessions can prove to be very tiring, inducing more vocal instability, with a potentially reduced phonetic coverage due to the pathology. In a context of speech synthesis, such medical application would require to study the impact of the vocal corpus' content and duration on the synthesized speech.

Speech matching a target speaker voice can be produced with a multi-speaker neural Text-to-Speech (TTS) system. However, it needs target speaker samples in the training corpus. Voice cloning methods, such as speaker adaptation and speaker encoding, offer more flexibility and can generate speech from speakers unseen during training [2,4,6].

Speaker adaptation relies on a second training step during which the pre-trained multi-speaker model is specialised, or fine-tuned, to produce only the target speaker voice. Each new speaker requires a fine-tuning step to obtain a custom model.

K. Ekštein et al. (Eds.): TSD 2023, LNAI 14102, pp. 293–303, 2023.
https://doi.org/10.1007/978-3-031-40498-6_26

Speaker encoding only trains on a multi-speaker corpus. A second model, called speaker encoder, outputs to the TTS model a vectorial representation of speaker features, called speaker embedding. To match another speaker, new audio samples are simply given as input to the speaker encoder.

Both approaches need relatively few data from the target speaker, obtaining very good results with ten minutes of speech, and good results with only ten seconds [4]. In this study, we use the speaker encoder approach, and the x-vector model in particular, as described in Fig. 1. Indeed, despite slightly lower results compared to speaker adaptation [2], it only needs one training phase, facilitating its generalisation to new speakers. This fits with the idea of being accessible, in the long term, for as many patients as possible.

This article presents first results on the impact of the target speaker corpus' phonetic content on speaker embeddings. The end goal medical application is detailed in Sect. 2. The experimental protocol is defined in Sect. 3, training settings and data in Sect. 4. Last, results are discussed in Sect. 5.

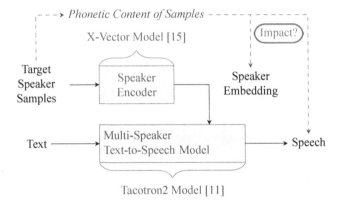

Fig. 1. Framework of the considered study. On this figure, we can see the overall architecture split into two main blocks: speaker encoder and multi-speaker TTS. Target speech samples are provided to control the identity of the target speaker. We investigate the impact of those input speech samples onto both the speaker embeddings and the output speech.

2   Medical Application

Dysphonia can be defined as an alteration of the voice timber, but also, more broadly, as a momentary or lasting disorder of the vocal function, felt as such by the subject or relatives [7]. Dysphonia can be of organic or functional origin, depending whether it is maintained principally by vocal gesture disturbances or caused by organic disorders. Here, only organic dysphonia are considered for voice cloning. Indeed, dysfunctional dysphonia symptoms, in most cases, can be greatly improved through speech therapy, and uttered speech remains understandable. As for organic dysphonia, while most symptoms can also be improved by speech therapy or surgery, for some patients uttered speech becomes very damaged and difficult to understand. This is especially true for degenerative organic dysphonia such as pharynx and larynx cancers [16] and amyotrophic lateral sclerosis. We believe voice cloning could be useful for such patients. Moreover, some pathologies such as stenosis, Riegel and Gerhardt syndromes, larynx and pharynx cancers, can require surgery. Post-surgery speech can be impossible, or difficult to utter and understand, with possible improvements or lasting effects. Voice cloning could also be a useful communication tool in this case, while it should not substitute with speech therapy and a regular use of natural speech. The end application would be a tool on which patients would type what they want to say, and which would "read" it with a voice as close as possible to their unaltered voice. Natural speech would still remain the main communication method for most patients, especially with their relatives. As a complement, the voice cloning tool could be used to boost intelligibility - and thus self-confidence - in daily interactions outside of their home. It could be a meaningful tool to broaden social interactions and improve patients' autonomy whenever their low intelligibility would represent a barrier.

Damaged voice can take various forms depending on pathologies, patients, and degrees of evolution. Common symptoms can include alterations of timbre or pitch, vocal irregularities, intermittent rhythm, and articulation disorders like a non-differentiation of consonants and vowels and even a disappearance of consonants. The variety and range of symptoms make it difficult to thoroughly simulate pathological voices from a healthy voice. For this study, extreme phonetic content strategies, described Sect. 3.2, are considered to simulate some of the symptoms: *MSW* and *Phn* which can be linked to random, intermittent speech, *Vowels* corresponding to a voice with consonant disappearance and *Phn-A* which is closer to a voice with consonant disappearance and vowel non-differentiation. The remaining strategy, *Sentences*, represents a speech baseline. Further studies could include actual dysphonia samples, once difficulties regarding their availability and protection are overcome.

3   Experimental Protocol

This investigation of the impact of the target speaker corpus' phonetic content on voice cloning comes in two parts. The first one focuses on the speaker encoder to determine whether there is an effect on the speaker embedding produced. The second one considers the entire voice cloning system, to determine whether there is an impact on the output cloned speech. For both parts, several sample sets are tested as input for the speaker encoder, with different durations and extreme phonetic content. If these experiments were to highlight an impact with a restricted field and extreme voices, then it would be legitimate to wonder about such a phenomenon for more usual phonetic contents, and for real dysphonic speech samples. Yet if it turns out to be independent from the phonetic content, then voice cloning systems could be directly offered to patients with voice disorders. Otherwise, solutions such as sample pre-processing or system modifications could be considered to adapt voice cloning models to patients.

3.1 Considered Models

The considered approach, displayed in Fig. 1, relies on two models, a speaker encoder model transmitting a speaker embedding to a multi-speaker TTS model. Their training can be separated in two phases, as in [6]: a first phase with the speaker encoder alone, then a second phase with the multi-speaker TTS model. For the latter, Tacotron2 is used [11], from the ESPNET toolkit[1]. WaveGlow [10] is used as vocoder instead of the original WaveNet of Tacotron2, for faster inference. The official NVidia implementation is used[2].

In voice cloning, speaker encoders usually come from speaker classification or speaker verification tasks. Speaker classification aims at determining which speaker a speech sample originates from, within a fixed set of speakers. Speaker verification seeks to determine whether two given speech samples are from the same speaker. The x-vector model [15] is frequently used for this task and takes as input variable-sized speech segments. It can be described with three blocks: frame-level layers, statistic pooling and segment-level layers. Extracted speaker embeddings, called x-vectors, are from the segment layers. The implementation used is from the Kaldi ASR toolkit[3]. Instead of a 512 dimension embedding, though, the model layers' size is reduced to 32, as we found that smaller embeddings better condensed speaker information.

3.2 Extreme Phonetic Content Sampling

To determine the phonetic content influence, samples are extracted from a female French voice (referred as Neb), containing 87 h of speech, from the SynPaFlex corpus [13]. They are constructed by randomly extracting *Sentences*, mono-syllabic words (*MSW*), phones (*Phn*), vowels (*Vowels*) or only "A" phones (*Phn-A*). While this extraction method is fairly simple, and the phonetic content strategies extreme, they fall within the scope of this study: a first investigation, whose results may open up to wider studies. Four sample durations - 1 h, 10 min, 1 min and 10 s - are considered to study the duration impact and to compare it with the phonetic content one. For each couple of strategy and duration, 100 samples are extracted. Using a large voice - here 87 h - is necessary to obtain several samples containing 1 h of "A" phones, for instance. Moreover, this voice has been used for French Text-to-Speech models training with good performance, being expressive without overacting. The samples described here are for the x-vector model inputs, to serve as reference from the target speaker. As in Sect. 4, we work under the hypothesis of the x-vector being rather noise-resistant, which would limit the impact of potential concatenation artifacts in our samples.

3.3 X-Vector Analysis

Two experiments are lead with the x-vector model, designed to determine whether sample duration and phonetic content have an impact on the x-vectors.

---

[1] https://github.com/espnet/espnet/tree/master/egs/libritts/tts1.
[2] https://github.com/NVIDIA/waveglow.
[3] https://github.com/kaldi-asr/kaldi/tree/master/egs/sre16/v2.

First, the aim is to know whether produced x-vectors are impacted by input sample duration. Indeed, SOTA shows that duration influences the output speech of a voice cloning system [4]. Differences between x-vectors of different duration classes could serve as a reference to study the impact of another parameter, here the phonetic content, on speaker similarity. Four sample durations are considered, presented in Sect. 3.2. A nearest neighbour-like classifier is implemented to classify x-vectors. Classes are known a priori and represent sample duration for the same speaker. The same classification method is used for varying phonetic content. This should determine if studied phonetic content strategies impact x-vectors enough to classify them per said strategy.

3.4   Cloned Samples Analysis

The x-vector experiments are completed with an analysis of speech samples produced by the complete voice cloning system. Two aspects are considered: speech quality and similarity to the target speaker. Tested samples were cloned samples obtained with Neb samples of different contents and strategies as input for the x-vector model. The text to synthesize is extracted randomly from the corpus to ensure the availability of the corresponding natural audio reference, with no overlap with the input samples for the x-vector model. It corresponds to interpausal cuts, as described in [14]. For each couple of duration and strategy, 100 samples are cloned.

To assess speech quality, we rely on a perception-related automatic measure. One popular approach is MOSNet [8] which is a recent neural-based automatic evaluation metric, trained to predict MOS perceptual scores, originally developed for voice conversion tasks. In this study, we prefer to use the WV-MOS model [1], which uses a wav2vec2.0 model [3] instead of the standard MOSNet architecture, to improve prediction proficiency. It is trained on the same data as standard MOSNet. The trained model used is available with the implementation[4]. For each of the 20 couples of strategy and duration, the WV-MOS score is computed for the 100 cloned samples.

For speaker similarity evaluation, cloned samples are given as input to a speaker encoder. The x-vector could have been used for this measure. However, it could be considered biased, as the model is part of the voice cloning system used in this study. Consequently, the Resemblyzer model [17] is used here. Resemblyzer is a speaker encoder producing 256-dimensions embeddings. The model used is the pre-trained model available in the implementation repository[5]. From each cloned sample, a resemblyzer embedding is extracted. A second resemblyzer embedding is also extracted from the corresponding natural sample. Cosine similarity is computed between these two embeddings.

4   Training and Data

Speaker encoder training requires a high number of speakers. Yet in [6], it seems more resistant to noise than the TTS model. Thus, it can be trained with lesser quality signals.

---

[4] https://github.com/AndreevP/wvmos.
[5] https://github.com/resemble-ai/Resemblyzer.

We assume their conclusions to be extendable to other speaker verification encoders such as the x-vector. This hypothesis serves as a basis to choose its training corpus. *CommonVoice* is an open-source multi-lingual corpus by Mozilla [9]. This community project allows volunteers to record speech samples via their recording device. The corpus contains more than 27k hours of speech in around 100 languages. Only the French part of the corpus is used here, with 1007 h of speech from 16,785 speakers. This is consistent with corpora used in SOTA voice cloning. Transcriptions belong to a pool of more than 2 million sentences, which ensures a diversity of sample content. However, using the text-independent version of the x-vector model, transcriptions are not given to the model. Due to the diversity of recording devices and background sound environments, sample quality is very variable. For reproducibility, the train, dev and test default sets are used for this study. No speaker appears in more than one set, guaranteeing that no test speaker was seen during training.

Tacotron2, more sensitive to corpus quality, is trained in two phases, on two different corpora. First, as in [5], a pre-training step is applied with a clean mono-speaker corpus to give the acoustic model a "warm start". The corpus used is FrenchSiwis [18], containing high-quality audio samples from a French female speaker and their transcriptions, aimed at speech synthesis. The model trains for 48 epochs, and stops with a patience mechanism set to 10 epochs. Then, it is trained on the multi-speaker Mufasa corpus [12] which is extracted from French audiobooks. As data quality in this corpus is more variable than in the FrenchSiwis corpus, we use WV-MOS score, presented in Sect. 3.4 as a criterion to filter the corpus. Through other experiments, we found that a 3.75 threshold offers, for this corpus, a good trade-off between model quality and speaker similarity of cloned speech. Therefore, all samples with a WV-MOS score lower than 3.75 are discarded. The training set contains 16 speakers. For each speaker, 10% of samples are randomly put in the dev set, except if it counts more than 500 samples, in which case 500 samples are put in the dev set.

The WaveGlow vocoder is trained separately. As it is a longer, costly step, it is not trained from scratch, but fine-tuned on French from the official English model. This second training phase is also executed on the Mufasa corpus, without WV-MOS score selection. All training was performed with Nvidia Tesla V100 SXL2 cards.

5   Results and Discussions

This section presents the results according to the two experiments conducted. First, a comparison of x-vector variations depending on duration and phonetic content strategies is done. Second, an analysis of the cloned speech in terms of quality and similarity to the target speaker is conducted.

5.1   Phonetic Content vs. Duration Impact

Duration classification within a phonetic content strategy has an accuracy of 0.32 for *Sentences*, 0.35 for *MSW*, 0.41 for *Phn*, 0.36 for *Vowels* and 0.42 for *Phn-A*. For a given strategy, x-vectors are not easily separable by sample duration. Yet, phonetic content classification is perfect for 1 h and 10 min duration. For 1 min and 10 s, the accuracy is respectively of 0.99 and 0.92. It shows that phonetic content strategies render significantly different x-vectors. The average dispersion for each class and the distances between class centroids, not detailed here, show that both class separation and distance are superior for phonetic content than for duration. These observations are illustrated here by the Principal Component Analysis (PCA) displayed in Fig. 2. This allows to conclude that studied extreme phonetic contents have a higher impact on x-vectors than duration. While increasing the recorded duration leads to a more stable x-vector, the phonetic content change the average x-vector generated.

It therefore remains to be seen whether those variations have an impact on the generated signal.

5.2 Cloned Speech Quality and Speaker Similarity

Speech quality and speaker similarity of cloned samples are evaluated with WV-MOS score and cosine similarity between resemblyzer embeddings, as described in Sect. 3.4.

In terms of cloned speech quality, WV-MOS scores are presented in Table 1a. Regarding duration, the only observable difference is for the *Sentences* strategy, for which cloned samples which received 1 h of speech as input of the x-vector model are of higher quality than those which received 10 s of speech. Except for this, within a given strategy, all duration result in cloned speech are of comparable quality. In terms of phonetic content strategy, for duration 1 h and 10 min, all strategies' cloned speech are of similar quality, except for the *Phn-A* strategy which has significantly lower WV-MOS scores. This later exception confirmed that the *Phn-A* strategy is more different than others as we can see in Fig. 2. On average, the difference is not visible probably because x-vectors for shorter durations are less stable.

In terms of cloned speech similarity, cosine similarity values between resemblyzer embeddings are presented in Table 1b. Once again, we observe very few differences even when significant considering either duration or strategy.

Overall, the differences and dynamics observed on x-vectors are not significantly measured in the signal generated by the voice cloning system. We may formulate some hypotheses to explain it.

Firstly, the precision of the measures, especially the similarity one, may not be sensible enough to capture the slight variations in the signal. It can explain partially the lack of differences but, by listening to some samples, no major differences between voices arise.

Secondly, variations in x-vectors are observed between voices of the same speaker. Inter-speaker distances may be much more important and therefore observed variations may be not significant. Nevertheless, some quality differences can be observed between very different configurations. For instance, a significant difference can be observed between the *Sentences* and *Phn-A* strategies, or between 1 h and 10 s durations.

Thirdly, the Tacotron2 model may not be able to take enough into account the speaker embedding conditioning. Thus the model may not learn well the link between the speaker embedding and the acoustic characteristics of the signal. It may not be due to the model itself but rather the quantity of data used to learn the model. Of course, this point should be investigated further.

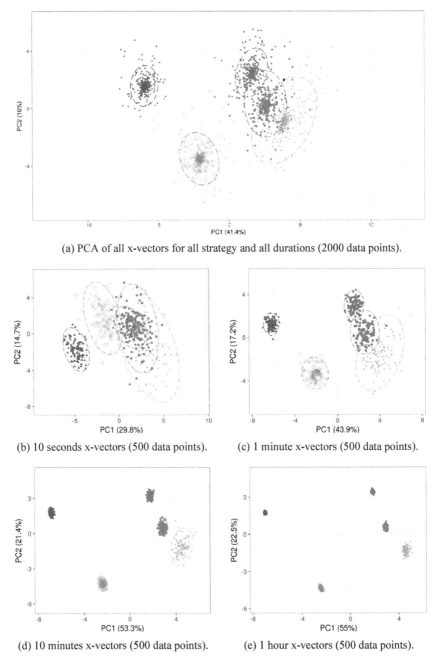

(a) PCA of all x-vectors for all strategy and all durations (2000 data points).

(b) 10 seconds x-vectors (500 data points).

(c) 1 minute x-vectors (500 data points).

(d) 10 minutes x-vectors (500 data points).

(e) 1 hour x-vectors (500 data points).

Fig. 2. Principal Components Analysis (PCA) of x-vectors. Strategies are grouped as follow: for *Sentences*; for *MSW*; for *Vowels*; for *Phn*; for *Phn-A*. Unit variance scaling is applied; SVD with imputation is used to calculate principal components. Percentage on axis show the part of the total variance explained. Prediction ellipses are such that with probability 0.95, a new observation from the same group will fall inside the ellipse.

Table 1. Automatic evaluation of the generated acoustic signal in terms of quality and similarity for various cloning voice sizes with various phonetic content strategies.

	Sentences	MSW	Phn	Vowels	Phn-A
1h	3.57 ± 0.09	3.55 ± 0.12	3.60 ± 0.08	3.59 ± 0.09	3.19 ± 0.12
10m	3.44 ± 0.09	3.47 ± 0.12	3.60 ± 0.11	3.50 ± 0.10	3.21 ± 0.12
1m	3.40 ± 0.09	3.55 ± 0.09	3.62 ± 0.09	3.51 ± 0.09	3.34 ± 0.10
10s	3.35 ± 0.10	3.37 ± 0.11	3.53 ± 0.10	3.42 ± 0.09	3.24 ± 0.09

(a) WV-MOS Scores

	Sentences	MSW	Phn	Vowels	Phn-A
1h	0.608 ± 0.013	0.609 ± 0.013	0.612 ± 0.014	0.595 ± 0.013	0.621 ± 0.012
10m	0.612 ± 0.013	0.611 ± 0.013	0.611 ± 0.012	0.592 ± 0.013	0.621 ± 0.012
1m	0.622 ± 0.014	0.607 ± 0.014	0.611 ± 0.014	0.600 ± 0.012	0.620 ± 0.012
10s	0.631 ± 0.013	0.622 ± 0.013	0.623 ± 0.014	0.609 ± 0.012	0.627 ± 0.012

(b) Cosine similarity between resemblyzer embeddings

Lastly, augmenting the diversity in the training dataset by increasing the number of voices may help the Tacotron2 generalize better. In our experiments, we use 16 speakers to train the model. Nevertheless, this number of voices can be too low either to interpolate or to find a similar voice. Augmenting the corpus size comes with other difficulties, like the control on the data quality. To alleviate this problem, we have applied filtering using a threshold on the MOS score. This method could help augment the corpus size automatically.

6 Conclusion and Future Work

With the improvement of voice cloning systems, it becomes conceivable to apply them to phonetically constrained voices, and more particularly to pathological voices. Linked to its medical application, this study focuses on the impact of extreme phonetic content. Quality and speaker similarity tests outline that the phonetic content and the duration of test samples have a limited impact on the quality except in some very particular cases. These results are an incentive for thorough studies on the links between phonetic content and cloned voice quality, and on voice cloning perceptive test conception. Whereas an impact is visible in speaker embedding representation, it was not significant when analysing the generated signal.

Many directions could be investigated in the future. First a listening test could be conducted to confirm the results we have obtained here. This could be the occasion to introduce other test speakers to investigate the inter-speaker behavior of the x-vectors in the context of voice cloning. Moreover, enriching the training corpus with new speakers may help the Tacotron2 generalize and improve the quality of the output speech. As mentioned earlier, an automatic filtering process could be proposed to do so. Other strategies maybe less extreme could be evaluated, for instance, removing one phoneme type (nasal, plosive, etc.). Finally, further studies could be led with samples from patients suffering from organic dysphonia, including tests with remediation strategies to overcome the impact of phonetic content.

Acknowledgements. This work was granted access to the HPC resources of IDRIS under the allocation 2023-AD011011870R2 made by GENCI.

References

1. Andreev, P., Alanov, A., Ivanov, O., Vetrov, D.: HiFi++: a unified framework for bandwidth extension and speech enhancement (2022). https://doi.org/10.48550/ARXIV.2203.13086
2. Arik, S.O., Chen, J., Peng, K., Ping, W., Zhou, Y.: Neural voice cloning with a few samples. In: Advances in Neural Information Processing Systems, pp. 10019–10029 (2018)
3. Baevski, A., Zhou, H., Mohamed, A., Auli, M.: wav2vec 2.0: a framework for self-supervised learning of speech representations (2020). https://doi.org/10.48550/ARXIV.2006.11477
4. Chen, Y., et al.: Sample efficient adaptive text-to-speech. In: Proceedings of the International Conference on Learning Representations (2019)
5. Cooper, E., et al.: Zero-shot multi-speaker text-to-speech with state-of-the-art neural speaker embeddings. In: IEEE International Conference on Acoustics, Speech and Signal Processing (ICASSP), pp. 6184–6188 (2020). https://doi.org/10.1109/ICASSP40776.2020.9054535
6. Jia, Y., et al.: Transfer learning from speaker verification to multispeaker text-to-speech synthesis. In: Proceedings of the Neural Information Processing Systems Conference, no. 32 (2018)
7. Le Huche, F., Allali, A.: La voix. Collection Phoniatrie, Elsevier Masson, 2e édition edn. (2010)
8. Lo, C.C., et al.: MOSNet: deep learning-based objective assessment for voice conversion. In: Interspeech (2019). https://doi.org/10.21437/Interspeech.2019-2003
9. Mozilla: CommonVoice, commonvoice.mozilla.org, consulted in December 2020
10. Prenger, R., Valle, R., Catanzaro, B.: WaveGlow: a flow-based generative network for speech synthesis. In: 2019 IEEE International Conference on Acoustics, Speech and Signal Processing, ICASSP 2019, pp. 3617–3621 (2019). https://doi.org/10.1109/ICASSP.2019.8683143
11. Shen, J., et al.: Natural TTS synthesis by conditioning WaveNet on Mel spectrogram predictions. In: Proceedings of the IEEE International Conference on Acoustics, Speech and Signal Processing (ICASSP) (2018)
12. Sini, A.: Characterisation and generation of expressivity in function of speaking styles for audiobook synthesis. Theses, Université Rennes 1 (2020)
13. Sini, A., Lolive, D., Vidal, G., Tahon, M., Delais-Roussarie, E.: SynPaFlex-corpus: an expressive French audiobooks corpus dedicated to expressive speech synthesis. In: Proceedings of the 11th International Conference on Language Resources and Evaluation (LREC), Miyazaki, Japan (2018)
14. Sini, A., Maguer, S.L., Lolive, D., Delais-Roussarie, E.: Introducing prosodic speaker identity for a better expressive speech synthesis control. In: 10th International Conference on Speech Prosody 2020, Tokyo, Japan, pp. 935–939. ISCA (2020). https://doi.org/10.21437/speechprosody.2020-191. https://hal.science/hal-03000148
15. Snyder, D., Garcia-Romero, D., Povey, D., Khudanpur, S.: Deep neural network embeddings for text-independent speaker verification. In: Proceedings of Interspeech (2017)
16. Steuer, C.E., El-Deiry, M., Parks, J.R., Higgins, K.A., Saba, N.F.: An update on larynx cancer. CA Cancer J. Clin. **67**(1), 31–50 (2017)

17. Wan, L., Wang, Q., Papir, A., Moreno, I.L.: Generalized end-to-end loss for speaker verification. In: IEEE International Conference on Acoustics, Speech and Signal Processing (ICASSP), pp. 4879–4883 (2018)
18. Yamagishi, J., Honnet, P.E., Garner, P., Lazaridis, A.: The SIWIS French speech synthesis database. Technical report, Idiap Research Institute (2017)

Towards End-to-End Speech-to-Text Summarization

Raul Monteiro[1,2](✉) [ID] and Diogo Pernes[1,3] [ID]

[1] Priberam, Alameda D. Afonso Henriques 41, 1000-123 Lisbon, Portugal
{raul.monteiro,diogo.pernes}@priberam.pt
[2] Instituto Superior Técnico, Universidade de Lisboa,
Av. Rovisco Pais 1, 1049-001 Lisbon, Portugal
[3] Faculdade de Engenharia, Universidade do Porto,
R. Dr. Roberto Frias s/n, 4200-465 Porto, Portugal

Abstract. Speech-to-text (S2T) summarization is a time-saving technique for filtering and keeping up with the broadcast news uploaded online on a daily basis. The rise of large language models from deep learning with impressive text generation capabilities has placed the research focus on summarization systems that produce paraphrased compact versions of the document content, also known as abstractive summaries. End-to-end (E2E) modelling of S2T abstractive summarization is a promising approach that offers the possibility of generating rich latent representations that leverage non-verbal and acoustic information, as opposed to the use of only linguistic information from automatically generated transcripts in cascade systems. However, the few literature on E2E modelling of this task fails on exploring different domains, namely broadcast news, which is challenging domain where large and diversified volumes of data are presented to the user every day. We model S2T summarization both with a cascade and an E2E system for a corpus of broadcast news in French. Our novel E2E model leverages external data by resorting to transfer learning from a pre-trained T2T summarizer. Experiments show that both our cascade and E2E abstractive summarizers are stronger than an extractive baseline. However, the performance of the E2E model still lies behind the cascade one, which is object of an extensive analysis that includes future directions to close that gap.

Keywords: Abstractive summarization · Speech-to-text summarization · End-to-end

1 Introduction

Broadcast news is mainly presented in large volumes of audio-visual multimedia, making it time-consuming to locate relevant information. S2T summarization systems help by identifying the most relevant content within human speech and producing a condensed form text suitable for the need. Extractive summarization selects relevant sentences or paragraphs from transcripts, but this method may sometimes lack cohesion and readability [6]. The rise of large language models from deep learning has enabled reaching high-level understanding of input documents, besides having impressive text generation capabilities. Thus, the research focus has been recently placed on abstractive summarization systems, where the generated summaries are paraphrased compact

© The Author(s), under exclusive license to Springer Nature Switzerland AG 2023
K. Ekštein et al. (Eds.): TSD 2023, LNAI 14102, pp. 304–316, 2023.
https://doi.org/10.1007/978-3-031-40498-6_27

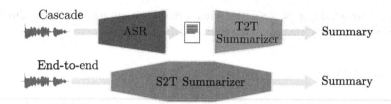

Fig. 1. Illustration of a cascade and E2E system for S2T summarization.

versions of the speech content. They are more natural, coherent, and fluent, i.e. ideally similar to a summary written by a human specialist.

S2T summarization is usually achieved using a cascade approach (see Fig. 1), where an automatic speech recognition (ASR) model generates transcripts, followed by a text-to-text (T2T) summarization model that produces summaries [18]. Deep learning, including attention-based architectures and self-supervised pre-training, has improved the performance of both models. Cascade abstractive systems using these components achieve strong results when trained on unpaired data for dialogue summarization tasks [24]. However, the transcripts produced by the ASR model may contain errors, so methods using confusion networks or language models have been proposed to improve robustness to these errors [11,23].

Cascade systems used for S2T summarization fail to utilize non-verbal and acoustic information that could be useful for summarization [22]. E2E modelling (see Fig. 1) has been proposed to address this issue in two different articles [9,21]. These systems do not make use of an intermediate speech recognition step and instead jointly optimise an acoustic and language model. However, E2E modelling requires large amounts of paired audio/summary data and the scarcity of publicly available large corpora on the broadcast news domain requires techniques to leverage external data.

This work proposes both a cascade and novel E2E models for S2T abstractive summarization of broadcast news. The former uses fine-tuned ASR and T2T abstractive summarizer on a broadcast news dataset. The E2E system follows the encoder-decoder paradigm and utilizes speech features extracted using a self-supervised pre-trained speech representation model as input [3]. It leverages external data from text corpora through transfer learning from a T2T abstractive summarizer. Both models are compared against an extractive cascade baseline and to each other using ROUGE scores and human evaluation. We release our source code publicly[1].

The remainder of this paper is organized as follows: in Sect. 2, we present the related work; in Sect. 3, we propose a new corpus of broadcast news in French, which is used to evaluate the models developed in this work; in Sect. 4, we describe the architectures of the cascade and novel E2E abstractive summarizers, how the latter benefits from the former through transfer learning and we introduce an extractive baseline; in Sect. 5, we detail the architecture and pre-training of the cross-modal adapter, which is the encoder of the E2E S2T abstractive summarizer that maps speech to textual features; in Sect. 6, we present the results for automatic and human evaluations; in Sect. 7, we

---

[1] https://github.com/Priberam/S2TSumm.

discuss the obtained results; Sect. 8 concludes this work and includes future directions for improving the performance of the E2E model.

2   Related Work

Automatic Speech Representation Learning and Recognition: Wav2vec 2.0 (W2V2) [1] is a transformer-based encoder-only model for extracting deep representations from raw audio waveforms, which was trained with self-supervised objectives. Evain et al. [3] found that speech representations extracted from W2V2 models trained on French data lead to better performance on several speech-related tasks than using human-tailored speech features like Mel filter bank (MFB) and Mel-frequency cepstral coefficients features (MFCC) [2,5]. Pasad et al. [12] used a metric called Projection Weighted Canonical Correlation Analysis (PWCCA) [10] to study the layer representations of W2V2 models. PWCCA was applied to compare the learned representations of each layer with external representations, for instance, MFB features and GloVe word embeddings [14]. It is uncovered that the pre-trained W2V2 models encode more semantic information in inner layers, whereas acoustic information is mostly represented in the outer layers.

W2V2 and its variants can be used as pre-initialization and directly trained for speech recognition using the Connectionist Temporal Classification (CTC) objective. The literature also contains fully supervised approaches like Whisper [17], which was jointly trained for ASR and speech translation using very large amounts of data crawled from the web.

Text-to-Text Abstractive Summarization: Most state-of-the-art approaches for T2T abstractive summarization make use of pre-trained large sequence-to-sequence (Seq2seq) language models like BART and fine-tune them on abstractive summarization datasets [7]. Rothe et al. [19] proposed an alternative approach in which encoder-only language models like RoBERTa [25] could be promoted to decoder modules, and the resulting encoder-decoder models could be fine-tuned for downstream tasks.

End-to-End Speech-to-Text Abstractive Summarization: To the best of our knowledge, only two works directly exploit E2E modeling of S2T summarization. Sharma et al. [21] used a restricted self-attention to enable processing long input audios with a transformer architecture. The authors first trained a randomly initialized model for ASR, and then trained it for S2T abstractive summarization using a 2000h corpus of instructional videos. Matsuura et al. [9] further leveraged a T2T abstractive summarization corpus using a text-to-speech voice synthesizer as a way of data augmentation. Both papers report better results than strong cascade baselines.

3   Dataset

For this work, we built a dataset for S2T abstractive summarization of broadcast news in French, that was built from articles that can be found in the EuroNews website[2].

---

[2] https://www.euronews.com/about.

Each news article from EuroNews has an audio, an abstractive summary of the news content and the article body. Since the latter is not always a perfect transcript of the audio, we employed an automatic procedure for selecting the news articles whose article bodies are perfect (or almost perfect) transcripts of the audios. An XLSR-based ASR model[3] was used to produce artificial transcripts from the audios. Afterwards, the word error rate (WER) evaluation metric was applied between the automatically generated transcript and the article body. A threshold for the WER of 45% was set, such that articles associated with higher values of WER were discarded. The remaining articles were randomly shuffled and separated into three distinct splits with sizes of 13 380, 1672 and 1673 for the *train*, *dev* and *test* splits, respectively, and this final corpus was named BNews[4]. The mean audio duration per article is about 87 s.

4   Model Architectures

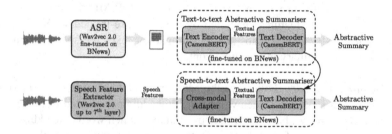

Fig. 2. Architectures of the cascade and E2E abstractive summarizers.

4.1   Cascade

The cascade abstractive summarizer requires both an ASR system and a T2T abstractive summarizer. Figure 2 illustrates the realization of the cascade and E2E abstractive summarizers.

Automatic Speech Recognizer: The ASR model was built from a W2V2 model[5] that was pre-trained on French speech data. The pre-trained model was loaded to a Wav2Vec2ForCTC object from the Transformers library of Huggingface[6]. This model consists of a pre-trained W2V2 model, followed by a linear layer and a softmax. The model is trained for speech recognition using the French sub-dataset of the Common Voice Corpus 10.0 (CV) with the CTC objective. The vocabulary contains 222 characters extracted from the *dev* split of the BNews corpus. The model was further fine-tuned on the latter from the checkpoint that showed lower WER on the *dev* split of

---

[3] https://huggingface.co/facebook/wav2vec2-large-xlsr-53-french.

[4] We are in contact with EuroNews to have a public license of this dataset.

[5] https://huggingface.co/LeBenchmark/wav2vec2-FR-7K-base.

[6] https://huggingface.co/docs/transformers/index.

the CV. The WER on the *test* split of the BNews corpus was $(18.8 \pm 0.3))\%$, where the `BasicTextNormalizer` from Whisper[7] was used for text normalization.

Text-to-Text Abstractive Summarizer: A publicly available pre-trained T2T abstractive summarizer[8] is used as the starting initialization for the model weights. The author of this model built it from two CamemBERTs [8], following the technique introduced by Rothe et al. [19], and trained it for abstractive summarization using the French sub-dataset from the MLSUM corpus [20]. The summarizer was further fine-tuned on the BNews training data. Only the weights of the decoder are updated during this fine-tuning. The checkpoint that showed maximum ROUGE-2 score on the *dev* split of the BNews corpus was selected.

4.2   End-to-End

The novel E2E implementation for S2T abstractive summarization proposed in this work does not directly use the audio waveform or MFB/MFCC features as input. Instead, it takes speech features generated by the same pre-trained W2V2 model that was trained for ASR. The S2T abstractive summarizer takes the speech features and converts them to a summary of the audio content.

Speech Feature Extractor: Following the same methodology used in [12], we computed the PWCCA scores[9] between word-level embeddings extracted from each transformer layer of the W2V2 base model and pre-trained French word embeddings, which were obtained in [4]. It is found that the 7th transformer layer is the one that generates representations more similar to word embeddings. For this reason, the speech feature extractor is composed of all the layers of the W2V2 model up to and including the 7th transformer layer.

Speech-to-Text Abstractive Summarizer: As is illustrated on Fig. 2, the decoder from the T2T summarizer is transferred to the S2T summarizer, which allows leveraging the MLSUM training data. The sequences of speech features do not lie in the same representation space as the textual features that the encoder of the T2T summarization model generates. For that reason, one must add an additional module that bridges the speech feature extractor and the decoder. This encoder is responsible for mapping sequences of audio features to sequences of textual features, and shall be hereby denoted as cross-modal adapter. The particular architecture of the cross-modal adapter and its pre-training are the subjects of Sect. 5. After being pre-trained, the whole S2T abstractive summarizer is fine-tuned on the BNews corpus, and the checkpoint with higher ROUGE-2 score on the *dev* split is selected for evaluation.

---

[7] https://github.com/kurianbenoy/whisper_normalizer.

[8] https://huggingface.co/mrm8488/camembert2camembert_shared-finetuned-french-summarization.

[9] https://github.com/google/svcca.

4.3   Extractive Baseline

The extractive baseline uses the same ASR system as the cascade abstractive summarizer. We adopted a simple centroid-based approach, where the sentence embeddings were provided by a publicly available unsupervised extractive CamemBERT-based model[10]. The summary is constructed by concatenating the top-k closest sentences to the centroid until a maximum number of words $\bar{w}$ is reached, where $\bar{w} = 24$ was set to match the average length of the *dev* split of the BNews corpus.

5   Cross-Modal Adapter

Given a dataset $\mathcal{D} = \{(w^{(i)}, t^{(i)}, r^{(i)})\}_{i=1}^{N}$ made of triplets of an audio waveform $w^{(i)}$, the speech transcript $t^{(i)}$ and reference summary $r^{(i)}$, the speech feature extractor generates an $L^{(i)}$-sized sequence of speech features $x^{(i)} = \{x_j^{(i)}\}_{j=1}^{L^{(i)}}$, $x_j^{(i)} \in \mathbb{R}^{768}$, from the audio waveform $w^{(i)}$, whereas the encoder from the T2T summarizer extracts a sequence of textual features or embeddings $y^{(i)} = \{y_j^{(i)}\}_{j=1}^{T^{(i)}}$, $y_j^{(i)} \in \mathbb{R}^{768}$ from the speech transcript $t^{(i)}$. The cross-modal adapter must be developed for mapping from sequences $x^{(i)}$ to $y^{(i)}$ (see Fig. 2).

5.1   Architecture

The architecture of the cross-modal is encoder-decoder. The encoder is a 1-layer BiL-STM and the decoder is a 1-layer forward LSTM, both of hidden dimension 768. Since the speech feature extractor generates speech features with an output frequency 50 Hz, whereas spoken text roughly contains 2–3 words per second, the encoder BiLSTM is preceded by a 2-layer convolutional neural network to reduce the length of the sequence of speech features from L to $\tilde{L} \approx L/4$. The cross-modal adapter contains several attention mechanisms, which follow closely the work done in [13]. Table 1 summarizes those attention mechanisms. The $\overrightarrow{h}_i^{\mathrm{e}}$, $\overleftarrow{h}_i^{\mathrm{e}}$ and h_t^{d} stand for encoder forward, encoder backward and decoder LSTM hidden states, respectively. The t-th textual embedding y_t is

Table 1. Different attention mechanisms used in the cross-modal adapter.

Attention	Intra-temporal Cross	Intra-decoder	EOS Generation
Query	h_t^{d}	h_t^{d}	y_t
Keys	$\{h_i^{\mathrm{e}} = [\overrightarrow{h}_i^{\mathrm{e}} \| \overleftarrow{h}_i^{\mathrm{e}}]\}_{1 \leq i \leq \tilde{L}}$	$\{h_{t'}^{\mathrm{d}}\}_{t' < t}$	$\{y_{t'}\}_{t-w \leq t' \leq t+w}$
Values	$\{h_i^{\mathrm{e}} = [\overrightarrow{h}_i^{\mathrm{e}} \| \overleftarrow{h}_i^{\mathrm{e}}]\}_{1 \leq i \leq \tilde{L}}$	$\{h_{t'}^{\mathrm{d}}\}_{t' < t}$	$\{y_{t'}\}_{t-w \leq t' \leq t+w}$
En. Scores	$e_{ti}^{\mathrm{e}} = h_t^{\mathrm{d}^T} W_{\mathrm{attn}}^{\mathrm{e}} h_i^{\mathrm{e}}$ $e'^{\mathrm{e}}_{ti} = \frac{\exp(e_{ti}^{\mathrm{e}})}{\sum_{j=1}^{t-1} \exp(e_{ji}^{\mathrm{e}})}$	$e_{tt'}^{\mathrm{d}} = h_t^{\mathrm{d}^T} W_{\mathrm{attn}}^{\mathrm{d}} h_{t'}^{\mathrm{d}}$	$e_{tt'}^{\mathrm{eos}} = y_{t'}^T W_{\mathrm{attn}}^{\mathrm{eos}} y_t$
Att. Weights	$\alpha_{ti}^{\mathrm{e}} = \frac{e'^{\mathrm{e}}_{ti}}{\sum_{j=1}^{L} e'^{\mathrm{e}}_{tj}}$	$\alpha_{tt'}^{\mathrm{d}} = \frac{\exp(e_{tt'}^{\mathrm{d}})}{\sum_{j=1}^{t-1} \exp(e_{tj}^{\mathrm{d}})}$	$\alpha_{tt'}^{\mathrm{eos}} = \frac{\exp(e_{tt'}^{\mathrm{eos}})}{\sum_{j=t-w}^{t+w} \exp(e_{tj}^{\mathrm{eos}})}$
Cont. Vectors	$c_t^{\mathrm{e}} = \sum_{i=1}^{L} \alpha_{ti}^{\mathrm{e}} h_i^{\mathrm{e}}$	$c_t^{\mathrm{d}} = \sum_{t'=1}^{t-1} \alpha_{tt'}^{\mathrm{d}} h_{t'}^{\mathrm{d}}$	$c_t^{\mathrm{eos}} = \sum_{t'=t-w}^{t+w} \alpha_{tt'}^{\mathrm{eos}} y_{t'}$

[10] https://github.com/ialifinaritra/Text_Summarization.

just a linear projection $y_t = W_{text}[h_t^d \| s_t^d \| c_t^e \| c_t^d]$, where s_t^d is the decoder LSTM cell state and $[\cdot \| \cdot]$ denotes vector concatenation.

Textual embeddings are continuously-valued on high-dimensional spaces. As such, there is not a direct way to stop the generation process at inference time. This problem is circumvented by training an additional attention mechanism and a neural layer for predicting the end of sequence. Given a set $\{\hat{y}_t\}_{t=1}^T$ of T (fixed) predicted textual embeddings, a restricted attention mechanism is applied on every $\hat{y}$ using a window of size w, which was set to 1 in all experiments. Details of the attention mechanism can be found in Table 1. A linear layer followed by a sigmoid function $\sigma(\cdot)$ are used to obtain the probability $p_t^{eos} = \sigma\left(W_{eos}[h_t^d \| s_t^d \| c_t^{eos}]\right) \in [0,1]$ of reaching the end of the sequence at time step t.

At inference time, the decoder of the cross-modal adapter auto-regressively generates $T = 512$ textual embeddings $\hat{y} = \{\hat{y}_t\}_{t=1}^T$. For each textual embedding, a corresponding probability $\hat{p}_t^{eos}$ of having reached the end of sequence is associated. A straightforward method to choose the end of sequence is to find the first instant t_π such that $\hat{p}_{t_\pi}^{eos} > \pi$, where $\pi \in [0,1]$ is a probability threshold. It was set to 0.5 in all experiments. Finally, the cross-modal adapter outputs a reduced sequence of textual embeddings $\hat{y}^{red} = \{\hat{y}_t\}_{t=1}^{t_\pi}$.

5.2   Pre-training

The pre-training of the cross-modal adapter encompasses three controlled steps, which are described below. The input speech features and target textual features were normalized such that each dimension had zero mean and unit variance.

Stage 1: At this stage, we used the same Common Voice corpus that was used to train the ASR model. A proportion of speech features from the sequence $x^{(i)}$ is randomly masked, where for every element of the sequence there is a probability $p_{mask} = 6.5 \times 10^{-2}$ of starting a masked span at that position with length $M_{mask} = 10$ (values identical to the ones used to train the W2V2 model). The cross-modal adapter is trained to minimize the mean squared error (MSE) between the reference embeddings $y^{(i)}$ and the ones predicted from the masked sequence $\hat{y}^{(i)}$.

Stage 2: We dropped the CV dataset and used the BNews corpus during this training stage. The objective remains to minimizing the MSE. Masking is no longer used and the default teacher forcing algorithm for training Seq2seq models is replaced by the peeling back algorithm introduced in [16]. For the j-th mini-batch or training step, we use linear decay for the teacher forcing ratio $\lambda(j) = \max(\epsilon, k - cj)$, where $\epsilon = 5.0 \times 10^{-1}$, $k = 1.0$, and $c = 8.0 \times 10^{-6}$.

Stage 3: The cross-modal adapter is now trained to predict the end of the sequence of textual embeddings, again using the BNews dataset. Given a $T^{(i)}$-sized sequence of predicted textual embeddings $\hat{y}^{(i)}$, predicting for every $\hat{y}_t^{(i)}$ whether it is the end of the sequence is a binary classification problem. Minimizing a binary cross-entropy loss suffices. All the model weights are frozen except for the ones directly associated with end-of-sequence prediction (W_{attn}^{eos} and W_{eos}), and one also makes use of the peeling back algorithm with linear decay, where $\epsilon = 0.0$, $k = 1.0$ and $c = 3.0 \times 10^{-4}$.

After this three-stage pre-training, the cross-modal adapter and the text decoder are jointly trained for abstractive summarization using the BNews dataset in a multitask objective consisting of the usual cross-entropy loss for summarization and the binary cross-entropy for EOS detection.

6 Evaluation

6.1 Automatic Evaluation

For assessing the performance of the different implementations developed in this work, we make use of the ROUGE package[11], more specifically, the ROUGE-1, ROUGE-2, ROUGE-L and ROUGE-Lsum metrics. The decoding for the cascade and E2E abstractive summarizers is performed with beam search. Table 2 compares the ROUGE scores for the extractive baseline and both cascade and E2E abstractive summarizers on the *test* split of the BNews corpus. We include the topline performance, which is simply the T2T abstractive summarizer from the cascade system applied on the gold transcripts (GT), and thus serves as an upper bound for the performance of the cascade abstractive summarizer. We also performed ablation studies for the following cases: the S2T abstractive summarizer is not fine-tuned on the BNews corpus after the pre-training of the cross-modal adapter (nFT); there is no fine-tuning and the cross-modal adapter additionally does not make use of its predictions for the end-of-sequence positions of the sequences of textual embeddings and uses instead the gold ones (G-EOS); the pre-training of cross-modal adapter described in Sect. 5.2 is not performed and the S2T abstractive summarizer is directly trained using the BNews dataset (nPre).

Table 2. Comparison between the ROUGE scores for the topline, baseline, cascade and end-to-end (E2E) on the *test* split of the BNews corpus. We show results without the final fine-tuning of the S2T abstractive summarizer (nFT), when using the ground truth end-of-sequence positions (G-EOS) and without the pre-training (nPre) of the cross-modal adapter. Every score is provided with a 95% confidence interval for the mean.

Model	ROUGE-1	ROUGE-2	ROUGE-L	ROUGE-Lsum
Topline (GT + T2T)	45.9 ± 1.4	33.0 ± 1.8	39.7 ± 1.6	41.6 ± 1.4
Cascade (ASR + T2T)	41.6 ± 1.2	26.2 ± 1.4	35.7 ± 1.2	37.6 ± 1.2
E2E	37.8 ± 1.2	23.7 ± 1.2	32.8 ± 1.2	33.9 ± 1.2
E2E (nFT)	30.0 ± 1.0	16.1 ± 1.0	25.9 ± 1.0	26.6 ± 1.0
E2E (G-EOS)	29.8 ± 1.0	15.9 ± 1.0	25.7 ± 1.0	26.5 ± 1.0
E2E (nPre)	16.8 ± 0.4	2.4 ± 0.2	12.6 ± 0.3	13.2 ± 0.3
Extractive	23.8 ± 0.8	8.3 ± 0.8	17.9 ± 0.8	18.8 ± 0.8

All the abstractive systems outperform the extractive baseline, which was expected given that the target summaries from our corpus are abstractive. The cascade abstractive

---

[11] https://huggingface.co/spaces/evaluate-metric/rouge.

summarizer yields worse scores than the topline model, which is due to ASR error propagation. On the other hand, the E2E model performs worse than the cascade model, as measured by ROUGE scores. This contrasts with the fact that, theoretically, E2E modeling allows leveraging non-verbal and acoustic information besides the linguistic one from transcripts, which is the only type of information that cascade systems have access to. Regarding the ablation studies, by comparing the performance of the E2E and E2E (nFT) models, it is found that fine-tuning the S2T abstractive summarizer after the pre-training of the cross-modal adapter significantly improves the ROUGE scores with a relative increase on the interval of 25%–50%. The similarity between the ROUGE scores of the E2E (nFT) and E2E (G-EOS) models allows us to conclude that the cross-modal adapter performs equally well either when using its own predictions for the end-of-sequence positions of the sequences of textual embeddings or when using the ground truth ones. Finally, the gap between E2E and E2E (nPre) proves that the proposed pre-training of the cross-modal adapter provides a very significant performance increase.

6.2 Human Evaluation

ROUGE metrics are simple automatic methods to evaluate the overlap between predicted and reference summaries. However, these metrics alone fail to evaluate important features like factual consistency (FC), relevance (R) and fluency (F). To evaluate these attributes, following the same procedure and criteria definition as in [15], we do pairwise comparisons between the summaries generated by the extractive baseline, the cascade and E2E systems. Given an entry of the dataset, we (one of the authors) were provided with the gold transcript and every pairwise combination of the summaries generated by the three systems. Afterwards, we were asked to rank the generated summaries according to the three criteria. For each criterion, we would evaluate whether the first summary is better than the second, tied with, or worse than the second summary. To make the evaluation process as unbiased as possible, the names of the models that generated each summary were not shown and the order with which they appeared was randomized. We randomly selected 30 examples from the *test* split of the BNews corpus and Table 3 shows the proportion of times that each system was considered the best for every pairwise comparison, according to each criterion. We show two examples of the evaluated summaries on Table 4.

The extractive baseline has been found to be very strong regarding factual consistency. This is consistent with the fact that extractive summaries are directly made of segments from automatically generated transcripts, and therefore factual inconsistencies may only come from ASR misspellings or unfortunate concatenation of sentences that together change the meaning of the original content. The cascade system is competitive against the extractive baseline in terms of factual consistency, but the E2E system performs very poorly on that attribute. Regarding relevance, the cascade and E2E systems are found to perform better than the extractive baseline. This was expected, since extractive summaries contain whole sentences that may include irrelevant information, or there may not exist sentences that give a comprehensive overview of the whole news. The cascade system also dominates the fluency attribute, and although the E2E model is generally more fluent than the extractive system, the difference is not as large as expected. The second example provided on Table 4 is illustrative of the cases when the

Table 3. Proportion of times that each model was considered the best in each pairwise comparison, according to each criterion with respect to factual consistency (FC), relevance (R) and fluency (F).

	FC	R	F
Extractive is better	0.17	0.10	0.13
Tie	**0.73**	0.07	**0.47**
Cascade (ASR + T2T) is better	0.10	**0.83**	0.40
Extractive is better	**0.63**	0.23	0.30
Tie	0.30	0.13	0.33
End-to-end is better	0.07	**0.63**	**0.37**
Cascade (ASR + T2T) is better	**0.60**	**0.57**	0.37
Tie	0.40	0.33	**0.53**
End-to-end is better	0.00	0.10	0.10

E2E model generates a repetitive summary, therefore compromising its fluency. When comparing only the abstractive summarizers, the cascade and E2E ones, we clearly see that the cascade system produces summaries that are better in all the three evaluated attributes, which is in line with the automatic evaluation with the ROUGE metrics.

7   Discussion

The results from automatic and human evaluation point out that the E2E abstractive summarizer underperforms with respect to the cascade one. This under-performance may be explained if one considers the several sub-modules of the cascade and E2E summarizers. Both make use of a W2V2-based model either for speech recognition or plain speech feature extraction. The T2T abstractive summarizer of the cascade system and the S2T abstractive summarizer of the E2E system share the same decoder, but differ strongly on the encoder. Thus, the limited performance of the proposed novel E2E implementation when compared with the cascade system must be sourced on the particular realization of the cross-modal adapter. We have strong reasons to believe that the large T2T summarization corpus (MLSUM [20]), to which the encoder of the T2T summarizer was exposed during its training for abstractive summarization, played a significant role. It is likely that this enormous amount of external data makes the text encoder generate much richer textual latent representations than the ones the cross-modal adapter could possibly generate, given that it only had access to the summarization training data from the BNews corpus during its development.

Table 4. Examples of summaries produced by the different summarizers.

	Text
Transcript	Des milliers de personnes rassemblées à Madrid pour dire "non" à la grâce des indépendantistes cata-lans, envisagée par le chef du gouvernement espagnol. En Espagne, des milliers de personnes se sont rassemblées ce dimanche à Madrid pour dire "non" à la grâce des indépendantistes catalans. (...)
Reference	Des milliers de personnes rassemblées à Madrid pour dire Non à la grâce des indépendantistes catalans, envisagée par le chef du gouvernement espagnol.
Extractive	Ces deux partis sont profondément opposés à l'initiative de l'actuele Premier ministre, Le socialiste Pedron Sanchez, qui souhaite acorder la grâce au leader séparatistes condamné pour la tentative de sécesion de 2017
Cascade	En Espagne, des miliers de persones se sont rasemblées ce dimanche à Madrid pour dire non à la grâce des indépendantistes catalans.
E2E	Des milliers de personnes se sont rassemblées ce dimanche à Madrid pour dire non à la grâce des indépendantistes catalans.
Transcript	La Belgique se dit prête à accueillir Jean-Pierre Bemba. Ce jeudi, le chef de la diplomatie belge, Didier Reynders, a annoncé que le pays était prêt à accueillir l'ancien dirigeant congolais, qui souhaite rejoin-dre sa famille, qui vit dans le pays. (...)
Reference	Le chef de la diplomatie belge l'a annoncé ce jeudi.
Extractive	Cet ancien home d'afaires devenue ensuite vice-président de la République démocratique du Congo, avait été condamné en première instance à 18 ans de prison il y a deux ans
Cascade	Didier Renders a finalement été acquité par la Cour pénale internationale, des acusations de crime de guere et de crimes contre l'humanité la semaine dernière qui a permis la mise en liberté conditionele de celui qui a été incarcéré pendant dix ans à La Haye.
E2E	Le chef de la diplomatie belge a annoncé que le pays était prêt à accueillir Jean-Claude Juncker. Ce jeudi, le chef de la diplomatie belge a annoncé que le pays était prêt à accueillir Jean-Claude Juncker.

8 Conclusion

We proposed a novel E2E model for S2T abstractive summarization of broadcast news in French. It leverages external data from T2T summarization corpora through transfer-ring the decoder from a T2T abstractive summarizer. Additionally, we proposed a clever pre-training of the cross-modal adapter that leverages external data from an ASR dataset besides the BNews corpus. We presented an extensive analysis that took into account automatic and human evaluations for assessing the quality of the generated summaries. Although the E2E model did not beat the cascade, our contributions helped to close the performance gap between the two approaches, as is shown by our ablation studies.

The low amount of abstractive summarization training data for pre-training the cross-modal adapter has been shown as the most likely source of the under-performance of E2E model. Future work should focus on enriching the training of the cross-modal adapter. For instance, by also transferring the text encoder from the T2T abstractive summarizer and carefully train it to process speech features as input. Another possible and not mutually exclusive direction would be the use of augmented data from T2T summarization corpora through speech synthesis to enlarge the training data. Finally, the lack of large corpora with speech/summary pairs severely jeopardizes any fully supervised approach for developing an E2E system. Future work on developing this kind of datasets is needed in order to improve the promising E2E systems.

Acknowledgments. This work was supported by the EU H2020 SELMA project (grant agree-ment No. 957017).

References

1. Baevski, A., Zhou, Y., Mohamed, A., Auli, M.: wav2vec 2.0: a framework for self-supervised learning of speech representations. In: Larochelle, H., Ranzato, M., Hadsell, R., Balcan, M., Lin, H. (eds.) Advances in Neural Information Processing Systems, vol. 33, pp. 12449–12460. Curran Associates, Inc. (2020). https://doi.org/10.48550/arXiv.2006.11477
2. Davis, S., Mermelstein, P.: Comparison of parametric representations for monosyllabic word recognition in continuously spoken sentences. IEEE Trans. Acoust. Speech Signal Process. **28**(4), 357–366 (1980). https://doi.org/10.1109/TASSP.1980.1163420
3. Evain, S., et al.: Task agnostic and task specific self-supervised learning from speech with lebenchmark. In: Thirty-Fifth Conference on Neural Information Processing Systems Datasets and Benchmarks Track (Round 2) (2021)
4. Ferreira, D.C., Martins, A.F.T., Almeida, M.S.C.: Jointly learning to embed and predict with multiple languages. In: Proceedings of the 54th Annual Meeting of the Association for Computational Linguistics, Berlin, Germany (Volume 1: Long Papers), pp. 2019–2028. Association for Computational Linguistics (2016). https://doi.org/10.18653/v1/P16-1190
5. Furui, S.: Speaker-independent isolated word recognition based on emphasized spectral dynamics. In: IEEE International Conference on Acoustics, Speech, and Signal Processing, ICASSP 1986, vol. 11, pp. 1991–1994 (1986). https://doi.org/10.1109/ICASSP.1986.1168654
6. Gupta, S., Gupta, S.K.: Abstractive summarization: an overview of the state of the art. Expert Syst. Appl. **121**, 49–65 (2019). https://doi.org/10.1016/j.eswa.2018.12.011
7. Lewis, M., et al.: BART: denoising sequence-to-sequence pre-training for natural language generation, translation, and comprehension. In: Proceedings of the 58th Annual Meeting of the Association for Computational Linguistics, pp. 7871–7880. Association for Computational Linguistics, Online (2020). https://doi.org/10.18653/v1/2020.acl-main.703
8. Martin, L., et al.: CamemBERT: a tasty French language model. In: Proceedings of the 58th Annual Meeting of the Association for Computational Linguistics, pp. 7203–7219. Association for Computational Linguistics, Online (2020). https://doi.org/10.18653/v1/2020.acl-main.645
9. Matsuura, K., et al.: Leveraging large text corpora for end-to-end speech summarization (2023). https://doi.org/10.48550/arXiv.2303.00978
10. Morcos, A., Raghu, M., Bengio, S.: Insights on representational similarity in neural networks with canonical correlation. In: Bengio, S., Wallach, H., Larochelle, H., Grauman, K., Cesa-Bianchi, N., Garnett, R. (eds.) Advances in Neural Information Processing Systems, vol. 31. Curran Associates, Inc. (2018). https://doi.org/10.48550/arXiv.1806.05759
11. Ogawa, A., Hirao, T., Nakatani, T., Nagata, M.: ILP-based compressive speech summarization with content word coverage maximization and its oracle performance analysis. In: IEEE International Conference on Acoustics, Speech and Signal Processing, ICASSP 2019, pp. 7190–7194 (2019). https://doi.org/10.1109/ICASSP.2019.8683543
12. Pasad, A., Chou, J.C., Livescu, K.: Layer-wise analysis of a self-supervised speech representation model. In: 2021 IEEE Automatic Speech Recognition and Understanding Workshop (ASRU), pp. 914–921 (2021). https://doi.org/10.1109/ASRU51503.2021.9688093
13. Paulus, R., Xiong, C., Socher, R.: A deep reinforced model for abstractive summarization. In: International Conference on Learning Representations (2018). https://doi.org/10.48550/arXiv.1705.04304
14. Pennington, J., Socher, R., Manning, C.D.: Glove: global vectors for word representation. In: Empirical Methods in Natural Language Processing (EMNLP), pp. 1532–1543 (2014). https://doi.org/10.3115/v1/D14-1162

15. Pernes, D., Mendes, A., Martins, A.F.T.: Improving abstractive summarization with energy-based re-ranking. In: Proceedings of the 2nd Workshop on Natural Language Generation, Evaluation, and Metrics, Abu Dhabi, United Arab Emirates, pp. 1–17. Association for Computational Linguistics (2022). https://doi.org/10.48550/arXiv.2210.15553

16. Peters, B., Correia, G., Mihaylova, T.: An exploration of teacher forcing techniques for neural machine translation (2018)

17. Radford, A., Kim, J.W., Xu, T., Brockman, G., McLeavey, C., Sutskever, I.: Robust speech recognition via large-scale weak supervision (2022). https://doi.org/10.48550/ARXIV.2212.04356

18. Rezazadegan, D., et al.: Automatic speech summarisation: a scoping review (2020). https://doi.org/10.48550/arXiv.2008.11897

19. Rothe, S., Narayan, S., Severyn, A.: Leveraging pre-trained checkpoints for sequence generation tasks. Trans. Assoc. Comput. Linguist. **8**, 264–280 (2020). https://doi.org/10.1162/tacl_a_00313

20. Scialom, T., Dray, P.A., Lamprier, S., Piwowarski, B., Staiano, J.: MLSUM: the multilingual summarization corpus. In: Proceedings of the 2020 Conference on Empirical Methods in Natural Language Processing (EMNLP), pp. 8051–8067. Association for Computational Linguistics, Online (2020). https://doi.org/10.18653/v1/2020.emnlp-main.647

21. Sharma, R., Palaskar, S., Black, A.W., Metze, F.: End-to-end speech summarization using restricted self-attention. In: IEEE International Conference on Acoustics, Speech and Signal Processing, ICASSP 2022, pp. 8072–8076 (2022). https://doi.org/10.1109/ICASSP43922.2022.9747320

22. Ákos Tündik, M., Kaszás, V., Szaszák, G.: Assessing the semantic space bias caused by ASR error propagation and its effect on spoken document summarization. In: Proceedings of the Interspeech 2019, pp. 1333–1337 (2019). https://doi.org/10.21437/Interspeech.2019-2154

23. Weng, S.Y., Lo, T.H., Chen, B.: An effective contextual language modeling framework for speech summarization with augmented features. In: 2020 28th European Signal Processing Conference (EUSIPCO), pp. 316–320 (2021). https://doi.org/10.23919/Eusipco47968.2020.9287432

24. Zhang, Y., et al.: An exploratory study on long dialogue summarization: what works and what's next. In: Findings of the Association for Computational Linguistics: EMNLP 2021, Punta Cana, Dominican Republic, pp. 4426–4433. Association for Computational Linguistics (2021). https://doi.org/10.18653/v1/2021.findings-emnlp.377

25. Zhuang, L., Wayne, L., Ya, S., Jun, Z.: A robustly optimized BERT pre-training approach with post-training. In: Proceedings of the 20th Chinese National Conference on Computational Linguistics, Huhhot, China, pp. 1218–1227. Chinese Information Processing Society of China (2021). https://doi.org/10.48550/arXiv.1907.11692

Multilingual TTS Accent Impressions
for Accented ASR

Georgios Karakasidis[1,3(✉)], Nathaniel Robinson[2], Yaroslav Getman[1], Atieno Ogayo[2],
Ragheb Al-Ghezi[1], Ananya Ayasi[2], Shinji Watanabe[2], David R. Mortensen[2],
and Mikko Kurimo[1]

[1] Department of Signal Processing and Acoustics, Aalto University, Espoo, Finland
`{georgios.karakasidis,yaroslav.getman,ragheb.al-ghezi,`
`mikko.kurimo}@aalto.fi`
[2] Language Technologies Institute, Carnegie Mellon University, Pittsburgh, USA
`{nrrobins,aogayo,aayasi,swatanab,dmortens}@cs.cmu.edu`
[3] Institute for Language, Cognition and Communication, University of Edinburgh,
Edinburgh, UK
`g.karakasidis@ed.ac.uk`

Abstract. Automatic Speech Recognition (ASR) for high-resource languages
like English is often considered a solved problem. However, most high-resource
ASR systems favor socioeconomically advantaged dialects. In the case of
English, this leaves behind many L2 speakers and speakers of low-resource
accents (a majority of English speakers). One way to mitigate this is to fine-tune a
pre-trained English ASR model for a desired low-resource accent. However, collecting transcribed accented audio is costly and time-consuming. In this work, we
present a method to produce synthetic L2-English speech via pre-trained text-to-
speech (TTS) in an L1 language (target accent). This can be produced at a much
larger scale and lower cost than authentic speech collection. We present initial
experiments applying this augmentation method. Our results suggest that success
of TTS augmentation relies on access to more than one hour of authentic training
data and a diversity of target-domain prompts for speech synthesis.

Keywords: accented speech recognition · data augmentation · low-resource
speech technologies · speech synthesis

1 Introduction

English is one of the most widely spoken languages in the world [11]. Like many languages, it is diverse and multi-dialectal [3]. ASR systems for English and other high-
resource languages are celebrated for high accuracy [19]. However, these ASR systems
are often tailored for a small number of dialects, due to limited data diversity [5]. Studies
have shown bias in English ASR systems against marginalized language varieties [15],
an ethical concern since this bias can disproportionately affect marginalized groups [16]
and immigrants [10]. Demonstrated ASR bias against non-native English accents [25]

G. Karakasidis and N. Robinson—Equal contribution.

© The Author(s), under exclusive license to Springer Nature Switzerland AG 2023
K. Ekštein et al. (Eds.): TSD 2023, LNAI 14102, pp. 317–327, 2023.
https://doi.org/10.1007/978-3-031-40498-6_28

is particularly concerning, due to the large and growing number of L2 English speakers [8]. Similar trends exist for other high-resource languages [4], but we direct our focus to English.

One potential strategy to accommodate a greater number of English speakers is to adapt existing trained English ASR models to different accents [28]. This requires labeled accented English speech data. However, labeled data in specific English accents is scarce [5], and collecting human speech for a large number of English accents is costly and time-intensive.

We propose a novel method: *produce L2-accented English for ASR training via text-to-speech (TTS) pre-trained for another language.* Accented speech can be approximated by passing English inputs through TTS for a language corresponding to the target accent. For example, English text through Spanish TTS will approximate Spanish-accented English. This strategy is inspired by the success of applying TTS speech for low-resource language ASR [6,20,21,27]. It is also inspired by the adaptability of commercial TTS systems such as Microsoft TTS, Google TTS and Amazon Polly to English accents. We chose Microsoft TTS because its online documentation[1] states that "All neural voices are multilingual and fluent in their own language and English" and indicates that English text prompts passed through another language's system will be rendered as accented English speech. In summary, we contribute:

- A novel method for accented ASR training by producing synthetic accented speech via a readily available foreign TTS system
- Reduced ASR error rates in some settings via our synthetic augmentation method
- Indications that synthetic accented speech augmentation relies on at least one hour of authentic data

2   Related Work

We are not the first researchers to investigate augmenting ASR training data via TTS. Multiple researchers have used TTS to extend ASR training data for a variety of languages including Mandarin [12] and low-resource languages in a variety of settings [27], including for languages with no TTS systems [20] and for children's ASR [9]. Others have leveraged TTS to replace a need for real speech features in training [17,24]. These TTS-based methods show promising results for improving ASR in low-resource settings. Our work, however, is the first to apply this approach to adapt ASR models to low-resource accents.

We are also not the first researchers to approach improving accented ASR. The Accented English Speech Recognition Challenge (AESRC2020) [22] garnered developments in the area from a variety of researchers, including accent embeddings and model layers [2,13]. [23] ranked first in AESRC2020 with 10.1% word error rate (WER) by data augmentation and ensembling accoustic models. [5] improved ASR by 33% in multiple accents by leveraging as little as 105 min of unannotated speech in a target accent with an adversarial transfer learning approach. Like these methods, our approach incorporates data augmentation and is largely unsupervised, incorporating a small amount of optional labeled data. However, we are the first researchers to take a multilingual TTS-based approach to accented ASR.

Table 1. Data statistics for authentic sets. n_a represents the number of TTS voices for synthetic data production.

Accent	train mins.	dev mins.	test mins.	n_a
Common Voice				
German	3.5K	396	438	18
Malaysian	66	6	18	4
Filipino	264	30	30	2
Arctic				
Arabic	37	9	55	32
Chinese	40	10	60	36
Hindi	37	10	42	2
Korean	44	12	51	8
Spanish	43	11	58	68
Vietnamese	45	11	56	2

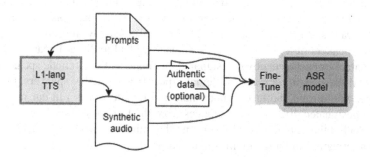

Fig. 1. Accented ASR via synthesized audio.

3 Methodology

Our method of accented English ASR via synthetic dataset curation is illustrated in Fig. 1. It requires (1) a generic pre-trained English ASR model; (2) a trained TTS system in the L1 language corresponding to the target L2-English accent; (3) a corpus of English sentences to use as TTS prompts; and, (4) optionally, a small amount of authentic accented speech data with transcriptions (which may serve as the English corpus). Accented ASR adaptation involves two steps: the data synthesis step consists of passing TTS prompts as input to the pre-trained TTS system (using a variety of TTS-voices as speakers if available) to produce automatically annotated synthetic audio. The training step involves fine-tuning the pre-trained English ASR model in the synthetic accented speech, along with the small amount of authentic accented speech, if available. We assume any authentic data set would be small, since this method is intended for low-resource language varieties.

In our experiments we explore the following methodological variations: fine-tuning on a small authentic dataset; fine-tuning on a large synthetic dataset combined with a small authentic dataset, with the authentic data up-sampled; and fine-tuning in two steps, first with a large synthetic dataset and subsequently with a small authentic dataset. (Details in Sect. 4).

3.1   Data

We tested our hypothesis on a total of nine accents, with authentic accented train, validation (dev), and test sets taken from the publicly available Common Voice (CV) [1] and L2-Arctic [26] databases. Table 1 contains statistics about the train/dev/test splits for all nine accents from both sources. More detailed specifications regarding the data preparation can be found on our github repository[2].

L2-Arctic is a corpus originally designed for the development of TTS systems for non-native English speakers. The small size of the dataset represents extremely low-resource settings in our experiments. It consists of six accents corresponding to L1 languages Arabic, Chinese, Hindi, Korean, Spanish, and Vietnamese, each of them represented by four speakers (two males and two females) with audio recordings spoken in clean environments. We split this data into separate train, dev, and test sets. We took great care to ensure that there was no overlap of voices or text prompts between the test set and the train and dev sets. Because L2-Arctic uses largely the same text prompts for all four speakers of a given accent, this meant we had to discard nearly half of the available data. For each accent we designated one male and one female speaker as test speakers and the remaining male and female speaker as train/dev speakers. (This also ensured we would train and test on both male and female voices.) In our main experiments we designated 40% of the utterances from the test speakers as our test set. We then constructed the train/dev sets by splitting the train/dev speaker files with an 80/20 ratio and afterward removing any files that had prompts contained in the test set. This allowed for a sizeable test set but resulted in small training amounts (see Table 1). Due to our concerns that the small train set may inhibit performance, we conducted some experiments where we allowed the train/dev sets to be as large as possible, though this resulted in very small test sets since we wanted to keep the sets of test prompts and train/dev prompts disjoint.

We used the eighth version of CV, a crowd-sourced dataset with messier audio than L2-Arctic. CV annotation only lists the speakers' country of origin, not L1 language. We selected German, Malaysian, and Filipino accents for our experiments because they mapped straightforwardly to L1 languages supported by Microsoft TTS.[3] Due to limitations in the number of speakers and their gender distribution for each language, splitting the CV dataset was less straightforward than L2-Arctic. We sampled 20% of the speakers for each accent, and used them for the accent's test set. From the utterances of the

---

[2] https://github.com/geoph9/accent-adaptation-through-tts.
[3] More details about the TTS voices can be found on our repository.

remaining 80% of speakers, we used 90% as the training set and 10% as the validation set. The German accent did not contain detailed speaker information (all of the prompts were uttered by the same client who seemingly corresponded to the same male speaker), so we used a random train/dev/test split where each subset consisted of 81%, 9%, and 10% of the whole set, respectively.

3.2 Model

Our baseline model is wav2vec 2.0 [2], which is an end-to-end neural network that consists of a convolutional feature encoder, a transformer, and a quantizer. In particular, we use the publicly available *wav2vec2-base-960h* model[4] which is pre-trained and fine-tuned on 960 h of transcribed audio from the Librispeech data set [18]. We followed the same training setup and hyperparameters for all fine-tuning experiments, with some small variations in batch size[5]. Our models were fine-tuned for 20 epochs with a learning rate of 1e-4. This procedure was done by first freezing the CNN feature encoder and updating the rest of the weights while training.

Table 2. Performance on controlled comparison. Underlined results in the **Synth.** column outperformed **Before Adapt.**. Best results across all experiments (including those in Tables 3 and 4) are **bold**.

Accent	Before Adapt.		Auth.		Synth.		Combined	
	WER%	CER%	WER%	CER%	WER%	CER%	WER%	CER%
CommonVoice								
German	32.77	11.61	8.42	2.12	60.58	27.72	**8.07**	2.05
Malaysian	44.59	18.84	**30.72**	**12.55**	42.12	17.76	34.81	13.98
Filipino	27.53	9.41	18.92	6.23	26.49	9.32	19.06	6.33
Arctic								
Arabic	19.85	7.75	**15.49**	**5.84**	23.71	8.33	17.47	6.68
Chinese	34.78	15.37	26.29	11.31	34.85	14.62	**25.69**	**11.10**
Hindi	17.26	6.73	**11.34**	**3.77**	17.49	5.56	12.30	4.17
Korean	19.51	7.65	15.92	6.10	26.98	10.84	**15.26**	**5.94**
Spanish	25.69	10.50	**21.06**	**8.21**	38.59	12.88	22.23	8.67
Vietnamese	42.25	19.43	**31.93**	14.30	47.27	20.60	33.50	14.73

4 Experiments and Results

We conducted a set of experiments to compare the effectiveness of synthetic to authentic accented audio, the results of which are displayed in Table 2. We used these same test sets for all experiments. **Before Adapt.** (baseline): We tested the wav2vec 2.0 model

---

[4] https://huggingface.co/facebook/wav2vec2-base-960h

[5] We initially opted for batch size of 128, which we used to produce results for German **Auth.** and all Filipino fine-tuned results in Table 2. However in subsequent experiments, this exceeded memory constraints. Accordingly we used a batch size of 96 for all other experiments.

Table 3. Performances on the larger synthesized sets.

Accent	Before Adapt.		Gutenberg synth.		Domain synth.	
	WER%	CER%	WER%	CER%	WER%	CER%
CommonVoice						
German	32.77	11.61	61.10	27.22	56.67	24.64
Malaysian	44.59	18.84	66.86	33.99	63.92	30.80
Filipino	27.53	9.41	34.27	13.29	39.32	15.18
Arctic						
Arabic	19.85	7.75	50.71	26.57	31.09	11.91
Chinese	34.78	15.37	41.53	19.11	32.57	14.38
Hindi	17.26	6.73	25.85	10.10	18.57	5.90
Korean	19.51	7.65	61.37	31.17	33.80	14.33
Spanish	25.69	10.50	35.94	15.16	34.41	12.39
Vietnamese	42.25	19.43	76.01	40.21	52.76	23.49

Table 4. Performances on the larger synthesized sets. <u>Underlined</u> results outperformed **Auth.**. Best results across all experiments (including those in Tables 2 and 3) are **bold**.

Accent	Before Adapt.		Comb. Up-samp.		Two-stage FT	
	WER%	CER%	WER%	CER%	WER%	CER%
CommonVoice						
German	32.77	11.61	8.78	2.20	<u>8.09</u>	**2.02**
Malaysian	44.59	18.84	36.13	14.93	36.08	15.20
Filipino	27.53	9.41	<u>18.51</u>	6.30	**18.00**	**5.93**
Arctic						
Arabic	19.85	7.75	18.66	7.18	17.89	6.90
Chinese	34.78	15.37	27.16	11.93	26.44	11.49
Hindi	17.26	6.73	11.91	3.98	11.74	3.93
Korean	19.51	7.65	18.91	7.30	17.49	6.56
Spanish	25.69	10.50	22.98	9.16	22.72	8.92
Vietnamese	42.25	19.43	32.66	14.55	31.95	**14.25**

off the shelf on the test set for each accent a. **Auth.**: Next, for each accent, we fine-tuned our model using the authentic train and dev sets $\mathcal{A}_a$ detailed in Table 1. **Synth.**: We then generated synthetic audio through Microsoft TTS, using the exact prompts from the authentic train and dev sets to produce new synthetic train and dev sets $\mathcal{S}_a$ for fine-tuning. We produced exactly one TTS file for each prompt, by uniformly sampling one of the n_a available Microsoft TTS voices.[6] (See Table 1 for n_a values.) **Combined**:

---

[6] We included voices for multiple TTS dialects corresponding to the L1 language for each accent (and more than one L1 language in the case of Malaysian) and sampled voices assigned to each accent uniformly without regard for TTS dialect.

Finally, we experimented fine-tuning on $\mathcal{A}_a$ and $\mathcal{S}_a$ combined. As expected, when using otherwise identical train and dev sets, authentic data was more effective than synthetic. However, for three of nine accents, combining the two was more effective.

Next, using the same test sets from Table 2, we experimented with a large amount of synthetic data. Initially, we used 28,104 prompts from the Gutenberg literature corpus[7] [7] to synthesize off-domain speech (**Gutenberg synth.** in Table 3). Then, due to the drastically different text domain of this corpus (compared to our small authentic test set), we constructed large TTS audio sets out of prompts corresponding to the authentic files from our data sources (**Domain synth.** in Table 3). For CV we sampled 25,000 prompts from the original dataset (excluding German, Malaysian, and Filipino accents) and produced TTS files as before to create $\mathcal{C}_a$. For L2-Arctic accents, the largest set of prompts we could create from combining all of the clean L2-Arctic prompts was 1853, resulting in only ~700 train and dev sentences per L1-language once we removed prompts appearing in the respective test sets. We made up for the scarcity by changing our TTS approach: instead of uniformly sampling a TTS voice for each prompt, we used up to 6 TTS voices for each prompt to produce a larger set $\mathcal{L}_a$.[8] Hence, this strategy resulted in training repeatedly on the same relatively small set of ~700 prompts.

Next, we incorporated the large in-domain synthetic sets, $\mathcal{C}_a$ for CV and $\mathcal{L}_a$ for L2-Arctic, with the small authentic sets $\mathcal{A}_a$ to fine-tune in two ways. First, we combined synthetic and authentic data and then up-sampled (i.e. duplicated) the authentic data to be as close to equal as possible to the synthetic data amount (**Comb. Up-samp.** in Table 4). Next, we kept synthetic and authentic sets separate, fine-tuning first on the synthetic, and then again on the authentic data (**Two-stage FT** in Table 4).

As discussed in Sect. 3.1, our primary splitting method left very few train and dev data for L2-Arctic accents (~40 min, as shown in Table 1). This could have a negative impact on both authentic and synthetic fine-tuning, since all of our synthetic augmentation methods for L2-Arcitc accents relied on the set of prompts present in the authentic train/dev sets. We ran additional experiments for three accents (Chinese, Korean, and Spanish), where we used all the prompts available with train and dev speakers for the train/dev data (again with an 80/20 split). This left only a small amount of viable test data that did not share any speakers or prompts with the train/dev data. (See **Test utts.** in Table 5 for the number of test utterances.) WER scores for three of our fine-tuning methods are in Table 5.

Table 5. WER for some L2-Arctic accents on small test sets with maximized train sets.

Accent	Auth	Comb. Up-samp	Two-st. FT	train hrs	test utts.
Chinese	26.1	**17.6**	21.9	1.8	49
Korean	17.5	**13.1**	15.6	1.9	15
Spanish	23.4	22.4	**19.6**	1.8	10

---

[7] https://github.com/geoph9/accent-adaptation-through-tts#synthesised-data-tts.
[8] Thus $|\mathcal{L}_a| = \min(n_a, 6) * N_a$, where $N_a \approx 700$ is the number of train/dev prompts available after removing prompts from the test set for a, $n_a = 2$ for Hindi and Vietnamese, and $n_a \geq 6$ for other L2-Arctic accents. See Table 1.

5   Discussion and Analysis

Table 2 demonstrates that augmentation with authentic data is preferable to synthetic data, though combining the two yielded slightly improved results for three of the nine accents (German, Chinese, and Korean). Synthesized audio files, even in the same small quantities as authentic data, improved over baseline CER for four accents (Malaysian, Filipino, Chinese, and Hindi). Table 3 shows that increasing the amount of synthetic data alone, whether using prompts in the target domain (**Domain synth.**) or out of it (**Gutenberg synth.**), was ineffective across accents. This strategy likely caused the model to overfit on synthetic speech. The **Comb. Up-samp.** and **Two-stage FT** methods, combining synthetic and authentic data, consistently improved error rates over the baseline but only improved over simple authentic fine-tuning by small amounts for two accents (German and Filipino). Results in Table 5 represent small test sizes, however they suggest that settings with more training data may be conducive to greater success in the **Comb. Up-samp.** and **Two-stage FT** methods. The three accents displayed demonstrate WERR[9] of 32.6% (Chinese), 33.6% (Korean), and 16.2% (Spanish) compared to **Auth.** fine-tuning.

We acknowledge a limitation of our experimental setup. Scarcity of authentic accented data made it difficult to find diverse, representative test sets. This highlights the significance of synthetic augumentation improving on simple authentic fine-tuning in some cases. Each authentic set alone was advantaged, since it came from the same source as the test set. One potential advantage of synthetic augmentation is the expansion of model capabilities to more general settings. We hope future researchers will explore the benefits of our augmentation methods with more diverse test sets.

We explore the possible effect of TTS audio characteristics on suitability for augmentation. In Table 6 we show the effectiveness (*eff.*) of synthetic data augmentation, represented as the WERR% of our best-performing method involving TTS audio, compared to the best-performing method without TTS audio, from Tables 2, 3, and 4. We also show measures of TTS quality: average intelligibility (*intel.*) measured by ASR WER% using our wav2vec2.0 model to recognize TTS audio; average naturalness (*nat.*) measured by MOS score[10] [14]; and faithfulness in approximating the target accent (*accen.*). For this last characteristic we hired two proficient English speakers to rate an audio segment from each TTS voice on a five-point scale, where 5 corresponded to such a strong accent as to render the audio unintelligible and 1 corresponded to no accent at all. From these human annotations we calculated two accent scores. To measure accent excess, we counted ratings of 4 as one point and ratings of 5 as two points, then divided an accent's total points by its number of TTS voices n_a. We calculated accent absence the same way, where a rating of 2 equaled one point, and a rating of 1 equaled two points. Table 6 shows average scores from the two evaluators, in the form: excess score/absence score.

Our analysis in Table 6 does not highlight any clear trends. Some accents with highly intelligible TTS and desirable accentedness (Filipino and Chinese) were more

---

[9] Calculated as $\frac{rate_{old} - rate_{new}}{rate_{old}}$.

[10] We took both intelligibility and naturalness measurements over the dev set used for **Domain synth.**, with maximalized dev sets for L2-Arctic accents.

effective, but so were Korean (with poor **intel.** and **accen.** scores) and German. Interestingly, naturalness seems inversely correlated with effectiveness. And both accents displaying excessive accentedness (German and Korean) were more effective.

In summary, results from Tables 2, 3, and 4 suggest that augmentation by synthetic accented speech should be accompanied by a small authentic dataset to prevent overfitting on synthetic speech. In Tables 2, 3, 4, and 5 we find that synthetic data augmentation was only effective when authentic train data exceeded one hour (German and Filipino in Table 4 and experiments in Table 5). This may be in part so that authentic speech can give a strong signal in fine-tuning and not be drowned out by synthetic speech. A related factor is the diversity of prompts for TTS. **Comb. Up-samp.** and **Two-stage FT** models for L2-Arctic accents trained repeatedly on the same ∼700 prompts and may have implicitly overtrained on them, rendering them ill-equipped to predict other prompts. This could explain why these two methods were ineffective in such settings but performed better for CV accents and in Table 5 (where larger training sets afforded larger prompt sets for augmentation).

Table 6. TTS quality analysis. *eff.* = effectiveness, *intel.* = intelligibility, *nat.* = naturalness, *accen.* = accentedness, shown as excess/absence of an accent.

Accent	*eff.* (↑)	*intel.* (↓)	*nat.* (↑)	*accen.* (↓/↓)
German	3.92	64.5	3.14	1.36/0.31
Malaysian	−13.3	68.6	3.41	0.88/0.13
Filipino	**4.86**	17.6	2.71	0.0/1.0
Arabic	−12.8	64.6	3.39	0.91/0.09
Chinese	2.28	**13.7**	3.16	0.07/1.01
Hindi	−3.53	20.6	**3.43**	0.25/0.50
Korean	4.15	93.2	3.07	1.94/0.0
Spanish	−5.56	51.8	3.22	0.80/0.43
Vietnamese	−0.06	89.8	3.17	2.0/0.0

6 Conclusion

The failure of many English ASR systems to accommodate non-native accents has a negative impact on the world's millions of L2-English speakers. We present a novel approach to assist in this problem, utilizing multilingual TTS systems with English prompts to approximate L2-accented speech and produce scalable augmentation data. We evaluated multiple realizations of this approach for ASR of 9 non-native English accents. Given our experiments and analysis, we find that TTS-based augmentation for accented ASR is best realized, and assists in error rate reductions for multiple accents, when accompanied by more than one hour of authentic speech and when sufficiently diverse target-domain TTS prompts are available.

References

1. Ardila, R., et al.: Common voice: a massively-multilingual speech corpus. arXiv preprint arXiv:1912.06670 (2019)
2. Baevski, A., Zhou, Y., Mohamed, A., Auli, M.: wav2vec 2.0: a framework for self-supervised learning of speech representations. In: Advances in Neural Information Processing Systems, vol. 33, 12449–12460 (2020)
3. Bhatt, R.M.: World Englishes. Ann. Rev. Anthropol. **30**(1), 527–550 (2001)
4. Cumbal, R., Moell, B., Águas Lopes, J.D., Engwall, O.: "You don't understand me!": Comparing ASR results for L1 and L2 speakers of Swedish. In: Interspeech 2021 (2021)
5. Das, N., Bodapati, S., Sunkara, M., Srinivasan, S., Chau, D.H.: Best of both worlds: robust accented speech recognition with adversarial transfer learning. In: Interspeech 2021, pp. 1314–1318. ISCA (2021). https://doi.org/10.21437/Interspeech.2021-1888. https://www.isca-speech.org/archive/interspeech_2021/das21b_interspeech.html
6. Du, C., Yu, K.: Speaker augmentation for low resource speech recognition. In: 2020 IEEE International Conference on Acoustics, Speech and Signal Processing, ICASSP 2020, pp. 7719–7723 (2020). https://doi.org/10.1109/ICASSP40776.2020.9053139
7. Gerlach, M., Font-Clos, F.: A standardized project Gutenberg corpus for statistical analysis of natural language and quantitative linguistics. Entropy **22**(1), 126 (2020)
8. Graddol, D.: The decline of the native speaker. Translation Today: Trends and Perspectives, pp. 152–167 (2003)
9. Kadyan, V., Kathania, H., Govil, P., Kurimo, M.: Synthesis speech based data augmentation for low resource children ASR. In: Karpov, A., Potapova, R. (eds.) SPECOM 2021. LNCS (LNAI), vol. 12997, pp. 317–326. Springer, Cham (2021). https://doi.org/10.1007/978-3-030-87802-3_29
10. Kulkarni, K., Sengupta, S., Ramasubramanian, V., Bauer, J.G., Stemmer, G.: Accented Indian English ASR: some early results. In: 2008 IEEE Spoken Language Technology Workshop, pp. 225–228 (2008). https://doi.org/10.1109/SLT.2008.4777881
11. Kuo, I.C.: Addressing the issue of teaching English as a lingua franca. ELT J. **60**(3), 213–221 (2006)
12. Laptev, A., Korostik, R., Svischev, A., Andrusenko, A., Medennikov, I., Rybin, S.: You do not need more data: improving end-to-end speech recognition by text-to-speech data augmentation. In: 2020 13th International Congress on Image and Signal Processing, BioMedical Engineering and Informatics (CISP-BMEI), pp. 439–444 (2020). https://doi.org/10.1109/CISP-BMEI51763.2020.9263564
13. Li, S., Ouyang, B., Liao, D., Xia, S., Li, L., Hong, Q.: End-to-end multi-accent speech recognition with unsupervised accent modelling. In: 2021 IEEE International Conference on Acoustics, Speech and Signal Processing, ICASSP 2021, pp. 6418–6422 (2021). https://doi.org/10.1109/ICASSP39728.2021.9414833. iSSN 2379-190X
14. Lo, C.C., et al.: MOSNet: deep learning-based objective assessment for voice conversion. In: Proceedings of the Interspeech 2019, pp. 1541–1545 (2019). https://doi.org/10.21437/Interspeech.2019-2003
15. Markl, N., McNulty, S.J.: Language technology practitioners as language managers: arbitrating data bias and predictive bias in ASR. In: Proceedings of the Thirteenth Language Resources and Evaluation Conference, pp. 6328–6339 (2022)
16. Martin, J.L.: Spoken corpora data, automatic speech recognition, and bias against African American language: the case of Habitual 'Be'. In: Proceedings of the 2021 ACM Conference on Fairness, Accountability, and Transparency, pp. 284–284 (2021)
17. Mimura, M., Ueno, S., Inaguma, H., Sakai, S., Kawahara, T.: Leveraging sequence-to-sequence speech synthesis for enhancing acoustic-to-word speech recognition. In: 2018

IEEE Spoken Language Technology Workshop (SLT), pp. 477–484 (2018). https://doi.org/10.1109/SLT.2018.8639589

18. Panayotov, V., Chen, G., Povey, D., Khudanpur, S.: Librispeech: an ASR corpus based on public domain audio books. In: 2015 IEEE International Conference on Acoustics, Speech and Signal Processing (ICASSP), pp. 5206–5210. IEEE (2015)

19. Radford, A., Kim, J.W., Xu, T., Brockman, G., McLeavey, C., Sutskever, I.: Robust speech recognition via large-scale weak supervision. arXiv preprint arXiv:2212.04356 (2022)

20. Robinson, N.R., Ogayo, P., Gangu, S.R., Mortensen, D.R., Watanabe, S.: When is TTS augmentation through a pivot language useful? In: Proceedings of the Interspeech 2022, pp. 3538–3542 (2022). https://doi.org/10.21437/Interspeech.2022-11203

21. Rossenbach, N., Zeyer, A., Schlüter, R., Ney, H.: Generating synthetic audio data for attention-based speech recognition systems. In: 2020 IEEE International Conference on Acoustics, Speech and Signal Processing, ICASSP 2020, pp. 7069–7073 (2020). https://doi.org/10.1109/ICASSP40776.2020.9053008. iSSN 2379-190X

22. Shi, X., et al.: The accented English speech recognition challenge 2020: open datasets, tracks, baselines, results and methods. CoRR arXiv:2102.10233 (2021)

23. Tan, T., Lu, Y., Ma, R., Zhu, S., Guo, J., Qian, Y.: AISpeech-SJTU ASR system for the accented English speech recognition challenge. In: 2021 IEEE International Conference on Acoustics, Speech and Signal Processing, ICASSP 2021, pp. 6413–6417 (2021). https://doi.org/10.1109/ICASSP39728.2021.9414471. iSSN 2379-190X

24. Ueno, S., Mimura, M., Sakai, S., Kawahara, T.: Data augmentation for ASR using TTS via a discrete representation. In: 2021 IEEE Automatic Speech Recognition and Understanding Workshop (ASRU), Cartagena, Colombia, pp. 68–75. IEEE (2021). https://doi.org/10.1109/ASRU51503.2021.9688218. https://ieeexplore.ieee.org/document/9688218/

25. Zhang, Y., Zhang, Y., Halpern, B.M., Patel, T., Scharenborg, O.: Mitigating bias against non-native accents. In: Proceedings of the Annual Conference of the International Speech Communication Association, INTERSPEECH, vol. 2022, pp. 3168–3172 (2022)

26. Zhao, G., et al.: L2-arctic: a non-native English speech corpus. In: Proceedings of the Interspeech, pp. 2783–2787 (2018). https://doi.org/10.21437/Interspeech.2018-1110

27. Zheng, X., Liu, Y., Gunceler, D., Willett, D.: Using synthetic audio to improve the recognition of out-of-vocabulary words in end-to-end ASR systems. In: 2021 IEEE International Conference on Acoustics, Speech and Signal Processing, ICASSP 2021, pp. 5674–5678 (2021). https://doi.org/10.1109/ICASSP39728.2021.9414778. iSSN 2379-190X

28. Zhu, H., Wang, L., Zhang, P., Yan, Y.: Multi-accent adaptation based on gate mechanism. In: Interspeech 2019, pp. 744–748. ISCA (2019). https://doi.org/10.21437/Interspeech.2019-3155. https://www.isca-speech.org/archive/interspeech_2019/zhu19_interspeech.html

Transfer Learning of Transformer-Based Speech Recognition Models from Czech to Slovak

Jan Lehečka$^{(\boxtimes)}$, Josef V. Psutka , and Josef Psutka

Department of Cybernetics, University of West Bohemia in Pilsen,
Pilsen, Czech Republic
{jlehecka,psutka_j,psutka}@kky.zcu.cz

Abstract. In this paper, we are comparing several methods of training the Slovak speech recognition models based on the Transformers architecture. Specifically, we are exploring the approach of transfer learning from the existing Czech pre-trained Wav2Vec 2.0 model into Slovak. We are demonstrating the benefits of the proposed approach on three Slovak datasets. Our Slovak models scored the best results when initializing the weights from the Czech model at the beginning of the pre-training phase. Our results show that the knowledge stored in the Cezch pre-trained model can be successfully reused to solve tasks in Slovak while outperforming even much larger public multilingual models.

Keywords: Transfer learning · Wav2Vec 2.0 · Transformers

1 Introduction

Transfer learning in speech recognition has been shown to be effective in improving accuracy and reducing the amount of training data required for new tasks. It is especially useful in scenarios where the amount of available training data is limited, such as low-resource languages or domains with specific acoustic characteristics. The aim of this paper is to identify a suitable transfer learning approach for two languages, Czech and Slovak. These two languages have many similarities, both in their written form and pronunciation.

In our experiments, we are comparing several methods of training the Slovak models for the target task of automatic speech recognition (ASR). Specifically, we are investigating the possibilities of transferring the knowledge from the existing pre-trained Czech model into Slovak ASR tasks. Since Czech and Slovak have a lot in common, we expect this transfer learning approach to be beneficial in the target Slovak tasks because it can reuse the already trained knowledge common to both languages while suppressing the non-Slovak information in favor of Slovak-specific knowledge during the transfer. In this paper, we investigate the benefits of this transfer learning approach.

We demonstrate the benefits of the proposed approach on three ASR datasets (described in detail in Sect. 4.3). Two of the used datasets (CommonVoice and

© The Author(s), under exclusive license to Springer Nature Switzerland AG 2023
K. Ekštein et al. (Eds.): TSD 2023, LNAI 14102, pp. 328–338, 2023.
https://doi.org/10.1007/978-3-031-40498-6_29

VoxPopuli) are public speech recognition datasets used very often for the bench-marking of ASR systems in many languages [2, 13]. The third dataset, MALACH, is the Slovak portion of the very unique and challenging speech recognition dataset containing testimonies of eyewitnesses of the Holocaust recorded during 90'. We consider the MALACH dataset to be extremely important dataset for several reasons: (1) it preserves extremely valuable testimonies from our recent history, which should not be forgotten and which, alas, cannot be extended or scaled up anymore because the number of direct witnesses of the Holocaust rapidly decreases to zero as time goes on; (2) every improvement in the speech recognition accuracy unlocks new valuable historical and cartographical infor-mation encoded in the spoken utterances for researchers and public searching in this vast archive; (3) since most of the speakers were very old at the time of recording and the testimonies were spoken under heavy emotions, it is a challeng-ing dataset to test the robustness, zero-shot performance and transfer learning ability of existing ASR models.

2   Transfer Learning from Czech to Slovak

As mentioned above, Czech and Slovak share many similarities not only in their written form but also phonetically. Czech orthography serves as a model for several other Balto-Slavic languages that use the Latin alphabet. Slovak can be regarded as its direct descendant from this perspective. Both languages use com-parable diacritics and have a similar, often interchangeable relationship between letters and the sounds they represent. The significant similarity between the two languages can also be attributed to the fact that they were both official languages in the same country for over 40 years (in Czechoslovakia). In this arti-cle, we will focus only on the graphemic aspect of these languages. For a more detailed comparison of Czech and Slovak in the context of acoustic modeling, please refer to [8, 9, 11].

In the Czech language, there are a total of 42 letters that are used. This includes the 26 letters of the basic Latin alphabet as well as 15 letters that have diacritical marks such as a caron [ˇ], acute [´], or a overring [˚]. In addition, there is a digraph [ch] that represents a phoneme /x/ (SAMPA is used in all cases of phonetic notation [15]) and is considered one of the letters of the Czech alphabet. There are two different ways to write a long /u:/ in Czech: [ú] and [ů], but they have the same pronunciation. One form cannot occur in the initial position, while the other occurs exclusively in the initial position or at the beginning of the root of a compound word.

The Slovak alphabet is the longest alphabet among Slavic and other Euro-pean languages, consisting of a total of 46 letters. It includes the 26 letters of the basic Latin alphabet that are also used in Czech. Additionally, there are 17 letters that have diacritical marks, which include diaeresis [¨] and a circumflex [ˆ] but do not include a overring [˚]. But only five of these diacritical letters differ from those used in Czech ([ä] [ľ] [ĺ] [ô] [ŕ]). Moreover, there are two addi-tional digraphs present in the Slovak alphabet, i.e. [dz] and [dž]. These letters represent phonemes /dz/ and /dZ/.

3   Wav2Vec 2.0

Wav2Vec 2.0 models have recently become a new state-of-the-art paradigm in ASR tasks outperforming the previous architectures by a large margin [3]. It is a deep neural network pre-trained to reconstruct the corrupted audio signals. The model consists of a multi-layer convolutional neural network (referred to as a feature encoder) followed by a multi-layer Transformer encoder [16]. The convolutional feature encoder processes the raw input signal and produces a sequence of latent-speech representations. Each of these latent-speech representations is a vector encoding one 20 ms-long frame of the input signal with only a small (5 ms) context being taken into account. The attention-based Transformer then converts latent-speech representations into contextualized speech representations while paying attention to the full context of the input signal.

The training of Wav2Vec models consists of two phases: self-supervised pre-training and supervised fine-tuning. The phase of self-supervised pre-training requires a large-scale unlabeled speech dataset, from which the model learns the contextualized speech representations by predicting masked frames. Moreover, the model is pre-trained also to solve a contrastive task over quantized speech representations, so the model is forced to map input frames into discrete speech units and correctly identify masked frames among a set of distractors. During this phase, the model does not have any orthographical information about the processed speech as it has access only to the raw audio signal, so it is pre-trained to catch and encode the meaning of individual audio frames only based on its context.

The pre-training phase is essential to equip the model with deep knowledge mined from tens of thousands of hours of unlabeled speech. This knowledge constitutes a great advantage over models trained from scratch using labeled data only. From this point of view, the pre-trained weights of the Wav2Vec model could be seen as a very clever initialization of the model weights for supervised training. In this paper, we are investigating the benefits of clever initialization also for the pre-training, i.e., not starting from random weights from scratch but using weights of a model pre-trained from much more speech data from a language that is somehow similar. This way, the model could preserve the information common to both languages and reuse it when solving tasks in the other language.

After the pre-training is done, the model transfers the pre-trained knowledge into the target ASR task within the fine-tuning phase. This is a supervised phase requiring the training speech dataset to be labeled. In order to decode the most probable sequences of graphemes, the model is additionally equipped with a final Connectionist Temporal Classification (CTC) layer [4]. CTC is an alignment-free method for grouping audio frames belonging to the same output token in order to convert a sequence of frame-level predictions into a much shorter sequence of output tokens. The CTC classification process can be described – in a simplified way – in 3 steps:

1. Assign the most probable output token to each audio frame.

2. Group sub-sequences with the same token into a single token.
3. Remove blank tokens.

Tokens could be any speech or language units, e.g., phonemes, graphemes, sub-word units, words, etc. In this paper, we experimented with grapheme-based predictions, i.e., we predicted the sequence of characters. We chose the grapheme-based output units because it has several advantages: (1) the fine-tuned model works with very small vocabulary (the size of the alphabet plus several special tokens), so the decoding is fast, (2) it avoids out-of-vocabulary problems (any sequence of graphemes can be predicted), and (3) it can be used as a stand-alone full-fledged end-to-end speech recognizer without any additional postprocessing.

4   Experimental Setup

In our experiments, we used existing pre-trained Wav2vec models or – when not available – we pre-trained new ones. We fine-tuned all pre-trained models on train and development parts of three Slovak ASR datasets. After that, we evaluated all models on the test part of relevant datasets. The test parts were held out during the whole fine-tuning process and had no speaker overlaps with train or development parts. We used implementation from `Fairseq` tool [10] for both pre-training and fine-tuning of models.

4.1   Pre-trained Models

In this section, we present all the pre-trained models we were experimenting with. We used three monolingual pre-trained Wav2Vec 2.0 models of the base size: Czech (denoted as `W2V2-cs`), Slovak (`W2V2-sk`), and a model transferred from Czech to Slovak (`W2V2-cs-sk`). To test the monolingual models against multilingual models, we also evaluated two popular large-scale multilingual models (Wav2Vec XLS-R and Whisper). We are listing the models along with detailed information in the rest of this section.

W2V2-cs. The `W2V2-cs` is a monolingual model pre-trained solely from the Czech speech. We used the publicly available model `ClTRUS`[1] [6]. It has been trained from 80 thousand hours of Czech speech from various domains, mainly from the VoxPopuli dataset [17] and records from Czech TV and radio shows.

W2V2-ck. The `W2V2-sk` is a monolingual model pre-trained solely from the Slovak speech. We didn't find any suitable public model, so we pre-trained a new base-sized model from scratch. Since Transformer-based models are known to scale well with the size of pre-training data, we tried to gather as much public unlabeled speech data as possible. We collected over 17 thousand hours of Slovak speech from various sources. The collection includes recordings from the

---

[1] https://huggingface.co/fav-kky/wav2vec2-base-cs-80k-ClTRUS.

Slovak portion of the VoxPopuli dataset [17] (12k hours), a mix of self-crawled records from Slovak TV shows (4.5k hours), the MALACH dataset (800 h) and the Slovak portion of CommonVoice corpus 13.0 [1] (24 h). We used Wav2Vec 2.0 architecture [3] and adopted the same hyperparameter setting as in the paper, i.e., we trained the base model (12 Transformer blocks, model dimension 768, 8 attention heads, and a total of 95 million parameters) for 400 thousand steps with a batch size of about 1.6 h. The pre-training took four days on a machine with eight NVIDIA A100 GPUs.

W2V2-cs-sk. The W2V2-cs-sk is a monolingual Slovak model which was not initialized randomly from scratch but rather from weights of the Czech model W2V2-cs. After the initialization, we pre-trained the model with the exact same setting and data as W2V2-sk. Thus, the only difference between W2V2-sk and W2V2-cs-sk is the initialization of weights. We expect this model to identify, preserve and transfer the useful knowledge common to both languages while suppressing the non-Slovak information in favor of Slovak-specific knowledge during the pre-training. In this paper, we are exploring if and how much this transfer learning approach is beneficial. We are releasing this pre-trained Slovak model publicly to the research community[2].

W2V2-XLS-R-300M. To compare monolingual models also with popular multilingual public models, we selected Wav2Vec XLS-R [2] as a representative of large-scale pre-trained cross-lingual models. The model was pre-trained on approximately 436 thousand hours of unlabeled speech data from 128 languages (including both Czech and Slovak). We experimented with the 300M variant, which has more than 300 million parameters, i.e., more than 3× more than the base Wav2Vec 2.0 model. We denote this model W2V2-XLS-R-300M.

Whisper-Large. Finally, we compared our models with Whisper-large [13], another popular model trained on 99 languages (including both Czech and Slovak) from 680,000 h of multilingual and multitask labeled data. This model differs from Wav2Vec models in two main aspects: (1) it is not an encoder-only model but has also a decoder serving as an audio-conditioned built-in language model, (2) the input is Mel spectrogram instead of the raw audio signal. We experimented with the large size of the model with 32+32 Transformer layers, dimension 1280, 20 attention heads, and a total of 1.55 billion trainable parameters. When decoding, we specified the language to Slovak, so the model didn't have to identify the language automatically from the input signal. As this model has already been fine-tuned on a large palette of datasets and tasks by authors, we didn't further fine-tune the model, and we used the downloaded weights directly.

---

[2] https://huggingface.co/fav-kky/wav2vec2-base-sk-17k.

4.2   Fine-Tuning

We prepared all training and development ASR data consistently for all datasets. Where necessary, we sliced long training audio signals on speech pauses not to exceed the length of 30 s. Longer utterances were discarded due to the memory limits of used GPUs during fine-tuning. We removed non-speech events and punctuation from the transcripts and mapped all words into lowercase. We fine-tuned all models with the same setting as the base model in [3], i.e., we trained for 80 thousand steps with a batch size of about 26 min per step, and the learning rate warmed up over the first 8 000 steps to a maximum value of 2×10^{-5}, where it was held for the next 32 000 steps, and finally decayed exponentially to zero. The weights of the feature encoder were frozen for the first 10 000 steps of the fine-tuning.

4.3   Fine-Tuning Datasets

We experimented with three datasets described in detail in the rest of this section. The statistics about individual datasets are tabulated in Table 1.

Table 1. Fine-tuning datasets. We show the total number of speech hours, the number of utterances, and the total number of words in transcripts (in thousands).

	CommonVoice			VoxPopuli			MALACH		
	train	dev	test	train	dev	test	train	dev	test
# hours of audio	14.2	2.9	3.1	29.2	1.9	1.7	94.3	2.0	1.2
# utterances	13 122	2 474	2 552	10 410	664	604	13 160	273	500
# words (in thousands)	48.0	11.0	10.2	233.2	14.6	13.4	645.8	14.0	8.3

CommonVoice. The CommonVoice dataset is a Slovak portion of the crowd-sourced project Mozilla Common Voice [1]. We used corpus version 13.0, containing 20 h of validated speech. We decided to keep also sentences reported as *difficult pronunciation* in our training data. All other reported sentences (e.g., *grammar or spelling*, *different language* etc.) were ignored.

VoxPopuli. The VoxPopuli dataset [17] is a large-scale multilingual speech corpus collected from 2009–2020 European Parliament event recordings. The Slovak portion contains 12.1 thousand unlabeled hours and 35 h with transcription. We ignored all train and development utterances without the raw transcription, decreasing the amount of transcribed data to 32.8 h.

MALACH. The Malach Archive preserves the memories of Holocaust survivors through audiovisual interviews in 32 languages. The recordings are characterized by natural speech with emotional outpourings and heavy accents due to the advanced age of the speakers (around 75 years old). Transfer learning can significantly increase recognition accuracy for such type of data, as it is difficult to find additional suitable data for acoustic modeling due to the nature of the corpus (more details can be found in [7]).

The Czech portion of the Malach data was released by the LDC in 2014 [12], comprising 400 randomly selected testimonies for training acoustic models. However, due to the manual transcription of only 15-minute segments of each testimony, the acoustic modeling process had access to only 100 h of Czech speech data. Theoretically, the available data could contain up to 800 speakers. The Slovak section of the Malach corpus was transcribed similarly to the Czech section, with 15-min segments of 400 testimonies transcribed for training. Additionally, 20 testimonies (10 men and 10 women) were fully transcribed to create the development and test portions of the Slovak corpus. In order to maintain consistency with other corpora and ensure a manageable test size, the size of the test set was limited to a reasonable level. A carefully selected subset of the transcribed data consisting of 500 sentences was utilized. To enhance the reliability of the results, all segments containing crosstalks were deliberately excluded from the test set, as they could potentially impact the findings. Therefore, this subset consisted only of continuous segments where either the survivor or the interviewer spoke, with no interruption or overlap from the other speakers.

4.4 Decoding

When transcribing the speech from fine-tuned models, we experimented with two decoding strategies: (1) using only the fine-tuned Wav2Vec model as a stand-alone end-to-end speech recognizer and (2) CTC beam search decoder using additional language information from a language model (LM) during the decoding. The decoding with strategy (2) usually improves speech recognition performance by bringing useful language information into the decoding process while penalizing improbable outputs in the target language.

For strategy (2), we trained one large-scale general-purpose n-gram LM to be used in all experiments for all datasets. As training data, we used web pages from the Common Crawl project[3]. We downloaded and processed 34 crawls from August 2018 to October 2021 following the same cleaning and deduplicating rules as in the English C4 dataset [14]. Together, we collected about 37 GB of cleaned and deduplicated Slovak text containing 5.6 billion words from more than 16 million web pages. To keep the LM of a practical size, we pruned all unigrams with counts lower than ten and higher-order n-grams with counts lower than 100. We trained the LM in lowercase as all fine-tuning transcripts were converted into lowercase. The final LM contained 2.5 million unigrams and 12 million n-grams

---

[3] https://commoncrawl.org.

in total. We used `KenLM` [5] toolkit to train the LM and `pyctcdecode`[4] tool to decode transcripts.

4.5   Evaluation

We compared models in terms of word error rate (WER). Since all transcripts were cleaned from punctuation and cast into lowercase before the fine-tuning, our fine-tuned models cannot predict punctuation or upper-cased characters, so we did not consider casing and punctuation differences with the reference as errors.

Note that although our models are not able to predict cased transcriptions nor punctuation, which usually makes the transcript difficult to read, we are, in all relevant applications, applying also a postprocessing phase on generated transcripts, in which a specially trained transformer-based large language model restores the casing and punctuations in the transcripts. We found this approach more beneficial than training the Wav2Vec models to predict directly cased words and punctuation for two reasons: (1) the text-based language model is more accurate in this task as it can work with larger context and have a better understanding of the syntax and semantics of the spoken words, and (2) the training of Wav2Vec models is less confusing because both cased words and punctuation tokens do not correspond to any distinguishable acoustic units and yet, they would have different target labels.

5   Results

The results of our experiments are tabulated in Table 2 (results with stand-alone Wav2Vec models) and Table 3 (results with Wav2Vec models using the language model in the decoder). When comparing corresponding values from both tables, we can confirm that including LM from Common Crawl into the CTC decoder significantly improves the ASR results for all models across all datasets.

Table 2. Evaluation results in terms of WER [%] scored by end-to-end grapheme-based models. These results show how individual fine-tuned Transformer models perform when used as a stand-alone ASR system without any language model involved.

	#params [in millions]	fine-tuned and evaluated on		
		CommonVoice	VoxPopuli	MALACH
W2V2-cs	95	13.85	11.58	14.81
W2V2-sk	95	**10.62**	10.09	13.60
W2V2-cs-sk	95	10.95	**9.76**	**13.30**
W2V2-XLS-R-300M	300	**9.44**	10.39	15.12

---

[4] https://github.com/kensho-technologies/pyctcdecode.

In the first row of both tables, we show the results of the Czech model W2V2-cs fine-tuned on the Slovak datasets. When compared with results in the second row from the Slovak model W2V2-sk, we can clearly see the Slovak model is better (which is expected), but moreover, we see that the difference is, in many cases, not so large (from 0.5% to 3.2% in terms of absolute WER reduction). This closeness confirms that Czech and Slovak have a lot in common, and we could get a reasonably good Slovak ASR system just by fine-tuning the Czech pre-trained model on a small amount of Slovak labeled speech. The larger the fine-tuning dataset is, the smaller the difference between the performance of the Czech and Slovak pre-trained models is.

Now, let's concentrate on the differences between the second row (Slovak model W2V2-sk pre-trained from scratch from the Slovak-only speech) and the third row (Slovak model W2V2-cs-sk initialized from the Czech model before pre-training). For two datasets (VoxPopuli and MALACH), we can observe a small but consistent decrease in WER gained by this transfer learning. However, for the CommonVoice dataset, we got the best results (among the base-sized models) from the pure Slovak model. After an analysis of the errors, we believe this is caused by an insufficient amount of training data. There are just 14.2 h of labeled Slovak speech in the training CommonVoice dataset. We observed many Czech forms of Slovak words in the transcripts from the W2V2-cs-sk model fine-tuned on the CommonVoice dataset, indicating that the model still has a lot of the original Czech-related knowledge even after the transfer to Slovak and that this amount of train labeled data is not enough to override the Czech-related knowledge in the model.

Table 3. Evaluation results in terms of WER [%] scored by models also incorporating the language model in the decoder. These results show how individual fine-tuned Transformer models perform when also adding the language model probabilities into the decoding process. Values decorated with an asterisk (*) are scored by a general-purpose ASR model without fine-tuning to the target dataset.

	#params [in millions]	fine-tuned and evaluated on		
		CommonVoice	VoxPopuli	MALACH
W2V2-cs	107	11.25	10.04	12.79
W2V2-sk	107	**8.68**	9.02	12.32
W2V2-cs-sk	107	8.82	**8.88**	**11.57**
W2V2-XLS-R-300M	312	**6.90**	9.09	12.17
Whisper-large	1 550	*34.61	*19.30	*27.49

The multilingual W2V2-XLS-R-300M scored the best result among all models on the CommonVoice dataset. We attribute this result to the fact that it was pre-trained on the whole CommonVoice dataset containing 7 thousand hours containing similar sentences (the domain of CommonVoice is a read speech primarily from Wikipedia sentences) in various languages. Thus, the pre-trained embeddings could better encode information in this dataset than other models, where the CommonVoice dataset was only a very small part of the pre-training corpus. However, although more than 3× larger, it did not perform better on the other two datasets, for which our smaller monolingual models performed slightly (VoxPopuli dataset) or significantly (MALACH dataset) better.

Finally, the results from the Whisper model are far from all fine-tuned models. Although this model was not directly fine-tuned on the target datasets, CommonVoice and VoxPopuli datasets were a part of the huge labeled training dataset of the model. These results, which correspond to the reported results in [13], suggested that general-purpose models – even the huge ones – do not always perform well on low-resources languages and tasks.

To sum up our results, the transfer learning between Czech and Slovak is, in most cases, beneficial, and the more labeled data for the target domain there is, the more we can benefit from this transfer by reusing the knowledge common to both languages. We also showed that monolingual models pre-trained on a single language can successfully compete with the much larger multilingual models.

6 Conclusion

In this paper, we compared several methods of training the Slovak ASR models and evaluated the models on three Slovak datasets. Our results showed that the proposed transfer learning approach from the Czech pre-trained model can bring significant reduction in terms of speech recognition WER, especially when the fine-tuning dataset is large enough.

Our base Wav2Vec 2.0 models performed better on two datasets (including the extremely important MALACH dataset) than 3× larger Facebook's XLS-R model and much better on all three datasets than 16× larger OpenAI's Whisper model. Since such a reduction of the model size while preserving or improving the performance could save a lot of energy required for the inference, we release the pre-trained Slovak model publicly for the research community.

Acknowledgments. This research was supported by the Ministry of the Interior of the Czech Republic, project No. VJ01010108. Computational resources were provided by the e-INFRA CZ project (ID:90254), supported by the Ministry of Education, Youth and Sports of the Czech Republic.

References

1. Ardila, R., et al.: Common voice: a massively-multilingual speech corpus. In: Proceedings of the 12th Conference on Language Resources and Evaluation (LREC 2020), pp. 4211–4215 (2020)
2. Babu, A., et al.: XLS-R: self-supervised cross-lingual speech representation learning at scale. In: Proceedings of Interspeech 2022, pp. 2278–2282 (2022). https://doi.org/10.21437/Interspeech.2022-143

3. Baevski, A., Zhou, Y., Mohamed, A., Auli, M.: Wav2Vec 2.0: a framework for self-supervised learning of speech representations. In: Advances in Neural Information Processing Systems, vol. 33, pp. 12449–12460 (2020)
4. Graves, A., Fernández, S., Gomez, F., Schmidhuber, J.: Connectionist temporal classification: labelling unsegmented sequence data with recurrent neural networks. In: Proceedings of the 23rd International Conference on Machine Learning, pp. 369–376 (2006)
5. Heafield, K.: KenLM: faster and smaller language model queries. In: Proceedings of the Sixth Workshop on Statistical Machine Translation, pp. 187–197 (2011)
6. Lehečka, J., Švec, J., Pražák, A., Psutka, J.V.: Exploring capabilities of monolingual audio transformers using large datasets in automatic speech recognition of Czech. In: Proceedings of Interspeech 2022, pp. 1831–1835 (2022). https://doi.org/10.21437/Interspeech.2022-10439
7. MALACH project (2006). https://malach.umiacs.umd.edu/
8. Mirilovič, M., Juhár, J., Čižmár, A.: Comparison of grapheme and phoneme based acoustic modeling in LVCSR task in Slovak. In: Esposito, A., Hussain, A., Marinaro, M., Martone, R. (eds.) Multimodal Signals: Cognitive and Algorithmic Issues. LNCS (LNAI), vol. 5398, pp. 242–247. Springer, Heidelberg (2009). https://doi.org/10.1007/978-3-642-00525-1_24
9. Nouza, J., Zdansky, J., Cerva, P., Silovsky, J.: Challenges in speech processing of slavic languages (case studies in speech recognition of Czech and Slovak). In: Esposito, A., Campbell, N., Vogel, C., Hussain, A., Nijholt, A. (eds.) Development of Multimodal Interfaces: Active Listening and Synchrony. LNCS, vol. 5967, pp. 225–241. Springer, Heidelberg (2010). https://doi.org/10.1007/978-3-642-12397-9_19
10. Ott, M., Edunov, S., Baevski, A., Fan, A., Gross, S., Ng, N., Grangier, D., Auli, M.: fairseq: a fast, extensible toolkit for sequence modeling. In: Proceedings of NAACL-HLT 2019: Demonstrations (2019)
11. Psutka, J., Ircing, P., Psutka, J.V., Hajič, J., Byrne, W., Mírovský, J.: Automatic transcription of Czech, Russian and Slovak spontaneous speech in the MALACH project. In: Eurospeech 2005, pp. 1349–1352. ISCA (2005)
12. Psutka, J.V., Psutka, J., Radová, V., Ircing, P., Matoušek, J., Müller, L.: USC-SFI MALACH interviews and transcripts Czech (2014). https://catalog.ldc.upenn.edu/LDC2014S04
13. Radford, A., Kim, J.W., Xu, T., Brockman, G., McLeavey, C., Sutskever, I.: Robust speech recognition via large-scale weak supervision (2022). https://doi.org/10.48550/ARXIV.2212.04356, arXiv:2212.04356
14. Raffel, C., et al.: Exploring the limits of transfer learning with a unified text-to-text transformer. J. Mach. Learn. Res. **21**(140), 1–67 (2020). http://jmlr.org/papers/v21/20-074.html
15. UCL. https://www.phon.ucl.ac.uk/home/sampa/
16. Vaswani, A., et al.: Attention is all you need. In: Proceedings of the 31st International Conference on Neural Information Processing Systems, NIPS 2017, pp. 6000–6010. Curran Associates Inc., Red Hook (2017)
17. Wang, C., et al.: VoxPopuli: a large-scale multilingual speech corpus for representation learning, semi-supervised learning and interpretation. In: Proceedings of the 59th Annual Meeting of the Association for Computational Linguistics and the 11th International Joint Conference on Natural Language Processing (Volume 1: Long Papers), pp. 993–1003. Association for Computational Linguistics, Online (2021). https://aclanthology.org/2021.acl-long.80

Automatic Pronunciation Assessment of Non-native English Based on Phonological Analysis

C. D. Rios-Urrego[1]([✉]), D. Escobar-Grisales[1], S. A. Moreno-Acevedo[1],
P. A. Perez-Toro[1,2], E. Nöth[2], and J. R. Orozco-Arroyave[1,2]

[1] Faculty of Engineering, University of Antioquia UdeA, Medellín, Colombia
cdavid.rios@udea.edu.co
[2] Pattern Recognition Lab, Friedrich-Alexander-Universität Erlangen-Nürnberg,
Erlangen, Germany

Abstract. The rapid development of speech recognition systems has motivated the community to work on accent classification, considerably improving the performance of these systems. However, only a few works or tools have focused on evaluating and analyzing in depth not only the accent but also the pronunciation level of a person when learning a non-native language. Our study aims to evaluate the pronunciation skills of non-native English speakers whose first language is Arabic, Chinese, Spanish, or French. We considered training a system to compute posterior probabilities of phonological classes from English native speakers and then evaluating whether it is possible to discriminate between native English speakers vs. non-native English speakers. Posteriors of each phonological class separately and also their combination are considered. Phonemes with low posterior results are used to give feedback to the speaker regarding which phonemes should be improved. The results suggest that it is possible to distinguish between each of the non-native languages and native English with accuracies between 67.6% and 80.6%. According to our observations, the most discriminant phonological classes are alveolar, lateral, velar, and front. Finally, the paper introduces a graphical way to interpret the results phoneme-by-phoneme, such that the speaker receives feedback about his/her pronunciation performance.

Keywords: Pronunciation assessment · Speech · English · Phonological Analysis

1 Introduction

English is the official language in over 50 countries and is widely used as a second language in many others. It is considered the language of international communication in business, academia, politics, and others [4]. Thus, there is a broad interest in learning this second language for speakers with a different native language. Typically, the English level is evaluated by a human, which is not always accurate due to subjective biases; for instance, evaluators may have different expectations and standards, leading to inconsistent and unreliable assessments [1]. Computer-based assessments can

K. Ekštein et al. (Eds.): TSD 2023, LNAI 14102, pp. 339–348, 2023.
https://doi.org/10.1007/978-3-031-40498-6_30

give a more objective and effective assessment of the English level by analyzing specific aspects of speech to provide feedback to users, which helps them identify their strengths and weaknesses. There are multiple tools for automatic assessment of English level, where grammatical skills, vocabulary knowledge, and others are evaluated using Automatic Speech Recognition (ASR) systems based on metrics such as word accuracy rate [8]. However, few tools evaluate or analyze deeply aspects of the English level, such as fluency, naturalness, or phonological precision, where it is possible to identify specific phonemes that can be more difficult to pronounce according to the native language in order to emphasize them in the learning process.

Automatic accent classification in speech recognition plays an important role in adapting systems to linguistic variations, improving recognition accuracy and robustness to different regions and contexts [21]. Therefore, many works have been addressed in the scientific community to classify accents. For example, in [13], a system based on Convolutional Neural Networks (CNNs) was trained and evaluated for classifying nine accents; the authors achieved an accuracy of up to 98.6%. Similar work was performed in [7], where the classification problem consisted of determining whether English speech samples are spoken by native speakers of English, Japanese, Dutch, French, or Polish. Again, this work using CNNs reported accuracies of up to 90% for discriminating the five accents. In [2], the authors used classical techniques and CNNs to recognize five accents (English, Arabic, French, German, and Hindi). They showed that the classical methods are not sufficiently efficient to solve this problem, and they obtained the best results with a deep learning approach with a mean accuracy of 90.2%. For the same corpus, in [17], five accents were evaluated (Arabic, English, French, Mandarin, and Spanish) using classical and deep approaches; in this case, the Mel-Frequency Cepstral Coefficients (MFCCs) obtained the best performance with an accuracy of 71.4%.

However, only some studies have investigated the level of pronunciation of each participant in addition to accent classification. A first approach to this can be found in [5], where the authors propose a model based on random forests and MFCCs to detect and correct automatic pronunciation errors in English classes. This work performed a bi-class classification (correct pronunciation vs. mispronunciations), obtaining accuracies of up to 74.7%. In [12], the authors propose an automatic pronunciation evaluation for non-native speakers based on robust models such as Wav2Vec 2.0 and HuBERT + bidirectional long short-term memory with the layer-wise contextual representations and the corresponding text. The authors achieved correlations of up to 0.82 when comparing model performance against human-labeled annotations. Following the same line of automatically evaluating the accent, in [16], a bidirectional long short-term memory layer in a neural network was proposed to predict human ratings of the accentedness of recorded speech. When the model prediction was compared with the human ratings, correlations of up to 0.57 were reported. Finally, in [10], a work that identifies pronunciation errors in non-native speech using spectrogram and MFCCs was presented. The authors evaluated each modality's performance and included their fusion for classifying some phonological classes, in addition to the error per phoneme. They observed that the fusion of both modalities achieved the best performance, and the erroneous phonemes found automatically are similar to those labeled manually.

Motivated by this, our study seeks to provide insights into the challenges faced by non-native English speakers in mastering English pronunciation and improving language learning and teaching strategies. Initially, we trained and evaluated Phonet[1], which computes the posterior probabilities of phonological classes from speech signals. Moreover, it considers several phoneme groups according to the place and manner of articulation.

Thus, we obtained the posterior probabilities for each audio from the target database to perform a classification between native English speakers vs. non-native English speakers for each phonological class and considered the fusion of these phonological classes. Finally, in each non-native English language, we obtained the most discriminative phonological class; then, we assessed weak phonemes in pronunciation to give feedback to each participant on which phonemes they had difficulty pronouncing compared to native speakers as a strategy to improve their pronunciation performance.

The rest of the paper is as follows: Sect. 2 describes the corpora considered for this study. Section 3, presents the methods used in the study. Section 4 shows the results and analysis of the study; and finally, Sect. 5 contains the conclusions and future work.

2 Data

2.1 TIMIT Corpus

In this work, the architecture used was trained and evaluated with the TIMIT database, which consists of 2342 sentences read by 630 speakers with different dialects of American English [6]. This corpus was developed mainly to train and evaluate automatic speech recognition systems. The TIMIT corpus includes time-aligned orthographic, phonetic, and word transcriptions as well as a 16-bit, 16kHz speech waveform file for each utterance. In addition, the TIMIT corpus transcriptions have been hand-verified. Test and training subsets, balanced for phonetic and dialectal coverage, are specified.

2.2 Speech Accent Archive

We used the Speech Accent Archive as the target corpus [20]. This dataset contains 2140 speech samples, each from a different talker reading the same reading passage in English (69-word paragraph). Talkers come from 177 countries and have 214 different native languages. Due to the large imbalance that exists in the database (English: 27%, Spanish: 7.5%, Arabic: 4.7%, etc.). We only considered the native speakers of the corpus (English), and the first 4 groups of non-native English speakers with the largest number of participants: Spanish, Arabic, Mandarin, and French. In addition, due to the idea of assessing the pronunciation level of each non-native speakers vs. native speakers, we chose a subset of English to assess each set of non-native speakers that will guarantee age and gender balance from the t-test and Chi-squared test, respectively. Therefore, each language was paired with the same number of English participants as follows: Spanish (162 participants), Arabic (102 participants), Mandarin (65 participants), and French (63 participants).

---

[1] https://phonet.readthedocs.io/en/latest/?badge=latest.

3   Methods

Figure 1 summarizes the architecture proposed in this work. Initially, we prepared the TIMIT corpus audios with their respective transcriptions to train Phonet. Then, we take the recordings of native and non-native speakers of English from the Speech Accent Archive and compute the phonological posteriors associated with each phonological class. Finally, we performed 2 approaches: (i) we classified between each set of non-native speakers, i.e., Spanish, Arabic, Mandarin, and French vs. their corresponding group of native speakers (English); this classification was performed using a Support Vector Machine (SVM), for each phonological class and considering the fusion of all of them. (ii) After finding the most discriminative phonological class for each set of non-native speakers, we performed a phoneme-level analysis to give feedback per phoneme on the pronunciation level of a specific speaker compared to a native speaker. Details of each stage are presented below.

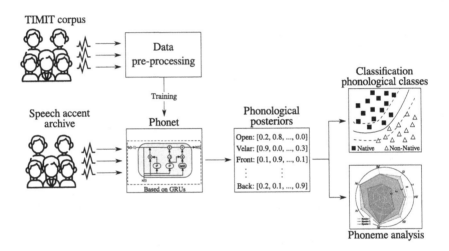

Fig. 1. Architecture proposed in this work.

3.1   Phonological Analysis

Phonological features are used to model the information about the place and manner of articulation of a speaker. These features are more understandable for clinicians than the standard high-dimensional features used in speech processing. Therefore, these features are typically used to model pathological speech, such as dysarthria, apraxia, and others [3,11]. Models of phonological analysis aim to detect the phonological class of a speech frame, where a phonological class is composed of a set of phonemes that share certain features, such as voicing, place of articulation, or manner of articulation. For instance, the phonological class "Alveolar" is a phonological class that groups the phonemes that are articulated with the tongue tip touching the alveolar ridge, which is the bony ridge behind the upper teeth. In this study, we used a toolkit called Phonet to estimate the phoneme articulation precision of different speakers and used these posteriors to classify native and non-native English speakers.

3.2 Phonet

This toolkit was proposed in [18], and it is designed to estimate phonological posteriors using bidirectional Recurrent Neural Networks (RNNs) with Gated Recurrent Units (GRUs). A speech segment of 400ms is defined as sequence size, and each element in the sequence is a frame of 25 ms with a time-shift of 10 ms. The model's input corresponds to the log-energy of the speech frame distributed into 33 triangular filters separated according to the Mel scale. This input is used to feed two bidirectional GRU layers with 128 cells. The output of the second bidirectional GRU is processed using N_c time-distributed dense layers, where N_c is the number of phonological classes. The model was trained following a multitask learning strategy to detect different phonological classes, and a Softmax activation function was used to get posterior probabilities. In [18], the model was trained with Spanish language utterances using the CIEMPIESS corpus to predict 21 phonemes distributed into 18 phonological classes. In this study, we trained the same model to predict phoneme articulation precision in English; therefore, we used the TIMIT corpus and considered 22 phonological classes: diphthong, back, closed, rounded, vowel, voiceless, postalveolar, open, velar, nasal, alveolar, bilabial, front, glottal, voiced, fricative, approximant, labiodental, dental, plosive, trill, and lateral. The notation of the phonemes is based on the International Phonetic Alphabet (IPA).

3.3 Classification and Analysis Stage

For the classification stage, we obtained a static representation for each phonological class, for which we calculated six different functionals: mean, standard deviation, skewness, kurtosis, maximum, and minimum. For this experiment, we considered classifying each set of non-native speakers vs. its corresponding group of native speakers using an SVM. This method allows discriminating N samples by finding a separating hyperplane that maximizes the margin between classes. We used a radial basis function as the kernel for the SVM, and its parameters were optimized upon a grid-search. The complexity parameter was varied as $C \in \{0.001, 0.005, 0.01, \cdots, 100, 500, 1000\}$ and the bandwidth of the kernel was varied as $\gamma \in \{0.0001, 0.001, \cdots, 1000\}$. We train, optimize and evaluate each phonological class individually and consider the fusion of all phonological classes forming a final vector of 132 features per participant (22 phonological classes × 6 statistics). All experiments are performed following a 5-fold cross-validation strategy. The results are reported in terms of mean and standard deviation computed along the folds. In the analysis stage, we consider it important to give feedback to the user on which phonemes are the most difficult to recognize in the system. For this, we consider a radar figure where we show for the most discriminative phonological class every mean posterior of each phoneme and compare it with the same phonemes of a native speaker (considered their target).

4 Experiments and Results

4.1 Training Phonet

Twenty-two phonological classes were trained and classified during the development of this work. In addition, it was guaranteed that each extracted phoneme had at least one or more phonological classes. The results show that the system's mean accuracy is 92.46% with a deviation of 3.16%. The lowest-performing phonological class is "Back" with an accuracy of 86.9%. In addition, the model for phoneme recognition proposed in [18] was trained with the TIMIT corpus in order to obtain a model that can recognize 51 phonemes of the English language. The system manages to predict the 51 phonemes with an accuracy of 67.7%.

4.2 Classification of Phonological Classes

The purpose of our study is to evaluate the pronunciation skills of non-native English speakers from Arabic, Chinese, Spanish, and French backgrounds. To achieve this goal, we apply a phonological approach to measure the accuracy of their pronunciation using Phonet to differentiate between native and non-native English speakers. We measure the confidence level of the classification to determine the degree of proficiency in English pronunciation. A higher score indicates a higher level of accuracy in differentiating between native and non-native English speakers. For instance, a high confidence score suggests that the speaker struggles with proper pronunciation.

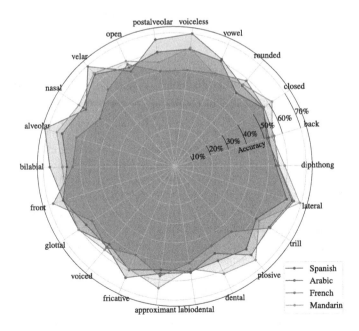

Fig. 2. Accuracy (%) of native vs non-native English speakers for all phonological classes.

The radar chart presented in Fig. 2 demonstrates the performance of the classification between native vs. non-native English speakers for all phonological classes. We could see that French speakers (red color), in general, have superior pronunciation skills compared to the other language groups, as their coverage area on the chart is relatively small.

Additionally, the performance of French speakers in the nasal class is relatively poor compared to the other languages, which shows that it is easier to identify a non-native speaker of Spanish, Arabic or Chinese than a French speaker. This result can be attributed to the presence of nasal phonemes (primarily vocal) that are specific to English and French and not present in the other languages [9,14,15,19]; thenceforth, French and English speakers pronounce the nasal class better than the Spanish, Arabic or Chinese speakers.

The findings of Fig. 2 led to conduct a detailed analysis of the most distinguishing phonological class for each language tested. For this analysis, we selected the class with the highest score for each language as the most discriminatory class. Specifically, we identified the Alveolar class as the most distinguishing class for Arabic, the Lateral class for Chinese, the Velar class for Spanish, and the Front class for French.

Table 1. Native vs non-native English speakers for all classes and the most discriminant class.

Native Language	Phon. Classes	Accuracy (%)	Sensitivity (%)	Specificity (%)	F1-score (%)
Arabic	All	80.6 ± 2.5	85.9 ± 2.7	75.3 ± 2.9	80.5 ± 2.5
	Alveolar	71.9 ± 3.1	68.4 ± 1.0	75.3 ± 5.7	71.8 ± 3.1
Mandarin	All	74.2 ± 2.8	78.5 ± 4.5	69.9 ± 1.9	74.1 ± 2.8
	Lateral	69.2 ± 3.2	71.7 ± 3.0	66.8 ± 3.5	69.2 ± 3.2
Spanish	All	72.0 ± 1.8	71.9 ± 2.0	72.1 ± 2.9	72.0 ± 1.8
	Velar	64.0 ± 0.9	73.6 ± 2.9	54.4 ± 2.4	63.7 ± 0.9
French	All	67.6 ± 2.0	74.3 ± 3.4	61.0 ± 5.0	67.4 ± 2.1
	Front	67.6 ± 1.5	79.7 ± 5.4	55.6 ± 5.0	67.1 ± 1.5

Table 1 presents the results of our analysis on the discriminant power of each language tested, which includes the averages for all classes as well as the most distinguishing class for each language. Arabic stands out as the most distinguishable language with an accuracy of 80.6% and 71.9%, for all classes and the Alveolar class, respectively, making it the easiest to differentiate between native and non-native English speakers. Chinese is the second most discriminant language, with an overall accuracy of 74.2% and 69.2% for the Lateral class. In Spanish, we obtained an accuracy score of 72% and 64% for all classes and the Velar class, respectively. In contrast, French, as shown in Fig. 2, is the least discriminant language with an accuracy score of 67.6% for both all and front classes. Our findings suggest that for Arabic, Chinese, and Spanish, all classes perform better in identifying non-native English speakers than relying on a single phonological class.

The alveolar class in Arabic may be more discriminant because it contains emphatic consonants that are not present in English, as reported in a previous study [14]. This difference in phonemes could explain why Arabic speakers can be more easily differentiated from native English speakers based on their pronunciation. On the other hand, the phonemes in the lateral class of Chinese and English are quite distinct, with Chinese phonemes being dental and English ones being alveolar, according to Wang [19]. Additionally, Spanish has a higher number of velar phonemes than English [15], which, like in Arabic, could contribute to its better discrimination. Finally, some elongated vowels that are common in English but not in the other languages fall into the front class [9], which may be why this class is more important for distinguishing native from non-native speakers.

4.3   Phoneme Analysis

To continue the analysis on the identification of the weakest phonological classes in each native language, we would like to perform an example of how the Phonet system can automatically generate feedback for each phonological class on the phoneme-by-phoneme pronunciation level, compared to a target (native speaker). Figure 3 shows the distribution from a radar plot of the mean posterior for three different speakers for the Alveolar phonological class. In particular, the Non-native 1 and Non-native 2 participants are Arabic native speakers of male gender and 55 and 43 years old, respectively. The Native participant is a native speaker from the USA, female, and 29 years old.

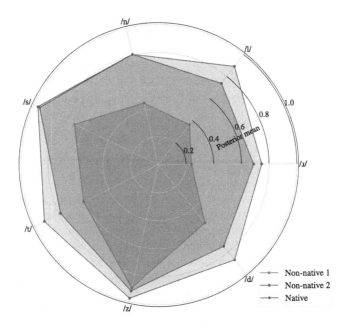

Fig. 3. Comparison of posterior means for the alveolar phonological class of 2 non-native and a native English speaker.

In Fig. 3, we can observe that the speaker Non-native 2 (blue color) has similar posterior means to the Native speaker (green color), even equaling in some phonemes such as /s/ and /n/; therefore, we could conclude that this participant has a high level of pronunciation in comparison with a native speaker of English. However, the opposite is the case when we compare the Non-native 1 participant (red color) with the native speaker; in this case, the difference in most of the posterior means of the native speaker vs. non-native speaker is evident. From this figure, we can conclude that this non-native speaker should focus on improving the pronunciation of all phonemes of the Alveolar phonological class, focusing on the phonemes , /l/, and /n/, which is where he shows lower performance compared to a native speaker and even to another person of the same native language.

5   Conclusions

The purpose of our study is to evaluate the pronunciation skills of non-native English speakers from Arabic, Chinese, Spanish, and French backgrounds; we consider training in English a tool called Phonet that allows calculating of posterior probabilities of phonological classes from speech for several groups of phonemes according to the place and manner of articulation. We consider evaluating each non-native speaker from each phonological class and also considering the combination of all of them. In general, the results suggest that Arabic and Mandarin speakers have greater difficulty pronouncing English than Spanish and French speakers. Particularly, when we performed an analysis at the phonological class level, it was possible to identify the Alveolar class as the most distinguishing class for Arabic, the Lateral class for Chinese, the Velar class for Spanish, and the Front class for French. In addition, it was possible to discuss, from previous work, the possible reason why these phonological classes allow to discriminate in a better way each non-native speaker from native speakers of English. Additionally, it was possible to observe that our system can automatically generate feedback for each phonological class on the phoneme-by-phoneme pronunciation level, compared to a target (native speaker) as a strategy to improve their pronunciation performance.

In future work, we will consider training a multilingual system that allows the automatic evaluation of pronunciation not only of English but of different languages. In addition, we will implement multi-class classification of the different non-native speakers involved in this work, including a variety of accents and dialects of each language.

Acknowledgment. This work received funding from UdeA grant # ES92210001 and CODI grant No. PI2023-58010, and PRG2017-15530.

References

1. Bachman, L., Palmer, A.: Language Assessment in Practice: Developing language Assessments and Justifying Their Use in the Real World. Oxford University Press, Oxford (2022)
2. Berjon, P., et al.: Analysis of French phonetic idiosyncrasies for accent recognition. Soft Comput. Lett. 100018 (2021)
3. Cernak, M., et al.: Characterisation of voice quality of Parkinson's disease using differential phonological posterior features. Comput. Speech Lang. **46**, 196–208 (2017)
4. Crystal, D., et al.: English as a Global Language. Cambridge University Press, Cambridge (2003)

5. Dai, Y.: An automatic pronunciation error detection and correction mechanism in English teaching based on an improved random forest model. J. Electr. Comput. Eng. (2022)
6. Garofolo, J.S.: Timit acoustic phonetic continuous speech corpus. Linguist. Data Consortium (1993)
7. Graham, C.: L1 identification from L2 speech using neural spectrogram analysis. In: Proceedings of Interspeech, pp. 3959–3963 (2021)
8. Huang, C., et al.: Accent issues in large vocabulary continuous speech recognition. Int. J. Speech Technol. **7**, 141–153 (2004)
9. Huerta, E.: Fonética comparada, español-francés, francés como segunda lengua para hispanohablantes, los fonemas complicados (2013)
10. Jenne, S., Vu, N.T.: Multimodal articulation-based pronunciation error detection with spectrogram and acoustic features. In: Proceedings of Interspeech, pp. 3549–3553 (2019)
11. Jiao, Y., et al.: Interpretable phonological features for clinical applications. In: Proceedings of ICASSP, pp. 5045–5049. IEEE (2017)
12. Kim, E., et al.: Automatic pronunciation assessment using self-supervised speech representation learning. arXiv preprint arXiv:2204.03863 (2022)
13. Lesnichaia, M., et al.: Classification of accented English using CNN model trained on amplitude mel-spectrograms. In: Proceedings of Interspeech, pp. 3669–3673 (2022)
14. Millar Cerda, M.A.: Los arabismos en la lengua española (1998)
15. Ocal, A.P.: Fonética contrastiva español/alemán, español/inglés, aspañol/francés y su aplicación a la enseñanza de la pronunciación española (1997)
16. Schnoor, T.T., et al.: Automatic accentedness rating using deep neural networks. In: Proceedings of Meetings on Acoustics ASA, vol. 45, p. 060013. Acoustical Society of America (2021)
17. Singh, Y., et al.: Features of speech audio for accent recognition, pp. 1–6 (2020)
18. Vásquez-Correa, J.C., et al.: Phonet: a tool based on gated recurrent neural networks to extract phonological posteriors from speech. In: Proceedings of Interspeech, pp. 549–553 (2019)
19. Wang, H.Y.: Estudio fónico del chino mandarín y del español (2001)
20. Weinberger, S.: Speech accent archive. George Mason University. Retrieved (2015)
21. Weninger, F., et al.: Deep learning based mandarin accent identification for accent robust ASR. In: Proceedings of Interspeech, pp. 510–514 (2019)

Language Generalization Using Active Learning in the Context of Parkinson's Disease Classification

S. A. Moreno-Acevedo[1,3(✉)], C. D. Rios-Urrego[1], J. C. Vásquez-Correa[3], J. Rusz[2], E. Nöth[4], and J. R. Orozco-Arroyave[1,4]

[1] GITA Lab., Universidad de Antioquia UdeA, Medellín, Colombia
santiago.moreno3@udea.edu.co
[2] Department of Circuit Theory, Czech Technical University in Prague, Prague, Czech Republic
[3] Fundación Vicomtech, Basque Research and Technology Alliance (BRTA), Donostia-San Sebastián, Spain
[4] LME Lab., Friedrich-Alexander Universität, Erlangen-Nürnberg, Germany

Abstract. Speech traits have enabled the evaluation and monitoring of the neurological state of different disorders, including Parkinson's Disease (PD) using classical and deep approaches. Considering that speech contains paralinguistic information, the native language of the speaker influences the performance of the trained models when classifying the presence of the disease. Although researchers have performed several studies using corpora from different acoustic and language conditions, there is no baseline for the accuracy of a system to classify PD in cross-language scenarios. This study evaluates the generalization capability of different classical and deep methods to discriminate between PD patients and healthy speakers. The experiments are performed in cross-language scenarios. In particular, an Active Learning (AL) strategy is considered to evaluate the influence of the training data selection to improve the model's performance under cross-language settings. The results indicate that models based on Wav2Vec 2.0 yielded the best results in detecting the presence of the disease in such non-controlled cross-language scenarios. In addition, the AL selection outperformed the results compared to a random selection of training samples. The considered AL based-approach allows to achieve high accuracies using a careful selection of training data in an adaptively manner. This is particularly important when dealing with non-annotated and limited data, such as the case of pathological speech modeling.

Keywords: Parkinson's Disease · Speech Processing · Active Learning · Deep Learning · Machine Learning · Cross Language

1 Introduction

Parkinson's Disease (PD) is a neurodegenerative disorder caused by the progressive loss of dopaminergic neurons in the substantia nigra of the brain [8]. PD

© The Author(s), under exclusive license to Springer Nature Switzerland AG 2023
K. Ekštein et al. (Eds.): TSD 2023, LNAI 14102, pp. 349–359, 2023.
https://doi.org/10.1007/978-3-031-40498-6_31

patients develop a group of speech impairments known as hypokinetic dysarthria. Speech symptoms associated to hypokinetic dysarthria include reduced intensity, harsh and breathy voice quality, increased voice nasality, mono-pitch, mono-loudness, imprecise articulation of consonants, and involuntary introduction of pauses [24]. Due to their non-invasive nature and low cost, speech signals have been used to evaluate different symptoms of patients suffering from neurodegenerative diseases [20,21].

Within the last years, the research community has been interested in evaluating PD using speech signals. Different methods for the classification of PD patients vs. Healthy Controls (HC) have been proposed. Classical approaches include Gaussian Mixture Models [3], Support Vector Machines (SVM) [22], and K-Nearest Neighbor [22]. In addition, Deep methods such as Convolutional Neural Networks (CNNs) [26], Recurrent Neural Networks with Long Short-Term Memory units [17], fully-connected networks [5], and combinations of them [13] have been used.

Paralinguistic information such as the presence and severity of PD is influenced by external factors like the native language of the speaker. Results from different studies have shown accuracies of up to 90%, when training and test sets have similar acoustic and linguistic conditions [18]. However, the scenario in which recordings of different languages are collected in different acoustic conditions has not been extensively explored.

In [18], the authors trained a CNN to classify PD with corpora from different languages with the aim to evaluate which additional information is learned by the network in addition to the presence of the disease. The authors found that the model acquires knowledge about the gender of the speakers in the first layers, while the native language learned in the last layers of the model. Moreover, in [16] the authors found that in the classification of PD vs. HC, the performance is not only a direct consequence of the influence of PD in the speech of the participants. Other factors such as age or the person's identity contribute to the overall accuracy of the models. One approach to adapting a model to multiple languages was performed in [27]. The authors proposed a methodology to classify PD patients vs. HC subjects in multiple languages by adapting the model using transfer learning. The findings showed that transfer learning strategies only improved the target corpus accuracy when the base model was sufficiently accurate. Additional studies have focused on paralinguistic data assessment from speech using Active Learning (AL) with the aim to select the most informative data to be labeled and included in the training set, reducing the annotation effort. For example, in [1], the authors discussed the difficulty of getting annotated data and explored the use of AL to select the best data to be annotated. They showed that the use of AL leads to competitive performance with limited training data. A similar approach was shown in [12], where the authors showed that using AL yields considerable improvements over the baseline model using random sampling.

To the best of our knowledge, most cross-lingual studies have used transfer learning strategies and other approaches have been poorly investigated. This work aims to establish a baseline about whether it is possible to find patterns in the speech of PD patients that can be shared among different languages and acoustic conditions. Moreover, the AL approach has not been applied to pathological speech classification, where the problem of getting high-quality data is more evident. We considered a strategy based on AL in the context of PD and analyze how a model generalizes to different languages. Hence, AL is used to teach the models information from a new language with the least possible amount of annotated data.

The rest of the paper is as follows: Sect. 2 describes the corpora. Section 3 shows the methods and models used in the pre-processing and classification tasks. Section 4 introduces the experiments and results, and finally, Sect. 5 contains the conclusions and future work.

2 Data

We considered three databases with recordings of PD patients and HC subjects native speakers of different languages: Spanish, German, and Czech. All patients were in ON-state during the recording session, i.e., under the effect of their daily medication, and were evaluated by specialized neurologists according to the Movement Disorder Society - Unified Parkinson's Disease Rating Scale (MDS-UPDRS-III) [6]. All recordings were collected in controlled acoustic conditions and down-sampled to 16 kHz. Table 1 summarizes the information of the participants.

Table 1. Clinical and demographic information of the speakers. Values are reported in terms of mean ± standard deviation.

	Gender	Spanish		German		Czech	
		Patients	Controls	Patients	Controls	Patients	Controls
Number of Subjects	Male	25	25	47	44	30	30
	Female	25	25	41	44	20	19
Age [years]	Male	61.3 ± 11	60.5 ± 12	66.7 ± 9	63.8 ± 13	65.3 ± 10	60.3 ± 12
	Female	60.7 ± 7	61.4 ± 7	66.2 ± 10	62.6 ± 15	60.1 ± 9	63.5±11
Years since diagnosis	Male	8.7 ± 5.9	–	7.0 ± 5.5	–	6.7 ± 4.5	–
	Female	12.6 ± 11.6	–	7.1 ± 6.2	–	6.8 ± 5.2	–
MDS-UPDRS-III	Male	37.8 ± 22.1	–	22.1 ± 9.9	–	21.4 ± 11.5	–
	Female	37.6 ± 14.1	–	23.3 ± 12.0	–	18.1 ± 9.7	–

Spanish: A total of 100 Colombian native speakers (50 PD patients and 50 HC subjects) are considered for this corpus [15]. Each participant performed different speech tasks including 10 sentences, one monologue, a read-text, isolated words, the rapid repetition of 6 diadochokinetic (DDK) tasks, sustained vowels, and modulated vowels. This dataset has approximately 5 h of audio material.

German: This corpus contains approximately 20 h of recordings from 88 PD patients and 88 HC subjects, all German native speakers [4]. The participants produced different speech tasks, including one monologue, a read-text, reading of question-answer pairs, 5 sentences, 7 isolated words, the rapid repetition of 8 DDKs, and sustained vowels.

Czech: This corpus consisted of 50 PD patients and 49 HC subjects, Czech native speakers [19]. A total of 4 speech tasks are included: one monologue, a read-text, a DDK, and sustained vowels. This dataset has approximately 5 h of audio.

3   Methods

Motivated by the aim of evaluating different models to classify between PD vs. HC subjects in different languages, we consider different methodologies based on three main paradigms: (1) classical methods using an SVM classifier with articulation features extracted from speech; (2) a ResNet-based CNN trained to classify Mel-scale spectrograms from PD patients vs. HC subjects [26]; and (3) a pre-trained Transformer model based on Wav2Vec 2.0 [2], fine-tuned to process the raw speech signals from the participants. All models are evaluated in a single-language approach and also in a cross-language scenario. Besides, an AL-based approach is implemented to evaluate its suitability to improve the accuracy when information from different languages is considered within the same model.

3.1   Articulatory Analysis

Articulation features model the ability of patients to control different muscles and limbs involved in speech production [14]. The features considered here are based on the energy content in the transition between voiced and unvoiced segments [14]. The transition segments are detected based on the presence of fundamental frequency (F_0). Once the border between unvoiced and voiced segments is detected, 40 ms of the signal are taken to the left and to the right. The spectrum of the transition segments is distributed into 22 critical bands according to the Bark scale, and the Bark-band energies are calculated. 12 Mel Frequency Cepstral Coefficients and their first two derivatives are included to complete the feature set. The source code to compute this feature set is available online via the Disvoice toolkit[1].

3.2   Convolutional Neural Network (CNN)

A ResNet-based CNN is used to avoid the vanishing gradient problem [7]. The architecture of the network has a total of 174k parameters and includes an input convolutional layer with 16 feature maps followed by 6 residual blocks and 3 main blocks with 16, 32, and 64 feature maps. The output of the residual blocks is reduced by an average pooling. The output layer is formed by a fully connected

---

[1] https://github.com/jcvasquezc/DisVoice/tree/master/disvoice/articulation.

layer. ReLu activations are considered in the hidden layers and a Softmax activation function is applied in the output to make the final decision. The input for the CNN corresponds to Mel-scale spectrograms of 500 ms length speech segments with a time-shift of 250 ms. The spectrogram is computed using Hanning windows of 32 ms and a step-size of 8 ms, forming 63-time frames per chunk. The time-frequency representations are transformed into a Mel-scale spectrogram with 128 Mel filters. Thus the CNN is fed with a spectrogram of 128×63.

3.3   Wav2Vec 2.0

We consider the Wav2Vec 2.0-base model [2] trained in English, which has demonstrated high performance in different speech classification tasks [10,11]. The main concept of Wav2Vec 2.0 is to develop representations of speech signals that are helpful for speech modeling via self-supervised learning. The architecture of Wav2Vec 2.0 consists of three main components: an encoder, a Transformer network, and a quantization module. Seven blocks compose the feature encoder. The temporal convolutions in each block are formed with 512 channels. As a result, the encoder output frequency is 49 Hz, with a 20 ms sample stride. The receptive field is 400 input samples (25 ms of audio). The transformer network is composed of 12 blocks, 8 attention heads, and a 768-dimensional feature vector. For self-supervised training, Wav2Vec 2.0 discretizes the output of the feature encoder to a finite set of speech representations via product quantization. Finally, the output of the quantized encoder is a 768-dimensional vector that feeds a classification stage of two fully connected layers with sizes of 768, and 256 hidden units, respectively. The Wav2Vec 2.0 model used had in total 9.3 M parameters.

3.4   Active Learning

AL aims to improve the performance of a model by iteratively selecting the most informative samples from a large pool of unlabeled data. This iterative process reduces the amount of labeled data required to achieve high accuracies, which is particularly useful when labeled data is expensive or hard to obtain. There are several strategies to select the most informative samples. One of the most popular is the entropy one [23], which involves selecting the samples with higher entropy, which is estimated as in Eq. 1.

$$H(x) = -\sum_{k} p_k \log(p_k) \tag{1}$$

where p_k is the assigned class probability by the Softmax layer. We use this criterion to select the samples that are included in the training set when adapting the model to the unknown language. Additional methods, like the ones based on margin separation [23] were considered as well, however, the most accurate results were achieved using the entropy criterion.

4   Experiments and Results

Three experimental scenarios are considered in this study: (1) **Single-language training:** We trained the models with the data from one language and test the models with data from the other two datasets. (2) **Two-language training:** The models were trained with data from two languages and tested in the remaining one. (3) **Sequentially added data:** The models were trained with information of two languages, while continuously adding information from the target one. We added 10%, 20%, 30%, 40%, 50%, and 60% of the target language to the train set and tested in the remaining 90%, 80%, 70%, 60%, 50%, and 40%, respectively. The selection of the samples to be added was done randomly, and via AL using the entropy query strategy. Speaker independence was guaranteed in all experiments.

The hyperparameter optimization in the classical approach was performed following a 10-fold cross-validation strategy. C and γ were selected from $\{1 \times 10^{-8}, 1 \times 10^{-8}, \cdots, 1, 10\}$ within the cross-validation according to the accuracy in the validation set. The Wav2Vec 2.0 was initialized with the original pre-trained weights. The classification layer was fine-tuned, while the other layers were frozen. We used a learning rate of 0.003, and 200 epochs with early stopping, and batches of 64 samples. The ResNet model was trained using 50 epochs with early stopping, and a batch size of 32.

4.1   Baselines

Aiming to set a benchmark for the different models, we performed the classification within the same language with a 5-fold cross-validation strategy (speaker-independent). The results obtained in Table 2 show the accuracies for each model and dataset when the training and test sets belong to the same corpus. Deep methods outperformed the results for all corpora, the highest accuracy of the ResNet model was observed with the Spanish corpus, while the Wav2Vec 2.0 yields best results for German and Czech.

Table 2. Baseline results in terms of accuracy (%) ± standard deviation.

Dataset	SVM	ResNet	Wav2Vec 2.0
Spanish	79.0 ± 5	**90.0 ± 4**	89.0 ± 7
German	72.7 ± 1	75.0 ± 6	**79.0 ± 4**
Czech	69.3 ± 4	68.8 ± 2	**74.0 ± 10**
Average	71.4	77.9	**80.7**

4.2   Single-Language Training

Table 3 shows the results when the models are trained with only one database and tested in the other two. The accuracies of these experiments range from

49.4% to 75.0%, depending on the method and language scenario. Wav2Vec 2.0 model yielded the best results for all corpora, with an average improvement of 7,3%. When the target language is Spanish, training with German audios showed the highest accuracy (75%). Using the PD-German corpus as test set, we obtain the most accurate result training with the PD-Czech dataset. Finally, for Czech as the target language, the best results are obtained when the training language is German.

Table 3. Results of the single-language training experiments. Values correspond to the accuracy in %.

Training	Test	SVM	ResNet	Wav2Vec 2.0
Spanish	German	53.4	52.3	60.2
	Czech	53.5	57.6	62.0
German	Spanish	54.0	67.0	**75.0**
	Czech	62.4	53.5	**72.0**
Czech	German	57.4	49.4	**68.2**
	Spanish	50.0	53.0	57.0
Average		55.1	55.5	**65.7**

The results indicated that Wav2Vec 2.0 is the method that generalizes better to unknown languages, achieving the highest accuracies (above 70%) when trained in German and tested in Spanish and Czech. These results could be explained because this is the largest corpus. The best result for German as a test language is achieved when training with Czech. This result is likely supported by the fact that patients in the German and Czech corpora are in similar neurological state severity. Another possible reason is that Czech is phonetically closer to German than Spanish.

4.3   Two-Language Training

The results observed in Table 4 correspond to the model trained with data from two languages and tested in the remaining one. Once again the Wav2Vec 2.0 model yielded the best results in the three scenarios. Notice that the results for the three languages are similar (around 72%). This is actually a very promising result considering that every test dataset in each scenario can be considered as a separate and independent test set. This result exceeds others reported in the literature where independent test sets (yet with the same language) are considered [9].

The ROC curves for the best outcomes of the Single-Language and Two-Language training experiments are presented in Fig. 1. According to the curves, when the test set is PD-German, the sensitivity of the model surpasses its specificity. This indicates that the model exhibits greater accuracy in identifying PD

Table 4. Results of the two-language training experiments. Values correspond to the accuracy in %.

Training	Test	SVM	ResNet	Wav2Vec 2.0
German + Czech	Spanish	46.0	50.0	**70.0**
Czech + Spanish	German	56.2	50.0	**72.7**
Spanish + German	Czech	51.5	49.5	**73.0**
Average		49.8	49.5	**72.0**

patients than HC subjects. Conversely, when the test languages are Spanish and Czech, the specificity slightly outweighs the sensitivity. In other words, the model demonstrates a higher capability in classifying HC subjects than accurately identifying PD patients.

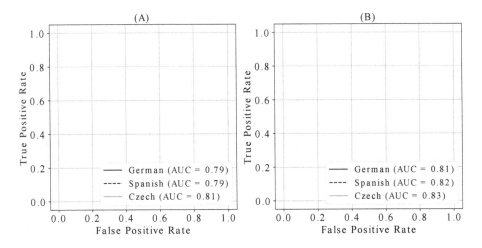

Fig. 1. ROC curves for each test set in the training experiments. (A) Best three results of Single-Language. (B) Results of Two-Language.

4.4 Sequentially Added Data

Since Wav2Vec 2.0 systematically showed the highest accuracy and the most promising generalization capability, we decided to use it in the sequentially added data experiments. In this case, small portions of the target language are removed from the test set and added to the training one. Two strategies to select those portions were compared: a random selection of samples vs. AL-based selection. Figure 2 shows the results of this experiment. Notice that the AL-based approach yields higher accuracies thanks to the intelligent selection of samples.

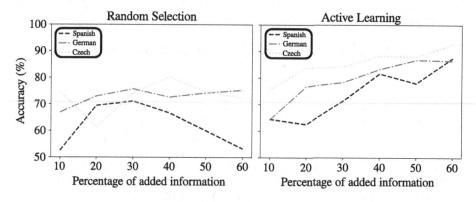

Fig. 2. Accuracy of Wav2Vec 2.0 in the sequentially added data experiments. Random selection (Left), and Active Learning selection (Right).

Figure 2 shows that when the samples to be added to the training process are randomly selected, the accuracy does not show any trend. Conversely, when the AL approach is used to select the samples, the performance systematically improves. Notice also that Czech and German only required about 20% of additional data to reach 80% of accuracy, while Spanish required around 40%. For all languages, the best result is observed at the final stage (50% to 60%). We believe that there is still a lot of investigation to do in order to reach similar results with the minimal number of additional samples.

5   Conclusions

This paper explores different scenarios where PD patients vs. HC subjects are discriminated even though recordings are collected in different acoustic environments and with speakers of different languages. Classical and deep models were evaluated, and the model based on Wav2Vec 2.0 showed the highest and most robust accuracies, even when the test set was formed with recordings of an unknown language. When the model was trained with recordings of two languages, the results were consistent, with accuracies above 70% in all cases. This paper also explored the use of an AL-based approach to adequately select the training data with the aim of improving the test results. The results showed that this method is more robust than a random selection approach, opening a new avenue to study strategies to combine several corpora to create a pattern recognition model.

Future work will include the evaluation of the neurological state of PD patients according to the MDS-UPDRS-III scale and the m-FDA scale [25]. Additionally, the study of strategies to interpret the outcomes of end-2-end models like Wav2Vec 2.0 is on the top priority for future research.

References

1. Abdelwahab, M., Busso, C.: Active learning for speech emotion recognition using deep neural network. In: Proceedings of ACII, pp. 1–7. IEEE (2019)
2. Baevski, A., et al.: wav2vec 2.0: a framework for self-supervised learning of speech representations. In: Advances in Neural Information Processing Systems, vol. 33, pp. 12449–12460 (2020)
3. Bocklet, T., et al.: Detection of persons with Parkinson's disease by acoustic, vocal, and prosodic analysis. In: Proceedings of ASRU, pp. 478–483 (2011)
4. Bocklet, T., et al.: Automatic evaluation of Parkinson's speech-acoustic, prosodic and voice related cues. In: Proceedings of INTERSPEECH, pp. 1149–1153 (2013)
5. El Maachi, I., et al.: Deep 1d-convnet for accurate Parkinson disease detection and severity prediction from gait. Expert Syst. Appl. **143**, 113075 (2020)
6. Goetz, C.G., et al.: Movement disorder society-sponsored revision of the unified Parkinson's disease rating scale (MDS-UPDRS): scale presentation and clinimetric testing results. Mov. Disord. **23**(15), 2129–2170 (2008)
7. He, K., Zhang, X., Ren, S., Sun, J.: Identity mappings in deep residual networks. In: Leibe, B., Matas, J., Sebe, N., Welling, M. (eds.) ECCV 2016. LNCS, vol. 9908, pp. 630–645. Springer, Cham (2016). https://doi.org/10.1007/978-3-319-46493-0_38
8. Jankovic, J.: Parkinson's disease: clinical features and diagnosis. J. Neurol. Neurosurg. Psychiatry **79**(4), 368–376 (2008)
9. Karan, B., Sekhar, S., Orozco-Arroyave, J.R.: Non-negative matrix factorization-based time-frequency feature extraction of voice signal for Parkinson's disease prediction. Comput. Speech Lang. **69**, 1–17 (2021)
10. Kim, D., Kang, P.: Cross-modal distillation with audio-text fusion for fine-grained emotion classification using BERT and wav2vec 2.0. Neurocomputing **506**, 168–183 (2022)
11. Makiuchi, M.R., et al.: Multimodal emotion recognition with high-level speech and text features. In: Proceedings of ASRU, pp. 350–357. IEEE (2021)
12. Malhotra, K., et al.: Active learning methods for low resource end-to-end speech recognition. In: Proceeding of INTERSPEECH, pp. 2215–2219 (2019)
13. Mallela, J., et al.: Voice based classification of patients with amyotrophic lateral sclerosis, Parkinson's disease and healthy controls with CNN-LSTM using transfer learning. In: Proceedings of ICASSP, pp. 6784–6788. IEEE (2020)
14. Orozco-Arroyave, J.R.: Analysis of Speech of People with Parkinson's Disease. Logos Verlag Berlin GmbH (2015)
15. Orozco-Arroyave, J.R., et al.: New Spanish speech corpus database for the analysis of people suffering from Parkinson's disease. In: Proceedings of LREC, pp. 342–347 (2014)
16. Ozbolt, A.S., et al.: Things to consider when automatically detecting Parkinson's disease using the phonation of sustained vowels: analysis of methodological issues. Appl. Sci. **12**(3), 991 (2022)
17. Quan, C., et al.: A deep learning based method for Parkinson's disease detection using dynamic features of speech. IEEE Access **9**, 10239–10252 (2021)
18. Rios-Urrego, C.D., Vásquez-Correa, J.C., Orozco-Arroyave, J.R., Nöth, E.: Is there any additional information in a neural network trained for pathological speech classification? In: Ekštein, K., Pártl, F., Konopík, M. (eds.) TSD 2021. LNCS (LNAI), vol. 12848, pp. 435–447. Springer, Cham (2021). https://doi.org/10.1007/978-3-030-83527-9_37

19. Rusz, J.: Detecting speech disorders in early Parkinson's disease by acoustic analysis. Habilitation thesis, Czech Technical University in Prague (2018)
20. Rusz, J., et al.: Objective acoustic quantification of phonatory dysfunction in Huntington's disease. PLoS ONE 8(6), e65881 (2013)
21. Rusz, J., et al.: Characteristics and occurrence of speech impairment in Huntington's disease: possible influence of antipsychotic medication. J. Neural Transm. 121(12), 1529–1539 (2014)
22. Sakar, B.E., et al.: Collection and analysis of a Parkinson speech dataset with multiple types of sound recordings. IEEE J. Biomed. Health Inform. 17(4), 828–834 (2013)
23. Settles, B.: Uncertainty sampling, pp. 11–20 (2012)
24. Spencer, K.A., Rogers, M.A.: Speech motor programming in hypokinetic and ataxic dysarthria. Brain Lang. 94(3), 347–366 (2005)
25. Vásquez-Correa, J.C., et al.: Towards an automatic evaluation of the dysarthria level of patients with Parkinson's disease. J. Commun. Disord. 76, 21–36 (2018)
26. Vasquez-Correa, J.C., et al.: End-2-end modeling of speech and gait from patients with Parkinson's disease: comparison between high quality vs. smartphone data. In: Proceedings of ICASSP, pp. 7298–7302. IEEE (2021)
27. Vásquez-Correa, J.C., et al.: Transfer learning helps to improve the accuracy to classify patients with different speech disorders in different languages. Pattern Recogn. Lett. 150, 272–279 (2021)

Author Index

Printed in the United States
by Baker & Taylor Publisher Services